The New Spirit of Islamism

About the author

Ezgi Başaran is a former journalist and a political scientist from Istanbul living in Oxford, UK. She gained recognition for her coverage of Turkey's Kurdish conflict, commencing her career as a reporter at *Hurriyet* in 2004. She later became the youngest editor of *Radikal*, the largest centre-left news outlet in Turkey, and the first woman to hold this position, after accepting an offer to write a daily column on Turkish politics. At the Southeast European Centre (SEESOX) in St Antony's College, University of Oxford, she served as the coordinator of the Programme on Contemporary Turkey, where she explored the intersection of journalism and academia. Ezgi has written on Turkish domestic politics, with her insights featured in major international media outlets such as the *BBC*, the *Financial Times*, *The Economist*, *The Wall Street Journal* and *The Washington Post*. Her book *Barış Bir Varmış, Bir Yokmuş* (Once upon a Time Peace) was published by Doğan Kitap in 2015, while her first English-language book, *Frontline Turkey: The Conflict at the Heart of the Middle East*, was published by IB Tauris/Bloomsbury in 2017. She holds an MPhil and a DPhil in Modern Middle Eastern studies from the University of Oxford and teaches a graduate politics course on the Middle East and North Africa at the same university.

The New Spirit of Islamism

Interactions between the AKP, Ennahda and the Muslim Brotherhood

Ezgi Başaran

I.B. TAURIS
LONDON • NEW YORK • OXFORD • NEW DELHI • SYDNEY

I.B. TAURIS
Bloomsbury Publishing Plc
50 Bedford Square, London, WC1B 3DP, UK
1385 Broadway, New York, NY 10018, USA
29 Earlfort Terrace, Dublin 2, Ireland

BLOOMSBURY, I.B. TAURIS and the I.B. Tauris logo are trademarks of Bloomsbury Publishing Plc

First published in Great Britain 2024

Copyright © Ezgi Başaran, 2024

Ezgi Başaran has asserted her rights under the Copyright, Designs and Patents Act, 1988, to be identified as Author of this work.

For legal purposes the Acknowledgements on p. vii constitute an extension of this copyright page.

Cover design: Adriana Brioso
Cover image © Pawel Czerwinski/Unsplash

All rights reserved. No part of this publication may be reproduced or transmitted in any form or by any means, electronic or mechanical, including photocopying, recording, or any information storage or retrieval system, without prior permission in writing from the publishers.

Bloomsbury Publishing Plc does not have any control over, or responsibility for, any third-party websites referred to or in this book. All internet addresses given in this book were correct at the time of going to press. The author and publisher regret any inconvenience caused if addresses have changed or sites have ceased to exist, but can accept no responsibility for any such changes.

A catalogue record for this book is available from the British Library.

A catalog record for this book is available from the Library of Congress.

ISBN: HB: 978-0-7556-5294-5
PB: 978-0-7556-5295-2
ePDF: 978-0-7556-5297-6
eBook: 978-0-7556-5296-9

Typeset by Deanta Global Publishing Services, Chennai, India

To find out more about our authors and books visit www.bloomsbury.com and sign up for our newsletters.

Contents

Acknowledgements		vii
Note on Transliterations		viii

1	Introduction: An indirect line of enquiry		1
	1.1	The purpose	1
	1.2	The construct	7
	1.3	The overview	13
2	The evolution of Islamism		15
	2.1	From Banna to Morsi	16
	2.2	From Zaytouna to the parliament	19
	2.3	From Milli Görüş to the AKP	23
3	The history of the interaction		27
	3.1	Erbakan, Ghannouchi and the MB	27
	3.2	The spread of frames for legitimacy	33
	3.3	Conservative/Muslim democracy and the Turkish model	35
		3.3.1 The origins of Conservative/Muslim democracy	36
		3.3.2 The origins of the Turkish model	40
		3.3.3 The EU and the Turkish model	43
4	The context, milestones and actors of the interplay		47
	4.1	The AKP in Cairo, the MB in Ankara and Istanbul	50
	4.2	The AKP in Tunis, Ennahda in Ankara and Istanbul	55
	4.3	The actors and interlocutors	61
		4.3.1 The elite actors	62
		4.3.2 The interlocutors and structure	63
		4.3.3 Brokers: Al Jazeera and Yusuf Al-Qaradawi	67
5	The tactics of success for Islamists		71
	5.1	Winning the system	77
	5.2	Service to people is like a prayer	82
	5.3	Protective alliances against the old regime	86

		5.3.1 Threats and alliances for the MB	87
		5.3.2 Threats and alliances for Ennahda	96
6	Brothers in search of their bourgeoisie		99
	6.1	Road to neoliberalism	101
	6.2	The economic vision of Ennahda and the MB	105
	6.3	Cultivating an Islamic bourgeoisie	111
7	The new spirit of Islamism		121
	7.1	Islamist longing for success	121
	7.2	Post-Islamism and managerialism	124
		7.2.1 What do Muslim youth want?	126
		7.2.2 Managerial awakening	129
		7.2.3 Cheap Islamization	133
8	Changing dynamics of the interplay		137
	8.1	Post-2013 period: Fear, isolation and activism	139
		8.1.1 The MB – the AKP	139
		8.1.2 Ennahda – the AKP	143
	8.2	Erdogan's U-turns vis-a-vis the MB	147
	8.3	The current crisis, democracy and Islamism	152
9	Conclusion: The sink, the cooker and Islamism		161

Notes 171
Bibliography 212
Index 236

Acknowledgements

I am indebted to Michael J. Willis, who taught me how to organize my thoughts and questions academically. He has tolerated my journalistic aspirations, demeanour and occasional hastiness and has guided me not only as a colleague but also as a kind friend. I would also like to thank Faisal Devji, Walter Armbrust, Eugene Rogan and Rory McCarthy, whose comments and insights made this work better.

I cannot thank my husband, Mehmet, my son Deniz and 'my girls' in Oxford enough for being there for me through my highs and lows. They made me feel safe and joyous in ways that only sisters can. I could not have completed this research without their support.

This book is dedicated to my late father, Prof Müjdat Başaran, and my beautiful mother, Prof Yelda Başaran, for shaping me into the person I am today. I was able to embark on this academic journey, beginning with an MPhil and continuing with a DPhil in my late thirties at the University of Oxford, simply because life around them taught me to be resilient and hopeful. So, *canım babam ve canım annem* – thank you for illuminating my path – always.

Transliterations

This book employs the IJMES transliteration system, but familiar Arabic expressions such as *sharia* whose meaning is known in English are spelled without diacritics. All Arabic and Turkish terms are italicized. Names already widely used in their English forms are used in their common spelling. All Arabic and Turkish texts have been translated into English by the author. However, on several occasions, a native Arabic speaker's assistance has been sought to avoid any misconceptions. Arabic names containing articles are shortened from their second appearance onwards (e.g. Yusuf Al-Qaradawi to Qaradawi).

1

Introduction

An indirect line of enquiry

1.1 The purpose

Allow me to recount a compelling anecdote; a vignette that served as the impetus for my research, ultimately culminating in the creation of this book: In the summer of 2013, I held the position of editor-in-chief at a prominent newspaper, diligently covering the Gezi Uprisings unfolding in Istanbul. As the protests intensified, reaching their fourth day, tensions soared. It was evident that Erdogan perceived these demonstrations as a formidable threat to his authority, evoking a mix of concern and fury within him. Surprisingly, despite this critical juncture, Erdogan chose not to delay his scheduled trip to Tunisia, an unfamiliar destination to many of us at the time. Tunis, instead of the customary metropolises like London, Washington, Berlin or Paris, became his chosen destination. Tunis, an 'obscure' city.

Let me clarify, our editorial team, comprising numerous seasoned journalists and reporters, including those with more experience than myself, found ourselves perplexed by Erdogan's decision. We struggled to comprehend why he would depart Turkey amid such tumultuous circumstances and venture to Tunisia, a nation that was relatively unfamiliar to us. Certainly, we were well-versed in covering the Arab Uprisings, fully aware of Turkey's Justice and Development Party's (*Adalet ve Kalkınma Partisi*, the AKP) support for the Muslim Brotherhood in Egypt (*al-Ikhwan al-muslimin fi Misr*, the MB) and the Tunisian Renaissance Party (*Ennahda*). However, the gravity of these alliances had yet to fully crystallize in our collective consciousness.

Subsequently, a series of profound events transpired within Turkey. The delicate peace process with the Kurdish community abruptly collapsed, followed by Erdogan's challenge to the outcomes of the 2015 elections, which witnessed the AKP losing a significant number of parliamentary seats. Yet,

Erdogan managed to secure a referendum triumphantly, paving the way for a transformation of Turkey's parliamentary system into a perplexing manifestation of hyper-presidentialism. Amid these tumultuous developments, a coup attempt sent shockwaves throughout the nation. The momentous events that unfolded commanded the focus and efforts of a multitude of journalists, opinion leaders, commentators and think tanks, impeding a comprehensive investigation into the intricate dynamics that underpinned the AKP's connection with Egypt's Ikhwan and Tunisia's Ennahda. Yet, within this backdrop, lay a multifaceted and significant narrative awaiting meticulous unravelling. A narrative that transcends the individual stories of Turkey's AKP, Egypt's MB and Tunisia's Ennahda, and instead, encapsulates the essence of the evolving spirit of Islamism itself.

From the fall of former Egyptian president Hosni Mubarak and President Ben Ali in Tunisia, Turkey's AKP maintained an intensive dialogue with the MB in Egypt and until 2013. Notably, delegations from the AKP, comprised of parliamentarians, ministers and accomplished mayors of major cities, undertook journeys to Cairo and Tunis. In turn, representatives from the MB, particularly members of the Freedom and Justice Party (FJP – *hizb al-hurriya wa'l adala*) and Ennahda, visited Istanbul and Ankara, where they embarked on a series of activities, including visits to municipalities and police stations, participation in workshops and conferences, and meetings with government ministers. What was the primary goal of these meetings, which were withheld from the public during that period? What topics and deliberations took place among these Islamist actors in the wake of the Arab Uprisings? What implications does this political confluence carry for the essence and ethos of Islamism? These inquiries sparked my curiosity and served as the impetus for this work, which examines two distinct sets of relationships: the affiliation between the AKP and the MB, as well as the connection between the AKP and Ennahda during the period spanning 2011 to 2013. The central argument put forth is that there existed a diffusion of tactics among these three prominent Islamist entities, which in turn sheds light on the ambitions and objectives of contemporary Islamist movements.

The selection of Ennahda, the Egyptian MB and the AKP as case studies was not intended for the purpose of comparing their strategies, discourse or praxis. This is not the gate through which this research enters the debate. Rather, it aims to elucidate the specifics of this political confluence, which presented an opportune moment for analysis due to the involvement of two Islamist entities – the Egyptian MB and Ennahda – that, for the first time in their respective histories, had participated in free elections, established political parties and subsequently assumed positions of power. In this sense, I agree with Talal Assad, when he claims that 'understanding any dominant concept of modern life is [...] perhaps best approached indirectly. A straight line isn't always the most useful way to explore things because it assumes not only that the endpoint is known but also that the shortest way to it from the starting point is always the best'.[1] In a similar vein Islamist ideas and actions are shaped and re-shaped precisely in this way – through their interactions with one another, rather than their interaction with the state or Islamic ideology.[2] Scholars of social movements also argue that a review of the interaction between actors is crucial for gaining a 'deeper insight into the complexities and agency involved in [any] process'.[3] The central question of this book arose from this line of thinking, which led me to focus on an indirect line – a political confluence – to determine Islamist actors' aspirations and goals.

In this book, I offer an alternative approach to comprehending Islamism, diverging from recent scholarship that primarily concentrates on case studies within a single country[4] or on cross-national comparisons[5]. Emphasizing transnational diffusion proves to be particularly rewarding as it presents a sobering counterpoint to those exceptionalist narratives of Islamism that accord priority to ideology as the principal causal explanation. De-exceptionalization, in this sense, does not imply that the goals and ideological evolution of Islamist actors in MENA are indistinguishable from those of their Western or Latin American counterparts. Rather, it allows me to avoid the two counterproductive lenses of studying Islamism: the neo-Orientalist trap that treats the actors and polities of MENA 'as largely homogeneous, closed, parochial, and resistant to change'[6] and the lens of 'postmodern/poststructuralist eulogisation of Islamism'.[7] Both approaches should be considered as traps for any research on the subject. This book demonstrates that Islamist parties, akin to any other political entity, encounter intricate trade-offs while navigating the demanding landscape of a newly competitive political system. It also represents an original contribution to understandings of contemporary Islamist politics, specifically developing a new analysis of transnational diffusion.

Two considerations justify my research topic and outline the puzzle I seek to unravel. First and foremost is the claim that the persistence of the ties between Islamist entities is fully explained by ideology. A simplistic and limiting assumption about transnational ties between Islamist actors is that they sought to create or join a utopian *ummah*. Thus, it is commonly asserted that these three Islamist actors with a shared ideological background – the AKP, the MB and Ennahda – have attempted to form an *Ikhwani* bloc in the Middle East. News outlets raised this belief, postulating that the transnational dialogue between the AKP, Ennahda and the Egyptian MB concerned 'their mutual interest in restoring the era of Islamic rule'.[8] Turkey's president Erdoğan had been accused by Turkey's opposition as being 'an offshoot of Ikhwan and Al-Qaeda whose main aim is to revive *ummah*' and 'a supporter of *Ikhwani* groups who diluted Turkishness within the *ummah*'[9] but was at the same time praised by Islamist and pro-government news outlets[10] as being '*ümmetçi* (promoter of the *ummah*)' due to AKP's close relations with the MB and Ennahda. Renowned scholars of Islamism, including Bassam Tibi and Gilles Kepel, saw the interplay in a similar vein. 'Well-informed observers know of the growing connections between the Muslim Brothers and the AKP, as Turkish Islamists claim a neo-Ottoman leadership of the Middle East. The Muslim Brothers are also growing outside of Egypt, including in the United States and Europe, thus becoming a transnational movement',[11] claims Tibi. Gilles Kepel's approach is akin to that of Tibi:

> The MB, Salafists of varied stripes and former Islamic fighters convened after April 2011, then once more in Istanbul in October under the auspices of Erdoğan's AKP and Qatar. The thought was to have Libya serve as the geopolitical hyphen between Ennahda's Tunisia and Morsi's Egypt, and thereby make one Brotherhood empire of eastern coastal North Africa. However, even within this movement, intertribal and regional conflicts prevailed over allegiance to a shared ideology.[12]

Kepel fails to explain what this 'one Brotherhood empire' would entail or aim to achieve. Although he acknowledges that allegiance to a shared ideology was frustrated by conflict and most probably national interests, his approach implies the existence of a pan-Islamist agenda.

Indeed, following its second term in 2007, the AKP undertook a deliberate positioning of itself as a representative voice for the Muslim world, particularly concerning the Palestinian-Israeli conflict. During this period, the party exhibited a greater alignment with Hamas rather than the Fatah faction of the Palestinian Liberation Organization. This strategic shift coincided with the appointment of Ahmet Davutoğlu as foreign minister, who expressed his desire to restore Turkey's prominence not only within the region but also in the wider Muslim world, embracing an Ottoman nostalgic perspective.[13]

Consequently, the AKP's efforts to strengthen ties with countries with Muslim-majority countries gave rise to a secondary interpretation, suggesting that Erdoğan harboured aspirations to transform Turkey in a manner reminiscent of Suleiman the Magnificent and reclaim a pre-Atatürk era when Turkey was not only fervently Muslim but also a regional powerhouse.[14] It is crucial to note that these analyses propose that the AKP's concealed agenda was not centred on establishing a theocracy,[15] but rather rooted in the concept of Neo-Ottomanism.[16] However, these points of contention can be challenged by considering the dynamics of the transnational dialogue that emerged between the AKP, the Egyptian MB and Tunisian Ennahda. Furthermore, they obscure our comprehension of the underlying principles of Islamism in the twenty-first century.

There is no denying the transnational aspect of 'Muslim politics'; however, this does not indicate the formation of a unified Muslim cultural entity or the establishment of a dominant transnational Islamic sphere. It is essential to approach politics and policymaking in a manner that surpasses the replication of the political paradigm prevalent during the Cold War era.[17] Through my research, I have demonstrated that the interplay observed between various Islamist actors did not embody a global Islamist political project as conceived in the 1980s, influenced by Jamal al-Afghani's conceptualization of *ummah* or *dar al-Islam*[18] – a territorial concept wherein sharia law holds sway. Contemporary Islamists, in contrast to their predecessors, exhibit a symbolic comprehension of global Muslim solidarity, which is mobilized in times of distress faced by Muslims worldwide. What Gilles Kepel referred to as the objective of constructing 'a Brotherhood empire' can be better explained through the lens of realist international relations theory as an interest-based relationship. For instance, during the period between 2011 and 2013, the exchange between the AKP and North African parties appeared to yield benefits for all parties involved. The North African parties acquired valuable technocratic knowledge from an Islamist party that was recognized by influential international actors as a success, thus strengthening their position within their respective governments. Simultaneously, the AKP extended its economic and geostrategic support, enabling it to exercise soft power in the region and establish broader avenues for economic investment.

The prospect of Islamist interconnectedness has been exaggerated as pan-Islamic solidarity and is perceived as a threat, especially in the West.[19] The dynamics of the Islamist movements, actors and parties are, however, complex and their goals follow divergent trajectories. An accurate problematization of these trajectories within Islamism requires the use of different perspectives to re-examine the Islamist actors' ways and means of conducting politics, the shifts in their theological teachings and discourses and their relationships with one another. The Islamist movements exhibit significant internal disagreements and clashes across a wide spectrum of issues such as the role of women within their movements and in society at large, the significance attributed to ethnic and tribal affiliations, the equitable distribution of rights, duties and privileges among different generations, the appropriate allocation of scarce local and national economic resources, the nature of international and transnational relations to be pursued, and the choice of allies.[20]

Furthermore, Islamists are deeply rooted in their local contexts, and nationalism often occupies a prominent position adjacent to their core ideological framework. In contemporary Islamist thinking, belonging to the global Muslim community – *ummah* – entails little more than encountering and responding to similar challenges faced by Muslims in different countries. While S. Sayyid views Islam as a master signifier in the polity of MENA countries,[21] Roy argues that Islam has never been a dominant factor but, rather, plays a legitimizing role[22] on ethnic and national factors and that Islamists have, since the 1980s, 'largely abandoned transnational militant solidarity and are centred on national politics, with an agenda based on three main points: a call to replace corrupt ruling elites, a conservative socio-cultural agenda, and robust nationalism'.[23] Put simply, 'Islamo-nationalism triumphs over pan-Islamism'.[24]

A second motivation for this research is to provide empirical evidence for an understudied aspect of the Arab Uprising era, that is, the relations between Islamist political parties.

It is true that the literature on Arab Uprisings covers a wide range of topics and approaches. Some studies analyse the impact of the revolutions on different Middle Eastern countries using frameworks like democratic transition, agency in democratization, contentious politics and democracy promotion.[25] Others focus on civil resistance since 2011,[26] examining the relationship between historical agency, structure and internal/external factors.[27] Some scholars explore broader questions, such as the implications of the 2011 revolutions for the MENA, while others examine the revolutions in the context of colonialism and argue that they are 'post-ideological'. Asef Bayat takes a micro-level approach, studying everyday contentions, ordinary people's routines and subaltern agency on the streets. There is also an examination of how Islamist movements influenced the revolts and the impact of the revolts on Islamism.[28] Works on Ennahda[29] and the Tunisian revolution, as well as articles on different aspects of the Turkish model,[30] are also available. However, there are limited examples focusing on the interactions between the AKP, Ennahda and the Muslim Brotherhood from 2011 to 2013.[31] Only a few books touch upon the symbolic and tactical diffusion between the AKP-Ennahda and the AKP-MB. While existing works offer valuable insights, they do not provide a comprehensive picture. Additional dimensions, such as the focus on transnational and trans-party dialogues during and after the revolutions provided by this research, would contribute to a more nuanced understanding.

Due to the absence of true democratic processes and the co-optation tendencies within Arab dictatorial regimes, the role of political parties, particularly Islamist parties, has been overlooked in the literature.[32] Political parties in the Arab world were viewed as a 'far cry from traditional Western-style political parties [that] seek to win elections and assume executive power [because] they were rarely given the opportunity to govern – [or even consider governing] – at local or national levels'.[33] Although political parties cannot provide a panoptic account to explain the malleability and transformation of an ideology, they possess the capacity to offer an enlightening subset of discourse production and implementation related to ideologies.[34] They are, in a way, agents capable of rendering ideologies palatable as well as contributing to the 'increase or decrease of ideological polarisation through what has been termed value cleavages'.[35] Moreover, they can influence the prominence of interest groups and foster ideological flexibility by shifting their focus to different electoral demands or presumed preferences during policy negotiations.

The period after the Arab Uprisings, however, unlocked a new avenue for studying party politics in the Arab world. Ennahda won 40 per cent of the seats and formed the first government in Tunisia in 2011, while the MB in Egypt, via its political party FJP, won 46 per cent of the seats; in 2012 its candidate, Mohammed Morsi, became the first democratically elected president of Egypt. Therefore, the victories of Ennahda and the Muslim Brotherhood at the ballot box offer a rare entry point for examining the practices and endeavours of Islamist entities as political parties.

1.2 The construct

Although I employed a grounded theory approach, it is important to note that I, too, made assumptions regarding this interplay. Considering the extensive body of literature on transnational Islamism and Turkey's shift in foreign policy towards the Middle East since 2009, as briefly mentioned earlier, it appeared reasonable to hypothesize that the interplay among these three Islamist entities could be linked to the formation of a transnational Sunni Islamist bloc guided by Islamist ideology. These assumptions have not compromised the grounded theory approach; rather, they have provided an opportunity to contrast an alternative explanation with the research findings.

The course of this research is the following. First, I seek to uncover the intricacies of the interplay that emerged in the wake of the Arab Uprisings of 2011. Despite the existence of numerous studies that discuss the promotion of a Turkish model for the Arab world and highlight the relationship between the AKP and North African countries like Morocco, Tunisia, Egypt and Libya as a notable example of this promotion, the literature fails to delve into the specifics of this interplay. Therefore, the primary objective is to bridge this gap by presenting tangible evidence. The second objective is to provide an explanation for the interplay, utilizing a diffusion framework and employing process tracing methods. By adopting these analytical tools, I mean to demonstrate the mechanisms through which ideas and practices were disseminated among Islamists and trace the trajectory of this interplay over time.

Before going any further, we need to establish a clear definition of diffusion and its relevance in this particular context. Typically, the diffusion framework is used to examine how protest tactics, repertoires, innovations or collective actions are transmitted from one group or individual to another.[36] However, diffusion processes also encompass the dissemination of interpretive frames constructed by actors to define issues, formulate problems and solutions, assign responsibility and mobilize political claims.[37] What distinguishes diffusion from broader forms of information dissemination or economic and diplomatic linkages is the active participation of both senders and recipients, as well as the introduction of new ideas into the discourse.[38]

In the context of this research, the new idea revolves around the AKP's provision of tactics aimed at assisting the MB and Ennahda in gaining and retaining political power. While these tactics may not appear as strategic innovations at first glance – since all political parties aspire to govern – this principle does not hold true for Islamist parties operating within authoritarian post-colonial regimes. For instance, despite Ennahda's long-standing pursuit of legality and inclusion in the Tunisian parliamentary system since its establishment in 1981, it lacked the means to govern effectively. The Egyptian MB faced a similar predicament, as did the Moroccan Justice and Development Party (PJD – *Parti de la Justice et du Développement*), which had to downplay its successes in local elections out of concern for agitating the king.[39]

Consequently, four categories of tactics were identified – crisis evasion, legitimization, winning elections and maintaining power – as part of the material diffusion explained by the AKP's assistance to Ennahda and the MB between 2011 and 2013. The symbolic diffusion, preceding the Arab Uprisings, was elucidated through frames such as Muslim/conservative democracy and the utilization of the Turkish model by the AKP, MB and Ennahda as a means to establish themselves as legitimate political actors. These tactics and frames are considered as evidence contributing to a deeper understanding of Islamist aspirations and strategies.

To investigate the relationship between the AKP, Ennahda and the MB following the Arab Uprisings, more than seventy elite actors from diverse socio-economic, cultural and national backgrounds were interviewed. Adhering to the process tracing method, the interviews were not randomly selected but carefully chosen based on a thorough examination of individuals involved in the interplay or possessing relevant knowledge. Conducted between 2018 and 2021, the interviews took place in Istanbul, Ankara, Tunis and London and followed a semi-structured format in various settings, countries and time periods. Importantly, each interviewee was unaware of what others had said or who the other interviewees were, ensuring independence and unbiased responses.

In accordance with Isaiah Berlin's formulation, academics and journalists are driven by the pursuit of truth. That still remains to be our primary objective. However, it is important to acknowledge the limitations inherent in the belief that there exists a singular, universally applicable truth, as this notion can be traced back to a Platonic understanding and poses certain challenges. While I do not intend to delve into an extensive epistemological debate or engage in an exhaustive analysis of the history of political ideas, I find it crucial to clarify my standpoint. Was I deceived by the interviewees or subject to party propaganda? There is no definitive answer to this question. Nonetheless, I took various precautions to mitigate such risks. First, I refrained from posing questions that explicitly sought to confirm whether individuals were seeking success. Instead, during the initial phase of the interviews, my focus was on uncovering the details surrounding the who, what, when and where of their encounters. Where did these meetings take place? Who was present? How frequently did they occur? What were the topics of discussion? Subsequently, the interviews shifted towards exploring the underlying motivations by asking the question, why. I approached this enquiry with an open-minded mindset. It was only towards the end that I gently probed them about the assumptions regarding their close relationship with the AKP following the revolutions. To validate the accuracy of the meetings, individuals involved and intermediaries, I cross-referenced each interview with one another.

Although exposing the thinking of elite actors and how these change over time cannot answer all our questions about Islamism, elite interviews allow us to identify what aspects are of utmost importance, which aspects are open to negotiation, and what remains uncertain.[40] Documenting elite perspectives and their processes of political learning is crucial for comprehending the trajectory of political actions. Political learning occurs at various levels of society, but the experiences and knowledge of political leaders are particularly significant for the reconstruction of democratic systems, as it involves challenging and discrediting old beliefs.[41] In the context of Islamism, elite interviews hold particular importance since the movements are largely organized around elite agents rather than solely ideas, as will be further explored in the subsequent chapter.

My position as a researcher had an impact on the collection of data. Prior to pursuing my MPhil and DPhil studies at Oxford, I held the position of editor-in-chief at a liberal-left newspaper in Turkey. Unfortunately, due to a government crackdown, the newspaper was shut down, and I had to suspend my professional activities to ensure the safety of my family. As a result, I was there for a known figure, albeit an unpopular one among many members of the AKP. Consequently, some of my interviewees hesitated to meet with me as they did not want to be perceived as engaging with a journalist from the opposing side. In the current Turkish context, the 'opposing side' encompasses individuals who do not pledge allegiance to President Erdoğan.

Nevertheless, throughout my research, those key individuals who were knowledgeable about the interplay or actively involved in it gradually distanced themselves from the AKP, with some even joining the opposition ranks. Despite initial obstacles, I was able to conduct interviews with nearly all relevant individuals from the AKP. Senior members of the MB and select Egyptian Islamist elites, who had sought refuge in Istanbul or Ankara, were also willing to participate in interviews. Only a small number of individuals declined or requested anonymity or pseudonyms for their involvement in the research. Fortunately, I had the opportunity to meet and interview all significant Ennahda members involved in the interplay before the *de facto* coup orchestrated by Tunisian president Kais Saeid.

While a valuable potential interviewee in Egypt would have been Khariat al-Shater, the then deputy Supreme Guide of the MB, his imprisonment made it impossible to arrange a meeting.

Another perspective to consider about this research involves the potential concern regarding generalization – a prevalent challenge often encountered in the realm of case studies. I may be criticized for focusing on an exceptional political confluence following consecutive revolutions in Tunisia and Egypt in 2011. Surely, it may be argued, this interplay cannot illustrate or explain all aspects of Islamist aspirations and objectives and it is also true that one study cannot capture the diverse array of Islamism that has emerged since the 1990s. Notwithstanding these points, I remain convinced that the interplay examined in this book does not stand as an isolated incident in the narrative of Islamism but rather represents a manifestation of the evolving goals of Islamists. The two-decade-long rule of Turkey's AKP, the rise and decline of the Egyptian MB's fledgling party FJP and Tunisia's Ennahda, once viewed as a model of reconciliation and consensus, make these three entities and their unprecedented interplay between 2011 and 2013 compelling examples for investigating change within political Islam. These entities have wielded and continue to wield substantial intellectual and organizational influence within Islamist movements. Egypt's MB, in particular, is considered a progenitor of Islamist politics, inspiring the establishment of similar movements across the Middle East, notably in Syria, Jordan and Palestine. Rachid Ghannouchi, the founder and president of Ennahda, is widely recognized as a prominent contemporary Islamist politician and thinker. Ennahda's path to governance in Tunisia since 2011 had demonstrated its alliance-building, consensus-based and power-sharing approaches, which reflect significant trends within political Islam and its party expressions.[42] Lastly, the AKP had long been championed by the West as a prime example of the fusion of Islamism, democracy and a market economy. Considering these three entities and the diffusion process that transpired among them allows us to examine contemporary Islamist aspirations and gain insights into their transformative nature.

Moreover, a sense of inevitability should not be projected onto this diffusion process in hindsight, as if it was natural for the MB and Ennahda to forge a close relationship with the AKP in the aftermath of the Arab Uprisings. First, the AKP is a non-Arab political party whose Islamist credentials are questioned within the realm of Islamism especially by the followers of the MB and Ennahda. Second, while the MB and Ennahda could have sought dialogue with established political parties worldwide or relied on their long-standing political strategies to acquire tactics on winning elections and governance, they did not. Third, the absence of a similar diffusion process between the AKP and the Moroccan PJD can be seen as a test case. Despite the PJD's leaders praising the AKP's reforms and electoral successes in the media and expressing interest in observing 'Turkey as an example to see how a faith-based, or an identity-based, political party could develop pragmatic policies to deal with the challenges',[43] there have been no meetings, personal connections or diffusion of tactics between the two parties.

According to a former foreign policy adviser to the AKP who participated in meetings between the AKP and the MB, attempts were made to establish contact with the PJD after the revolutions in Egypt and Tunisia, but the PJD showed no interest, seemingly existing 'in a different dimension'.[44] In this 'other dimension', King Mohammed VI of Morocco, known as the Commander of the Faithful, holds ultimate authority over legitimacy. The PJD was co-opted by the regime into the political system in 2011, transitioning from the main opposition party to becoming part of the executive branch through ministries. However, the PJD's inclusion was carefully structured so that it had to cooperate with stalwarts of the existing political order.[45] As the aspirations and legitimacy of the PJD were shaped within the boundaries set by the Moroccan monarchy, the AKP's tactics were of restricted relevance.

During this research, a recurring theme of success emerged organically in every interview and subsequently took centre stage in this research, without any deliberate manipulation or influence. The Egyptian MB sought to understand the specific components of a 'success model', commonly referred to as the Turkish model, which had been constructed and advocated by a diverse array of actors including Western policymakers, think tanks, Turkish soft power entities, Arab intellectuals, Islamist organizations and academics.

In 2011, Turkey was still perceived as the preferred Muslim power by the West, given its NATO membership, ongoing EU accession process and strong integration with European markets. In essence, the AKP, with its Islamist background, was seen as a European actor that had successfully implemented a market-friendly economic programme leading to economic prosperity. From this standpoint, the AKP's model held normative appeal for both the Egyptian MB and Ennahda in Tunisia. It provided a pathway for these parties to be recognized as viable political actors both domestically and internationally. Thus, the attempts by these Islamist groups and other ideological entities suppressed by national or international actors to emulate transnational movements are not unique.[46] This pattern reflects a broader trend where actors seek to align with established models to gain legitimacy and recognition in the global arena.

What is this model and why is it considered successful? It has been described and labelled by various scholars in different ways, including terms such as post-Islamist, Islamic liberalism, Islamo-democracy, Muslimhood model, conservative populism, institutional Islamism, conservative democracy or neo-Islamist model.[47] Olivier Roy simply referred to its adherents as 'new Islamists'.[48] While I agree with the scholarly view that characterizes the AKP's model as post-Islamist, it is important to emphasize that it is also 'shaped by the geopolitical reconfigurations that have occurred in the post-Cold War era'.[49] In keeping with this historical context, I conceptualize the pursuit of success as an endeavour to integrate Islamist praxis into the framework of neoliberal rationality, as understood by the Islamists themselves. Neoliberal rationality, according to Foucault, pertains to any conduct that can be systematically adjusted and modified in response to changing circumstances.[50] The diffusion process aimed to equip Ennahda and the MB with tactics and frameworks that could facilitate the most adaptable conduct to achieve success. This adaptation, I argue, prompts the Islamist movements in question to shift their agendas, modus operandi, and attention from the core tenets of Islamism to 'banality of governance'. This is not surprising, as neoliberal rationality extends beyond economic policies and encompasses the incorporation of market principles to institutions and societal entities.[51]

S. Sayyid, in the second edition of *Fundamental Fear* (published in 2003), summarizes the conundrum of Islamists as if he had access to the interviews I conducted:

> The major difficulty faced by Islamists, despite all their rhetoric of Islam as a total system, a complete way of life, is that when it comes down to it, far too many of them have a very limited idea of what 'a way of life' is. [. . . Hence] it is not surprising that so many Islamists are considered unequal to the task of managing the complexities of contemporary governance. Their capacity to make the trains run on time or make sure the garbage is collected is often put into question.[52]

Remarkably, the chapters in which I lay out the structure and details of the diffusion process between the AKP, Ennahda and the MB, bear witness to how garbage collection had become a symbolic as well as a practical issue among these actors. 'There is great need for Islamists to demonstrate great skill in dealing with the banality of governing'[53] continues Sayyid. This book, to some degree, features this endeavour of the Islamists and sheds light on their goals.

1.3 The overview

The following chapter outlines the evolution of the MB, Ennahda and the AKP. It serves as a second introduction to the book while situating the interplay already within the broader context of Islamism. Chapter 3 then describes the historical background of the relationship between the AKP's predecessor movement, *Milli Görüş* and the MB in Egypt; and Ennahda in Tunisia since the 1980s. The purpose of Chapter 3 is to demonstrate the extent of the relationship prior to the 2011 uprisings by explaining the use and diffusion of two frames as signposts towards legitimacy and success: The 'Turkish model' and the 'Muslim democracy/Conservative democrat' model.

Chapter 4 chronicles pivotal events and meetings from 2011 to 2013 between the parties. It sets out the structure of the diffusion, as well as identifying the key actors, institutions and brokers who helped craft this relationship. The fifth chapter categorizes and explains the tactics shared by the AKP with Ennahda and the MB, all of which the AKP believed to be principal components in its success. Then, the process tracing method was employed to examine the correlation between these tactics and the AKP's history of governance, particularly its success and crisis management approaches. Process tracing involves employing descriptive inferences to elucidate the evidence on event sequences and processes within a given case, aiming to develop or test hypotheses about causal mechanisms.[54] This method entails utilizing various sources, including histories, archival documents, interview transcripts and other relevant materials, to verify whether the hypothesized or implied causal process suggested by a theory is evident in the observed sequence of events.[55] Thus, Chapter 5 of the book involves an interplay between explaining the tactics employed during the AKP's rule in Turkey since 2002 and those transferred to the MB and Ennahda, illustrating how these tactics were shaped by the AKP's experiences and derived from its proven methods. This approach, often referred to as 'correlation mapping', seeks to identify *prima facie* evidence of other diffusion processes, whether material or ideational (such as diffusion through normative power).[56]

Chapter 6 begins exploring Islamists' encounters with neoliberalism and continues explaining the economic vision of the MB and Ennahda and why the AKP's economic strategy appealed to them. It demonstrates the crux of the AKP's economic strategy – the cultivation of an Islamic bourgeoisie – and how this was diffused and translated to Ennahda and the MB. This chapter also provides the most tangible causal inference of the diffusion process. Chapter 7 attempts to expound on the meaning of 'success' for these actors. In the broadest sense, the pursuit of success at all costs and the formation of an entrepreneurial self are key social tenets of the neoliberal system.[57] The first part of the chapter discusses Islamists' longing for success, and their managerial spirit in attaining this success by engaging with *The New Spirit of Capitalism* by Boltsanki et al.[58] The second part of the chapter attempts to incorporate the discussion into a post-Islamist[59] framework. Finally, Chapter 8 presents a summary of how the relationship between the AKP, the MB and Ennahda evolved from the 2013 Egyptian coup to 2022, highlighting Erdoğan's remarkable U-turns regarding the MB and Ennahda. This last section adds to the evidence that the primary motivation in the interplay of these parties was neither Islamic activism nor the establishment of a Sunni bloc.

2

The evolution of Islamism

If the ambition is contributing to the deliberation of a 'new spirit of Islamism' by demonstrating the changing goals and aspirations of the Islamists in the post-Arab Uprising era, unpacking Islamism's emergence and evolution are imperative. Despite a plethora of literature and sources, Islamism remains an enigmatic socio-political phenomenon, and scholars struggle to explain the changing faces of its followers.[1] The Orientalist or culturalist approach to studying Islamism, in which Islam and Muslim culture are treated as constant variables, results in a reductionist and rigid understanding of political Islam. Insufficient and prejudiced views on the politics of Islam also stem from the use of modernization theory as a primary analytical paradigm. With its inherent secular bias and clear demarcation between the traditional and the modern, modernization theorists are inclined to view political Islam as inherently regressive, stagnant and totalitarian and exaggerate the notion that Islam dictates every aspect of Islamist politics.

From a postmodernist perspective, on the other hand, Islamism can be understood as a response to the aspirations of Muslim societies for cultural autonomy, alternative political systems and moral frameworks in the face of universalizing secular modernity.[2] Hence, the argument goes, Islamism emerged as a reaction to the challenges posed by postmodernity, characterized by the proliferation of multiple truths and the erosion of certainties. As Muslims grappled with the perceived intrusion of modernism into their cultural spheres, the advent of postmodernism pushed them to seek certainty and coherence through tangible moral principles and stable cultural identities to which they could anchor themselves. I am inclined to agree with the postmodernist approach; however, with a certain caveat: Islamism does not merely involve a quest for cultural authenticity, as emphasized by postmodernists but instead, it encompasses a political agenda and choices intertwined with twentieth-century Western ideas, ranging from liberal to totalitarian perspectives.[3]

In a similar vein, Islamist movements emerged not due to a failure to adapt to modernity, but rather as responses to what they perceived as the shortcomings of 'systems and ideologies hostile to Islam [. . .]'.[4] Islamists held that the post-colonial ruling regimes remained dependent on the former colonial powers, rendering them inherently illegitimate. They drew 'strength from the widespread deficiencies of these post-colonial states in the Middle East: massive corruption, overreliance on coercion, and the failure of Arab Socialism in Egypt, Syria, Iraq, and Algeria'.[5] Concomitantly, while many states adopted a secular model influenced by Europe, certain elites in countries like Iraq, Turkey and Tunisia believed that rapid nation-building required a cohesive religious and linguistic identity. This emphasis on religious homogenization and the reorganization of religious communities in relation to political power further politicized Islamist movements.[6]

Certain regional and international developments also had a significant impact on the standing of Islamist movements. The defeat of Arab states led by Egypt's president Gamal Abdel Nasser in their conflicts with Israel, particularly the failure to regain Palestine in 1967, played a pivotal role. Prominent scholar Yusuf al-Qaradawi, for instance, links the displacement of Palestinians from their land and the establishment of Israel in 1948 (known as *an-nakbah*, meaning 'catastrophe') and the Arab defeat in 1967 (*an-naksah*, meaning 'setback') to the awakening of Islamism.[7] This defeat further eroded the credibility of nationalist-populist Arab regimes. Following Nasser's death, which occurred a few years after the 1967 defeat, discourses centred on liberation, Marxism and socialism lost their rigour. Despite the presence of other populist regimes in the region, such as in Iraq, Syria, Libya and Algeria, with similar structures and narratives, the tide had turned irreversibly. 'A new force was maturing rapidly, namely, Islamism'[8] to fill the ideological vacuum.

2.1 From Banna to Morsi

Against the backdrop of European colonialism, particularly evident through the establishment of the Suez Canal Company in Ismailiyya, Egypt, Hasan al-Banna, the founder of the Muslim Brotherhood, witnessed the repercussions of foreign control. Influenced by prominent thinkers such as Jamal al-Din al-Afghani (1839–97), Afghani's student Muhammad Abduh (1849–1905) and Abduh's follower Rashid Rida (1865–1935), Banna came to believe that Islam held the remedies necessary to combat the perceived degeneration caused by colonial rule. What began as conversations in Ismailiyya's coffeehouses eventually led to the formation of the Society of Muslim Brothers (*Jam'iyyat al-Ikhwan al-Muslimin*) in 1928.

Banna advocated for the establishment of an Islamic order (*nizam islami*), with the core element being an Islamic state. He argued that the path to resolving societal issues lay in the gradual Islamization of both society and the state through the implementation of *sharia*, the Islamic legal framework. Banna believed that by embracing this vision, Muslims would rediscover their authentic selves.

Considered as one of the primary ideologues of Islamism, Sayyid Qutb was not initially a member of the Brotherhood and even criticized several MB leaders in the aftermath of the 1952 Free Officers revolution led by Gamal Abdel Nasser. Qutb later joined the MB and was arrested by the Nasser government. He was then released on the grounds of ill health but rearrested and, in 1965, executed. Nasser's repression of the MB during the 1950s and 1960s, jailing and torturing its members and denying them access to the legal political arena, had been paradigmatic for the MB.[9] The MB's persecution and Qutb's execution caused frustration and anger within the organization, leading to the increased prominence of radical ideas.[10]

During the 1970s, under the presidency of Anwar Sadat in Egypt, the MB found a favourable environment in which to operate. Sadat, who succeeded Nasser, released imprisoned Brotherhood leaders as a counterbalance to leftist forces.[11] It was also during this period that Hasan al-Hudaibi, the second Supreme Guide of the Brotherhood, indirectly criticized the views of Sayyid Qutb. In his notable work 'Preachers not Judges (*du'at la qudat*)', Hudaibi argued that *jihad* against a man-made state solely because the latter is not based on *sharia* was illegitimate.[12] He also advocated for non-violent means to further the MB's goals.

During the 1980s, the MB faced a complex and divergent set of circumstances under the rule of Hosni Mubarak. The Islamic Revolution of 1979 in Iran provided a boost to the Brotherhood's aspirations. However, within Egypt, the group encountered 'conflicting currents'. One example of this was their participation in parliamentary elections through alliances with the centrist-nationalist Al Wafd Party in 1984, 1987 and 1995. This approach received criticism from hardliners within the Brotherhood who feared it would compromise the movement's integrity.[13] Nevertheless, by engaging in these elections, the Brotherhood 'plunged into formal politics, expanded its social network, and reached out to liberal and secular forces'.[14]

Until the 1990s, the MB maintained its unwavering objective of establishing an Islamic state in Egypt, firmly rooted in its ideology of *tawheed* (unity of

God), emphasizing the comprehensive involvement of Islam in all aspects of life and politics. However, similar to other Islamist movements worldwide, the MB began publicly embracing the civic and religious virtues of democracy in the early 1990s, demanding its full implementation within the Egyptian political system.[15] While engaging in electoral politics, the MB pursued a strategy of coexistence with the Mubarak regime, employing appeasement, concessions and alliances. It is important to note that the MB did not abandon its commitment to *sharia* law, and from the mid-1990s, their rhetoric exhibited a dual emphasis on democracy and *sharia*.[16] The movement proposed the establishment of 'a civil state theoretically promising equality for all citizens regardless of religion or gender, accompanied by the active use of language advocating personal freedom'.[17] However, there is limited evidence to support the translation of these theoretical principles and rhetoric into practical implementation. Notably, the MB deputies consistently opposed the liberalization of laws pertaining to the rights of non-Muslims and women, citing their perceived violation of *sharia*. This firm stance serves as evidence of the MB's unwavering conservatism and uncompromising approach towards gender issues.[18]

However, it was also during this period that a notable divergence in strategy, practice and ideology surfaced within the MB, with the younger generation espousing the idea of a civil state that incorporated an Islamic framework, rather than the complete implementation of *sharia* within the state apparatus.[19] This internal divide within the MB has been characterized as a generational clash between the younger members and the older, established figures, or alternatively, as a division between reformists and conservatives. The reformist faction, comprised of the younger generation, expressed criticism towards the MB's rigid and authoritative internal structure, while the conservative old guard remained 'staunchly committed to long-term religious missionary work (*dawa*) and the preservation of the movement's unity'.[20]

In the aftermath of the 9/11 attacks, the MB, like many other mainstream Islamist movements, felt the need to reframe its message to the West. During the 2005 presidential election campaign, the Brotherhood sought to present itself as 'open, moderate, and democratic'. However, its credibility as an opposition party was called into question due to its cautious and sometimes insufficient support for the *Kifaya* (Enough) movement, which emerged in late 2004 to protest against corruption and authoritarianism in the Mubarak regime. While some of the younger members of the Brotherhood expressed solidarity with the *Kifaya* movement through their writings on platforms such as Islam Online and

Al Jazeera.net, this did not fully satisfy the political supporters of *Kifaya*, who consisted of Nasserists, liberals, secularists and leftists.[21]

By the late 2000s, the leadership of the MB had come to realize that their long-term goal of establishing an Islamic state in Egypt was not achievable in the near future.[22] During this time, the Brotherhood refined its core political beliefs, emphasizing the importance of popular sovereignty, free elections and fair representation for all citizens, regardless of gender.[23] However, a persistent challenge remained until the 2011 uprisings: the need to clearly differentiate between the Brotherhood as a political movement and its role as a religious organization. In the years leading up to the revolution, the conservative wing of the Brotherhood held sway, although this did not mean that the reformist faction had been completely marginalized.

Following the 2011 uprisings, the MB became increasingly divided along generational and ideological lines regarding the path forward. The establishment of the Freedom and Justice Party (FJP) further intensified tensions, particularly between those advocating for a party-oriented approach and those emphasizing the importance of maintaining a broader social movement. Another source of conflict – between the *hizb* (party) and the *haraka* (social movement) – emerged. The literature and my findings highlight the emergence of a younger generation, particularly within the FJP, that looked to the Turkish model as a source of inspiration. However, the older generation remained sceptical of certain aspects, particularly in terms of conforming to the expectations of a secular state. This generational divide led to differing perspectives on Islamic governance, with the youth embracing a more post-Islamist outlook[24] and viewing the AKP as a model, while the older guard continued to prioritize an Islamizing agenda, adhering to the concept of '*shura*'.[25] What brought all these factions within the MB together was the opportunity for power and a consensus on the acceptance of 'the procedural aspects of democracy noting that *shura* consultation is mandated by Islam and was practised by the Prophet Muhammad himself'.[26]

2.2 From Zaytouna to the parliament

To comprehend the emergence and evolution of Ennahda, it is crucial to examine the key actors and state-building process in post-independence Tunisia. The nationalist movement in Tunisia began with the Destour Party in 1920, but it was eventually challenged by the more radical Neo-Destour Party, which became the dominant force in Tunisian nationalism. However, even within the Neo-Destour

Party, a division arose between its leader, Habib Bourguiba, and its secretary-general, Salah Ben Youssef. This rivalry for power reflected not only personal ambitions but also deeper societal dynamics, representing differing visions for Tunisia's future. Bourguiba embodied a modern, secular and Western-oriented perspective, while Ben Youssef advocated for an Arab-Islamic identity as the foundation of the state. In between these viewpoints were millions of Tunisians who embraced elements of both the West and their Arab-Islamic heritage.[27]

After winning the power struggle, Bourguiba became Tunisia's first president and implemented a top-down modernization agenda. He targeted sectors that had supported his rival, Ben Youssef, particularly the ulama and religious institutions. Bourguiba incorporated the ulama into government ministries and utilized their fatwas to legitimize his policies, aiming to control Islamism and seek retribution for their support of Youssef.[28] He introduced a series of Jacobin reforms that were met with disapproval from devout Tunisians. Bourguiba, who stated on several occasions his admiration for Turkey's founder, Atatürk, integrated the *sharia* court into the state judicial system, introduced a Personal Status Code, which prohibited polygyny, gave women the right to divorce, set a minimum age for marriage and ended male repudiation. Bourguiba justified these reforms by claiming to reinterpret Quranic commands through *ijtihad* while maintaining that he was not anti-Islam.

The Islamist movement in Tunisia, initially known as *Jamaa Islamiyya*, in 1972, emerged as a discussion group centred around Zaytouna University, the oldest Islamic teaching institution in the Middle East. This gathering was primarily driven by a sense of alienation, as religious institutions had been targeted and marginalized after Tunisia gained independence. The exposure to books published by the Muslim Brotherhood in Egypt further influenced Tunisian Islamists, creating ideological links with figures like Banna and Qutb. However, the formation of the movement in the 1970s was not the result of a mere importation of MB ideology, but rather an adaptation to Tunisia's evolving needs and modern tendencies.[29]

Two years later, in 1981, the group made a significant move by announcing its new name, the Islamic Tendency Group (*Mouvement de tendance islamique* – MTI), reflecting its progressive approach and adaptability to changing societal and political contexts.[30] This marked a pivotal moment for Tunisian Islamism as it aimed for legal recognition and inclusion in the political and public spheres. Rachid Ghannouchi, co-founder of MTI and later Ennahda, expressed the feelings of exclusion and displacement among his generation, who perceived their Arab-Islamic identity being overshadowed by Westernization.[31]

The MTI manifesto explicitly rejected violence and advocated for a multi-party system, positioning itself as a mainstream entity from the beginning. However, instead of gaining recognition, the emergence of the MTI faced harsh repression. Bourguiba, feeling threatened by its existence, vowed to eradicate the perceived Islamist threat,[32] leading to the imprisonment of MTI leaders shortly after its establishment. They were eventually released in 1984. During this period, the MTI broadened its agenda to include human rights, further reforms, democratization and social justice. To strengthen its support base, the MTI encouraged its followers to take up positions within the government, military, police force and trade unions. They also made efforts to influence the main student union, UGET, by attracting sympathizers. Although the government's refusal to officially include the MTI in the Tunisian political landscape did not lead to violent resistance, the movement sought to infiltrate the system through informal means. Their recruitment strategies and initiatives to gain control over syndicates, unions and certain government positions mirrored the operations of the MB in Egypt. With the ascension of Ben Ali to power, the MTI leaders were released from prison and saw an opportunity to establish a closer relationship with the regime. It was a time of potential change, with the MTI considering participation in the 1989 elections.

Ben Ali rebranded his party as the Democratic Constitutional Rally (*Rassemblement Constitutionnel Démocratique* – RCD) to mark the end of the Bourguiba era, while the MTI renamed itself Ennahda to avoid explicit Islamic references. Ennahda adopted a more moderate tone in public, stating it did not seek to undo secular reforms or oppose the Personal Status Code. However, as their recognition as a political party was pending, they participated in the 1989 election by fielding independent candidates nationwide. The election results were concerning for the Ben Ali regime, with Ennahda garnering 30 per cent of the votes while other opposition parties received less than 5 per cent combined. However, the regime downplayed Ennahda's support, reducing their official vote share to 14.5 per cent and claiming a 99 per cent endorsement for Ben Ali as president. Furthermore, the regime refused to recognize Ennahda as a political party and portrayed Islamists as a threat to social order due to their alleged dogmatism, contrasting it with the regime's supposed tolerance. Ghannouchi, infuriated by these portrayals and the election rigging, left for Algeria, and later imposed self-exile in London. Ennahda was officially banned, and many members were imprisoned by 1992. Ghannouchi's time in exile shifted his perspective on politics and altered his approach to integrating Islam within a modern state structure.

Ennahda has consistently sought recognition as a political party, unlike its ideological counterpart, the MB. However, it had only one opportunity to participate in an election in 1989, with its candidates running as independents due to repression and the threat of arrests. While its rhetoric occasionally became more radicalized due to internal divisions, government crackdowns prompted a prevailing approach of conciliation and compromise. Nevertheless, Ghannouchi had been advocating for democracy and the importance of parliamentary power since the 1980s. In 1995, Ennahda's congress in Switzerland marked an official declaration of the movement's revised approach, termed Islamic democracy, where *sharia* law would be the foundation of the state, implemented through elected councils within a democratic and multi-party system.[33]

Ennahda endured imprisonment and exile for nearly two decades from its foundation to the fall of Ben Ali in 2011, leading to debates and self-reflection within the movement.[34] Some saw this period as an opportunity for reform, while others questioned the future of Ennahda.[35] The truth lies in between: Ennahda was not extinguished, but it required significant effort to revive and reform the movement after the Uprising. A confidential document circulated among Ennahda elites in 2004 acknowledged that the movement had overreached in its confrontation with Ben Ali, advocating for a more compromising and pragmatic approach.[36] According to this document, the leaders also seemed to be embracing a market economy.[37] What these snapshots indicate is that Ennahda's ideological revision preceded the strategic changes seen in the post-2011 period, suggesting that it was not solely driven by political competition.[38]

During the 2011 election campaign, Ennahda portrayed itself as a progressive alternative, advocating for women's rights and economic stability. It made concessions on issues such as *sharia*, women's status and blasphemy, demonstrating a willingness to dilute its religious ideology in response to public resistance.[39] While internal divisions emerged during the drafting of the Tunisian constitution in 2014, Ghannouchi interpreted *sharia* as more of a philosophy and way of life rather than a legal code. As a result, they decided against explicitly referencing sharia in the constitution.

One of the founders of the AKP, Beşir Atalay (former deputy prime minister 2011–14), states that he went to Tunisia in 2018 and met with Ghannouchi:

> During our long chat, I asked Ghannouchi how he managed to persuade Ennahda's base in not including *sharia* in the new Tunisian constitution. He replied that he employed *ijtihad* [interpretation of Quranic legal codes by a qualified Islamic scholar]. I praised him and said, 'Please continue to produce such *ijtihads*!'[40] The

majority of Ennahda's leadership either spent years in the West in exile or were educated there. They knew that attempting to Islamize Tunisia would cause a nuisance to the public. They knew that the only solution is more democracy.[41]

A delegation of academics and journalists affiliated with the AKP visited Tunisia in 2012, including Mümtazer Türköne. Their purpose was to exchange ideas and compare the experiences of Turkey and Tunisia.

> I said to them [Nahdawis], let's collectively, lift the burden of establishing an Islamic state from the shoulders of Ennahda. I realized that day that Ghannouchi who once advocated for God's sovereignty, intends to relieve Ennahda of that burden as well. This exemplified the distinction between Islamism in opposition and Islamism in power.[42]

In the 2014 elections, Ennahda formed an alliance with Nidaa Tounes, Tunisia's main opposition party at the time, which was characterized by a general 'fear of Islamism'.[43] By adopting a more centrist position and making concessions on religious matters, Ennahda demonstrated that it was not the rigid Islamist party its opponents feared. The decision to drop the demand for *sharia* as the source of legislation and the inclusion of the secular Nidaa Tounes party in the cabinet were significant steps which constituted 'a formal organisational break with [Ennahda's] religious, cultural, and social activities'.[44]

In a 2016 congress, Ghannouchi proclaimed that Ennahda was no longer an Islamist party but a party of 'Muslim democrats', reflecting a process of rebranding and relabelling.

2.3 From Milli Görüş to the AKP

Milli Görüş, the precursor of the AKP, is a Turkish Islamist movement led by Necmettin Erbakan in the 1970s. Its core beliefs were anti-Western and anti-finance capital, with the aim of establishing an Islamic order. Erbakan's parties, originating from *Milli Görüş* – the National Order Party (*Milli Nizam Partisi* 1970–1) and the National Salvation Party (*Milli Selamet Partisi* 1973–80) – were forcibly disbanded by the Turkey's state due to alleged anti-secular activities.

Ghannouchi sees similarities between the evolution of the Turkish and Tunisian Islamist movements:

> At first, both Tunisian and Turkish Islamists rejected and fought the visions imposed by Atatürk and Bourguiba. They later realized, however, that they could

not completely eradicate the legacy, so they decided to engage in dialogue with it. They recognized the importance of finding common ground with this legacy. This is the central idea behind these two Islamic projects in Turkey and Tunisia.[45]

Divergent from the cases of Ennahda and the MB, the development of 'the Islamic project in Turkey', as referred by Ghannouchi, and its culmination in the establishment of the AKP, can be best understood through a political economy perspective. In the early years of the Turkish Republic, secularism was not merely a political stance, but also viewed as a prerequisite for national economic progress. The replication of the Western industrial model without the perceived interference of Islamic values was deemed essential for achieving economic development.[46] Consequently, businesses with religious or Islamic orientations were systematically marginalized due to the perceived insignificance of their contribution to the Turkish economy.

The Republican elites held significant control over the economy, and regional disparities further exacerbated political grievances, which were voiced by emerging Islamist parties as early as the 1970s.[47] However, a shift occurred with the emergence of the centre-right Motherland Party (*Anavatan Partisi* – ANAP) and its leader Turgut Özal in the mid-1980s. This period witnessed the partial integration of devout Anatolian businesspeople into the core of the economic realm.

Turgut Özal's rise to power in Turkey, in the aftermath of the 1980 coup that saw the imprisonment or exile of leftist leaders, played a significant role in reshaping a society that saw success and the accumulation of wealth as symbols of status. The elevation of certain materialistic aspirations, such as establishing personal businesses, marrying, owning property, cars and household appliances, as well as enjoying comfortable financial situations were conspicuous during this period. Television advertisements showcased families who had achieved such milestones, and happiness became associated with a scale of consumption and easy acquisition.[48] Concurrently, Özal's policies aimed to rejuvenate the market by fostering competition between Muslim businessmen and traders and the secular bourgeoisie. This encouragement resulted in the flourishing of an Islamic business class, whose members commonly referred to as the Anatolian Tigers or Calvinist Muslims, highlighting their distinct background and entrepreneurial drive.[49] The emergence of this new class of entrepreneurs played a significant role in shaping the trajectories of Islamist movements in Turkey.

Erbakan and his *Refah Partisi* (RP – Welfare Party), founded in 1983, rose to prominence in the 1994 local elections by winning the mayorships of twenty-eight cities, including Istanbul and Ankara. The following year, after the 1995 general elections, Erbakan became prime minister through a coalition government formed with Tansu Çiller's centre-right *Doğru Yol Partisi* (DYP). The 1990s in Turkey were marred by political and economic instability, characterized by increased military control over politics and escalating violence between the state and the banned Kurdish group, PKK. This violence resulted in extrajudicial killings of prominent Kurdish figures by the state. These troubling circumstances reached a climax with a military intervention, often referred to as a 'postmodern coup'[50] in Turkish political discourse, on 28 February 1997, which forced the resignation of the coalition government. Erbakan's RP was dissolved due to its perceived Islamist agenda, and shortly after, *Fazilet Partisi* (The Virtue Party), founded ten months after the coup, also met a similar fate. In addition to the political turmoil, the Turkish economy suffered a severe collapse in 2001. The formation of the AKP began as a response to this 'postmodern coup' and the accompanying economic crisis.

Following the 2001 economic crisis, Islamist strands associated with Erbakan faced setbacks, while pro-business factions found common ground within the AKP. Importantly, as Navaro-Yashin highlights, by the time the AKP assumed power, both secularists and Islamist bourgeoisie were already deeply implicated in the capitalist consumption market. This influenced how they constructed their identities, with Islamists becoming actively involved in shaping and participating in this market alongside their secular counterparts.[51]

In the 2002 elections, the AKP emerged victorious by presenting itself as a fresh start, promising to rectify the country's issues such as corruption, stagnant services, excessive state expansion and the unfair political representation of the Republican elite.

Thus, it can be asserted that the genesis of the so-called Turkish model can be traced back to the tumultuous era of the 1980 military junta, from which it gradually evolved and was subsequently moulded by the Özal reforms that provided fertile ground for the ascent of religious factions.[52] With the rise of the AKP to the helm of power in 2002 that the model reached its zenith, signifying a deliberate strategy on the part of the Turkish state to harness and moderate the mobilizations of both the leftist movements of 1968 and the Iranian revolution of 1979.[53]

One of the founders of the AKP and former deputy prime minister, Beşir Atalay, recalled the sentiment at the time of the break from Erbakan:

> There were no major disagreements or schisms among the parties about how we should build the strategy and discourse because we all understood the

conditions required for the AKP to take power in a country like Turkey. We had a strong grasp of national and international conjunctures of the time. Of course, as devout Muslims, we were aware of our identity and never discussed that. We knew that promoting democracy and individual liberties, would benefit our base the most – the religious Muslim strata.[54]

İbrahim Kalın, an academic and long-time chief adviser (2009–23)[55] to President Erdoğan and the head of Turkey's intelligence agency since June 2023, provided a noteworthy depiction of the AKP in his contribution to the Oxford Handbook of Political Islam. Kalın emphasized that Erdoğan and Gül, upon parting ways with Erbakan, embarked on a transformative path, 'they [adopted] a radically different perspective and redefined their political ideology and [. . .] identity based on cosmopolitan values, conservative politics, liberal economic policies, and a globalist and pro-active foreign policy, [. . .] in contrast to Islamist movements that aim to establish a *sharia* state'.[56]

As per Ali Bulaç, a discerning Turkish Islamist intellectual, the ascent of the AKP to power was accompanied by a solemn pledge to shed its '*Milli Görüş* shirt', disavowing Islamism and eschewing the path of religious politics. Bulaç contends that the AKP's strategic manoeuvres during the EU accession process, such as the abolition of the death penalty and the decriminalization of extramarital relations (*zina*), served as tangible evidence of the party's capacity to embrace policies that were either at odds with or transcended the confines of Islamic principles.[57] Moreover, the AKP's economic, cultural and social initiatives drew inspiration from Western reform programmes, further reinforcing its departure from its *Milli Görüş* roots. Notably, given *Milli Görüş*'s staunchly anti-EU stance and their somewhat ambivalent stance on embracing a market economy, the AKP's policy directions, coupled with its self-identification as a Muslim/conservative democrat, were hailed as 'path-breaking' both within the Islamist movement and in the context of Turkish democratization.[58]

The next chapter delves into the interplay between *Milli Görüş* and Ennahda and the MB during the 1980s to highlight the long-standing relationship between Turkish Islamism and these movements, predating the Arab Uprisings by several decades. It further expounds on the divergent paths *Milli Görüş* and the AKP took, as well as the purpose Muslim Democrat and Turkish model frames serve.

3

The history of the interaction

Within the realm of political sociology, scholars conceptualize the transfer and adoption of new ideas, policies and strategies through diffusion mechanisms. Diffusion does not imply political contagion; rather, it is a strategic process heavily influenced by the character, positioning and intentions of the actors involved.[1] The actors in a diffusion process are dependent on the heuristics within a bounded rationality[2] which affect the applicability of the policies and tactics diffused and, thus, the implications of the overall process. Put in another way, the actors' history of interpersonal relations and the diffusion context produce intuitive decisions – cognitive shortcuts – that may or may not benefit their parties.[3] Therefore, it becomes crucial to familiarize ourselves with the actors and their relations with each other over time and space in order to grasp the extent of diffusion.[4] For this reason, this chapter will first revert back to the early 1980s to explore the interaction between Turkish Islamism, Ennahda and the MB in Egypt. Next, it will discuss the ideational dimension of diffusion, specifically examining the evolution of two frames: Muslim/conservative democracy and the Turkish model.

3.1 Erbakan, Ghannouchi and the MB

In the late 1960s and early 1970s, Turkish Islamists became acquainted with the literature of the MB. Nureddin Şirin, a Turkish Islamist who faced imprisonment on charges related to *Turkish Hizbullah* and *Selam ve Tevhid*,[5] revealed that Muslims in Turkey gained access to the writings of Banna and Qutb through translations provided by the International Islamic Federation of Student Organizations (IIFSO) based in Kuwait.

Mehmet Fuat Doğu, the former head of Turkey's intelligence service, the Milli İstihbarat Teşkilatı (MİT) (1961–4/1966–71), personally oversaw the translation of Qutb's 'Social Justice in Islam' (*al-adala al-ijtima'iyyah fi l-islam*) into Turkish (*İslam'da Sosyal Adalet*)⁶. The motivation behind this translation was to mobilize Islamic sentiment as a counterforce to communism. However, when Qutb's most radical work, 'Signposts along the Road' (*ma'alim fi'l-tariq*), was translated into Turkish by an Islamist publisher called *Hilal Yayınları*, just four months after Qutb's execution by the Nasser regime, the same intelligence organization, MİT, moved to ban the book in 1966.⁷ This time, the fear of Islamism, rather than communism, posed a threat to the Kemalist establishment. Nevertheless, this intervention did not dissuade Turkish Islamists from studying and discussing the Ikhwan literature of the MB.

In 1968, an Islamist train conductor employed by the Turkish State Railways (*TC Devlet Demiryolları*) took it upon himself to translate and distribute Qutb's commentary on the Quran, 'In the Shade of the Qur'an' (*fi zilal al-Qur'an*), to major cities.⁸ By the end of the 1960s, a group of prominent Islamists in Turkey began to perceive Qutb's works and his criticisms of the nation-state system as problematic. As a result, they started advocating for 'national piety' and a distinctively 'Turkish Islam' as a counterpoint to the discourse propagated by the MB.⁹ However, the *Milli Görüş* movement continued to endorse and disseminate these translated works within Turkey.¹⁰

During the 1980s, the allure of Banna and Qutb's ideas among young Muslims in Turkey diminished, mirroring a similar trend within Tunisian Islamism. The writings of Qutb and al-Banna were gradually deemed disconnected from the reality in Tunisia, and authors like Baqir al-Sadr and Ali Shariati gained prominence in the 1980s as their works resonated more with the local context.¹¹ In Turkey, Islamist circles began to view the ideology of the Muslim Brotherhood as a historical source rather than a practical guide for addressing contemporary challenges.¹²

Turkish theologian İsmail Kara identifies several factors contributing to this disengagement. Firstly, during the 1980s, the MB seemed to be stagnating, lacking new ideas and relying on their existing body of work. Second, the Iranian revolution had a profound impact on Islamist movements worldwide. Efforts to translate Qutb's and Banna's works were eclipsed by a focus on making the writings of figures like Rouhallah Khomeini, Morteza Motaharri, Musa Sadre and Ali Shariati accessible to Turkish Islamists. Additionally, following the 1980 military coup in Turkey, a new trend emerged among Islamists that advocated for a critical examination of Islamism itself, drawing on the experiences of the MB and the Iranian revolution. İsmet Özel's work exemplified this approach, calling for a re-evaluation of contemporary Islamic thought and its reductionist treatment of tradition.¹³ Devout Turks rejected Qutb's proposed forms of resistance, perceiving them as exclusivist and rigid, as Turkish Islam represents a synthesis of Sufi Islam, mystical traditions and Turkish nationalism.¹⁴ For instance, Necip Fazıl Kısakürek, an influential figure for Turkish Islamists and nationalists, including Erdogan, once criticized Qutb's works as 'deviant branches of the right path'.¹⁵

Nonetheless, the interaction between the MB in Egypt and Islamist movements in Turkey extended beyond the translation of a few books. According to *Ikhvanwiki*, an archive of MB news, articles and dossiers, the Egyptian MB maintained contact with two Islamist factions in Turkey: *Milli Görüş* and the Sufi tariqa known as *Nurcus* (followers of Bediuzaman Said-i Nursi, referred to as *Nurcular* in Turkish). It is noteworthy that *Milli Görüş*, led by Erbakan, never enjoyed harmonious relations with the *Nurcular* or its offshoot, the Gülen movement. This discord arose from pronounced disparities in rhetoric, approaches to the state, and mobilization methods. While Erbakan maintained amicable ties with the MB, the Nur movement expressed opposition to this alliance.

Mehmet Kırkıncı, a respected *murshid* (teacher) within the *Nur* movement, claims to have met Mustafa Mashhur, the fifth Supreme Guide of the MB (1996–2002), in Istanbul in 1996. Kırkıncı was disappointed when Mashhur requested that Nur members support Erbakan's Milli Görüş. In response, Kırkıncı endeavoured to explain to Mashhur how the Nur path differed from both Milli Görüş and the MB. He emphasized that while thousands of Egyptians had suffered and lost their lives due to MB activities, including figures like Al-Banna and Qutb, none of the followers of the *Risale-i Nur* had experienced such hardships. Instead, he argued that 'not a single *Risale-i Nur* student has ever suffered a nosebleed, but they are all enlightened in their Islamic faith'.¹⁶

İhsan Süreyya Sırma, a Turkish Islamist who maintained personal connections with MB leaders, asserted that Erbakan provided political guidance to the MB, 'because Ikhwan was a movement of *tabligh* (propagator of faith and cause – *dawa*), not of politics, they [the MB members] would listen to Erbakan and take notes'.¹⁷ Another disciple of Milli Görüş, Necip Yavuzer, claimed that when MB leaders visited Erbakan and expressed grievances about the repression under the Mubarak regime, Erbakan advised them to form alliances with other political parties and participate in parliamentary activities. He warned that failure to do so would result in complete shutdown by Mubarak's government.¹⁸ It was then, Yavuzer claims, that the MB allied with the nationalist Al Wafd Party. The impact of Erbakan's advice remains uncertain, but in the 1984 elections, the MB-Wafd coalition garnered 13 per cent of the votes and secured fifty-eight seats, with eight going to the MB.[19] This marked the MB's initial strategic alliance to gain parliamentary representation.

Since the late 1980s, Rachid Ghannouchi, the founder of Ennahda, has been widely recognized by Turkish Islamists. His initial published work in 1988, titled '*Filistin Sorunu ve FKÖ*' (The Palestinian Conflict and the PLO), delved into the Palestinian struggle. In 1994, he presented his perspectives on Islamist movements worldwide in a book formatted as interviews with him, entitled '*Raşid Gannuşi ile İslami Hareket Üzerine Söyleşiler*' (Conversations on Islamist Movements with Rachid Ghannouchi). One of his most renowned works, 'Public Liberties in the Islamic State' (*al-hurriyat al-'ammah fid-dawlah al-islamiyya / İslam Toplumunda Vatandaşlık Hakları*),[20] was translated into Turkish in 1996, three years after its original Arabic publication. During this period, Turkish Islamist movements were largely dominated by advocates of Milli Görüş.

Notably, Ghannouchi's subsequent works on secularism and the role of women were published under the rule of the AKP, predominantly after 2010.[21] Ghannouchi takes pride in acknowledging that his ideas have influenced the founders of the AKP as well as a broader constituency within the Turkish Islamist landscape.

> Seven of my books have been translated into Turkish and are very well known. I was walking down the street in Istanbul's Fatih district one day when a group of young people approached me and paid their respects. My friend Loutfi was with me at the time, and he joked that if you run for office in Turkey, you'd have a good chance of winning. I was in exile in Britain back then.[22]

In a 2004 book authored by former AKP MP Mehmet Metiner (2011–18), it is mentioned that Rachid Ghannouchi was invited to Istanbul in 1989 by Erbakan to commemorate the 536th anniversary of Istanbul's conquest. During this visit, Recep Tayyip Erdoğan, who served as the head of the *Refah Partisi*'s Istanbul branch at the time, played the role of host to Ghannouchi and reportedly 'never left his side'.[23] This event potentially marked one of the earliest significant encounters between Erdoğan and Ghannouchi.

Ghannouchi distinguishes *Milli Görüş* from the AKP and holds Erbakan in high regard as one of the founders of Islamism.

> Necmettin Erbakan came from a different generation of Islamists. I consider him as a professor, as a sheikh and a role model for me much like Maududi and Hasan Al-Banna. He was descended from this lineage. I met him many times during conferences and conventions in Turkey and elsewhere. For example, during the

first Gulf War in 1990, Islamic leaders gathered in Jordan, Saudi Arabia and Iraq and Iran to oppose the war. Hasan Al-Turabi, Erbakan, Ghabi Hussein of Pakistan, Algerian leaders . . . I represented the Tunisian Islamic movement. I also met Erbakan after he became Turkey's prime minister. He hosted me many times. I admired his personality, his oratory, his vision, and courage.[24]

Recai Kutan, Erbakan's long-time comrade, claimed that Ghannouchi saw Erbakan as a mentor and that Mahdi Akef (2004–10), the MB's seventh Supreme Guide, referred to Erbakan as 'a Godsend *mujaddid* (reformist)' and praised his *taqwa* (piety, fear of God, following of the truth), ideas and projects.[25]

The relationship between Erbakan, the leaders of the MB, and Ghannouchi became more prominent after the success of Erbakan's *Refah Partisi* in Turkey's municipal elections in 1994, which saw Tayyip Erdoğan elected as the mayor of Istanbul. Subsequently, in the 1995 Turkish general elections, Erbakan formed a coalition government with the centre-right *Doğru Yol Partisi* (True Path Party). That same year, Egypt's Supreme Court had sentenced fifty-four MB members to hard labour in prison on charges of belonging to an illegal organization, a ruling that marked the nadir of the MB's deteriorating relationship with the Mubarak regime.[26] According to Fethullah Erbaş, a member of the *Refah Partisi* at the time, the party's leader, Erbakan, asked him to go to Egypt along with two others – Mehmet Elkatmış and Ahmet Dönmez – and observe the trials. 'We went to the airport and saw that Erbakan had arranged a private jet for us so that we wouldn't waste time', he recalls. 'In Cairo, we were greeted by Banna's son, Saif al-Islam al-Banna, observed the trials, and even spoke with the judges.'[27]

During Mubarak's visit to Ankara in 1996, then prime minister Erbakan and he had a heated exchange, in which Erbakan told Mubarak to 'tolerate the MB'.[28] According to *Kitabiyat*, the two-volume memoir of the former leader of the Arab League, Amr Moussa, Erbakan went so far as to request the release of the imprisoned MB members, to which Mubarak responded, 'We do not want them: if you want them you can have them.'[29]

Erbakan's affinity with the MB was publicly reciprocated during his short rule as prime minister. The MB's then leader, Mahdi Akef, who would later become the seventh Supreme Guide, told the Turkish secular newspaper *Cumhuriyet* on 28 November 1996 that Erbakan was the MB's representative in Turkey, causing such outrage within the secular establishment that Akef later issued a statement on the MB website claiming that his words had been misconstrued.[30] However, on the same page as the statement are several photos of Erbakan and Akef holding hands triumphantly for the *Milli Görüş* crowds.[31]

When Abdullah Gül and Recep Tayyip Erdoğan split from Erbakan's movement and founded the AKP in 2002, Ghannouchi attempted to mediate:

> I tried to bring Erdoğan, Gül, and Erbakan together. I tried to persuade Erbakan that these people are your students, and you should be proud of them because your dream of ruling Turkey, your Islamist vision, has won. So, you must be pleased because your students rule the country. He considered what I said before responding, then said: 'they are the students who left my class before completing their education under me, so I am not happy'.[32]

Erbakan accused the founders of the AKP of 'changing Islam'.[33] He felt that the AKP had been established by those whose Islamist aspirations had been shattered by the 28 February coup and whose main goal became immediate power.[34] Erbakan was dissatisfied with the pragmatic break made by his disciples and saw it as a rupture with the core tenets of Islamism. A Tunisian media figure, Mehdi Ben Hamida, who visited Turkey in 1997 when Erbakan was prime minister, sees Erbakan and Ghannouchi as belonging to the same school of thought and politics. He compares them with Erdoğan: 'Erbakan and Ghannouchi tried to persuade voters through sermons, books and slogans, while Erdoğan managed to put food on people's tables, build roads, canals, subways and transportation networks.'[35]

As these incidents demonstrate, the interaction between Turkish Islamism, the Egyptian MB and Ghannouchi revolved around Erbakan and resulted from his personal efforts. The extensive list of attendees at Erbakan's funeral is a testament to the strong relationships he had cultivated not only with the Egyptian MB but also with Islamist groups from various countries worldwide, including Malaysia, Tunisia, Morocco, Jordan, Pakistan, Sudan, Indonesia and Kuwait.[36]

Despite their long-standing connections with Erdoğan's mentor, Necmettin Erbakan, and their claim of being ideologically closer to *Milli Görüş* than the AKP, the leaders of the MB and Ennahda chose to draw lessons from the AKP following the 2011 revolutions. According to my interviews with Nahdawis (Ennahda members), the AKP was seen as the organization that successfully implemented Ghannouchi's ideas of integrating Islamist entities within secular and democratic settings, becoming the first major success story for an Islamist party.

The MB in Egypt, for its part, had initially preferred to remain allied with Erbakan's *Milli Görüş* when Tayyip Erdoğan and Abdullah Gül – the former president of Turkey 2007–14 – broke away and founded the AKP. Although the MB did not consider the AKP to be sufficiently Islamist, it nevertheless forged an extensive dialogue with the party due to its success while Erbakan's movement gradually faded into obscurity. Thus, for both the MB and Ennahda, achieving success took precedence over strict ideological alignment.

3.2 The spread of frames for legitimacy

Ideas, frames, innovations and tactics spread in both domestic and transnational contexts – across nations, social movements and organizations, as well as political parties. What primarily spreads are narratives, or more specifically, success stories. While the literature on diffusion often emphasizes contentious politics or government agencies to illustrate the transfer of policies between national contexts, it is not uncommon for political parties to learn from foreign regimes in their quest for assuming power.[37] Party-to-party diffusion is also not exclusive to Islamist entities in the broader Middle East. For instance, in the mid-1990s, Tony Blair of Britain was influenced by Bill Clinton's 'New Democrat' campaign in 1992, and Germany's Linke party claimed to have adopted tactics from Greece's Syriza party following their electoral victory in 2015.[38]

As shown by experiences of exiting authoritarian regimes in southern Europe, Latin America and Eastern Europe, social movements, and parties find themselves in a position of strong agency during transitional periods but are frequently unprepared following the collapse of an authoritarian regime.[39] Hence, they turn to foreign success stories for guidance or inspiration. The notion of success may vary for political parties depending on the prevailing opportunity structure at the time. Niche parties may perceive themselves as successful if they can participate in a coalition government, while mainstream parties strive for assuming office.[40] The strategy to retaining success sometimes relies on the emulation of foreign parties' policies and tactics deemed to be successful.[41]

Models, policies and strategies that are deemed successful are curated by networks of actors 'in discursive frames and rhetorical tools but in a loose and broadly generative fashion surrounded by narratives and social fictions'.[42]

What sets Islamist entities, particularly the MB and Ennahda, apart is their prolonged engagement in underground or semi-underground activities, compelled by the incessant repressive, confrontational and co-optation cycles imposed by their authoritarian regimes. In this regard, the trajectory of Turkish Islamism significantly deviates from that of Ennahda and the MB. As demonstrated earlier, the Turkish Islamist movement promptly established a political party during the 1970s. Despite encountering setbacks and facing pressure from Turkey's secular establishment, bolstered by the military, Islamists in Turkey have adeptly 'transform[ed] themselves to answer the challenges that they have faced';[43] thus enhancing their survival and consolidation of power in a methodical and refined manner over the ensuing decades.

The MB, however, 'remained an integral organization with low levels of professionalization and also failed to unify the Islamic field once it ultimately established its party'[44] due to the Salafist presence in Egypt. While it participated in parliamentary elections, it was perpetually compelled to maintain a low profile and conform to the regime's regulations in order to 'fend off repression and maintain their organizational existence'.[45] However, when the MB sought to capitalize on its social legitimacy to politically mobilize the lower-class beneficiaries of its philanthropic structure, the Mubarak regime escalated its repressive measures and dismantled the spaces it had previously permitted the MB to operate in during the 1980s, thus undermining both the regime's own legitimacy and that of the MB. Similarly, Ennahda was banned as a movement in Tunisia from 1992 and only attained legal recognition following the downfall of the Ben Ali regime in 2011. Henceforth, elections provided a pivotal juncture for the MB and Ennahda, not solely to seize political authority but also to solidify their legitimacy, thereby distinguishing them from non-Islamist counterparts with regards to the diffusion of strategic approaches during this convergence.

For Islamist entities such as the MB, Ennahda or the AKP, it became imperative to craft a novel 'commodity' of Muslim politics that both international and domestic audiences would 'buy'. In many respects, the crux of this diffusion involved leveraging the 'political opportunity' structure arising from the Arab Uprisings to showcase that Islamists possessed the legitimacy and aptitude to govern as political actors. The leadership of these three parties forged alignments, thereby initiating a diffusion process that engendered political learning foci.

The mechanisms of diffusion can be succinctly categorized as emulation, coercion, learning and competition, each of which can be further distinguished based on whether they facilitate direct or indirect channels of influence.[46] Put differently, the process of diffusion can be compelled through military power, employing tactics like military interventions or incentivized through civilian power, offering rewards such as trade agreements, financial support and technical assistance. These two forms of diffusion are classified as material diffusion.

Ideational diffusion, on the other hand, encompasses socialization and emulation, involving the transmission of frameworks, narratives and symbolic representations. As substantiated by the evidence presented in Chapters 4, 5 and 6, the process of diffusion within the scope of this research comprises both material incentives, such as technical and financial aid provided by Turkey to Tunisia and Egypt between 2011 and 2013, as well as ideational incentives manifested through discursive and symbolic elements, which will be examined in the subsequent section.

3.3 Conservative/Muslim democracy and the Turkish model

The frames, Muslim Democracy (or conservative democracy) and the Turkish model, as well as the concept of legitimacy, I believe, play a crucial role in comprehending the political convergence that unfolded in the aftermath of the Arab Uprisings. Scholars of social movements define framing as 'the conscious strategic efforts by groups of people to fashion shared understandings of the world and of themselves that legitimate and motivate collective action'.[47] These frames, mentioned earlier, provide insight into the nature of diffusion between 2011 and 2013 because they represent interpretative meanings intentionally attached to events, actions, plans and actors in order to legitimize them 'through appeal to values and appropriateness'.[48] Moreover, they act as 'compelling and effective [tools] to bring the movement's message to the people'.[49] Following the Uprisings, 'adopting frames which were distinctly Islamist (i.e., advocating a fully-fledged Islamic state), or secularly democratic (no mention of Islamic principles as a political framework) would have alienated important segments of Egyptian and Tunisian society from the outset'.[50] Invoking a tried-and-tested, internationally acknowledged model, on the other hand, would serve the purpose of gaining legitimacy and reinforcing the political standing of Ennahda and the MB in 2011.

According to Tarrow, framing starts with a domestic claim and becomes international through convergence and communication.[51] Muslim/conservative democracy and the Turkish model are prognostic or orientational frames. Snow, who first coined the term 'frame', argues that framing is regularly achieved by social movement leaders.[52]

Prognostic frames offer specific remedies, solutions and tactics for achieving objectives, addressing the question of 'what needs to be done'.[53] On the other hand, orientational frames pertain to people's fundamental beliefs and attitudes, providing direction and focusing on action.[54] It is important to note that orientational and prognostic frames do not necessarily stem solely from the core ideology of the political actor. It is a misconception to view frames as 'merely and simply ideologically derived'.[55] Instead, they represent a mid-range concept that identifies the development of political ideas motivating movement actions while remaining rooted in grassroots praxis.[56] In the case of the Muslim/conservative democracy frame, frames are 'not identical to, or isomorphic with, existing ideologies, but are novel blends of the old and the new, the past and the present'.[57] However, it is not implausible to expect an interplay and transitivity between the ideology and the frame.[58] For example, Esposito et al. see the frame of Muslim democracy as signifying 'a dynamic political and intellectual wave shifting across the Muslim world'.[59]

The use of these orientational and prognostic frames by the AKP, Ennahda and the MB along with the diffusion of specific tactics outlined in Chapters 5 and 6, distinguish this political confluence. Various entities such as European and American embassies, policymakers and democracy-promoting organizations like the National Endowment for Democracy (NED), National Democratic Institute (NDI), International Republican Institute (IRI) and the Konrad Adenauer Stiftung rushed to fill the void during the transitional period following the 2011 revolutions in Tunisia and Egypt. They engaged with groups actively involved in the revolution. While Ennahda held meetings with representatives from French and German parties and the MB claimed to have attended several embassy meetings, these encounters did not become regular or progress beyond informal discussions.[60]

3.3.1 The origins of Conservative/Muslim democracy

The AKP's founders first used the 'Conservative/Muslim democracy' frame in their rift with the *Refah Partisi* and after the AKP's inception in 2001. They positioned the AKP as a 'conservative democrat' party, drawing parallels to Christian Democratic parties in Europe, and consciously avoided Islamic terminology.

Numerous efforts have been made by AKP elites to elucidate the AKP's interpretation of conservative democracy. Yalçın Akdoğan, a long-time advisor to Erdoğan, former deputy prime minister (2014–16), and AKP Member of Parliament (2011–18), even authored a book titled 'The AKP and Conservative Democracy'[61] in 2004. However, the term remained somewhat ambiguous until it was abandoned by Erdoğan in 2013, and there was never a consensus among Turkey's Muslim intellectuals regarding the definition and content of conservative democracy.[62] Nonetheless, in the AKP's 2023 vision document, they still assert that they have developed and institutionalized the political identity of the conservative democrat, which has subsequently 'become a source of inspiration that sets an example for other countries in the region'.[63] Esposito characterizes the AKP as a conservative democratic party whose governance policies were not influenced by Islam, instead emphasizing pragmatism, democracy and pluralism, with a focus on fostering a prosperous future for all Turkish citizens.[64] In this respect, I agree with Taşkın who contends, we can argue that 'conservative democracy is an ideological construct that has been strongly inspired by the legacy of [Turkey's] centre-right politics'.[65]

According to prominent Turkish Islamist Ali Bulaç, 'they [the founders of the AKP] wanted to take power' and to accomplish this, they devised a reconciliation doctrine.

> They identified three influential actors shaping Turkey and the Islamic world: the US, the EU, and Israel on the global stage, and the military, bureaucracy, and big capital domestically. Their strategy involved reconciling with these forces. They also recognized the growing presence of their Anatolian religious base in urban areas. To secure electoral victories and maintain power, they embraced the identity of 'conservative democrats' and distanced themselves from Islamism.[66]

We should consider the origin of Muslim/conservative democracy is linked to a broader debate on the strategic shifts within Islamism, that is post-Islamism. Two prominent scholars, Olivier Roy and Asef Bayat, have contended that the objectives and undertakings of Islamist politicians have undergone transformation since the mid-1990s. The term 'post-Islamism' was coined in Bayat's seminal essay published in 1996, which examined reformist tendencies in post-Khomeini Iran and highlighted the evolution of Islamist ideas, approaches and practices. According to Bayat, the post-Islamist trajectory commenced in 1988, coinciding with the conclusion of the Iran-Iraq war. Bayat argued that Islamists acknowledged the inadequacies of their strategies due to internal contradictions or societal pressures, prompting a pragmatic departure. During this phase, they reinvented themselves by relinquishing certain foundational principles of Islamism and instead began formulating their project and discourse by combining Islam with notions of individual choice, freedom, democracy and modernity.[67] Another significant point emphasized by Bayat, closely tied to the arguments presented in this research, is that the rise of post-Islamism was prompted by the legitimacy deficit experienced by Islamism itself.[68]

As Benhabib eloquently puts it, the Arab Middle East was gripped by a profound crisis of legitimacy.[69] One contributing factor to this crisis was the prevailing Western narrative on counterterrorism, which decisively subsumed all Islamist groups and linked the stability and security of Western democracies to the ability of 'Muslims to tamp down on violence in the name of religion'.[70]

In the aftermath of 9/11, Ghannouchi made a resolute declaration to the international community, emphasizing Ennahda's commitment to non-violence and disavowing any association with al-Qaeda. He also acknowledged that Ennahda had acted too hastily during the 1989 election, needlessly confronting the regime. A crucial driving force behind this approach was the desire to dismantle the cynical appeals made by Arab dictators to the West. Figures like Egypt's president Hosni Mubarak and Tunisia's president Ben Ali would essentially convey to their Western counterparts, 'It's either us or Bin Laden'. Faced with such a choice, Westerners – despite their professed dedication to democracy – would naturally lean towards supporting autocrats over theocrats.[71]

Ghannouchi's perspective on the compatibility of Islamic principles and democratic governance is elucidated in his book titled *Public Liberties in the Islamic State*,[72] which he completed while in exile in London. This influential work has emerged as 'one of the influential tracts in contemporary Islamic political thought' that advocates democracy and pluralism'.[73] Ghannouchi argues that the notion of sovereignty has been erroneously interpreted as exclusively belonging to God, primarily due to Qutb's initial conceptualization of the term.[74]

In Ghannouchi's formulation, God's sovereignty (*hakimiyya Allah*) operates to impede despots from 'monopoliz[ing] wealth, power, and law-making, [as well as] against clerics who monopolize the right to interpret God's will and who claim to speak in His name'.[75]

Ghannouchi contends that the *sharia*, understood as broad guidelines rather than rigid legal codes, provides the framework for democratic governance by the people (*hakimiyya as-shaab*) or their representatives.[76]

This means that in the 1990s, Ghannouchi's ideal democratic governance '[was still] conditional on the existence of an Islamic state [similar to] the first Islamic state in Medina that lasted 14 centuries and comprised all the required criteria, that is, people, territory, a government and law'.[77] Thus, Ghannouchi's formulation of Islamic/Muslim democracy diverges from the early propositions of the AKP's founders regarding 'conservative democracy' when they initially assumed power.

Nevertheless, the former prime minister of Tunisia (2013–14) and a key Nahdawi, Ali Larayedh, asserts that it was Ghannouchi who laid the groundwork for Islamists to embrace the concept of Muslim democracy, given his credibility as an Islamist thinker. Larayedh further argues that it was the AKP, under the leadership of Erdoğan, that translated Ghannouchi's ideas into action by establishing the party and achieving successive electoral victories.[78] Similarly, Rafik Abdessalem, the former Tunisian Minister of Foreign Affairs (2011–13) and Ghannouchi's son-in-law, describes the exchange of ideas between Ghannouchi and the AKP in a similar vein. He portrays Ghannouchi as the originator of the Muslim democracy concept, while Erdoğan is depicted as a pragmatic politician driven by the pursuit of power rather than as a thinker.[79] According to Abdessalem and Larayedh, these perspectives are also shared by other members of Ennahda. For example, according to Maha Somrani, who worked at Ennahda's youth 'everyone knows, especially young people, that Erdoğan is a student of Sheikh Rachid [Ghannouchi]'.[80]

Khalil Amiri, former Secretary of State for Scientific Research (2016–20) and coordinator of Ennahda's 2019 electoral manifesto, argues that it is not a question of giving intellectual credit to either Ghannouchi or the AKP's founders for adopting frames that revolved around democracy:

> In all honesty, the concept of compatibility between Islam and modernity was prominently articulated in Ghannouchi's books in the late 1980s. However, its roots can be traced back even further to Taha Abdurrahman, a Moroccan thinker who espoused ideas on the harmony between Islam and modernity as early as the 1970s. The AKP acknowledges being influenced by Sheikh Ghannouchi's writings and progressive perspectives. From the outset, Ghannouchi has been a proponent of innovative ideas for the Muslim project, advocating for its alignment with democracy, liberty, and modern governance. Ghannouchi's affirmation that there is no contradiction between Islam, democracy, and modernity holds significant weight, particularly in persuading Muslim individuals, especially the youth, as scholars like him possess a unique authority that politicians do not possess.[81]

It could be argued that the AKP was influenced by Ghannouchi's ideas and reformulated them to fit the Turkish context. It could also be claimed that Ghannouchi himself transformed his ideal democratic governance, abandoning the prerequisite of *sharia*, because Ennahda did not push for it to be included in the new Tunisian constitution in the plenary sessions from December 2013 to January 2014.[82] However, what is even more significant is that the movement of the Muslim/conservative democracy frame between the AKP and Ennahda indicates that the diffusion of ideas had already begun prior to the material diffusion that ensued after the Arab Uprisings.

The AKP's self-identification as conservative democrat initially 'lured many in the Arab Spring countries, Tunisia being the first among them because it was a way of avoiding the clutches of extremism and the risk of slipping back into another form of dictatorship disguised by religious rhetoric'.[83] Following the 2011 revolution, one of the key objectives of both Ennahda and the AKP was to underscore the notion that not all Islamists, or rather 'Muslim politicians' as they preferred to be addressed, should be seen as homogeneous entities. Former Ennahda MP Oussama Sagheir explained:

> The idea of [adopting the term] Muslim democrats is founded on two premises: First, Ennahda must be transformed from being seen as threat to a political party capable of working within the state. Second, we want to set Ennahda apart from other Islamist parties and movements. Many European countries put everyone under the same banner of political Islam. Salafists, Al-Qaeda, Daesh, Nahda, Ikhwan, the AKP. Muslim democrat as a concept was a different way of presenting ourselves.[84]

Many of the interviewees from Ennahda, the MB and the AKP shared the concerns and goals defined by Sagheir. This was a critical driver of the diffusion process between the AKP, Egyptian MB and Ennahda in the aftermath of the Arab Uprisings: the desire to change the image of Ennahda and the MB from a threat to a competent political party.

It should be noted that the MB never adopted or used the Muslim/conservative democracy frame in its rhetoric. For the MB, the Turkish model was a more fluid and useful frame for gaining legitimacy than the Muslim/conservative frame, even before the revolution, as the following section will explain.

3.3.2 The origins of the Turkish model

Upon assuming power in 2002, the AKP garnered accolades from global powers, who hailed it as a successful paradigm for harmonizing Islam with democracy and the free market, urging its replication across the Muslim Arab world. Notably, in 2004, US president George W. Bush and British foreign secretary Jack Straw commended the AKP for steering Turkey towards a democratic path. Esteemed international media outlets like the New York Times and The Economist, alongside renowned think tanks such as the Brookings Institute and the Carnegie Endowment for International Peace, consistently extolled the AKP as a bridge between political Islam and democracy. Academic circles contributed to this discourse by illustrating how the AKP skilfully integrated Islam into the global system, showcasing its efficacy.

The Bush administration, with its 'US democracy promotion toolkit, particularly highlighted the AKP as an exemplar of "good Islamists," turning the model narrative into a source of symbolic capital in domestic, regional, and international politics, effectively validating the party's policies, approaches, and governance methods'.[85] Turkey's experience with the AKP further reinforced the prevalent liberal argument that authoritarian secular regimes in the MENA region were approaching their end, and that if reformist Islamist actors were to ascend to power through elections, they could pave the way for a democratic trajectory. Contrary to the widespread acclaim, it is important to note that not everyone – particularly certain prominent journalists and academics from Turkey – shared the positive sentiment towards the AKP and its model of combining Islam and democracy.

Cihan Tuğal describes the Turkish model 'in two words: Islamic liberalism'.[86] In his book *The Rise and Fall of the Turkish Model*, Tuğal analyses the phenomenon through a political economy lens. He highlights that the Turkish model gained traction among global business elites and was embraced by international media outlets due to its ability to fortify the free-market economy while accommodating political Islam within the international financial system.[87] An examination of academic discourse on the Turkish model between 2002 and 2014 reveals that the concept originated in the West, with each scholar emphasizing different aspects.[88] These characteristics encompassed the AKP's alignment with global markets, its economic policies and its democratic reforms, all of which were influenced by Turkey's EU accession process. Depictions of the Turkish model varied depending on the specific period within the AKP's extended rule. For instance, from 2002 to 2007, the Turkish model was portrayed as representing a pro-Western, secular, democratic, capitalist and moderate Muslim state.[89] However, during the period encompassing the events of the Arab Uprisings (2008-11), the dominant Western academic narrative regarding AKP Turkey underwent a shift, with interpretations ranging from perceiving it as a radical Islamist party to a more benign Islamist party, and even as a potential model for post-revolutionary Arab states.[90]

Ennahda leaders frequently expressed their desire to emulate the model of Turkey's AKP, particularly 'its early shift from its Islamist origins toward a vote-seeking centre-right platform'.[91] This strategic move was intended to counter potential discrediting from Western observers and secular Tunisians who perceived 'Ennahda as a direct contradiction and a threat to the country's modernist legacy'.[92] When asked about the kind of Islamist party or model Ennahda aspired to be, 'not a single respondent listed the Egyptian Muslim Brotherhood as an inspiring example, [but] the vast majority of respondents said

Turkey's AK Party, which they perceived at the time as representing a winning combination of piety, prosperity, and democratic credibility'.[93]

While Abdelkarem Harouni, president of the Ennahdha's *shura*, describes the AKP as a 'party that combined Islam, democracy and economic boom',[94] Naofel Jamali claims that the 'AKP is like us, they are Muslim democrats'.[95] According to Meherzia Labidi, 'AKP people are good Muslims, closer to Islam than many in the Gulf countries. I do not know if this means they are Islamist. I am very suspicious of that term.'[96]

In the 2005 parliamentary elections in Egypt, the MB secured a historic success, winning eighty-eight seats and becoming the biggest opposition bloc. This development fuelled debate within the movement about how much effort should be devoted to political participation. As a result, the old guard, fearing complete destruction by the regime, withdrew from the municipal elections of 2008. However, simultaneously, a younger and more pragmatic strand of the movement was in search of ideas that would help them gain greater influence in Egyptian politics. Turkey's foreign policy shift towards the Middle East and the international promotion of the Turkish model coincided with the aspirations of younger MB members for political participation and the exploration of relevant strategies. Accordingly, a close, but primarily intellectual connection between the MB and the AKP developed at that time. For example, the AKP's then political ally, the Gülen movement, which served as its international lobbying machine, hosted a panel entitled 'Is Turkey's AKP a model for the Arab world' at Washington's Century Foundation in 2008.[97] Ibrahim Al-Hudaibi, then an MB member, 'editor of the MB's official web page,[98] and great-grandson of Hassan Al-Hudaibi, the MB's second Supreme Guide after Banna's death, participated in the panel. He emphasized the AKP's wise and responsible approach by avoiding antagonism towards any segment of Turkish society.[99] This public endorsement marked the earliest acknowledgement of the Turkish model by a prominent MB figure. According to Amr Darrag, a senior MB member and former Minister of Planning and International Cooperation under the Morsi government, 'the West began marketing a Turkish model to them around 2007'.[100]

While the MB viewed itself as the pioneering force of Islamism, focusing on exporting ideas and expertise rather than importing them, it closely monitored developments in Tunisia and Turkey.[101] The interviews conducted for this research revealed the members' confidence within the MB. However, these interviews also demonstrated that the MB went beyond mere observation of the AKP's model and actively engaged in learning from it for practical reasons.[102] Previously, the MB had the freedom to adopt radical postures, but these posed significant challenges following the revolution. When confronted with the opportunity of the first free elections in 2012, the MB needed to demonstrate 'its accountability to a wider global audience'.[103] As Sallam argues, 'the success of a fellow Islamist party, [the AKP], served as a useful example for the Brothers in this endeavour'.[104]

While 'the FJP's functionaries privately scoffed at the idea that the Brotherhood was to "emulate" the experience of the Islamist activists in Turkey',[105] in public they praised the policies of the AKP and Erdoğan. The MB's Freedom and Justice Party published its official party newspaper *Freedom and Justice* (*al-hurriya wal 'adala*) on 22 October 2011, with chairman Mohamed Morsi and editor-in-chief Adel Al-Ansari. The inaugural issue included an exclusive interview with Jehan Sadat, the wife of former Egyptian president Anwar Sadat. The headline prominently featured her statement: 'I wish Ikhwan's party would be like Erdoğan's party'.[106]

However, the FJP never used the terms conservative/Muslim democracy or Turkish model when defining itself:

> We are the Freedom and Justice Party, a civil party with an Islamic frame of reference, founded by the Muslim Brotherhood for all Egyptians, of different creeds and races and social positions, without discrimination. The party undertakes its activities within the scope of constitutional legitimacy and works for the rejuvenation and development of the nation and seeks to fulfil the hopes and aspirations of the Egyptian people, including the objectives of the January 2011 revolution.[107]

While not explicitly mentioned, it was widely understood that 'in conceptualizing the FJP, its architects found inspiration in Turkey's AKP which had spearheaded a new model of Islamic democratic governance'.[108]

3.3.3 The EU and the Turkish model

The EU played a significant role in framing AKP-led Turkey as a model for Islamist parties and movements, and this role needs to be briefly examined. This transposition of the EU model to Turkey and Turkey subsequently becoming a model for other Muslim-majority countries, or more specifically, Islamist movements and parties, was influenced by various factors. One of the reasons behind this transposition was that 'the EU's democracy promotion efforts in the southern Mediterranean in the context of the Arab Uprisings'[109] were ineffectual 'because, especially in Tunisia, the EU was seen as hypocritical and unwelcomed as the young activists believed that the EU played a key role in maintaining the Ben Ali regime for decades'.[110] Therefore, the Turkish model discourse was 'connected to the interests of the United States, and [. . .]the European Union, to influence parts of the world beyond their direct control via a more trusted regional leader, i.e. Turkey'.[111] In the aftermath of the Uprisings, the EU's engagement with actors central to the revolutions, especially in Egypt and Tunisia, greatly increased. It became 'actively involved in many projects in Tunisia and Egypt today, promoting a certain form of polity whereby democracy is procedural, the economy is neoliberal, and cultural actors are encouraged to be entrepreneurial and competitive'.[112] When the EU was not actively involved, its most recent protégé – the AKP – filled the void with marked composure.

The EU's influence over Turkey went through a transformative phase, reaching its peak between 1999 and 2006–07. During this time, Turkey was officially declared a candidate country for EU membership at the Helsinki Summit in 1999. This declaration, along with the prospect of launching accession negotiations, created an optimistic environment and a strong impetus for democratic reforms. As a result, Turkey embarked on an extensive reform process, initially under a three-party coalition government from 1999 to 2002 and later under the AKP from 2003 to 2007.

To meet the so-called Copenhagen Criteria for EU membership, Turkey adopted nine legislative packages and made significant amendments to its 1982 constitution in 2001 and 2004. These reforms aimed to align Turkish laws and institutions with European standards, with a focus on fundamental rights based on the European Court of Human Rights (ECHR) provisions, which took precedence over Turkish laws and the constitution. The EU believed that these changes would ensure the preservation of liberal democracy in Turkey.

However, after 2013, authoritarian tendencies started to emerge in Turkey under the AKP government, contrary to the expectations of the EU. The reason for this can be attributed to the nature of EU accession process, which predominantly revolved around legal and institutional checklists. The EU-led reforms in Turkey focused on legalistic measures, emphasizing the means rather than the ends of the rule of law. While there were efforts to reform laws and strengthen administrative and judicial institutions to protect individual rights, there was insufficient emphasis on addressing the structural issues of power to ensure pluralism and prevent majoritarianism. The EU did not make structural reforms a precondition for starting membership negotiations with Turkey. This aspect of Turkey's EU accession process is crucial in understanding the true nature of the AKP's Turkish model and its diffusion to the MB and Ennahda.

After the EU's enlargement in 2004, discussions arose regarding the potential limitations of European integration, with concerns that it had become a neoliberal zone where market forces dominated all policies and actions of the EU. Critics argued that EU accession processes perpetuated neoliberal policies and strategies.[113] A review of Commission reports on candidate countries in 1998 and 1999 revealed a lack of emphasis on social policy or social protection, except for minority rights.[114] This neglect occurred despite the rising income inequalities in many accession countries.[115] Privatization of pensions and healthcare was encouraged, with the main concerns revolving around financial stability, expenditure levels and price deregulation.[116] It became evident that a neoliberal agenda was embedded in the enlargement process from the beginning, with support from supranational organizations like the IMF and the World Bank.[117] Then, Lenz and Nicolaidis contend, the EU model can be reduced to 'a toolbox of governance, from which individual elements can be authentically drawn, while others are simply deemed inappropriate in a different context'.[118] This was precisely the AKP's key takeaway from the EU accession process, incorporating select elements into its own model. This toolbox of governance – with different contents – as will be seen in Chapters 5 and 6, was diffused to Ennahda and the MB.

The AKP's eager participation in the EU accession process helped it to create a façade of normalization and democratization. As Çınar argues, 'foreign policy has been used to offset the AKP's legitimacy deficit and [. . .] EU norms had provided the AKP with strategic resources'.[119] While Erbakan's *Refah Partisi* did not and could not offer a 'strategic alternative to the pro-Europe, pro-US, pro-Israeli policy of the Kemalist state, simply because such an alternative does not exist',[120] the AKP used the EU accession process to thwart the military's interference in politics and provide a 'credible alternative to the obsolete and often corrupt political establishment' through its 'technocratic cadres and experience in urban management'.[121]

Additionally, The AKP benefited from the EU accession process by acquiring a technocratic and strategic toolbox of governance that aligned with a comprehensive neoliberal agenda aimed at meeting the demands of global competition.[122] While the specific contents of the toolbox provided by the EU to Turkey may differ from those used by the AKP for Ennahda and the MB, the managerial ethos of finding effective solutions, sustaining competitiveness and ensuring survival remains similar.

The AKP not utilized its close relationship with the EU until 2007 to cultivate an international image as a party that is both Muslim and democratic, as well as supportive of market principles but also 'learned by doing' how to concoct a toolbox of tactics to gain domestic and international consent. This included strategies such as manufacturing societal consent for privatization and financialization, as well as crisis management and manipulation, which are core tenets of neoliberalism.[123]

The literature on the Arab Uprisings now agrees that 'what was being marketed to the Arab world [following the revolutions of 2011], not only by advanced capitals, Western governments, but also by countries such as Turkey and Qatar [was] the project of a mainstream neoliberal economic agenda'.[124]

The concerted efforts of the United States, the EU and the AKP in creating the Turkish model played out as follows: the AKP privatized the majority of the luxury estates, resolved overemployment in bureaucracy, created urgent resources for the Treasury and improved public services,[125] all of which led to its second and more significant victory in the next election. The boom in the economy after the deep economic and political crises of 2001 'consolidated [the AKP's] position as a dominant party within a multi-party system'.[126] Therefore, the most conspicuous reason the AKP became a success to be emulated after the Arab Uprising was its economic policy, which appealed more widely than just to its Islamist base and led to its election victories. For the MB and Ennahda, whose intentions and ability to govern were in question, adopting and – more importantly – declaring to domestic and international actors that they would adopt the AKP model meant, in essence, the possibility of economic improvement[127] and was, therefore, a ticket to legitimacy.

This will be discussed further in Chapters 5 and 6 but, just as an example at this point, Ghannouchi's response to my question regarding his relationship with Erdoğan is revealing:

> We talk about mutual interests of our countries and also touch upon developments in the region. I am not an adviser to Erdoğan. He is a friend, and I respect him, and commend his achievements, particularly in transforming Turkey's economy into the 21st largest globally. This is a remarkable success considering the previous state of the Turkish lira.[128]

4

The context, milestones and actors of the interplay

In the prelude to the Arab Uprisings, Turkey increasingly positioned itself as a 'trading state',[1] aiming to bolster its status as a regional powerhouse through economic and cultural ties. A pivotal moment came in January 2009 during a World Economic Forum panel in Davos, where then prime minister Erdoğan found himself engaged in a heated exchange with Israeli president Shimon Peres regarding Israel's assault on Gaza, resulting in the tragic loss of 1,200 Palestinian lives. In a display of fiery indignation, 'One minute! One minute! *Olmaz* [Not ok]!' interrupted a furious Erdoğan as he abruptly left the podium, capturing the admiration of Muslims worldwide and catapulting him into the role of a hero.[2] Former Tunisian prime minister Ali Larayedh asserts that Erdoğan emerged as a global leader in the Muslim world,[3] while Ajmi Lourimi, an executive member of Ennahda's *shura* (consultative council), believes that Erdoğan and his AKP party fulfilled the role of the sought-after leader in the Arab Muslim world, which had been predominantly governed by monarchies or military dictatorships.[4]

In the aftermath of the notable 'one minute' incident, interactions between members of the MB, Ennahda and the AKP intensified through their participation in conferences, workshops and panels organized by pro-Palestinian Islamist NGOs based in Turkey. One noteworthy event occurred five months later when prominent MB figure Sheikh Yusuf al-Qaradawi attended a conference organized by FIDDER (Filistin Dayanışma Derneği – Palestinian Solidarity Association) at an Istanbul hotel. The conference commenced with a Quran recitation from the Al-Aqsa Mosque in Jerusalem, connected live to the venue.[5]

Bassem Khafagi, the former community relations director of the Council on American-Islamic Relations (CAIR) and a presidential candidate in Egypt in 2012, explains that during the 2001 rift between Erbakan and Erdoğan, the MB collectively aligned themselves with Erbakan rather than Erdoğan. However, the transformative impact of the 'one minute' incident led to a new perception of Erdoğan within the Middle East.

> During the Davos panel, Amr Moussa, a prominent Egyptian intellectual, appeared indecisive while Erdoğan boldly expressed his strong criticisms of Israel. Witnessing this display of determination, the MB recognized that Erdoğan possessed the qualities of a capable leader, prompting them to view him as a more favorable partner compared to Erbakan's movement. It was not because Erdoğan was deemed more Islamic than Erbakan, as they were aware of the contrary, but because they observed Erdoğan's assertiveness.[6]

Following the 'One minute!' incident in July 2009, the Turkish think tank TESEV conducted a survey in seven Middle Eastern countries to gauge perceptions of Turkey. The results showed that 75 per cent of respondents held a positive view of Turkey, surpassing even Egypt, often regarded as the Arab world's political leader. Additionally, 77 per cent of respondents from the region called for Turkey to play a larger role in the Arab world. Surprisingly, despite Turkey's secular political system, 61 per cent of respondents considered Turkey a model for the Arab world.[7] Consequently, after the Arab Uprisings, 'the AKP felt compelled to clarify its identity more strongly in Islamic terms to more effectively communicate with its Arab counterparts and continue assuming a regional leadership role'.[8]

This was consistent with the vision of the then foreign minister Ahmet Davutoğlu, who advanced the idea of a new Islamic civilization led by Turkey in his 2001 book *Stratejik Derinlik* (Strategic Depth). Davutoğlu boasted in a speech to the Turkish parliament in 2011 of having 'implemented what he had written in his book, *Strategic Depth*'.[9] While he was dubbed 'the Turkish Kissinger'[10] due to his assertive foreign policy, his book *Strategic Depth* was considered by the AKP elite to be a political manual to be followed step by step, rather than an academic treatise. Although Davutoğlu's policies were approved by the AKP base, they were criticized in Turkey's opposition circles as well as by Western and Arab media for having a neo-Ottoman and pan-Islamic agenda. However, it may also be argued that Turkey's support under Erdoğan and Davutoğlu for Islamist governments following the Arab Uprisings stemmed not from ideological connections with Islamism but from Turkey's economic aspirations in the Arab world, and that the AKP's vision was to create economic solidarity among Muslims.[11] The interviews conducted for this book, which will be presented extensively, appear to support this argument regarding the AKP's relations with Ennahda and the MB. Nationalistic in their own right, neither

Ennahda nor the MB sought strategies or tactics from the AKP to realize the dreams of Erdoğan or Davutoğlu. During our interview, Davutoğlu himself vehemently denied having a neo-Ottoman or pan-Islamic vision, but expecting him to acknowledge such ambitions would be unrealistic.

> We did want to be a strong actor in the Middle East, but who wouldn't? This cannot be considered a crime. We have never attempted to intervene in any country's domestic affairs or to change regimes. But I've always maintained that those establishments in the Middle East were Cold War era products and doomed to fail. Until the protests began in Syria, Egypt, Libya, or Tunisia we had stable diplomatic and economic relations with the existing regimes. We did not have any problem with Mubarak. If we had a regime change aspiration, say in Syria, 2005 was a better time because of the Hariri assassination.[12]

For the AKP, its alliance with the MB and Ennahda helped it to be considered an Islamist party with a mission to protect Muslim interests in the region. The aim was not to establish global or regional Islamic rule but to maintain economic and strategic alliances. Although Erdoğan claimed that the 2008 global recession had 'passed us by',[13] it certainly placed limits on the AKP's neoliberal programme. Therefore, the AKP started to seek new opportunities, especially in the Middle East. According to Tuğal, in terms of new neoliberal gains, 'the AKP leaders saw an imperial possibility after 2011 [the Arab Uprisings] and further intensified the party's [reference] to Islamist themes' to appeal to the devout in the broader region.[14]

According to a high-level Turkish diplomat, economic relations between Egypt and Turkey had improved since the implementation of the trade agreement in 2007. In 2009, Turkey's trade with Egypt amounted to 2.9 billion dollars, and it established top-flight technology manufacturing plants in Cairo employing 60,000 Egyptians.[15] The Turkish Foreign Ministry also had a stable relationship with its Egyptian counterparts. While the Egyptian foreign minister, Ahmed Abu al-Gheit (2004–11), had become friendly with Davutoğlu, the Minister of Trade and Industry, Rachid Mohamed Rachid (2004–11) would stay at President Erdoğan's house when he visited Turkey.[16] There was, thus, a cordial relationship with the Mubarak regime, as claimed by Davutoğlu earlier. Conversely, as Labbad stated, 'even though Cairo inaugurated two rounds of strategic dialogue with Ankara, these produced nothing tangible, owing to Cairo's lack of a clear vision as to what it hoped to gain from Turkey'.[17] Neither the volume of the trade nor the strategic cooperation was good enough for Turkey. However, with Morsi in power, economic cooperation was likely to go more smoothly. Turkey had given a 2-billion-dollar loan[18] to Egypt, while Egypt had promised 'an 8-billion-dollar investment opportunity to Turkish businessmen'.[19] This promise was further embellished with an assurance that the well-being of the Turkish business elite in Egypt would be looked after at the presidential level. For example, when President Morsi visited Erdoğan in September 2012 in Ankara, he acknowledged that 'there are one or two Turkish companies that experience difficulties, but we will fix those problems too'.[20] A former AKP MP claimed that 'during Morsi's brief rule, RO-RO [roll-on, roll-off ferries] expeditions increased significantly. For the first time, we could cross the Rafah Border as an AKP team and bring aid to Gaza. Do you realize what this means? There was a lot more to do in terms of electricity and tourism bids. We would rebuild Egypt and both of us would benefit from that'.[21]

As this MP's statement demonstrates, the AKP had a combination of goals, both economic and geostrategic. The AKP's conservative constituency, especially the small to medium-sized entrepreneurs from Anatolia, would invest in the 'new markets in the Middle East, Africa and Central Asia whose people were predominantly Muslims, [which would eventually] contribute to strengthening Turkey as a regional power'.[22] The emphasis on the Rafah Border is also critical. In November 2012, the then foreign minister, Davutoğlu, accompanied with his Arab counterparts and a team of AKP members, crossed Rafah, which is the only crossing point between Egypt and the Gaza Strip. It was a tour de force for Turkey that Arab ministers were able to step into Gaza, where the Arab-Israeli conflict is most visible and bitter and made the news as 'a historic visit'.[23] Coupled with Erdoğan's 'One minute!' episode, the AKP believed that the Gaza visit proved that, with the MB in power in Egypt, it would become one of the most influential powers in the region.

4.1 The AKP in Cairo, the MB in Ankara and Istanbul

'As Muslims, where we all go is a two-cubic-meter hole. Listen to the voices of the people [. . .]. Without a doubt, the people desire change',[24] said Prime Minister Erdoğan to Hosni Mubarak on 1 February 2011. In the days that followed, Erdoğan continued to address Mubarak, calling on him to step down. In solidarity with the protests in Tahrir Square, Turkish Islamist groups, led by organizations like Mazlum-DER and the IHH, organized demonstrations in Turkey. One notable protest[25] took place in front of the Egyptian Consulate in Istanbul, featuring Ashraf Abdul Ghaffar, a senior member of the MB, who praised Turkey as an example for Egypt. Shortly after, Egypt's ambassador to Ankara, Abdurrahman Selahaddin, delivered a letter from Egypt's foreign minister to Turkey's foreign minister, Ahmet Davutoğlu, expressing the Egyptian government's dismay with Erdoğan's comments regarding the transfer of power and a transitional government.[26] Both Erdoğan and high-ranking members of the MB had already started planning for the post-Mubarak era even before Mubarak's resignation was announced on 11 February 2011.

The first official visit from a foreign country to Cairo in the aftermath of the revolution was, unsurprisingly, that paid by Turkey's president Abdullah Gül on 2 March 2011. Gül's visit, accompanied by Davutoğlu, was intended to show support for the Egyptian revolution without favouring any one element of it. During his day-long visit, Gül was greeted by Field Marshal Mohammed Hussein Tantawi and met with the Wafd Party leader Siyad El-Badawy, the former secretary-general of the Arab League Amr Moussa, the former director of the International Atomic Agency Mohammed El Baradei, a group of young people who actively participated in the revolution and the supreme leader of the MB Mohammed Badie, at the Turkish Embassy in the Giza district.[27]

Turkey's stance of maintaining an equidistant relationship with all elements of the revolution changed after this trip. 'Several advisers to Erdoğan began coming to Cairo and meeting with the executives of the MB, and this drew the attention of other sectors of Egyptian politics, especially from the *fuluul* – members of the old regime', recalls the then chief correspondent of Turkey's national television *TRT*'s Cairo office, Mehmet Akif Ersoy. 'Every day, someone from the AKP government was landing in Cairo. The aim was to forge a close economic and military relationship with the upcoming Egyptian regime. They did, however, put all of their eggs in one basket, the MB basket.'[28] The interactions between AKP officials and the MB became intense to the point that they had little time to meet with anyone outside of MB circles. 'For example, Amr Moussa wanted to meet with our guys [the AKP]; they said no, not right now. Some of Erdoğan's advisers mistakenly assumed that the MB represented all of Egypt and that simply talking to them was sufficient. Those advisers misled Erdoğan in that respect.'[29] It is hard to determine whether it was the advisers or President Erdoğan himself who made the choice to focus exclusively on the MB during meetings.

Erdoğan's visit to Cairo showcased the strong relationship between the AKP and the MB at the highest level. Accompanied by several AKP deputies and ministers, as well as a delegation of businesspeople, Erdoğan was warmly welcomed by a crowd of supporters, including members of the Muslim Brotherhood with banners reading 'Erdoğan the hero' and 'Erdoğan, a huge welcome from the Brothers'.³⁰ According to Reuters, the crowd consisted of 'Islamist groups such as the Muslim Brotherhood, who approve of Erdoğan's bringing Islamists into mainstream Turkish politics'.³¹ Erdoğan addressed the crowd in Arabic: 'Turkey and Egypt hand in hand. Greetings to Egyptian youth and people. May God's peace be upon you.'³² This – 'Turkey and Egypt hand in hand' – was a slogan that had already appeared on several billboards in Cairo.³³ Chanting for Erdoğan, sometimes in Turkish, continued in front of the Kempinski Hotel where he was staying.³⁴

Erdoğan's visit to Cairo had both public and discreet aspects. In a public interview with anchorwoman Mona Shazly, Erdoğan sought to address concerns about secularism and reassure Egyptians that it was not a threat.³⁵ He emphasized that as the president of a secular state, he recognized the importance of treating Muslims and non-Muslims equally. Erdoğan recommended that Egypt adopt a secular constitution and expressed hope that his speech would change public perception of secularism.³⁶ It is worth noting that this interview took place at the AKP headquarters in Ankara and was broadcast on Erdoğan's second night in Cairo, prior to his meeting with politicians at the Turkish ambassador's residence, where the interview had not yet been seen.

Ayman Nour, an Egyptian politician who identifies as a liberal, was among the select few invited to the dinner arranged in honor of Erdoğan. Nour's political journey began as a member of the *Al Wafd* Party but he later departed in 2001 to establish *Hizb Al-Ghad* (Tomorrow's Party) in 2004. He made history in the 2005 presidential elections as the first candidate to challenge Mubarak, although he ultimately secured second place. Unfortunately, Nour faced accusations of forgery, leading to imprisonment until his release in 2009. He had shared a prison cell with Mohammad Morsi, demonstrating their close friendship. Nour made another attempt in the first post-revolution presidential election, but his nomination was withdrawn due to legal reasons. Upon Nour's arrival at the Turkish ambassador's residence on 13 September 2011, Erdoğan had not yet arrived. However, prominent figures from the MB such as Mohammad Badie, Mahdi Akef, Gomaa Amin, Khairat Al-Shater and Mahmoud Ghozlan were already present. Nour reminisced about the friendly encounter, sharing an amusing anecdote about being teased by MB members for his liberal stance. "'Ayman, you are a liberal, why are you here? This place is for true Muslims, and Erdoğan is our man," they said. I laughed but did not comment', Nour recalled. When Nour later discovered that Erdoğan had advocated for secularism in Egypt, he playfully turned the tables and teased the MB members, suggesting that their perception might have been misplaced: "'I think your man may actually be my man. He talks about secularism! Maybe you people were out of place that night, not me!"'[37]

Erdoğan's comments on secularism provoked discontent among MB leaders and raised doubts about his commitment to Islamism.[38] While Mahmoud Ghuzlan, the spokesperson of the MB at the time, remarked that 'Egypt differed from Atatürk's secularist Turkey under Atatürk', Essam El Erian, the deputy leader of the FJP, 'wished to believe that there had been a mistranslation'.[39] Nevertheless, Erdoğan's interview resonated positively with seculars, liberals and Coptics. During his visit, Erdoğan also met with Coptic Pope Shenouda III, who, despite his ailing health, warmly welcomed Erdoğan and expressed gratitude for his remarks on secularism. The Pope acknowledged that Erdoğan had articulated sentiments that Egyptian leaders had failed to convey to their people, appreciating his stance on the matter. 'You managed to say things that the leaders of my country failed to deliver to my people', the Pope said, according to a high-level bureaucrat who was present at the meeting, 'I appreciate it very much.'[40]

Despite the varied responses to Erdoğan's interview on secularism, the connection between the MB and the AKP persisted, both publicly and privately. Additionally, Erdoğan's discreet visit to Saif al-Islam al-Banna, son of Hasan Al-Banna, further solidified their relationship. To maintain confidentiality, Erdoğan refrained from using his official car adorned with the Turkish flag. While I received confirmation of this visit from multiple sources,[41] the specific topics discussed during the meeting remain undisclosed.

Following the revolution, the MB initially announced its intention to refrain from participating in the presidential race, adopting a stance of being a kingmaker rather than a candidate, as per their principle of 'participation, not domination'. Additionally, they sought to avoid confrontation with other forces within Egypt and the Western world, aligning with the cautious approach of Ennahda. They initially planned to contest only 30 per cent of parliamentary seats, as instructed by the *shura*. However, the same *shura* later reversed its decision as 'the Brotherhood became emboldened and could not rein in its political ambitions'.[42] Eventually, the MB contested 50 per cent of the seats and fielded a presidential candidate. One influential figure in this shift was Khairat al-Shater, the then deputy general guide and the *shura*'s preferred choice for president. However, he was disqualified due to legal reasons, leading to Mohammad Morsi being designated as 'the spare tyre'.[43] Through meetings with al-Shater, Brown observed the evolution of the MB's approach, with al-Shater becoming more assertive in his political stance as time progressed, expressing confidence in their potential victory in the elections.[44]

In the period between Mubarak's fall and the presidential election, a public rift emerged within the MB. Prior to the revolution, the MB was influenced by conservative figures who held control over decision-making bodies, facilitated by Mahmoud Izzat and Shater. The generational divide within the MB was not apparent before 2011 due to limited political participation. However, after the revolution, more members of the MB became willing to express their opinions and criticism. Dissent initially emerged within the youth wing, but gradually expanded to other groups. The main point of contention revolved around the MB's focus on participating in elections. A faction of members believed that the ousting of Mubarak was insufficient and argued for a revolutionary approach to completely overthrow the old regime.[45]

Examining the AKP's influence on the MB's vacillating stance towards participation in the first presidential election yields inconclusive results. While AKP and MB interviewees denied direct involvement, there are indications of some level of influence. Shater, a prominent figure within the MB, exerted pressure on the *shura* to contest the elections and nominate him, suggesting internal dynamics at play.[46] Additionally, the AKP believed that holding elections promptly was the best approach and advised the MB accordingly. The former director of the Islamist NGO IHH (*İnsani Yardım Vakfı* – Humanitarian Relief Foundation) claimed that 'it was because of the AKP that the MB changed its mind on participating in the presidential elections. It was wrong because this led the MB to shoulder the whole burden of the revolution'.[47] A source who closely followed the AKP's relations with the MB claimed that 'the AKP pushed really hard for the MB to participate in the presidential elections to the point of pestering the Ikhwanis'.[48]

A phone call that the Al Jazeera general director Wadah Khanfar recalls having with Davutoğlu is also illuminating. According to Khanfar, the Turkish officials were vigilant about the perils of military rule and made sure to convey their concerns to the Egyptian counterparts they encountered.

> On the night of Mubarak's ousting and the military assuming power, Davutoğlu called me to discuss the situation. He expressed concerns about the military's control, drawing from Turkey's experience. He predicted that it wouldn't last long and emphasized the need for a civil government. And I said, what are you talking about? Let us rejoice.[49]

Consensus among the interviewees affirms Shater's prominent position as the most frequently encountered 'Egyptian official' by AKP teams. A former AKP MP claims that Shater not only visited Turkey 'countless times' during and after the election campaign but that the AKP team usually held their meetings in Shater's office in Cairo.⁵⁰ These exchanges likely influenced Shater, as evidenced by his integration of Erdoğan's persona into his presidential campaign, even prompting the circulation of a video dubbing him 'Egypt's Erdoğan'.⁵¹ As previously mentioned, it is challenging to ascertain the precise nature of the AKP's role. However, drawing from these anecdotes, it is reasonable to suggest that AKP's influence may have permeated Shater's approach and, by extension, influenced the MB. Since Shater served as the primary point of contact for the AKP, only a select few encountered Mohammad Morsi, including Davutoğlu, who claimed that he met Morsi for the first time after his election as president. Davutoğlu clarified that their support for Morsi stemmed not from his affiliation with the MB but rather his electoral victory, implying that the AKP's primary objective in post-revolution Egypt was the establishment of democratic practices and institutions.⁵²

The dialogue between the MB and the AKP resumed unabated after Morsi became president, but this time more publicly. The AKP's fourth General Assembly in September 2012 in Ankara was a spectacle that demonstrated Erdoğan's status in the Muslim world. The attendees included Khalid Meshal of Hamas, Rashid Ghannouichi of Ennahda, Ali Osman Muhammad of Sudan, Lutfi Hasan Ishaaq of Indonesia, Hasin Sowan Elmkrish of Libya's Justice, and Construction Party and, of course, President Morsi of Egypt.⁵³ Morsi was the sole foreign leader granted the opportunity to address the AKP audience. In his nearly fifty-minute speech, he lauded the AKP's accomplishments while preserving its distinct identity and expressed gratitude to the AKP, particularly President Gül and Prime Minister Erdoğan, 'for being the first people on the face of this earth to support the Egyptian revolution and my taking office'. Morsi strategically emphasized the alignment between Egypt and Turkey on key issues like the Palestinian cause and the Syrian crisis, underscoring the need for enhanced collaboration.⁵⁴ Upon concluding his address, Morsi was warmly received by Erdoğan himself, unaware that his speech would later be broadcasted to hundreds of thousands of AKP supporters at a campaign rally in Turkey in 2015, shortly after he had been sentenced to death.⁵⁵

4.2 The AKP in Tunis, Ennahda in Ankara and Istanbul

The day after his visit to Cairo, Erdoğan arrived at Tunis's Carthage Airport on 15 September 2011, where he was greeted by a vibrant crowd reminiscent of the one in Cairo. Banners displaying slogans such as 'Jerusalem is our home' and 'Erdoğan, young people want freedom' adorned the scene, accompanied by waving Tunisian, Turkish and Palestinian flags.[56] Erdoğan and his son Bilal engaged with the enthusiastic crowd, exchanging handshakes and conversations. Rachid Ghannouchi, also present, welcomed Erdoğan, praising his efforts in service of Islam.[57]

Erdoğan's primary objective during his first visit to Tunisia after the revolution mirrored that of his Egyptian tour: to emphasize the compatibility of Islam and democracy, highlighting the ability of an Islamist party to effectively govern a secular state.[58] This message was intended for both Western and Arab audiences.

During his joint press conference with caretaker prime minister Beji Caid Essebsi, Erdoğan reaffirmed his stance on secularism in Tunisia. He stated,

> A secular state treats all religious groups equally, whether they are Muslims, Christians, Jews, or atheists. This is the essence of the matter. It may spark debate, but it is our belief. Regarding Ennahda, we will respect the will of the Tunisian people. However, most importantly, Tunisia will demonstrate that Islam and democracy can coexist harmoniously. Turkey, with a population that is 99 percent Muslim, sets an example. If we can achieve it, it is attainable. There is no need to obstruct this path.[59]

The Ennahda leaders responded differently to Erdoğan's advocacy of secularism compared to the MB. While the MB found his comments inappropriate, the Ennahda saw them as advantageous. Ennahda had worked hard to align itself with the AKP to reassure the Tunisian people, especially the secular population.

The Nahdawi Lourimi claims that 'Ennahda, since the beginning saw AKP's successes as its own and was genuinely thrilled with every electoral victory'.[60]

Lotfi Zitoun, a former Ennahda minister and advisor to Ghannouchi, suggests that initially there was an idea of cooperation between democratic Islamic movements, but there was no formal association known as 'Ikhwani'.[61]

According to then Ennahda MP Ounnissi, the AKP's initial plan may have been to establish something akin to the Socialist International, where socialist parties from various countries come together.

> I personally attended an AKP meeting where I represented the European wing of Ennahda. It was evident that the AKP harbored ambitions of integrating not only Ennahda but also other parties such as the Moroccan PJD, the MB in Egypt, and groups from Sudan, Libya, and Mauritania under an umbrella organization. The AKP aimed to exert influence over the entire sphere of Islamist parties, and Ennahda was just one component within this larger framework.[62]

During this period, key Ennahda figures made it clear that they had no intentions of imposing *sharia* law. Hamadi Jebali even highlighted that his own daughter was not veiled, emphasizing Ennahda's commitment to pluralism. These statements closely mirrored the arguments put forth by AKP leaders.[63] However, the excessive focus on the AKP began to irritate certain Tunisians, particularly Tunisian nationalists who emphasized that Tunisia had a rich history predating the rise of Erdoğan. They believed that Tunisia's visibility on the world stage should not be solely dependent on the AKP's recognition.[64]

Nonetheless, as with Erdoğan's visit to Cairo, there was a delicate balance to his stand in Tunisia. While assuring that secularism should not be feared, he also aligned himself with the Islamists by highlighting the Palestinian issue and strongly condemning Israel. This gesture resonated with the Ennahda electorate. Additionally, Erdoğan's last-minute visit to the Zaytouna Mosque, the symbolic birthplace of Ennahda's mother movement, the MTI, further solidified his Islamic credentials. These actions were aimed at showcasing his understanding and respect for the history of Islamist groups like the MB in Egypt and Ennahda in Tunisia.

On 23 October 2011, almost a month after Erdoğan's visit, Tunisia was to hold its first free vote to elect the constituent assembly – the assembly that would pave the way for the post-revolution constitution. Ennahda, finally legalized as a political party in March 2011, fielded candidates in every constituency but they expressed a more modest ambition, emphasizing their willingness to govern in a coalition and declining to pursue the presidency while seeking the position of prime minister.[65]

Beşir Atalay, the then deputy prime minister of Turkey (2011–14), claimed that he had been appointed by the AKP's higher echelons (in practice, Erdoğan himself) to engage in meetings with delegations from the MB and Ennahda.

> They [the MB and Ennahda teams] travelled to Turkey to learn why and how the AKP had achieved success. The main reason why I was chosen to meet these groups was that I was one of the AKP's founders and had coordinated the drafting of all the election manifestos, strategy documents and government programmes up to that point. Ennahda's first visit came shortly after the revolution and just before their first election. The head of the delegation was Ali Larayedh, and the second man in charge was Lotfi Zaitoun. Their second visit took place following the election.[66]

The meetings between the AKP and the MB/Ennahda delegations were deliberately kept discreet to avoid giving weight to claims of an emerging Ikhwani bloc supported by the AKP – a claim made by Gulf countries and *ancien régime* elements in Egypt and secular groups in Tunisia and Turkey. Indeed, concerns about provoking secular elements in Tunisia were valid, as other political parties centred their election campaigns on the perceived intentions of Ennahda to establish a theocratic state. Secularists portrayed Ennahda in a caricatured manner, stoking fears that their rise to power would result in the enforcement of hijab, erosion of women's rights protected by the Personal Status Code, and the banning of alcohol and beachwear, potentially harming the tourism industry.[67]

Beşir Atalay believes that the AKP's suggestions may have influenced Ennahda so that they managed to calm the waves of anxiety directed at them:

> During my two meetings with the Ennahda delegation, I told them not to form a government alone. Even today, Ennahda gives us credit for this. Thanks to your guidance, they say, we formed a coalition and could move forward in 2011. Later, they [Ennahda] were also clever enough to appoint Moncef Marzouki as president and omit Ghannouchi from the [initial] picture. Of course, we did not dictate their government composition name by name, but we kept underlining that if they did not rule in a coalition, they would not be able to make any advances in a place like Tunisia.[68]

Ennahda secured 37 per cent of the vote, capturing 89 seats out of 217 in the National Constituent Assembly in October 2011, and formed a coalition government known as the Troika, along with Ettakol (Democratic Forum for Labour and Liberties – *at-Takattul ad-Dīmuqrāṭī min ajl il-'Amal wal-Ḥurriyyāt*) and the CPR (Congress for the Republic – *el-Mo'tamar min ajl el-Jomhūriya*). Ennahda's electoral success was attributed to its meticulous grassroots campaigning and its compelling narrative of cultural revitalization 'which reflected traditional identities, and it compared itself with the Turkish AKP party, under whose leadership Turkey has enjoyed the kind of economic prosperity that Tunisians crave'.[69] Tuğal concurs that the allure of the Turkish model, combining religious principles, economic achievements and global acceptance, played a pivotal role in Ennahda's victory, despite years of persecution and organizational challenges.[70]

One month into their government, Ennahda's leader, Rachid Ghannouchi, and Prime Minister Hamadi Jebali visited Istanbul and held talks with Erdoğan. According to Ghannouchi, he and Erdoğan discussed 'the main problems of the Muslim world' and looked for ways to strengthen cooperation between Turkey and Tunisia 'because we believe the closest experience to Tunisia's is the Turkish experience'.[71] Shortly thereafter, Tunisia's new Minister of Foreign Affairs and

Ghannouchi's son-in-law, Rafik Abdessalem, visited Ankara, where he met with his Turkish counterpart, Ahmet Davutoğlu, as well as Prime Minister Erdoğan and President Abdullah Gül.[72]

Abdessalem, speaking at a panel organized by SETA (*Strateji Ekonomi ve Toplum Araştırmaları Vakfı* – the Foundation for Political, Economic and Social Research) titled 'Arab Spring, Turkey and Tunisia', expressed that

> many people consider the Tunisian model as representing a peaceful political change and democratization process and I think the Turkish model very much influences the Tunisian model; it is a by-product of the Turkish model. We learned and continue to learn a lot from Turkey [. . .] Turkey demonstrated that Islam and democracy are compatible. Tunisia is about to prove that Islam, Arabism, and democracy can coexist.[73]

His fellow panellist, Davutoğlu, addressing Abdessalem with warmth and camaraderie, hailed his visit as one of great importance, representing not only the Tunisian government but also the dignity and struggle of the Tunisian and Arab peoples. Davutoğlu assured Tunisia of Turkey's unwavering support, pledging to assist in every step and project undertaken by the Tunisian government, as their success would resonate throughout the region:

> Tunisia's success is Turkey's success. We will not let Tunisia fail [. . .] This is why our institutions and experience will be at your service.[74]

It was not only Davutoğlu who linked the successes of Tunisia and Turkey. According to Ajmi Lourimi, an executive member of Ennahda and MP, who had been arrested in 1991, sentenced to life imprisonment and subjected to severe torture by the Ben Ali regime, 'Erdoğan [was] eager for the success of a moderate experience like Ennahda's [because] it exemplified the model championed by Erdoğan himself.'[75]

As part of Ankara's commitment to sharing practical knowledge with Tunisia, Tunisia's Nahdawi regional development and planning minister, Jamel Eddin Al-Gharbi, held meetings with his Turkish counterparts, Cevdet Yılmaz, Ertuğrul Günay and Veysel Eroğlu. Following Al-Gharbi's visit, Turkey's president Abdullah Gül, accompanied by Beşir Atalay and Cevdet Yılmaz, made a historic visit to Tunisia as the first foreign president to visit the country after the revolution, just as he had done in Egypt. During the visit, the two countries signed three protocols focusing on cooperation in transport, tourism and technology. Gül also announced that Turkey's Exim Bank would provide a credit of 500 million dollars to Tunisian businesspeople.[76] Following lunch with Rachid

Ghannouchi, Gül joined him in visiting the Zaytouna Mosque and partook in prayers, following the example set by Erdoğan.[77]

Away from the public eye, the development ministers of both countries, Yılmaz and Gharbi, continued their meetings in the following months. During Yılmaz's second visit to Tunisia in less than six months, he announced Turkey's commitment to provide Tunisia with 100 million dollars as an endowment, along with 400 million dollars in loans.[78]

As Ali Larayedh, a senior Nahdawi and the interior minister at the time, confirmed, Turkey's financial and political support of Tunisia was apparent until the end of 2014:

> When we started determining the state's budget after the revolution, one of the funding resources we had was from Turkey. There were several Turkish banks that facilitated the loan process by following presidential orders. They also assisted us with the security systems.[79]

According to Meherzia Labidi, an executive member of Ennahda in charge of relationships with civil society and a former VP of the Parliament, the unconditional and prompt nature of Turkey's support proved to be its most salient aspect:

> When Tunisia required genuine assistance in its municipalities and combating terrorism, Turkey was the only country that provided military and municipal equipment without any conditions. They immediately helped us, which I will never forget, as I was part of the constitutional committee in parliament around 2013-14. In contrast, European countries offered help but with a list of conditions, such as purchasing specific items from them. Turkey's quick and unconditional response was greatly appreciated, and Tunisians know that it was Erdoğan and Turkey that aided us.[80]

As Labidi mentions, Turkey helped Tunisia tackle the resurgence of terrorist attacks in addition to offering financial and political support. 'Terrorism was a fundamental issue for us', according to Fethi Ayadi, Ennahda MP, 'and we talked about how to fight terrorism in most of our meetings with the AKP. And the Tunisian army received logistical and technical help from Turkey'.[81]

The fall of Ben Ali's regime in 2011 allowed radical groups to emerge openly, with imprisoned individuals utilizing their time in confinement to build networks. This resulted in a significant surge in membership for the prominent Salafist group *Ansar al-Shari'a*, which established branches throughout Tunisia.[82] The outbreak of the Syrian Civil War further fuelled the problem, as many Tunisians were drawn to join ISIS in the conflict. In addition, high-profile attacks such as the 2013 assault on Tunisian soldiers in the Chambi region and the 2015 mass shooting at a tourist resort in Sousse demonstrated that Tunisia itself had become a breeding ground for religious violence.[83] The presence of Tunisians fighting for ISIS and affiliated groups was disproportionately high, reflecting the growing influence of Salafi-jihadism within the country.[84]

In March 2016, the Tunisian city of Ben Gardane, located on the border with Libya, was targeted by an ISIS group attempting to establish a vassal entity. It is widely believed that Turkey's assistance and support played a crucial role in preventing the invasion of Ben Gardane by ISIS.[85] According to Abdel Jalil Tamimi, Turkey provided significant financial aid to Tunisia under delicate circumstances. However, Tamimi argued that Turkey should aim to foster positive relations with all political parties in Tunisia, rather than relying solely on one specific party, namely Ennahda.[86]

Nevertheless, it was evident from Erdoğan's speeches that he was determined to ensure a smooth governance experience for Ennahda, as a testament to their motto of 'Islamists can govern'. It was crucial during this time to differentiate Ennahda from Salafist and radical groups, thus reinforcing Ennahda's vision of reconciling Islam and democracy.[87]

4.3 The actors and interlocutors

When discussing the concept of emulating a 'model', it is important to distinguish between the narrative of the model and the actual structural processes at play. In the case of the Turkish model, it primarily pertains to the AKP rather than Turkey as a whole. It is worth noting historical examples such as the influence of Germany's efficient bureaucracy on American social policy actors between 1890 and 1914. During that time, stories of Germany's successful administration and social policies inspired progressive policymakers in the United States, leading to the adoption of similar ideas in addressing social challenges caused by industrial capitalism.[88]

In our current context, although ideas may have originated from Turkey and spread to Egypt and Tunisia after the Arab Uprisings, the dynamic between 2011 and 2013 unfolded primarily among political parties: the AKP, Ennahda and the Egyptian MB's FJP. Turkey, Tunisia and Egypt were not just structures or sources of inspiration in this interplay; they served as backdrops against which the limitations on Islamist political behaviour were cultivated in their respective previous regimes or as reminders of the obstacles that the AKP had overcome and that Ennahda and the FJP had to face. This is another reason why international relations models are not adequate for construing the interplay between the AKP, Ennahda and the Egyptian MB, even though the actors in question employed foreign policy tools and institutions. This was not merely state-to-state interaction, which would not be unusual given that the receiver states – Tunisia and Egypt – were in a turbulent transition period.

4.3.1 The elite actors

Diffusion operates across three levels: relational, non-relational and mediated (brokerage).

Relational diffusion involves direct interpersonal networks, while non-relational diffusion pertains to the dissemination of ideas, tactics and frames through mass media. Mediated diffusion typically involves the involvement of non-governmental organizations (NGOs). This process typically begins with a triggering event or stimulus, which creates a medium or milieu through which ideas travel from the sender to the receiver. In the case of the AKP, the triggering event was the onset of protests in Tunisia and Egypt.

Within the diffusion process, four types of actors can be identified: innovators, early adopters, late adopters and non-adopters. Innovators are the first to embrace an innovation, while early adopters play a crucial role in legitimizing the innovation. Late adopters tend to adopt the innovation after careful consideration, while non-adopters refrain from adopting it altogether. The literature on diffusion does not provide a systematic explanation for why certain actors choose to adopt diffused policies while others do not.[89] In this particular diffusion process, the innovators were Ahmet Davutoğlu, Rachid Ghannouichi of Ennahda and Tayyip Erdoğan. Early adopters included Beşir Atalay and Abdullah Gül. Potential early adopters within Ennahda may include former prime minister Ali Larayedh, former foreign minister Rafek Abdesselam, and Ajmi Lourimi, an executive member of Ennahda's *shura*.

While it seemed to many ordinary Nahdawis that 'all parts of the Arabic world follow Erdoğan [as] a successful person who raised the standards of welfare of his people',[90] as explained in the previous chapter, Ghannouchi was not merely an adopter of a Turkish model, nor did he stand idly at the receiving end of the diffusion process. Despite political factions such as the moderates and Salafists led by influential figures such as Abdelfattah Morou and Mohammed Khouja within Ennahda, it was primarily Ghannouchi's thoughts and writings that shaped the party's political trajectory.[91] In summary, 'Ghannouchi is one of the rare examples of Islamic leaders whose authoritative voice has influence in both the West and the Arab World.'[92]

An early adopter unit emerged within the MB immediately after the fall of Mubarak, led by influential figures Khairat El-Shater, deputy chair of the movement and the initial presidential candidate; Amr Darrag, former senior MB member and development minister; and Abd Al-Moneim Aboul Futuh, former leader of the MB's youth wing. 'Even before Morsi became president, delegations started to work with one another', Darrag recalled. 'The Egyptian delegation had gone to Turkey and visited municipalities. After I became minister, I had two important meetings, one with Prime Minister Erdoğan and the other with President Abdullah Gül. Ali Babacan, Turkey's finance minister at the time, joined our meeting with Erdoğan. During that meeting, we agreed on a two-million-dollar credit deal.'[93]

If Ghannouchi's and Erdoğan's positions in the diffusion process were crucial, so was that of Ahmet Davutoğlu. According to Bülent Aras, political scientist and close associate of Davutoğlu, the latter has not only 'changed the rhetoric and practice of Turkish foreign policy [and provided] a new framework for pursuing it, thanks to the willingness of Erdoğan and Gül, [but also] he is known as the intellectual architect of the AKP'.[94] Davutoğlu served as Erdoğan's chief foreign policy adviser from the beginning, then as foreign minister and finally as prime minister. Davutoğlu devised a scheme in which specific NGOs and think tanks played a significant role in publicizing the election of a pro-democracy and pro-market Islamist party.

Known as 'total performance', this mechanism sought to mobilize the support of NGOs, business communities and civil organizations, integrating them into the new foreign policy vision. These groups gained influence in the formulation of foreign policy, contrary to the past when their involvement was limited.[95] This went beyond traditional lobbying, as the NGOs and their directors, selected by Davutoğlu, were directly involved in bureaucratic operations. Furthermore, these NGOs served as key interlocutors in the diffusion process.

4.3.2 The interlocutors and structure

Ahmed Gaaloul, former Ennahda MP, Secretary of State in the Ministry of Youth and Sports and member of Ennahda's *shura* has close ties to Ghannouchi from their time as refugees in the UK and claimed that 'there was the dissemination of ideas between Ennahda and the AKP, but the relationship was not structural, [meaning] it was not maintained through party institutions but interpersonal and spontaneous relations. AKP's help for Ennahda derives more from friendship. It is good, but it is not enough'.⁹⁶ Indeed, the relationship with the MB and Ennahda was not conducted through Turkey's state apparatus and usually bypassed the Turkish embassies in Cairo or Tunis. For example, meetings in Cairo of the AKP and the MB/FJP delegation almost always took place not on state premises but at the FJP's headquarters in central Cairo, Shater's office or the Kempinski Hotel, where AKP members almost always stayed when they visited the city.

Key non-state actors or interlocutors coordinated these meetings while also organizing symposia, workshops and conferences, which would provide opportunities for interaction between the teams of the AKP, Ennahda and the MB, as well as opportunities to meet prominent politicians and scholars in the wider Muslim world. Conferences are a common trait of diffusion strategies and have a 'multiplier effect on strategic planning and discourse around a set of problems as well as structuring opportunities for transnational [. . .] work'.⁹⁷

The diffusion structure was a combination of interpersonal meetings, in which AKP-affiliated actors shared their experiences, and broader encounters such as conferences. Sayyida Ounissi claims that after the revolution 'there were a lot of seminars organized in Turkey and a special interaction was managed between the AKP and Ennahda'.

> The youth and women's branches of the AKP and Ennahda parties regularly met to collaborate and exchange ideas. Businessmen from both sides also attended seminars and conferences together. Additionally, the AKP's municipal departments interacted with local Ennahda representatives, and the AKP provided training on media management and online activism to Ennahda members.⁹⁸

Oussama Sagheir, Ennahda MP, recalls that he had 'been to Turkey and met with AKP people during our [Tunisia's] first municipal elections [after the Arab Uprisings] to see how they [the AKP] ran their municipal election campaigns, and later I organized a conference here [in Tunis] on the relationship between Turkey and Tunisia'.⁹⁹ According to Nidhal Gharbi, who 'was present in some meetings and youth exchange programmes between Ennahda and the AKP', representing Ennahda's youth bureau in Medjez El Bab, 'as Nahdawi young people we got information about the AKP's election campaigns. We are also invited by the AKP to Turkey at election times to observe'.¹⁰⁰ The AKP and Ennahda delegates also met regularly at each other's party congresses.¹⁰¹

The key AKP participants in the dialogue were advisers to Erdoğan and Davutoğlu, SETA academics with expertise in Islamic theology or Middle

Eastern politics, and individual Turkish correspondents, who acted as fixers for meetings. According to one of these key players, 'the MB members who communicated with [the AKP] were all highly and usually Western-educated people. One of them was a Harvard University graduate and the other was from Durham University'.¹⁰² Amr Darrag corroborates this information, claiming that although members of the MB old guard were not opposed to the learning process, they did not attend meetings. 'I can say that it was mostly FJP members who took an active part in the process. Many of them were young people who spoke several languages. I was 53 at the time and the oldest person in this group', he recalled. 'The rest were in their late 20s and 30s, with backgrounds in international relations or with work experience in multinational corporations.'¹⁰³

Think tanks, legal associations and academic initiatives play pivotal roles in transition periods and diffusion processes around the world by forging relations among key actors.¹⁰⁴ The primary interlocutors in this diffusion process were Turkey's SETA, the governmental organization TIKA (*Türk İşbirliği ve Koordinasyon Ajansı Başkanlığı* – Turkish Cooperation and Coordination Agency) and the Yunus Emre Foundation (*Yunus Emre Enstitüsü*). Talip Küçükcan, a former AKP MP and one of the co-founders of SETA claimed that 'SETA played an essential part as a facilitator. When the MB or Ennahda people wanted to meet AKP people, we, as SETA, arranged the meetings'.¹⁰⁵

SETA is often referred to as 'the AKP's think tank' because many of its fellows not only worked actively in Turkey's foreign policy as part of Davutoğlu's so-called 'total performance' but had also at some point become AKP members or MPs and wrote op-ed columns in pro-government newspapers such as *Star*, *Yeni Şafak*, *Sabah* and, recently, *Karar*.¹⁰⁶ As can be seen, the think tanks led by SETA that disseminated the 'Turkish model' discourse in Washington and the Arab world are not autonomous and have a tangled relationship with the AKP government.¹⁰⁷ As with the diffusion process, it is also important to stress that SETA opened a Cairo branch to be able to operate on-site with ease. Prime Minister Erdoğan, at a conference of trade attachés on 25 April 2011, acknowledged parts of this new foreign policy apparatus: 'In addition, we disseminate Turkey's soft power, Turkey's message of peace to the whole world through TIKA, the Yunus Emre Institutes, the TRT, and the Presidency of Turks Abroad and Related Communities.'¹⁰⁸

Another soft power apparatus, established in January 2010 and led by Erdoğan's long-time senior adviser İbrahim Kalın, was the Office of Public Diplomacy (*Kamu Diplomasisi Koordinatörlüğü* – KDK). Cemallettin Haşimi, who succeeded Kalın at the end of 2012, claims that the KDK's main aim 'was to deliver the experience of new Turkey to other countries and regions'.[109] Haşimi was also among those who regularly met with Egyptian and Tunisian delegates. In 2014, when he hosted thirty Tunisian government and civil society figures at the KDK headquarters, he highlighted the importance of a political strategy that would enable the Tunisian government to manage crises while preventing coups, violence and terrorism.[110]

Aside from KDK and SETA, Turkey opened its first TIKA branch in 2012 in Cairo, thanks to a protocol signed during the Morsi presidency. TIKA's Tunis office was also opened in February 2013 along with an industrial zone that would house 1,000 Turkish businesses, creating 25,000 jobs.[111] It had not been possible to open a TIKA branch in Cairo during the Mubarak era, owing to TIKA's reputation. Although TIKA claims to exist 'to provide aid, technical assistance, and information in developmental issues and preserve and promote Turkish and Ottoman culture', it is covertly linked to the Turkish Intelligence Agency, MIT (*Millî İstihbarat Teşkilatı*). For example, it is common practice for TIKA officials to join MIT at some point or vice versa. The most prominent example of this flow is MIT's director between 2010 and 2023, Hakan Fidan, who was appointed to TIKA in 2003 before being transferred to MIT. It was this relationship with the intelligence that caused the Mubarak regime – and later Saudi Arabia, Jordan and Israel – to limit TIKA's presence in the region, since they saw 'the organization as trying to inject Turkey's influence into highly sensitive issues [such as the Palestinian issue, the status of Jerusalem and the Gaza blockade]'.[112]

However, since the AKP and the MB hold similar attitudes towards the Palestinian issue, TIKA's presence in Cairo – approved by President Morsi – would be beneficial to both parties in terms of exerting soft power. Similarly, it was during Morsi's period in office that the Yunus Emre Foundation, which in 2010 opened its Cairo office on the same street as TIKA in the Giza district with the aim of promoting the Turkish language and culture, expanded its activities significantly.[113] There is an intriguing story behind this foundation, which was established in 2009 to counter the influence of the Gülen movement's Turkish schools, especially in Africa. In the aftermath of the fallout between the AKP and the Gülen movement, the Yunus Emre Foundation in Cairo, according to a Turkish bureaucrat, took over almost all the cultural and educational activities that the Turkish Embassy in Egypt had previously coordinated.[114]

In summary, the AKP structured its relationship with the MB and Ennahda through foundations and NGOs in an unregulated, unrecorded fashion. For this reason, in part, while official visits at a presidential or ministerial level between

Ankara, Cairo and Tunis made the news, little information about the nature of the dialogue has been made public.

4.3.3 Brokers: Al Jazeera and Yusuf Al-Qaradawi

As shown earlier, the diffusion mechanism between AKP, the MB and Ennahda is a relational and social enterprise, in which tactics, ideas and frames are conveyed through personal contacts and organizational connections. However, 'most scholars recognize that direct network ties and relational diffusion are only part of the story'[115] and that brokers may also be involved. The role of the broker is to bridge otherwise unconnected entities in a diffusion process. The other function of brokers such as mass media or international activist networks is to 'mobilize external support for local or national struggles in an attempt to enhance their political leverage when pressing claims on domestic governments'.[116] In addition to the interpersonal contact of elite actors and interlocutors within the AKP, Ennahda and Egyptian MB, brokers such as Al Jazeera TV and IUMS (*Al-Ittiḥād Al-'Ālamī li-'Ulāmā' al-Muslimīn* – International Union for Muslim Scholars) and its former president, Sheikh Yusuf Al-Qaradawi, aided the diffusion process. These brokers are vehicles of 'vertical transnationalism which [are] evolved, sponsored, and funded by state or non-state actors',[117] intending to connect local actors to the larger polity. Media outlets such as Al Jazeera 'often perform the function of [diffusing tactical repertoires] and thus play an important role as indirect channels of diffusion'.[118]

Qaradawi was considered one of the most influential Islamic scholars who died in September 2022. He was even 'characterised by some observers as something of a papal figure in Sunni Islam'.[119] Born in Egypt, he graduated from Al-Azhar University with a PhD in 1973 and was part of the MB until he went into exile in Qatar. He claimed that he declined an invitation from the MB to be its Supreme Guide. He is the author of 120 books, more than half of which have been translated into Turkish. Although some countries – including the Gulf countries and Egypt – believe he has ties with terrorist groups, his teachings on Islamic jurisprudence are regarded as being 'located between the fundamentalists who rely on ancient sources of the *sunna* and the Quran and the more moderate from the new stream. Ennahda's leaders also reflect this intellectual and theological trend called *wassatiyya*, which Qaradawi developed from a Quranic verse interpreted as justifying Islam's moderate nature'.[120] According to Ajmi Lourimi of Ennahda, 'Yes, this is the concept we adopt; it is more or less the same thing as the concept of Muslim democracy.'[121]

The actors involved in this diffusion process have close personal ties with Qaradawi. Ghannouchi, for example, had previously served as the vice president of IUMS. A recently published photograph of Erdoğan and Qaradawi demonstrates that their relationship dates back to 1998, before the foundation of AKP;[122] additionally, both the MB and the Palestinian Hamas regard him as a spiritual guide.[123] During and after the Arab Uprisings, Qaradawi's involvement in Islamist politics increased through his popular television show on Al Jazeera, his social media accounts, and visits to Istanbul. Similarly, statements issued by IUMS, which before the Uprisings referred primarily to the troubles of Muslims around the world and thus were not seen as 'fundamentally threatening to the regional autocracies', changed into documents forcefully supporting the revolutions.[124] Qaradawi wrote a series of articles in the FJP's official newspaper, *Freedom and Justice* (*al-hurriya wal 'adala*), praising and 'encouraging the newspaper to profile itself as the voice of freedom and truth'.[125]

Qaradawi demanded that all Arab nations, but particularly the MB, cut their ties with Israel until the Gaza strip was liberated. Although Egypt did not sever ties with Tel Aviv, 'a long line of Arab nations expressed their support for Hamas, including Arab Foreign Affairs Ministers in the Gaza strip, thus [enabling] Hamas to [score] political achievements'.[126] Hence, although Qaradawi's influence has its limits, almost all the major Muslim political figures pay heed to him because he is popular in Muslim societies around the world. For example, he was one of the most quoted figures in Turkish newspapers in reports of the Arab Uprisings.[127] A 2018 public opinion survey[128] conducted by YouGov with 16,497 respondents in Bahrain, Egypt, Iran, Jordan, Kuwait, Morocco, Lebanon, Qatar, Saudi Arabia, Tunisia, Turkey and the United Arab Emirates found that Qaradawi, along with Erdoğan and Ghannouchi, had one of the highest approval ratings among religious leaders.[129]

One year prior to the Arab Uprisings, on 25 June 2010, Qaradawi made a significant public appearance in Istanbul, when he hosted the annual meeting of IUMS in Grand Cevahir Kongre Merkezi – a meeting that Qaradawi described as a watershed moment for the Islamic world. The event brought together more than 500 Muslim clerics from various parts of the globe. During the press conference on the first day, Qaradawi emphasized that due to their leaders' hesitancy in addressing the Palestinian issue, 'Arab countries need a couple of Erdoğans' who could actively champion this cause.[130]

Qaradawi played a crucial role as a mediator between the AKP and various Islamist groups worldwide, particularly the MB, both before and after Morsi's removal from power. He consistently organized the annual meetings of the

International Union of Muslim Scholars (IUMS) in Istanbul, providing a platform for senior MB members to engage with other Islamist groups and scholars. In these gatherings, Qaradawi hailed Erdoğan as a guardian and beacon of hope for Islam.[131] He went as far as urging Turkish citizens to support Erdoğan in the 2014 presidential election, citing Turkey's progress in various domains and adding that Erdoğan's presidency would bring prosperity not only to Turkey but also to the entire *ummah*. Unsurprisingly, Erdoğan reciprocated Qaradawi's support. He vehemently protested when Egypt's president Sisi requested Interpol to issue a red notice for Qaradawi in 2014.[132] Additionally, when several Gulf states included Qaradawi and several Qatari organizations on a list of terror sanctions, Erdoğan voiced his strong objections.[133]

Indeed, the meetings involving Qaradawi can be seen as a form of mediated diffusion facilitated by influential figures acting as missionaries. These individuals serve as bridges, connecting different groups and allowing them to become aware of each other's perspectives and ideas.[134] Qaradawi played a significant role in legitimizing Erdoğan and the AKP within the Muslim world, effectively contributing to the diffusion process. As a broker, Qaradawi's prominent position influenced the content and dissemination of information among these otherwise disconnected sites, shaping the narrative and perceptions within the network of Islamist groups.[135]

Following the Arab Uprisings, Istanbul and Doha emerged as destinations par excellence for those with an Islamic orientation, and for senior MB members to meet to decide on the movement's course.[136] Doha became a global power broker, thanks to the presence of Al Jazeera's headquarters in the city since 1996. The 'Al Jazeera effect', according to Cherribi, assists Arabs in overcoming government censorship and embracing notions of freedom and democracy in the face of authoritarian regimes. Al Jazeera supported the agendas of Ennahda and the MB and 'remain[ed] a staunch supporter of democratic political Islam, which sees the emancipation of [their] ideology as the only way for [them] to gain greater acceptance'.[137] Wadah Khanfar, the general director of the channel from 2003 to 2011, argued that an Islamist president would ensure a democratic transition during the Egyptian presidential election period.[138] He also acknowledged that 'there is and always has been an element of advocacy about Al Jazeera's role. Its reporting opened the minds of a generation of Arab young people [and] told them their voices mattered which gave them hope. For the first time, through Al Jazeera, that generation felt connected to the rest of the world'.[139]

Khanfar played a pivotal role in cementing a profound alliance between the Egyptian MB and the AKP. His significance in this regard can be traced back to his enduring camaraderie with Ahmet Davutoğlu, forged during their respective affiliations at Malaysia's International Islam University, as affirmed by numerous sources. It is worth noting that Khanfar's visits to Turkey, both preceding and succeeding the Arab Uprisings, further fortified this bond. A scholar from Georgetown University reveals that a Turkish diplomat stationed at the Doha embassy divulged how this friendship served as an impetus for Al Jazeera to allocate more airtime to news items concerning Turkey.[140]

Hakan Albayrak, a prominent figure within Turkish Islamist circles, expounded upon Khanfar's role, ascribing Turkey's resonance, and favorability among the Arab populace to his unwavering efforts. Albayrak articulates how Al Jazeera, for a considerable period, assumed an almost quasi-official Turkish channel, with Khanfar singlehandedly endowing the 'one minute incident' with legendary status. This, in turn, contributed to Turkish president Erdoğan being hailed as a contemporary incarnation of the revered figure Selahaddin on the streets of Arab nations. 'We should thank Wadah for his efforts in bringing Arabs and Turks together'[141] Albayrak wrote. Subsequent to his departure from Al Jazeera, Khanfar founded the Al Sharq Forum, a notable think tank whose activities prominently feature Istanbul as their backdrop.[142] These i gatherings, held nearly every year, serve as a platform where scholars specializing in political Islam from both Western and Muslim realms convene. Additionally, youth groups hailing from the Middle East and the Maghreb region find a vital space for engagement within this influential forum.

To conclude, the Arab Uprisings set in motion a process of diffusion, resulting in a convergence between the AKP, Ennahda and the MB in Egypt. Various actors, interlocutors and brokers played integral roles in facilitating this dynamic. However, it is crucial to delve deeper into the nature of this diffusion and examine what other elements were disseminated beyond the Turkish model or the concept of Muslim democracy. Were policies or tactics of greater significance in this context? Furthermore, it is imperative to explore the aims and objectives of the AKP, Ennahda and the MB during this period. These intricate questions will be the focal point of the subsequent chapter, seeking to unravel the multifaceted dimensions of this intricate process of diffusion.

5

The tactics of success for Islamists

The apex of the diffusion process between the AKP, Ennahda and the MB in Egypt transpired during the transitional period that ensued after the revolutions. In order to elucidate the developments that unfolded during this critical phase, it becomes imperative to delve into a series of pertinent inquiries. First, it is crucial to ascertain the precise components that were diffused. Did the AKP, for instance, proffer policy frameworks for Ennahda and the MB to adopt? Second, it becomes essential to conceptualize and delineate the contours of this diffusion process. What factors influenced the selection of this specific toolbox for diffusion? These inquiries assume paramount importance as they shed light on the objectives and aspirations of the Islamist actors involved. It is hoped that addressing these queries, which have remained inadequately explored within the existing literature, will establish a contextual foundation for subsequent chapters. In these forthcoming sections, I will endeavour to explicate why this political convergence revolves around the notion of success, how Islamist entities navigate their actions, and what aspirations they harbour when not engaged in opposition or resistance to Western colonization – two prevailing themes often invoked in defining Islamism.[1]

Ennahda and the MB in Egypt considered the AKP as a yardstick for evaluating effective governance. The geographical proximity, cultural similarities and shared history between these entities played a role in this perception. According to Sayyida Ounnissi, a former Ennahda MP (2014–20), the AKP's ability to maintain its hold on power over an extended period was a source of fascination. The AKP's proficiency, discipline and professionalism left a lasting impression on Ennahda. In the words of Ounnissi, the AKP was seen as an electoral 'wow machine' due to its remarkable success in elections.[2]

This description of the AKP as a 'wow machine' aptly encapsulates the diffusion process. What was disseminated from the AKP to Ennahda, and the MB was a collection of insights into the workings of a political machine that had achieved success within a political culture dominated by an Islamist-secular or Islamist-anti-Islamist dichotomy. Thus, the tactics diffused represented the essential components on which the AKP believed its success relied. In the post-Uprisings era, success, as defined by Ennahda and the MB, entailed triumphing in elections, attaining, preserving and solidifying power. The diffused tactics pertained to four key areas: (1) winning elections; (2) providing efficient services through local municipalities; (3) employing gradualism and building domestic and international alliances to maintain legitimacy and undermine opponents and remnants of previous regimes; and (4) implementing neoliberal economic strategies that would, in theory, enable Ennahda or the MB to cultivate a loyal bourgeoisie.

It is pertinent to acknowledge that the AKP harboured significant misconceptions regarding the social structures of both Egypt and Tunisia, as well as the internal dynamics of Ennahda and the MB. This could potentially explain why the theorization of these tactics did not yield optimal results for Ennahda and the MB. In the realm of transnational diffusion, once the process is set in motion, it follows two distinct paths: the attribution of similarity and theorization.

The attribution of similarity involves the formation of social bonds and personal networks that facilitate the transmission of information along established communication channels, enabling individuals who identify with one another to adopt each other's modes of action. Theorization, on the other hand, entails the process by which individuals in one country simplify or 'nationalize' the ideas of actors from other countries, adapting them to their own circumstances.[3] It is typical in many diffusion processes worldwide, such as the spread of Bolivarianism from Venezuela under President Hugo Chávez to other Latin American countries like Ecuador, Nicaragua and Honduras, for receiving parties to selectively adopt ideas based on their domestic context.[4] Amid times of urgent crisis or uncertain conditions, the diffusion process often takes the form of 'lesson-drawing', wherein institutional solutions are selectively adopted and tailored to address specific problems.[5] Indeed, the tactics diffused from the AKP were not tailor-made for the Egyptian or Tunisian contexts.

To examine the correlation between the diffused tactics and the AKP's history in power, as well as their congruence with its success and crisis management, I employ process tracing as a methodological approach. This approach allows for an analysis of the evidence pertaining to the processes, sequences and conjunctures of events within a specific case. By doing so, it facilitates the development or testing of hypotheses regarding the mechanisms that potentially explain the case, while also enabling the exclusion of extraneous variables that may hinder our understanding of the underlying question.

As mentioned earlier, the theorization and applicability of the diffused tactics in the Tunisian and Egyptian contexts may be seen as extraneous variables that could obscure the answer we seek. This is where process tracing is useful, as it analyses 'the evidence on processes, sequences and conjunctures of events within a case for the purposes of either developing or testing hypotheses about mechanisms that *might* causally explain the case',[6] side-lining extraneous variables if necessary.

I argue that the observed diffusion process, reminiscent of the diffusion of EU policies to candidate countries and neighbouring nations, represents a social learning process characterized by active engagement rather than a passive 'downloading' of new rules and institutional 'software'.[7] In this active engagement, Ennahda and the MB sought to 'acquire and incorporate new norms and new understandings into one's belief systems'.[8]

Two postulations can be made regarding the toolbox that the AKP provided to Ennahda and the MB from 2011 to 2013. Firstly, it appears that specific policies were not diffused, but rather, selective tactics were shared that could be utilized during times of crisis to bolster the political standing of these entities. The focus was on fortifying their positions and navigating challenging circumstances effectively.

Secondly, the tactics that were diffused seemed to be stripped of ideological canon. They were not intended to invoke Islam as a means of acquiring or maintaining power. Instead, the essence of the diffusion process revolved around the notions of normalizing, legitimizing and evading crises. The style adopted was managerial, aimed at providing expedient solutions to problems that arose. Complex issues, including ideological and social considerations, were simplified into practical complications that required a step-by-step approach for resolution.

Managerialism is an under-theorized concept that holds various meanings, contingent upon the academic discipline in which it is explored, such as sociology, economics or politics. In the realm of management studies, managerialism refers to a set of beliefs that facilitate the smooth and efficient operation of an organization. When considering managerialism in a broader context beyond corporate settings, it shares similarities with Foucault's concept of governmentality. Governmentality can be defined as 'the techniques and procedures for directing human behaviour. Government of children, government of souls and consciences, government of a state'.[9] At the heart of both managerialism and governmentality lie the principles of rationality and organizational efficiency. These principles underpin the management of diverse entities, be they corporations, societies or states, with the aim of achieving effective governance and optimal outcomes.[10]

The AKP accomplished the enterprises of 'normalisation', 'crisis management' and 'institutionalisation' in a similar way to how a corporation reacts to crises, with a managerial toolbox. Extensive research demonstrates that crisis management involves a strong managerial dimension, including critical decision-making during emergency responses, organizational coordination and effective public communication. These characteristics are applicable across a range of crises, from major events like 9/11 to disasters such as the NASA Challenger space shuttle incident.[11]

The managerial and prescriptive aspects of the formula diffused in these two sets of relations seem analogous to the legislative reform packages (the so-called Copenhagen Criteria) that the AKP had to adopt to further its EU accession process between 2003 and 2007. In this sense, the AKP provided strategies for success to Ennahda and the MB in a manner akin to how it received strategies from the EU. The key difference lies in the conceptualization of success, thus impacting the contents of the formula or checklist. The diffused tactics from the AKP resembled the managerial performance of maximizing input-output and optimizing organizational efficiency within a firm.[12] In this scenario, the AKP assumed the role of an external actor possessing knowledge and expertise, akin to that of a business management consultant for Ennahda and the MB. This role acknowledged the AKP's capacity to provide guidance and support based on its own experiences and expertise.

In the context of Tunisia and Egypt, the term 'crisis' refers to the collision and contestation between various competing forces, such as the military, civil society and Salafis who emerged as the primary agents in the post-uprising period.[13] Armbrust, in his ethnography of the Egyptian revolution, suggests that the revolution itself constituted a crisis, in which no one could 'anticipate the future [but] sense the present acutely'.[14] This reflects the notion that crises encompass real and immediate dangers, problems, or challenges that challenge 'widely held beliefs that such events should not and cannot occur within a particular context'.[15]

From this perspective, the rise to power of Ennahda and the MB following the initial free elections can be seen as a second crisis. These entities had endured persecution under previous regimes for decades, and the fault lines between secular/liberal forces and Islamists had become deeply entrenched within society. The sudden emergence of Ennahda and the FJP as pivotal actors in shaping the trajectories of Tunisia and Egypt raised questions for many, particularly those with secular leanings. How could two Islamist parties – Ennahda and the FJP – suddenly become pivotal in determining the trajectories of Tunisia and Egypt? For the secular-minded, this turn of events could be considered another crisis – a crisis that both the secularists and the remnants of the old regime had to manage and one that Ennahda and the MB had to survive.

Beşir Atalay admitted the need to devise a careful strategy to avoid similar crises when forming the AKP:

> In 2002 [the year that the AKP emerged], we had several questions in mind: how could the AKP gain and maintain power? Back then, the AKP was viewed as an Islamist party. We realized we needed to expand our reach beyond the Islamist label. The formation of alliances with various segments of society was the most important component of our strategy. For example, allying with the liberals. To do so, we knew we needed to broaden the areas of freedom. The second alignment was with the EU. Thanks to the EU, we managed to widen our alliances to international levels. All these steps were carefully thought out. No coincidences, no spontaneous moves.[16]

The meticulously planned steps taken by the AKP served as tools for the process of normalization. The concept of normalization is inherently ambiguous, since its meaning depends on the perspective of the actor making the claim. However, for the period between the collapse of the regimes and the first elections in Tunisia and Egypt, it proves to be a useful concept. In this context, normalization refers to a series of measures aimed at elevating Ennahda and the MB from the political fringes to the mainstream.

The normalization of the Turkish Islamists began in the 1990s and 'the AKP's willingness and ability to *"look and act normal"* in the perception of a wide range of domestic and external actors explains many of its accomplishments'.[17]

The former Nahdawi prime minister, Hamadi Jebali, offered his perspective on normalization in an interview in 2006, claiming that Ennahda's aim was not to establish *sharia* but rather to show that Ennahda 'in the social and political world, [is] just *one party like the others*'.[18] Indeed, the research conducted by Mecham et al. on the goals of Islamist movements also indicates that 'Islamist parties, particularly in Morocco, Turkey, Indonesia and Malaysia, are becoming increasingly *normalized* participants in their political systems, [. . .] alongside a shift in emphasis in their party platforms'.[19] Being perceived as a 'party like others' encapsulates the essence of normalization for the MB and Ennahda following the uprisings. It reflects 'a genuine desire to be welcomed as responsible actors within the international community'.[20] The process of party institutionalization serves as the initial step in this trajectory of normalization.

In the present context, party institutionalization refers to the ability to mobilize and expand the party's support base, as well as the establishment of efficient internal operations.

Weber explains that the emergence of politics as a profession (*Beruf*) occurs by transforming an amateur apparatus, which is 'very often manned by students who say to a man to whom they attribute leadership qualities, "we will do what needs to be done if you tell us what it is."'[21] However, it is important to note that the internal structure and organizational operations of Ennahda and the MB cannot be described as amateurish. While these movements may have originated with a group of students and a charismatic leader, over the course of several decades, they have evolved into complex and sophisticated entities with distinct hierarchies and functional bodies.

However, as Weber observes, a political party can be likened to a massive apparatus or machine. The successful operation of this machinery necessitates the presence of full-time, paid political entrepreneurs both within and outside of parliament. These individuals are subject to strict bureaucratic control and are equipped with the skills required to engage in canvassing efforts and secure a significant number of voters.[22]

The machine that produced AKP's success was a highly institutionalized party structure with over 13.5 million members,[23] offices in eighty-one cities,[24] youth and women's organizations, specific training programmes for young people, and propaganda and lobbying bodies. According to Erdoğan, 'the AKP has no parallel in Turkey in terms of membership and institutional bodies'.[25] The professionalism of the AKP partly explains why movements such as Ennahda and the MB – which are much older than the AKP and had experience participating in elections in Tunisia and Egypt when permitted – would want to learn from it.

Nahdawi Mohammed Ali Azaiez explains the takeaways Ennahda looked for in the AKP as a political party:

> We [Ennahda] asked a lot of technical questions. We were particularly interested in how the AKP MPs manage their bureaus and so on. Because, here in Tunisia, MPs work alone, and most don't even have an office. We saw that Turkish MPs have a large team of assistants and experts. Yes, it has a lot to do with money, but we looked closely at how a successful party operated.[26]

The MB could not admit that it was inexperienced and knew little about governing, Wickham claims.[27] However, my research proves otherwise. The

MB – at least its party, the FJP – was aware of its limitations, which was why it sought the AKP's advice on such matters. The transitional period following the Uprisings provided an opportunity for full engagement in political processes in Tunisia and Egypt, and this required different tools to tackle a broader range of challenges. As Brown contends, 'in Egypt in 2012, the Brotherhood's leaders [had] to answer questions that [had] never been asked before. They can refer to the epistles of their founder, Hassan al-Banna, for inspiration, but not for practical guidance on detailed questions'.[28]

Former FJP minister Darrag elucidated the practical implications of collaborating with the AKP team, which, for instance, facilitated the FJP team in preparing President Morsi for international engagements.

> If Dr Morsi were about to meet with a minister from another country, we would prepare extensive briefings for him. He would talk to these people and impress them with his detailed knowledge. It was an entirely new thing for us. During Mubarak's time, we couldn't meet with foreigners like this because it was considered espionage. We learned this kind of stuff from the AKP.[29]

This example demonstrates the extent of inexperience on the part of the MB.

Similarly, before the Uprisings, Ennahda, like other Tunisian political parties, 'lacked clear policy goals, [was] highly personalistic'.[30] A Nahdawi, who wished to remain anonymous, argues that 'Ennahda was like a charity organization whose leadership had been in exile for the last decade. So, anyone with some expertise and experience would be welcomed. And it was the AKP who got in touch with us [Ennahda] first. What Ennahda looked for back then was success and power, and the AKP had both'.[31]

5.1 Winning the system

Over the past four decades, eighty-nine parliamentary elections in twenty-one countries have involved one or more Islamic parties, as reported by the Inter-Parliamentary Union.[32]

However, their performance in these elections has often been underwhelming, with these parties typically receiving only a small share of the vote.[33] Interestingly, this lacklustre performance may not necessarily be attributed to unfair election practices or fear of retribution from authoritarian regimes.[34] In fact, prior to the 2000s, Islamic parties often fared worse in elections that were more routine and relatively freer in Muslim-majority countries. In response to these challenges, many Islamist parties have strategically shifted their stances and adopted more liberal positions over the past several decades. The aim has been to appeal to median swing voters and broaden their electoral appeal.[35] The AKP, with its liberal economic policies and effective management of electoral campaigns, exemplifies this transformation within Islamist parties.

In the autumn of 2011, the AKP mentored Ennahda and the MB's FJP in several elections.

Tunisia's constituent assembly elections were scheduled for October 2011, followed by Egypt's parliamentary elections in November 2011 and January 2012. Egypt's presidential election took place in May and June of 2012.

In preparation for Tunisia's constituent assembly election in October 2011, Ennahda actively observed and studied the AKP's extensive and advanced electoral experience.[36] According to Moussa Ben Ahmed, a member of Tunisia's Nahdawi party, the core objective of the relationship between Ennahda and the AKP was to learn the intricacies of winning elections in Muslim-majority countries like Turkey and Tunisia.[37]

Fethi Ayadi, an Ennahda MP (2019), who had been in exile in France before the revolution, asserts that Ennahda delegates visited Istanbul to meet with the AKP's election campaign management teams.[38] In turn, the AKP's teams also visited Tunisia to assist in refining their election strategies. Mohammad Ali Azaiez, an adviser to the minister for investment, development and international cooperation (2019) within Ennahda, mentioned a meeting in which a delegation from Nahdawi met with Foreign Minister Ahmet Davutoğlu, three AKP MPs and the then mayors of Ankara and Üsküdar. The objective of the meeting was to learn about electoral campaign skills.[39] Furthermore, Ennahda delegations were regularly invited to Turkey during general or mayoral elections. This exchange of knowledge and expertise demonstrated the active engagement between Ennahda and the AKP, with Ennahda seeking to gain insights into successful electoral campaigns from the experienced AKP.

Following Ennahda's success in the parliamentary elections of October 2011, where they secured 89 seats out of 217, attention shifted to the upcoming presidential election in Egypt during the summer of 2012. The AKP's involvement with the Muslim Brotherhood's FJP intensified, and their meetings became more frequent. In Egypt, neither the liberal nor secular forces, nor the MB, were fully prepared to contest the election. Decades of military rule had deprived these forces of the experience of open politics. However, the MB had long been anticipating such a historic moment and seized the opportunity presented by the changing political landscape.[40]

While the MB had previously fielded independent candidates in several elections from 1983 onwards, including the 1987, 1995, 2000, 2005 and 2010 elections, the rationale behind seeking advice on elections from the AKP may not be immediately apparent. However, a closer examination reveals that the conditions for participating in elections under Mubarak's authoritarian regime differed significantly from those in the post-revolutionary context.

Under Mubarak's rule, elections provided the MB with an opportunity to propagate its ideas and disseminate its ideology more broadly in society. Shehata refers to this as a form of 'political *da'wa*', an act of inviting people to embrace Islam.[41] Furthermore, during those elections, the primary aim of the MB was not to seek office or maximize votes, as both goals were unattainable under Mubarak's regime.[42] Instead, their participation in the elections and the dissemination of their message were seen as victories in themselves.

However, with Mubarak out of the picture, the MB faced its first free elections and sought advice from a party used to seeking both votes and office, that is, the AKP. Shehata ends his discussion with the prediction that with the founding of the FJP, the MB's electoral strategy may change and the FJP may 'function increasingly like an "ordinary" political party and participate in elections with the primary objective of winning seats, influencing policy and gaining power. Exploring such transformations, as well as their implications for the Muslim Brotherhood organization, is surely a worthy subject for future research'.[43] Indeed, this is precisely how this book aims to contribute to the literature, by demonstrating as clearly as possible the strategic and aspirational transformations of the Islamist entities in question.

'When they [the MB] decided to run, they figured that they needed to examine how political parties prepare for elections', a former AKP MP recalled. 'Where is the closest place that holds elections? Turkey, of course. Turkish Airlines back then had six flights a day between Turkey and Egypt. They used to come in the morning, find out what they wanted to know and leave again in the evening. They wanted to learn everything about elections. From A to Z.'[44] The AKP MP, who was in Cairo throughout the FJP's election campaign, claims that the biggest challenge proved to be conducting opinion polls. 'They had not done it before and told us that it wasn't possible. We explained how to conduct an opinion poll, but they still told us it was not feasible because they did not have the voter demographics to hand.'[45] There was a reason for the MB to see political polling as unfeasible, although it was not apparent to this AKP official. The Egyptian government agency CAPMAS (the Central Agency for Public Mobilization and Statistics) was the only entity authorized to conduct polling of any kind, including market or media research, both of which are also notoriously difficult to conduct in Egypt. For obvious reasons, CAPMAS had not approved political polling for any party other than Mubarek's ruling National Democratic Party. This incident can be seen as an example of the AKP's misconceptions and lack of expertise about the MB and Egypt's political structure, as mentioned earlier.

Unlike in Egypt, the AKP, and particularly Erdoğan, considers election polls an essential part of their political activity. Indeed, the AKP conducts opinion polls not only during election periods but whenever they introduce a new reform or launch a game-changing initiative.[46] For the AKP team it was inconceivable not to use polls in an election campaign 'because, in our experience, it is crucial to see the big picture and have a base level in terms of the MB votes'. Instead of conducting a robust opinion poll in Egypt, 'we did some research using other methods, and we found evidence of serious popularity for the Salafists, especially around the Nour Party. The MB people said we were wrong, but the result of the election proved us right. The Salafists had a significant level of popularity'.[47]

The AKP's influence extended beyond the FJP campaign and also had an impact on other presidential candidates in Egypt. Abdul Moneim Aboul Fotouh had to leave the MB when he declared his intention to run for presidency in 2012. He had previously served as the leader of the MB's youth wing in the late 1970s and later became an influential medical doctor heading the Arab Medical Union. Over time, his ideological views evolved from condoning violence to embracing a more democratic and liberal perspective, particularly during the first decade of the 2000s.

In the period leading up to the elections, Aboul Fotouh met with then prime minister Erdoğan and Ennahda leader Ghannouchi. While the exact date of the meeting remains unknown, it highlights the connections between Aboul Fotouh and these influential Islamist figures. As an independent presidential candidate in 2012, Aboul Fotouh ran his campaign separately from the FJP but used the AKP in an unexpected manner.

'We could not believe it when we saw Fotouh's banner on the streets of Cairo', one former AKP MP remembered. The banner showed an image of Erdoğan's smiling face with a quotation allegedly from him, saying, 'I can't recommend what the Egyptian people should choose, but if I were an Egyptian, I would choose Aboul Fotouh.'[48] 'We told him [Fotouh] that it was not a clever idea, but he went ahead with it anyway. His banner was a great example of how much influence and positivity the AKP's name sparked on the Egyptian streets back then.'[49] While no AKP interviewee could confirm that Erdoğan had actually made such a statement or given consent for the banners, the fact that the banners remained in place suggests that Erdoğan did not have any objections to them.

When it came to the elections, the AKP's then political marketing and publicity chief, Erol Olçok, was the key person appointed to assist both the MB and Ennahda with their campaigns. Olçok had a personal relationship with Erdoğan and managed all AKP campaigns from the party's inception until his death during clashes between military officials and civilians in the attempted coup in Istanbul on 15 July 2016.

In November 2011, just before the first round of parliamentary elections in Egypt, Olçok visited Cairo and held meetings with members of the FJP. These meetings were not intended to be made public, as the AKP preferred to keep them confidential. A TRT correspondent in Cairo at the time, who was from the state channel and not considered an anti-AKP news outlet, attempted to greet Olçok during the meeting at the Kempinski Hotel Cairo. However, he was promptly expelled from the room, and his contract with TRT was terminated.[50] Only later, through a court order, was his contract renewed after several months. The meeting was never reported in Turkey. Given the sensitive political climate and the potential for backlash, it was in the best interest of the AKP and the FJP to keep their dialogue discreet and minimize any perception of external influence.

In addition to Erol Olçok, the AKP team consisted of two scholars affiliated with the think tank SETA, two translators and two AKP ministers who joined on the second day of the meeting. Yehia Hamed, the then senior adviser to President Morsi and the Minister of Investment, was among the MB members present at the meeting. 'We sat in on two sessions with the marketing director of AKP, Erol Olçok. He gave us a lot of tips on what a party should do in terms of political marketing. He had experience, some of which was very relevant, and some of which was not.'[51] During the two-day workshop, Olçok 'explained to the MB the methods and tricks for running a successful election campaign, including techniques of propaganda, publicity, and advertising'.[52]

Similar meetings were also held with Ennahda in 2011, 2014 and 2019, where ideas and experiences about elections were exchanged.[53] 'Erol [Olçok] came to Tunis to help with the October 2014 parliamentary elections', a former senior Nahdawi recalled.[54] Ajmi Lourimi, who was at the time in charge of Ennahda's communication, remembers meeting Erol Olçok and discussing the importance of having a unified discourse as a party:

> Olçok emphasized the importance of unifying our discourse to avoid controversies, suggesting that it would be beneficial to have experts address specific subjects rather than politicians, as it enhances credibility. We never talked about ideology because what we needed to learn was the modern ways of winning elections and succeeding in governance.[55]

Rabeb ben Lotief, the 2019 Ennahda MP for Tunisians in the Americas and the rest of Europe (including Turkey), was among the Nahdawis who held meetings with an AKP delegation just before the 2019 Tunisian elections:

> The AKP team was specialized in elections and stayed with us for two days. They had suggestions about slogans, photos, and logos we use on Twitter and Facebook. All photos had to be taken professionally, they said. They advised us to use light, bright colours and devise short messages and hashtags. They also showed us how to promote the hashtags by sending to all Nahdawis.[56]

Ennahda's outlook as a vote-seeking, centre-right platform was underscored at its 2016 Congress, in which it announced the separation of the political party and *da'wa* (propagation). 'We do not deny our Islamic background', claimed Bechir Yousifi, a member of Ennahda's youth wing from Medenine, 'but we left *da'wa* so the NGOs and charities can take care of it. We want to focus solely on politics and creating a strong party'. He defined a strong party as a 'party that can govern, able to reform, guide, and deliver political programmes. A party that is well institutionalized with transparent organizations and funding. That's why within Ennahda now there is no link between politics and the *da'wa*'.[57] The AKP may have had some influence as an example for the gradual expulsion of Islamic rhetoric and the separation between preaching and politics within Ennahda; at least, that is what several interviewees contended:

> Ennahda had various relations with foreign parties, but the relationship between Ennahda and the AKP is distinctive because we learned from the AKP how to separate religion and politics. Even after the revolution, old habits linked with being a *da'wa* movement continued to surface. So, the AKP for us was a successful model that separated Islam from daily political practice.[58]

This diffusion of electoral tactics indicates that Ennahda and the MB's younger cadres, who filled most of the positions within the FJP, wanted to abandon their single-issue niche party status and 'framed success in terms of attaining office'[59] in the same way as other mainstream parties.

5.2 Service to people is like a prayer

In addition to campaign strategies and effective messaging, an important topic of discussion between the AKP and the MB and Ennahda teams was how to govern municipalities. Why was this such an important issue for diffusion? The answer is twofold. First, Islamist movements in the Middle East had been actively engaged in providing social welfare services, such as healthcare, education and financial aid, to marginalized communities. They filled the gaps left by local entities that were closely associated with authoritarian clientelist regimes. This phenomenon, referred to as 'social Islam' by Bayat, involved the provision of goods, healthcare and informal study groups conducted through mosques that were independent of state control.[60] Therefore, socializing Islam was in this sense a mobilizing tool for these movements, as they sought to address the needs of the underprivileged and socially marginalized populations.

Second, the provision of such services was interpreted within the framework of *da'wa*. By framing the delivery of efficient services as a religious duty, Islamist movements were able to mobilize their base and encourage active participation in these initiatives. This, in turn, contributed to the sustainability of the services provided.

The voting behaviour of individuals in support of Islamist parties that provide social welfare services highlights the complex interplay between ideology, reputation and electoral success in the Middle East. While the provision of social services through charities may serve as a form of *da'wa* for Islamist entities, electoral support for these parties does not necessarily indicate a complete alignment with their ideological underpinnings. Rather, it often stems from the recognition and satisfaction with the efficiency and quality of the services delivered.

For Islamist parties, the implications of this phenomenon are multi-dimensional. On one hand, their reputation as effective providers of local governance and social welfare can bolster their standing in political processes. However, as Cammett and Luong argue, it is essential to recognize that ideology and reputation are not synonymous, and merely having an ideological stance is not sufficient to win the support and trust of the public.[61] Reputation plays a crucial role, however during times of transition when 'Islamist parties no longer operate in a quasi-legal environment, their reputations can be easily undermined if they fail to live up to their messages or appear to contradict their principles and ideologies'.[62]

Therefore, in the aftermath of the Arab Uprisings, when the reputations of Islamist parties as reliable social welfare providers were not firmly established, both Ennahda and the MB saw value in seeking guidance from the AKP whose leader had risen to power through his tenure as mayor of Istanbul. It is noteworthy that while the MB had experience in providing social services, Ennahda had been repressed since the early 1990s and had not had the opportunity to develop a strong base in local government or offer extensive social services.

The AKP is a service-oriented party and accommodates this trait within Islamist rhetoric, such as 'serving people is equal to serving God (*Halka hizmet Hakk'a hizmettir*)'. This slogan both served the AKP's secular approach to everyday politics and gave its Islamist base incentive to engage and participate in politics. Controlling municipalities, or its grip on power, lies at the heart of the AKP's success. For example, Qaradawi, in a speech highlighting Turkey's development, specifically mentioned the AKP's municipalities as benchmarks for the country's progress.[63] Since the 1990s, municipalities in Turkey have become 'the institutional vanguards of a socio-political project that attacks the established order and one of the chief mobilizers of people on the ground against this order',[64] because they sit on the boundary between state and politics and have a certain degree of autonomy. The AKP's mother movement, *Refah Partisi* (RP), reaped the seeds sown by the grassroots community services in the 1994 local elections, gaining 327 municipalities, including Istanbul and Ankara. Erdoğan, then a member of the party, was one of the beneficiaries of RP's powerful mayoral influence. For the AKP, this socio-political project was to extend and consolidate its base by 'merging ex-Islamists, the urban poor, intellectuals, business families, and professionals around a neoliberal "democratic" program'.[65] It utilized the autonomy and resources of the municipalities to achieve that goal. Understanding the AKP's transformation from Islamism to post-Islamism is also closely linked to its community experience. Erdoğan's tenure as the mayor of Istanbul led him to 'shift his focus from lofty ideals of building a new Islamic society and state'[66] to mobilizing the voter base through service delivery.

The first woman to run Tunisia's State Fund, Boutheina Ben Yaghlane, was appointed by Ennahda and believes that 'the success of the AKP began with its municipality work, which reinforced its relations with the people. This made people focus on their work'.[67]

Adel Ben Amor, a member of Ennahda's *shura* and adviser to the Minister of State for Transport and Logistics, also sees that 'municipalities enabled the party to widen its base. Any new party, not only Ennahda, should learn about this aspect'.[68]

Yaghlane's observation aligns with reality. The AKP's expertise gained since 1994, first through the RP's mayoral positions and later within the AKP, was transformed into a mechanism for social mobilization. This involved computerized lists, neighbourhood maps, neighbourhood management commissions and party-appointed head observers responsible for voter districts. A personalized style of face-to-face mobilization was at the core of the AKP's success.⁶⁹ Both the MB and Ennahda expressed their interest in learning and adopting this crucial aspect of the AKP's approach.

As White claims, the computerized lists and neighbourhood maps, with a neighbourhood management commission and a party-assigned head observer responsible 'for about 300 people in a voting district [... and] a perfected face-to-face personalized style of mobilizing' were at the heart of the AKP's success. This was the most important aspect and one that interviewees from both the MB and Ennahda claimed their parties would like to learn about and emulate. Here, it is important to emphasize one other feature of AKP's style of local governance. The AKP – via its municipalities – advocated pro-market and neoliberal policies promoting a massive expansion of social housing whose contracts 'awarded by the central government to local municipalities also fuelled distributive politics in the form of jobs, contracts, and subsidized housing, which, in turn, played a key role in consolidating and expanding the AKP's electoral base'.⁷⁰

Khanfar recollects that the AKP representatives made multiple visits to Egypt to demonstrate effective service delivery techniques to the MB.⁷¹ Mesut Özcan, a former adviser to Davutoğlu and current Deputy Director of the Ministry of Foreign Affairs Strategic Research Department, concurs with this view: 'Our [the AKP's] delegations had underlined the importance of services time and time again. You should focus on dynamic communities, we said'.⁷² According to Mohamed Hgazy, a former youth leader from Alexandria, the MB sent teams to Istanbul to study the AKP's municipal operations. These teams included individuals from the MB who were later assigned roles within the municipalities. For instance, one participant eventually became part of one of Alexandria's governance bodies.⁷³

President Morsi's presidential committee had visited Turkey and toured districts of Istanbul and Ankara. 'We also were given a tour of the police departments. One time, we went to a very nice factory in Ankara that had a garbage recycling facility. We wanted to import that technology so as to create a full recycling facility of our own'⁷⁴ says Yehia Hamed, Egypt's former minister of investment. According to a former AKP MP who was a crucial figure in the diffusion process, 'we [the AKP] also helped them restructure their municipal services. We have connected many municipalities to different places in Cairo to make services more efficient'.⁷⁵

In May 2013, 150 refuse disposal trucks worth 25 million USD were loaded onto ships berthed in Mersin Port, to be sent to Egypt.⁷⁶ The refuse trucks were a gift, symbolic of the emphasis placed by the AKP on efficient services, as Cairo's refuse situation worsened in the aftermath of the revolution owing to the collapse of multiple state practices and, between 2011 and 2013, became a political issue.

The general sanitation problems on the streets had made a deep impression on the AKP team, who had to live in Cairo during and immediately after the election period. Memories of dirty streets appeared to be very vivid in their minds. 'Even the Kempinski Hotel was under a heavy layer of dust. I went to a mosque once and could not pray because of the filth inside',[77] one AKP bureaucrat claimed. A former AKP MP recalled seeing the corpse of a horse on the street very close to the FJP offices in Cairo.

> On the third day, I went up to the FJP office and asked them if they could do something about the horse and told them the body had been lying there untouched for three days. They looked at me and asked, 'What horse?' I couldn't believe my ears. It was impossible for them to miss it, but even when they look at it, they don't see.[78]

These anecdotes may perhaps imply a sense of Turkish superiority over Arabs, reflecting discriminatory rhetoric associating uncleanliness with Arabs. While these remarks may carry elements of racism, they also highlight the AKP's concern for the success of the MB. The AKP officials recognized that failing to meet the basic needs of the people could quickly make or break a political actor. Erdogan, in particular, repeatedly criticized Turkey's main opposition party, CHP, for its alleged corruption and garbage issues.[79] Another example can be found in the AKP's 2019 recent local election campaign for the March 2019 elections, which highlighted old pictures of Istanbul filled with refuse.[80]

5.3 Protective alliances against the old regime

The Arab Uprisings dismantled the extant 'ruling bargains' in Tunisia and Egypt as the transitional periods redefined 'the roles, functions, and the structures of institutions (political parties and organizations, the armed forces, the executive), personal actions and initiatives'.[81] The AKP sees itself as the founder of a 'new Turkey', in which the ruling bargains of the old secular elite and the military were broken up, and the power dynamics of the political landscape altered. The 'new Turkey' narrative, which entered the political jargon through Erdoğan's speeches in and around 2010, symbolized a counter-hegemony to the old Kemalist establishment. As Davutoğlu once expressed it, 'new Turkey' was not only a slogan but a new design project.[82] The tactics deployed in forming alliances and managing threats were based on the AKP's experiences in constructing this so-called 'new Turkey'.

Both Ennahda and the MB are experienced in self-preservation against regime threats. However, the interviews for this research demonstrate that building alliances with various actors – both domestic and foreign – and taking precautions against the military were some of the topics that these three entities discussed in the aftermath of the revolutions in Egypt and Tunisia. Why, though, would Ennahda and the MB need to heed the AKP's cautionary tales? The first reason was that the AKP practised a strategy of building alliances and curbing the military's role in politics while it was in power, not in opposition. Neither Ennahda nor the MB had had the opportunity to put their self-preservation methods to test while in power. As Roy explains, 'the Islamists [the MB and Ennahda are] obliged to search for allies as they control neither the army nor the religious sphere. And even if they are able to find allies among the Salafists – the religious conservatives – and the military, these two groups are nevertheless not prepared to allow them to become dominant. The Islamists [have] to negotiate'.[83] The second reason was that these tactics had, in the eyes of the MB and Ennahda, been effective in Turkey. 'One of the most important accomplishments of the AKP was to end the era of military coups in Turkey', observed the president of Ennahda's *shura*, Abdelkarim Harouni.

In examining the influence of the AKP's alliance-building tactics on the Muslim Brotherhood (MB) and Ennahda between 2011 and 2013, it is crucial to acknowledge the inherent complexity and unpredictability of the causal inference.[84] AKP's impact on the actions of Ennahda and the MB is an exogenous variable that is 'too complex or unpredictable to be brought into theory'.[85] Consequently, I employ the process tracing method to delineate the micro-correlating events[86] that transpired during this period, with the aim of elucidating the extent to which the AKP's strategies were congruous with the transitional experiences of the MB and Ennahda.

5.3.1 Threats and alliances for the MB

After the revolution, the locus of major forces within society and the state unleashed in Egypt was more complicated than in Tunisia. The MB was confronted with three major and unfamiliar challenges: 'its newfound legality, its involvement in party politics, and its being thrust into the centre of the institutional political sphere'.[87] Second, a large proportion of Egyptian revolutionary groups and a faction within the MB as well believed that rushing into elections in November 2011 – ten months after the fall of Mubarak – without fully eliminating elements of the old regime from state apparatuses would be contrary to people's demands and it would appear that the MB was hijacking the revolution and negotiating with the army. The Supreme Council of Armed Forces (SCAF), which took power after Mubarak's fall, had soon come face-to-face with the MB. The standoff that ensued 'was not based on different views over democracy, achieving the Uprising's objectives, or meeting the people's demands; rather, it was about each side's share of power and political privileges'.[88]

The former Egyptian parliamentarian and author of several books on Islamism and the MB, Amr Al-Shobaki, argued at that time that Egypt could learn from Turkey's experience of establishing civil-military relations.[89] However, the AKP did not see themselves as on the same page as the MB on this matter: 'We were unable to persuade them of the danger that the old regime, with its remnants in the military and judiciary, posed. That was our biggest headache with the MB',[90] recalled a former AKP MP.

On 14 June 2012, two days before the presidential election, the Egyptian Supreme Court, comprised of judges appointed by former president Mubarak, ruled that the first democratically elected parliament should be shut down and the constitution suspended on the grounds of misapplication of election rules by independent candidates. The media reported that the court's ruling was 'condemned as a coup by Islamists, liberals and scholars' in Egypt. However, the AKP team had a different story to tell regarding the reaction of the Islamists and the MB.[91] One AKP member telephoned the MB members with whom he was in contact when he learned of the parliamentary shutdown to find that the MB members were not as shocked or as enraged as he was. He telephoned Ankara to consult on the matter and, with Ankara's approval, went to the FJP election office.

> When we entered the office, we noticed MB people eating *knafeh (künefe)*. They greeted us joyfully and offered the dessert. Their complacency astounded me. I tried to urge them to take action such as organizing protests or sit-ins, to prevent the parliament from closing down. I told them that, if the parliament were to be suspended, you would have to make decisions about everything from the electricity administration to foreign policy. And in two months, you'll be labelled a dictator. The parliament is the most important insurance policy. They [the MB people] didn't seem to mind. Not because they were stupid but because they did not know how the system works. They were fixated on winning the presidential election. That day I realized that this show was likely to culminate in a coup.[92]

The divergent responses of the MB and the AKP to the interventions of the *ancien régime* can be attributed to several factors. During the 1980s, both the Turkish junta and the Mubarak regime in Egypt provided a limited degree of political space for Islamist movements, such as Milli Görüş in Turkey and the MB in Egypt, as a counterbalance to leftist and more radical Islamist factions. However, these concessions were restricted, with both the MB and Milli Görüş adhering to the rules that allowed them only minimal and regulated representation in their respective parliaments, thereby preventing any significant alteration to the status quo. As Bayat contends, 'the challenge faced by Turkish Islamism in its encounter with strong secular sensibilities and the Turkish military had brought about the emergence of a post-Islamist AKP'.[93] Put another way, the arrival of the AKP, which adopted a distinct strategy from its predecessor, the *Refah Partisi*, signalled the initiation of a solution for Turkey's Islamists in addressing the threat posed by the military. Conversely, the MB in Egypt did not undergo a comparable transformational process, which may explain the differences in their approaches.

Needless to say, however, neither the MB leadership nor the Morsi government was naive about the perils posed by the remnants of the Mubarak regime. In this situation, the MB implemented a parallel strategy. In August 2012, shortly after assuming office, President Morsi forced several powerful officials to retire, including the former head of the SCAF Hussein Tantawi, the defence minister, the army chief of staff and senior generals within the navy and air force. He also annulled a constitutional decree used by the military to oversee presidential processes. The Morsi government's moves were deemed provocative, as they appeared to be 'animated by an endless reservoir of distrust and dismissiveness toward their opponents'.[94] In theory, a Brother such as Morsi ruling Egypt could bring about a total disruption of the regime structure and the military's privileged position. What, however, happened in reality?

Although Morsi's steps appeared to be a bold reshuffling of the army, it later transpired that the changes were dictated by the military itself, which was embroiled in its own turf wars.[95] The Morsi government had enacted no legislation to limit the military's privileges, and the latter's position remained unchecked, autonomous and opaque, as it had been during Mubarak's time. The Morsi government made no attempt to prosecute army officials for human rights violations or other wrongdoing. The constitution was drafted by a committee appointed by the SCAF in 2012. The military retained sole control over its budget, estimated to be 15 per cent of Egypt's GDP.[96] The MB seemed to have assumed that, if it did not antagonize the military, the two sides would eventually find a balance in sharing power.

Nevertheless, the previous tacit agreements would be superseded by new ones, with unprecedented consequences, as witnessed in the coup of the summer of 2013 and the subsequent crackdown on the MB. According to AKP members, the MB failed to foresee this outcome.

While its strategy to contain military threats was becoming counterproductive, the MB was also failing to follow the AKP's advice to forge protective alliances. In November 2012, President Morsi issued a decree that granted him and the Islamist-led assembly expansive power and exempted presidential decrees from constitutional scrutiny. With this move, he lost the support of the liberals, secularists, and leftists forever. Within one brief year, 'the Egyptians who had initially cheered him wanted him to go'.[97] At that point, 'many Egyptians (69 per cent) disapproved of the job performance of the country's leadership – a dramatic drop from the 63 per cent approval rating in November 2012. Nineteen per cent of Egyptians in June [2013] said they supported the FJP, a sharp decline from early 2012 when 67 per cent of Egyptians expressed support'.[98]

According to a high-level Turkish bureaucrat who was present in Cairo during Morsi's government, 'even though Ikhwan [the MB in Egypt] had promised that they would not interfere with individual lifestyles, just as the AKP had promised in its first two tenures, they could not persuade the technocratic cadres of the *ancien régime* who thought that Ikhwan's promises were just *taqiya* [a precautionary concealment of Islamic belief and practice]'.[99] The perception of the MB's *taqiya* or fear of an Islamist takeover of the Egyptian state may have contributed to Morsi's unpopularity. However, these were not the primary reasons in the context of food and water shortages, rising prices for basic supplies and an increase in street crime. Although the MB blamed these problems on a military plot,[100] the responsibility laid on its shoulders.

The AKP in Turkey has navigated the complex relationship between the military and society's anti-military sentiment with a measured and gradual approach. Unlike its predecessor, Erbakan's *Refah Partisi*, the AKP refrained from attempting to depose all ruling secularist elites, at least until 2011. This conciliatory tone resonated with a diverse array of non-Islamist politicians, intellectuals and voters who subsequently joined its ranks.[101] This gradual approach to dismantling the status quo did not equate to submission; rather, the AKP actively resisted military and judicial intervention in politics.

A pivotal moment in the AKP's tenure occurred during the 2007 presidential elections, which marked the end of the term of the staunchly Kemalist tenth president, Ahmet Necdet Sezer. Despite the largely ceremonial nature of the position, the president wielded considerable power in vetoing constitutional amendments. Sezer had overturned twenty-two draft bills proposed by the AKP on various issues, thereby providing a protective shield for the secular establishment against the perceived Islamist agenda of the AKP. When the AKP nominated Abdullah Gül for the presidency, it anticipated three likely outcomes: Gül's almost certain victory due to the AKP's parliamentary majority; Gül's facilitation of AKP-proposed bills as president; and the symbolic significance of a First Lady wearing a head covering residing in the presidential mansion in Ankara for the first time since modern Turkey's foundation.

To avoid this scenario, nationwide rallies known as *Cumhuriyet Mitingleri* (Republican Rallies) were organized. The AKP ignored them and nominated Gül. The main opposition party, the CHP, boycotted the first round of parliamentary elections. On the same night, the chief of general staff of the Turkish army posted a threatening memorandum on the army's website, declaring that he would do whatever it took to guard the secular republic, an event that was dubbed the '*e-muhtıra*' (e-ultimatum) in Turkish political jargon. The AKP did not back down and repeal Gül's nomination but adhered to its original plan. The crisis culminated, in 2007, in an early general election, in which the AKP received 46 per cent of the votes and Gül became the eleventh president of Turkey. The second challenge came in 2008, when the AKP, with the help of nationalist party MHP (*Milliyetçi Hareket Partisi*), was able to pass a constitutional amendment that liberalized restrictions on wearing head coverings at universities and in civil service. As a result, the chief public prosecutor issued an indictment against the AKP for violating the separation of religion and state. In July 2008, the Constitutional Court voted six to five not to ban the party.

These two incidents provided the AKP and its base with invaluable learning experiences, the principal among which was that if it stood firm against threats from the secular establishment, it would eventually triumph. 'We stand our ground; we never bow down except when we pray'[102] had become Erdoğan's motto.[103] In the AKP's thinking, it would be a fatal mistake to yield to groundless threats from the *ancien régime*, such as the Egyptian Supreme Court's decision to close down parliament two days before the presidential election. Hence, at that time, the AKP delegation tried to push the FJP to 'stand its ground', though to no avail.

The then deputy prime minister of Turkey, Beşir Atalay, states that he was frank with delegates from both the MB and Ennahda whom he had met a couple of times in the aftermath of the regime's collapse.

> I went through step by step what kind of obstacles and challenges the AKP had encountered in its first years in power. I emphasized the need to form alliances

with different segments of society. I said to them, do not envy the Iranian model. Its governance is a bad example for Muslims. Please, I said to the Egyptians, please be cautious when it comes to the military. I told them that their guardianship is worse than what we had in Turkey.[104]

In its first years in office, the AKP was 'nearly obsessed with garnering support from a diverse group of voters because of their fear of the military elite and another possible coup d'état'.[105] When it faced perceived existential threats, the AKP set about diligently forming critical alliances that would help it to consolidate certain blocs that stood on the fracture lines of Turkish society. One such alliance was with the liberal intellectuals, who provided significant intellectual and media support during the aforementioned 2007–8 crises, the Ergenekon and Sledgehammer trials and the 2011 constitutional amendment referendum, all of which sealed the deal for the AKP's consolidation of power. Another alliance that enabled the AKP to push back was that with the Gülen movement, which staged the high-profile trials mentioned earlier with fabricated evidence, thanks to its members in the police and the judiciary, and acted as the AKP's international lobbying agent until 2014. When the AKP fell out violently with its former partner Gülen, it allied itself with the ultra-nationalist bloc led by MHP (*Milliyetçi Hareket Partisi* – Nationalist Movement Party). In short, it took the AKP nearly a decade to take a stand and another decade to fully control the state. It formed alliances according to its needs while discarding old partners. The media and scholars often fail to note that 'the transition that produced the Turkish model was much slower and more precarious than the pace of change unleashed in Egypt, Tunisia and beyond'.[106]

According to the interviewees, the AKP tried to explain precisely this to the MB team. 'I have seen more than once that "our guys (*bizimkiler*)" told Morsi to go slowly and be flexible on specific issues',[107] claims a former AKP MP. The former adviser to then foreign minister Davutoğlu, Mesut Özcan, had met with Yasser Ali, an adviser to President Morsi, and asked him about the MB's vision for Egypt.

> Yasser Ali told me that the AKP is very successful in economic policies and overcoming the military's challenges. But, he said, we'd do the same in less time. I could sense his pride. In the back of his mind, he was thinking, 'We are Ikhwan. We are Egyptian civilization. Who are you, Turks? You were in Central Asia yesterday.' Of course, he was not as blunt about it as I just was, but you get that feeling. So, I told him that the Islamist parties in Turkey, beginning with Erbakan's party, have been an integral part of the Turkish political system since

the adoption of the multi-party system in 1946. Furthermore, Turkey's active EU accession process, initiated in 1999, played a significant role in attracting foreign investment and revitalizing the economy. In Egypt, you have neither of these conditions, and you tell me that you are going to act fast. I told him it was a mistake, but he was too cocksure to listen.[108]

According to Wickham, the MB's soft underbelly was not its ideological rigidity but its hubris, which stood in the way of forming alliances with other sectors of society – such as the revolutionary camp, the leftists and the secular–liberals – to confront elements of the deep state.[109] The MB discarded the gradualism of the past after achieving victory in the elections following the revolution and moved hurriedly, Hamid claims.[110] A further factor contributing to the MB's complacency was its inexperience. As all the Egyptian interviewees confirmed, none of their previous interactions with the regime could have provided them with the knowledge they would need when in power. Another problem was the movement's *shura*, which consisted of the old guard, and 'placed its political party on a very short leash – appointing the FJP's leaders, approving its platforms, and even deciding which movement members should move over to the party'.[111]

The then prime minister Ahmet Davutoğlu highlights the same problem, emphasizing the importance of alliances for survival.

> Ikhwan endured the same challenges that any movement transitioning from a *da'wa* entity to a political party would endure. I've warned them several times that they cannot manage a political party under the auspices of a religious movement. A political party should treat each citizen equally and respect all identities. Because Ikhwan was unable to separate the FJP from the movement, the Copts felt ill at ease. We always stressed that the Copts should feel comfortable. Make Christians part of the party, if possible, we suggested. When I became the prime minister, I appointed an Armenian intellectual as my senior adviser. This appointment aimed to demonstrate that that merit, rather than religious identity, should be the guiding principle in decision making.[112]

According to the AKP actors involved in the diffusion process, the MB had implemented some of the AKP's suggestions:

> We repeatedly urged the MB delegation to consider the significant Christian population and the influential Christian elites in Egypt. We advised them to be brave and avoid the Salafist path. Morsi listened to us and bravely stated on TV, 'Christians are my brothers'. Despite attempts by Salafists to pit the MB against the Coptic Pope, the MB did not fall into that trap. Our insistence and suggestions on this issue influenced Morsi's decision to publicly reach out to the Christians.[113]

It is important to note that, in Egypt, the elite intelligentsia is composed mainly of Sunni Muslims. However, a certain degree of pluralism and coexistence with non-Muslims holds some symbolic value and, more importantly, may be considered – in the eyes of Egypt's 'secularized intelligentsia'[114] – as a sign of democratic maturity.

While the approach of the former AKP MP cited earlier demonstrates the importance attributed by the AKP to forming alliances with, or at the very least not antagonizing other social groups, Davutoğlu's words highlight the practicality of symbolic gestures such as – in his case – appointing an Armenian scholar as a senior adviser. As he implied, the significance of winning the hearts of the Coptic Christians was critical not merely because they hegemonized the elite intelligentsia, but because an alliance with the Copts – symbolical or structural – could open up avenues of elite consolidation for the MB. Although the Copts and seculars constitute a small proportion of Egyptian society, their exclusion from the early stages of the transition 'created an atmosphere of distrust at the outset that was worsened overtime'[115] and hampered any possibility of elite coherence, which is one of the main factors determining the success or failure of a transitional period.[116]

Not only the AKP, but also Tariq Al-Zomor, the leader of the Salafist Building and Development Party, warned the FJP and the Morsi government about the military's encroachment. Al-Zomor, who had been imprisoned for twenty-five years for involvement in the assassination of former Egyptian president Anwar Sadat, recounted a conversation with Morsi, where he expressed his concern about the Supreme Court's ruling, influenced by the military's request. 'Dr Morsi asked me what my recommendation was, and I said that, as Islamist groups, we were behind him; we should get five million people out on the street and protest: that way, we could stop a possible coup.'[117]

According to Zomor, President Morsi was not convinced that a coup was likely because he believed that the United States would not allow it to happen. Another reason may have been that the MB was attempting to strike a deal with the military in a bid to acquire more freedom to manoeuvre when the crowds began their sit-in at Tahrir Square to force Mubarak to resign in 2011. Young Egyptians saw the MB's negotiations with the military as a betrayal of the revolution.[118] This episode at the height of the revolution may have led the MB leadership to assume that the initial accord between them and the military was still in effect.

Salah Abdel Maqsoud admitted that the MB misjudged the military's actions. 'We made two critical errors. First, we assumed that, after the 25

January revolution, the Egyptian military would not attempt a coup. Second, we anticipated a strong international reaction to the junta.'[119] This blunder was based partly on the belief that President Morsi had maintained a cordial relationship with high-ranking military officers. However, this was not a delusion concocted by MB members.

'I met with a high-ranking army officer close to Sisi one month before the coup. He told me that the military loved Dr Morsi because he called army officials every time, he made a foreign visit and asked them what they wanted, and then structured his visits to fulfil the army's requests', Zomor claimed.

Why, then, did this seemingly amicable relationship culminate in a bloody coup? The goal of the amicability was reverse co-option, incorporating the military into the MB's own processes so that the army did not pose a threat and would also – potentially – legitimize the MB government. Remarkably, this strategy mirrored Mubarak's long-standing method of engaging with Islamist groups. According to Springborg, the Muslim Brotherhood oscillated between cultivating alliances with authoritarian figures and impulsively retaliating against them, never achieving a stable midpoint that would allow for cooperation with other political forces in forming a cohesive and unified civilian opposition.[120] Kandil, similarly, contends that Morsi and the MB, even at the pinnacle of their power, harboured distrust towards other political factions and relied on their past oppressors within the military and security apparatus.[121]

The AKP appeared to have recognized the emergence of an anti-Morsi coalition, not necessarily due to a deep understanding of the tensions and trends within Egyptian society, but rather due to the efforts of the Turkish Intelligence Agency (MIT). In an August 2013 television interview, Davutoğlu revealed for the first time that Hakan Fidan, the head of MIT, had been dispatched to Cairo fifteen days prior to the coup to alert President Morsi of the 'probable coup' as the MIT had gathered relevant information. Pro-AKP media outlets reported that Fidan had presented President Morsi with a list of recommendations.

The AKP seemed to have noticed the strengthening of an anti-Morsi bloc, not necessarily due to a deep understanding of the tensions and trends within Egyptian society but rather because of the efforts of the Turkish Intelligence Agency (MIT). Davutoğlu, in a television interview in August 2013, disclosed for the first time that the then head of MIT (2010–23), Hakan Fidan, had been dispatched to Cairo fifteen days prior to the coup to alert President Morsi of the 'probable coup' as the MIY had gathered relevant information.[122] Pro-AKP news outlets reported that Fidan had presented President Morsi with a list of suggestions.

1) To strengthen your presidency's legitimacy, reach out to all sectors of Egyptian society, and organize consultation meetings with members of other political parties. 2) We understand how much you value our close relationship. Turkey appreciates this; however, you should arrange foreign visits to countries like the USA and Iran. 3) Focus on tourism to revitalize the economy. 4) Clean the streets of Cairo. Use the garbage trucks we provided. 5) Send us government bureaucrats for training.[123]

Fidan's suggestions provide further support for the overarching patterns of collaboration between the AKP and the MB following Mubarak's ousting. They also serve as an official account of the dynamics at play during this process, highlighting the emphasis on plurality, and the pursuit of accommodations with global and regional powers.

5.3.2 Threats and alliances for Ennahda

According to the interviews conducted for this research, the AKP advised Ennahda to form coalitions with secular and left-wing parties in the Tunisian Parliament, especially during the transition and constitution-writing period. The discussions on the new constitution began after the parliamentary elections in November 2011 and lasted for two years, with the draft ready to be put to a vote in late January 2014. The coalitions and alliances formed during that period enabled Ennahda to maintain its hold on power, mirroring the AKP's strategy of forging alliances with the liberal intelligentsia and the EU, which aided in gaining during its initial terms and safeguarded it against the secular establishment and military in Turkey. The AKP's tacit and cross-class coalition had attracted support from various groups including 'housewives, public employees, pro-EU, mostly urban, educated voters'.[124] Similarly, Ennahda had a history of reaching out to other opposition parties from the early 1980s in a way that the MB did not.

The alliance with the Mustapha Ben Jaffar's Ettakatol Party linked Ennahda to the old Tunis opposition elites while the alliance with Moncef Marzouki's Congress for the Republic (CPR) connected them to emerging revolutionary elites – both important constituencies.

Zeinab Brahmi of Ennahda acknowledges that 'diversity management was the most important task' facing Ennahda after the revolution highlighting similarities between Turkey and Tunisia 'in terms of the political and social cleavages'. To navigate these challenges, she said, 'we focus on how the AKP managed disagreements and differences in Turkey, because, in the end, that is the reality of a country everyone must deal with'.¹²⁵ The interviewees from Ennahda's side uphold the view that the party's decision to form a coalition following the first free elections was a deliberate strategy to manage diversity within Tunisian polity.

Ridha Driss, one of the key actors who advocated Ennahda's announcement of a 'Muslim democracy' at the tenth Congress in 2016, claims that Ennahda did not and does not rule alone, for three reasons:

> First, Tunisia's electoral law prevents any single party from gaining a majority of votes. Second, as we transition from an unjust state to a democratic one, it is crucial to form coalitions involving all parties and collectively learn democratic about governance. Third, situated in a volatile region, with Libya and Algeria in constant flux next door, we must fortify the Tunisian national core to effectively face these challenges.¹²⁶

To protect Ennahda, the existing fault lines in society needed not to be permitted to solidify. Ennahda was confronted with 'an anti-Islamist backlash from large sectors of the secular and modernist sectors of society due to its initially ambiguous position on its commitment to liberal democracy'.¹²⁷ This ambiguity contributed to the general apprehension towards Islamism. Consequently, Lourimi argues, 'We worked with moderate secularists [after the first election] rather than Muslim extremists, because we believed that the country should be led by a strong centre composed of moderate Muslims and secularists. We did not wish to build a broad Islamic front against a secular front'.¹²⁸

Between crisis and consolidation come moments of 'anchoring' for political parties and actors. The anchors in the political sense are strategic decisions made in times of crisis that define the path of the political actor/party and the country's transitional period.¹²⁹

Although the Nahdawis claim they did not fear a similar end to that of the MB, the Egyptian coup impacted Ennahda's political path and precipitated Ennahda's decision of 2016 to split the practices of politics and preaching. Certain segments within Ennahda rationalize this decision by alluding to the first amendment of the constitution, which states that 'Tunisia is a free, independent, sovereign state; its religion is Islam, its language Arabic, and its system is republican'. Through this amendment, the Nahdawis claim that Islamic values and principles are automatically applied to society and that Ennahda's initial self-relegated task of preaching Islamic values to the people is thus redundant. As a result:

> Now we [Ennahda] want to focus on politics. If people want to focus on religion, they can do it through religious organizations. We, as a party, need to deal with administration, economics, and foreign relations. We decided to separate *da'wa*

and politics after discussing the issue for 18 months with Tunisian figures who do not belong to Ennahda and scrutinizing the experiences of Morocco, Algeria, and Turkey.[130]

Others believe that the separation of *da'wa* and politics resulted from Ennahda's evolution since its foundation in the 1980s, and that, 'if Ennahda had not wanted its fortunes to wane and become a nostalgic entity, it would have had to reinvent itself. Of course, an impulse for self-preservation might have been behind the decision to split *da'wa* from politics, after seeing what happened in Egypt in 2013'.[131] Lotfi Ziotun claims there had also been pressure from the Tunisian public:

> Ennahda felt the need to announce that it was no longer an Islamist party because there was pressure from society. The first election that made Ennahda the leading party was right after the revolution. People's minds were still not set. However, in the next election, it was apparent that the Tunisian sentiment rejected the prospect of having an ideological party in power. The Tunisian elite, the intelligentsia, academics, and artists made that clear.[132]

As seen, Ennahda was more reactive to and conscious of threats, and it proposed solutions that would appease the prominent forces in Tunisian politics. For example, during Tunisia's constitution-writing period, a video of Ghannouchi was leaked to Facebook, showing a speech made in a meeting with Islamist leaders on 10 October 2012, in which Ghannouchi stated that while Ennahda had polled higher than expected in the elections, the secular elites retained hegemony over the national discourse due to their control over the media and economy, so Islamists had to tread very carefully.[133]

As shown in this chapter, the tactics diffused from the AKP can be summarized as two-tier formulae that would bring about the success that Ennahda and the MB saw in the AKP rule. The first tier encompassed checklists aimed at legitimizing the MB's party, the FJP, and Ennahda as competent political parties and assisting them in navigating the first few years of a transitional period shaped by unavoidable crises. The second tier entailed prescriptions for state, party and elite consolidation. This is analogous to the Gramscian power structure, in which the state equals political society plus civil society.[134] In this sense, while forming alliances was a formula that would aid elite consolidation, curbing the military's role acted as a strategy for state consolidation. Additionally, managing the municipalities and the elections can be viewed as part of the party consolidation process. The final strategy diffused from the AKP pertained to economic management. In the next chapter, I will set out the economic strategies that helped to solidify the AKP's status vis-à-vis the state and society.

6

Brothers in search of their bourgeoisie

It is easy enough to chant a slogan such as 'Islam is the solution' – a slogan adopted by Islamist movements from the end of the 1980s across the MENA region[1] – when oppressed and excluded from the political game. It is even easier for movements to propose nebulous solutions to economic grievances that primarily draw attention to the corruption of the ruling establishment when they are not in a position to deliver a comprehensive economic vision. However, when they ascend to power in the aftermath of a crisis – in this case, a crisis that has shaken the status quo – it is imprudent to reiterate ideological slogans without concurrently developing actionable and feasible strategies. This was the formidable challenge facing both the Tunisian Ennahda and the MB/FJP when they emerged victorious from the first free elections held after the Arab Uprisings in Tunisia and Egypt respectively.

The Islamist movements, especially the MB in Egypt, had been filling the gap in social provision with their charities, as a result of the government's retreat from welfare. As mentioned in Chapter 5, the MB's charity work may have contributed to the belief that it would fight corruption and deliver services to the have-nots and have played a role in its victory in the first elections. In other words, 'the Islamic machine' – a term Masoud uses to describe the MB's charity structure – helped the MB to win the election; however, the voters soon realized that the MB had over-promised and withheld their initial support.[2] Thus the Islamists' initial and perceived advantage over other political parties waned quickly after Ennahda and the MB/FJP assumed power. Tacit and utopian promises of a 'return to Islam's Golden Age', previous charity work: none of this proved enough. The population, and especially the young, needed to believe that their needs would be met and their material lives improve. As the son of an Egyptian Islamist put it, '[T]he last thing youth are thinking about is religion. [...] They need money, they need to get married, a car, and they don't have anything to do with anything else.'[3]

Although certain parts of the era are still understudied, the literature on the Arab Uprisings of 2011 has effectively elucidated the political, cultural and economic factors that contributed to the downfall of the regimes in Egypt and Tunisia. The Uprisings crossed ideologies and classes,[4] railing against a system that the protesters saw as illegitimate. Roughly construed, the peoples of Tunisia and Egypt revolted against decades of oppression and the neoliberal policies, ostentatious corruption and cronyism of the ruling elite at a time when almost 40 per cent of the population was living below the poverty line. Just before the Uprisings, the gulf in living standards between the affluent and the impoverished had reached alarming levels. For example, the majority of Egyptians relied solely on Islamic charities to make ends meet and access essential social services.[5] This stark contrast in living standards was exacerbated by the privatization, deregulation and globalization of various which led to unequal distribution of benefits and significant external debt, amounting, in the case of Tunisia, to 48 per cent of annual GDP.[6] Given the sheer number of studies on the adverse effects of neoliberal policies introduced during the 1990s and 2000s in Arab economies and the socio-economic plight of the people, the Uprisings should not have surprised anyone.[7]

When asked about the outlook for Arab Uprising countries in 2011, the French scholar Bertrand Badie suggested that it would be delusional to anticipate swift democratization, since the former autocracies had eviscerated the social strata rendering them incapable of instigating the necessary processes for democracy and modernization.

According to Badie the only path to optimism lay in emulating the successes of emerging powers like Turkey, Brazil and India, which gradually established democracies by leveraging their economic performance and fostering a genuine middle class that embraced the principles of democratic governance.[8] Olivier Roy echoed these sentiments emphasizing the need for Egypt and Tunisia to navigate the challenges of austerity by seeking a 'historic compromise' with the liberals: 'A coalition that is conservative in politics and morals but neoliberal in economics, and thus open to the West. In this respect, the model is the AKP in Turkey.'[9]

The common – and Western – assumption was that the policies of the Washington Consensus had been poorly implemented in the economic systems of Egypt and Tunisia, resulting in societal grievances that led to the overthrow of the existing regimes.

This is, as Armbrust contends, interpreting the anger on the streets of Egypt and Tunisia in 2011 as purely directed at the corrupted state elites – *haramiyya* (thieves) – which is akin to pointing at a tree but missing the forest.[10] Egypt and Tunisia had already experienced three decades of neoliberal transformation and the regimes of Mubarak and Ben Ali 'were considered to be at the forefront of instituting neoliberal policies in the Middle East'.[11]

It is fair to claim that the cause of the Arab Uprisings was not that the countries in question had applied neoliberal policies less effectively than the Western economies but that neoliberal policies were so well applied that they created uneven development, social and economic disparities and cronyism.[12]

The international financial institutions, for their part, assumed the grievances of the Egyptians and Tunisians as a 'response to the absence of capitalism'.[13] The words of the then president of the World Bank, Robert Zoellick, reveal the simulated economic paradigm pushed at Egypt and Tunisia:

> The key point I emphasized in this speech is that it is not just a question of money. It is a question of policy. [. . .] Keep in mind [that], the late Mr Bouazizi was basically driven to burn himself alive because he was harassed with red tape [for] locating a poor fruit vendor stand. Quit harassing those people and let them have a chance to start their small businesses.[14]

This was exactly the approach that the AKP would, step by step, teach Ennahda and the MB to foster.

6.1 Road to neoliberalism

This research is neither about globalization nor the trajectories of capitalism or original moorings of neoliberalism. However, it is impossible to escape these socio-economic systems if we are to conceptualize success and discuss the Islamists' economic vision. This section will, therefore, first explain the Islamists' relationship with capitalism and neoliberalism and then juxtapose these accounts with the diffusion process.

The West has usually defined Muslim-majority countries in terms of what they are not, as it did with post-communist societies: 'They are not proper capitalist societies because they do not have a recognizable capitalist class, [their] institutions cannot work, or they have the wrong characterizations.'[15] However, as historian Maxime Rodinson asserted in 1974, 'The alleged fundamental opposition of Islam to capitalism is a myth, whether this view is put forward with good intentions or bad'.[16] Many Islamists indeed started their careers in the 1970s and early 1980s as socialists with Marxist tendencies. While Mustafa

Al-Siba'i, the author of *Socialism of Islam*,[17] argued in 1960 that socialism would be an appropriate remedy for the economic, social and political ailments of Muslim countries,[18] other prominent Islamic thinkers, such as 'Sayyed Abol-Ala Maududi, Sayyid Qutb and Mohammad Baqir Al-Sadr, tried to present an Islamic alternative to capitalism and communism based on the moral teachings of Islam'.[19]

During the 1970s and 1980s, Islamist thinkers envisioned an economic system based on the Islamic values of equal prosperity, protection of property rights and social justice – a system 'situated between the two major economic systems of the time, capitalism and communism'.[20] Qutb had contended that an economic system developed around Islam's values would serve social justice which, in his thinking, was inconceivable in either capitalism or communism. The teachings of Iranian thinker Ali Shariati, who argued against the Western capitalist system because of its materialistic treatment of society, also had significant influence. In these writings, the authors all endeavoured to propose a forum in which Islamic moral considerations could coexist with threads of both capitalism and socialism.[21]

Qutb's *The Battle between Islam and Capitalism* was written in a historical context in which authoritarian nationalism emerged, modelled on European fascist movements. Communism was propagated, at the time, by 'intellectuals of European descent and/or Western-educated Egyptians, [and] turned into a real mass movement during World War II'.[22] These ideologies rivalled for domination. Qutb, as the main proponent of the idea that Islam, as a complete system, provides the best economic and ideological framework, 'not only guaranteeing the salvation of the individual soul but the realisation of social justice on earth for the whole of humanity',[23] proposed that Islam's taxation solutions – *zakat* and limits on excessive wealth accumulation – were the solution to unequal wealth distribution.[24] However, intellectual and practical attempts to Islamize economies failed in Iran, Pakistan and Sudan; thus, 'the ideals of an Islamic economy fell short of the economic and political realities on the ground'.[25]

The penetration of neoliberal policies in the Middle East dates to the early 1970s following the 1967 Arab defeat and the 1973 oil crisis, 'through the aid conditionality or debt-relief programmes of the IMF and the World Bank' primarily instigated by the United States and the United Kingdom.[26] In the late 1970s, the Open Door (*Infitah*) policy of Egypt's then president Anwar Sadat (1970–81) promoted foreign investment and a market-oriented economy, signalling a break with the USSR. Coupled with the oil boom of the Gulf countries, to which many workers flocked and from which they sent remittances home, and the emergence of the Islamic Republic in Iran, the Islamists in Egypt found themselves in a burgeoning environment for business.

During this period, the Islamist intelligentsia moved away from socialism, claiming that it was essentially opposed to Islamist principles such as trust in the market rather than the state and the importance of private property. The global discrediting of the Left and the demise of the Soviet Union were additional factors driving this shift. It was not difficult for Islamists to accept capitalism and its mode of production in the end, because Islamism has always emphasized the centrality of private property.[27] The implementation of economic reforms prescribed by the World Bank and the IMF resulted in the prosperity of Islamist enterprises, leading to the emergence of a distinct Islamist elite who 'invested heavily in the banking and financial sectors'.[28]

Amir argues that Islamism aligns itself with capitalism and is in the service of imperialism, despite its claims to the contrary. According to Amin the MB, for example, had supported the passing of the laws in parliament that would reinforce private property to the detriment of tenant farmers' rights. He contends that Islamism is reactionary and contrary to the rights of women and anti-Muslims, but its base – 'the nouveaux riches, the comprador bourgeoisie' – support and benefit from 'current imperialist globalization' while the agenda of the elite Islamists is 'lined up behind the dominant powers in the world scale'.[29]

Neoliberalism, a combination of *globalization* and *financialization*

> generates the fact that *no place*, or almost no place in the world [where] human activities, production forces, relations of distribution of material and cultural goods among the classes, relations of power, alliances or antagonisms among nations and peoples, everyday habits and modes of life, travel, and settlement [are defined], remains 'outside' the global constraints or is immune to the effects of financialization.[30]

In the context of global neoliberal convergence, 'the requirements of globalization leave very little room for manoeuvre for national policymakers to try out alternative economic policies to deal with the increased vulnerability of citizens exposed to the full force of globalization'.[31] It seems that the Islamists who were inclined towards a neoliberal vision since the late 1980s 'have [too] arrived at common technical solutions, based on a common set of problems'.[32] The implicit narrative of progress and success encoded in neoliberalism is impervious to counter-evidence. It is true that neoliberalism as a coherent theory has been hammered by a storm of criticism, but the process of policy implementation has been a success from Latin America to Central and Eastern Europe.[33]

Mona Atia calls the convergence of Islamism and neoliberalism 'pious neoliberalism' but also contends that 'the patterns and processes involved in Islamic neoliberalism are not unique to Islam but are indicative of a particular combination of religion and economic rationality [. . .] in the contemporary moment'.[34] By process and patterns, Atia refers to the neoliberal economic reforms in Egypt during the 1990s, such as the privatization of state industries, retreat of the welfare state, currency devaluation and subsidy elimination, all of which led to the creation of a 'pro-business, consumption-driven economy focused on drawing in international investment, promoting unregulated markets and unfettered competition, and extending market logic into all components of social life'.[35] Collectively, these initiatives fostered the establishment of a pro-business, consumption-driven economy and led to the emergence of a new, 'more virtuous economic actor dubbed *homo Islamicus*, who will be disciplined enough to refrain from corrupt practices and who will inspire workers to greater productivity by engaging them in culturally appropriate ways'.[36] Unlike the ideal Muslim in the minds of Qutb and Maududi, *homo Islamicus* strives for material success and individual excellence;[37] he is a translation and operationalization of 'the Hayekian prescription of free political order'[38] into contemporary Islamist politics.

Homo Islamicus, a close cousin of *homo economicus*, 'may well represent the contemporary equivalent in the Muslim world of the Protestant Reformation', claims Beinin. '*Homo Islamicus* is [. . .] an entrepreneur who works hard for material gain and his spiritual purity will be rewarded here on earth in the form of shared profits and social recognition.'[39]

The Protestant work ethic of the Enlightenment era, which 'emphasizes economic freedom to acquire private property, to exchange goods and services, and to succeed or fail according to a person's merits'[40] is, in the twentieth century, an extension of prosperity theology. This cannot be seen as a fringe movement, as it is preached today by Pentecostalists and three of the four largest US churches.[41] The Protestant ethic is also redefined by the Universal Church 'with enterprise and urbanity, fulsomely embracing the material world where we see here Pentecostalism meets neoliberal enterprise'.[42] Prosperity theology, while making the crass capitalistic pursuit of wealth palatable to the conscience of the religious, 'reinforces the Calvinist tenet of individual responsibility for material success, and its darker corollary, individual responsibility for one's failures – a key justification for dissolving the welfare state'.[43]

Tayyip Erdoğan is a great practitioner of the neoliberal mindset: for example, in his thinking, 'if the conditions of the lower classes deteriorated, this was because they failed in their quest for good education, submission to work or the acquisition of a Protestant work ethic, discipline and flexibility, [they are not fit enough to survive] in a Darwinian new liberal world'.[44] Erdoğan is known to berate citizens who complain about their economic hardships, telling 'the poor to pull themselves together and do something for themselves, instead of expecting the government to do it for them'.[45] 'Rise and start doing business' would be his slogan.

6.2 The economic vision of Ennahda and the MB

Thematically, the economic pledges of Ennahda and the MB had sounded similar for the two decades preceding the Uprisings: to wipe out corruption, end cronyism, create more jobs for young people and end poverty via 'market-driven growth coupled with protections for the poor and social justice for all'.[46] Nevertheless, neither organization had devised a practical, policy-driven economic programme until the elections of 2011, as they had been forced to linger in opposition with no prospect of gaining power. Neither Ennahda nor the MB had opposed the respective *ancien régime* neoliberal policies in their country; instead, both saw corruption as the biggest problem. Moreover, the MB, comprising a considerable number of small to medium-sized businesses, had benefited both from President Sadat's Infitah (Open Door) policies in the mid-1970s and Mubarak's neoliberal reforms in the 1990s. Such benefits were denied to Ennahda, as many of its members were forced to live outside Tunisia. It is important to note that, compared to the privileges enjoyed in Egypt by crony allies of Mubarak and his son Gamal,[47] the gains of businessmen affiliated with the MB were small, since they were always seen as part of the opposition rather than the ruling coalition whose needs were met by generating rents.[48]

With the 2011 Uprisings and the fall of the dictators, the economic complexities of Tunisia and Egypt became more pressing than ever for the MB and Ennahda, as the elections approached, and they were ill-prepared to address the issues. A top Egyptian banker in Islamic finance who had 'dealt frequently with Brothers after they came to power' claimed that the MB had a very poor grasp of Islamic finance and sought advice from Islamist bankers abroad, who were also 'market-oriented technicians, with limited economic imagination'.[49]

In a 2004 document entitled 'The Muslim Brotherhood's Initiative on the Principles of Reform in Egypt (*mubadarat al-ikhwan al-muslimin hawl mabadi' al-islah fi misr*),[50] the MB offered several economic prescriptions based on ideas derived from Banna's 'Economic Order (*al-nizam al-iktisadi*)'. This was no comprehensive economic vision but it did include the 'prohibition of usury and gambling, which are considered as sinful, promoting social solidarity to reduce income gaps, restricting luxuries and upholding the right to private property as long as it does not harm the public interest'.[51] A year later, in 2005, the MB published another document called 'The Muslim Brotherhood's Initiative for Domestic Reforms in Egypt (*mubadara jamaa'a al-ikhwan al-muslimin lil-islaah al-dahili fi misr*)' on what it believed to be the reforms necessary. This included the MB's observations and suggestions in thirteen areas: political reform, social reform, economic reform, electoral reform, judicial reform, Al-Azhar reform, the cultural field, women, Coptic brothers and sisters, education, scientific research, fighting poverty and foreign policy. The section on the economy, after reiterating opposition to usury and extravagant expenditure, especially at the state level, and vowing to increase punishments for fraud and corruption, emphasized the freedom of economic activity and the right to ownership, as Islam dictates. The part that closely resembled the AKP's economic strategy concerned privatization: 'We are working to encourage the private sector to participate in major public projects that are subject to privatization.'[52] Needless to say, the MB's vision did not propose an economic plan that was structurally different from the Mubarak era neoliberal policies. Furthermore, while in parliament, MPs close to the MB argued for higher wages and supported strikes against further privatization initiatives, the leadership offered no anti-market rhetoric;[53] on the contrary, pro-business approaches were lauded.

Similarly, Ennahda lacked a comprehensive understanding of the global and Tunisian economies and required advice on technical policy.[54] Its economic programme was prepared hastily for the election by inexperienced activists and adopted the Keynesian model in which the private sector plays a more significant role.[55] Similar to the policies of the MB and Mubarak era, Ennahda's proposals differed little from Ben Ali's neoliberal programme. The key divergence may be that Ennahda's programme claimed to 'emulate Turkey in its attempt to re-moralize the economy by promoting individual virtue'.[56] How, though, did the AKP promote individual virtue, and how would that 're-moralize' the economy? An examination of Ennahda's programme does not supply satisfactory answers, but we know that the AKP promoted a Protestant version of the individual work ethic with the dictum 'service to people is a prayer to God', and this dictum together with 'an unambiguous embrace of the market'[57] seemed to be adopted by Ennahda to construct its model of '*homo Islamicus*'.

A document written by Ennahda's president, Rachid Ghannouchi, was published in April 2011 under the title 'On the Problematique of the Islamists' Economic Programme (*huwl ishkaliya al-barnamaj al-iqtisadi lida al-islamiyyin*)'. The document had seven parts – representing seven observations – on how Ennahda saw problems in and solutions to the economy. It argued that the Islamic economy integrates the political, social and cultural spheres and brings its leaders closer to their citizens. While claiming that both capitalism and socialism had failed, it argued that a 'Third Way' – an Islamic developmental path – would be successful in Tunisia.[58] The AKP, when it first assumed power, also 'reframed an Islamic moral stance to fit a Third Way party image that partly emulate[d] the former political approaches of Tony Blair, Bill Clinton, and Gerhard Schröder, which were crucial for the neoliberal restructuring of the economy and transformation of the state along liberal–democratic lines'.[59] The Third Way was not the only reference to embracing an AKP approach: the fifth section of Ennahda's document was devoted to praising Turkey's economy and its efficient services, especially in the municipality of Istanbul.

'They [the AKP] reduced Turkey's debts by a third within three years, brought inflation and unemployment down to the rates of developed countries, and their economy escaped the 2008 crisis that hit the capitalist economies', asserted Ghannouchi. 'There is no apparent reason for these successes other than Islam, as the Islamists, like their secular colleagues, have studied at the same universities, mastering the same sciences, technologies, and modern knowledge. However, they are superior to them because they are also competent in [the tenets of] Islam.'[60] Ghannouchi fails to explain how Islam protected the Turkish economy from the 2008 crisis; his allusion to the Turkish example can be seen as simply an attempt to bolster the idea that Islamists can govern successfully. Conspicuous throughout the document is the reduction of Islamism to a moral identity that helps only if its actors are trained in the same way as their secular counterparts. In general, Ghannouchi's article and 'Ennahda Movement Programme for Freedom, Justice and Development in Tunisia',[61] a document published in October 2011, display a dedication to 'free enterprise capitalism, emphasizing the role of small and medium-sized enterprises.'[62] This commitment aligns with the AKP's economic vision from very early on. Ennahda's economic vision, which became evident after 2011, was not influenced by Islamist thinkers but rather encompassed a liberal ethos and neo-managerial logic stressing the responsibility and autonomy of its members.[63]

Similar to Ghannouchi's argument earlier, the MB contended that 'if honest and competent people are put in high state positions, Egypt can harness its people's talents, and pockets of wealth, which would allow for healthy economic development'.[64] Therefore, like Ennahda, the MB offers virtuousness as an economic policy. Inside this virtuous outer wrapping – of pledges to promote social justice and end corruption – would be found 'all sorts of pro-market reforms and structural adjustment programmes with the (secular) blessing of foreign investors and international organizations such as the IMF and the World Bank'.[65] For the MB, Ennahda and the AKP limiting the state's role and establishing good governance were good enough precepts for moralizing the economy.[66]

According to former FJP minister Amr Darrag, the MB team was looking for answers to this question: 'How did Turkey raise its GDP from 2,500 dollars to 10,000 dollars during the AKP's time in power? This was the important thing to us. We were not going to learn Islamic ideology from Turkey! They [the AKP team] were not interested in learning anything about Islam from us either.'[67] Ennahda was on the same page as the MB in this regard. 'How Turkey managed to attract international and domestic investments was a good model for us. We thought that the Turkish export policy was one of the best policies', says Ridha Driss, executive member of Ennahda. 'The AKP succeeded in promoting Turkish products worldwide. In Tunisia, we are also focusing on what we call the export of added value. We want to export services and technology.'[68] Both Ennahda and the MB, therefore, sought actionable and specific economic tactics.

Therefore, the most important topic in the dialogue between the MB and the AKP – and between the AKP and Ennahda – was improving the economy. However, the methods of accomplishing that goal have become a point of contention within the MB's old guard. For example, according to Darrag, the MB believed that 'whenever it is possible, institutions should be built in compatibility with Islamic principles. For us, for example, loans and interest are not advisable. We do not want to lower inflation or raise interest rates for the sake of a healthy economy'.[69] The literature on the MB's economic stance demonstrates that Darrag's words do not represent general attitudes within the movement but perhaps resonate with the rhetoric of the old guard.

The dialogue between the MB's eighth and last Supreme Guide, Mohammad Badie, and the then-Turkish ambassador to Egypt shows another example of this rhetoric. Although, as explained in Chapter 4, the Turkish Embassy was not involved in the dialogue, the then-Turkish ambassador, at the Turkish Foreign Ministry's request, visited Badie at the MB's headquarters in Cairo's Al-Moqattam suburb on one occasion in 2011. A senior bureaucrat revealed that the Turkish ambassador advised Badie on key factors for maintaining a stable country. The ambassador suggested that Egypt should consider engaging in IMF negotiations, citing Turkey's positive experience with this approach since 2000. It was emphasized that Egypt's cooperation with the international economic system would lead to greater benefits.[70] Badie listened to the Turkish ambassador without interrupting, then turned to his aide, who was taking notes and asked him not to record what he was about to say. 'I understand very well, but not everyone in our movement does', Badie told the Turkish ambassador. He continued half-jokingly, 'It would be nice of you to drop in on my predecessor, whose office is downstairs, and tell him what you just told me. See if you can convince him.'[71]

Was Badie's playful remark an indication of a rift within the *shura* regarding how to approach the economy? Hardly. Even if a consensus had been lacking in the *shura*, it did not affect the MB's path, which was pro-foreign investment and well-disposed to the IMF. In fact, it was not the MB but the Salafists within the parliament calling themselves the Al Nour Party – which was later shut down – who had protested against an IMF loan while the Morsi government was in negotiations. The Salafists claimed that foreign loans amounted to usury, which is against Islamic law. The MB, for its part, was seeking ways to present the IMF loan as a palatable option for the Islamist electorate. When the meetings between the Morsi government and the IMF regarding a $4.8 billion loan were terminated, Abdel Khaleq al-Sherif, head of the Muslim Brotherhood's advocacy and guidance department, asked Al-Azhar to issue a collective fatwa on the permissibility of accepting the IMF loan to aid President Morsi.[72]

As President Morsi took his place in the front seat, the MB *shura* tried to preserve its hegemony over the movement and the newly founded FJP. The FJP's leadership cadres, however, were filled with young, Western-educated, ambitious technocrats who would soon recognize their limited room for manoeuvre. This constraint was exemplified by a prominent MB strategist, Khairat Al-Shater, mentioned in Chapter 4. 'Before doing anything, especially involving economic steps, Morsi used to consult Shater. Shater decided everything, from the gas pipeline that would pass through Israel to the distribution of billboards on Cairo streets,'[73] claims a former AKP MP. Former Brother and presidential nominee Aboul Foutuh corroborated this information in an interview with Alison Pargeter. According to Foutuh, Shater was 'running everything like a puppet show from behind ... Egypt had two presidents, a real one, Shater, and an official one, Morsi.'[74] Following his release from prison in 2011, Shater emerged as a key figure in shaping a new Egypt, engaging in meetings with foreign ambassadors, executives from multinational corporations and Wall Street firms, as well as various United States senators and officials,[75] namely pro-democracy, pro-free market and tolerant of other religions. It was an ironic image, since Shater had led the conservative wing of the MB, strengthening his influence by placing allies in critical positions in the movement since the beginning of the 2000s. Moreover, he marginalized reformist figures such as Abdel Moneim Aboul Foutuh while maintaining the MB's connections with Salafi movements.[76]

Inspired by Qutb's 'emphasis on a strong organization', Shater developed 'his managerial mind' and 'developed training and research manuals for private sector clients, [and] lectured aspiring management consultants on doing business'[77] from the mid-1980s. With this mindset, he tried to shape the FJP's economic policies along with – or sometimes against – a small clique of young technocrats. As Roy put it, 'Morsi's economic model was neoliberal: he is surrounded by "Chicago Boys", who swear by the free market. He is in favour of deregulation, the end of subsidies and an opening to the global market.'[78] By 'Chicago Boys', Roy alluded to the young cadres of the FJP who had been educated in the West and returned to Egypt after the Uprisings, rather like the Chilean or Mexican students who studied economics in the United States – especially at Harvard, Yale, MIT and the University of Chicago[79] – and promoted anti-socialist and neoliberal policies when they returned to their countries in the 1980s. As an engineer, businessman and Deputy General of the MB (2011–13), Al-Shater had business relations with Turkey, predating the 2011 revolution. In 2003, he and his business partner, Hassan Malek, also an MB member, opened two branches of a Turkish furniture superstore, İstikbal, in Cairo.[80] In 2005, Malek and Shater brought the Turkish menswear brand Sarar to City Stars mall in Cairo. Turkey's trade attaché and leading businesspeople attended the opening.[81] Malek and Shater had spent four years in prison together on charges of illegally funding the MB and were released in 2011 when the Mubarak regime fell.

Malek and Shater amassed their wealth during the Mubarak era, benefiting from its free-market policies. The FJP government, therefore, aimed to preserve the system as it was, and even continued to follow policies initiated by SCAF 'such as anti-labour legislation to discourage strike action by workers and plans to cut subsidies'.[82] The issue partly arose from the MB's perspective on the Egyptian economy and the underlying causes of the Arab Uprisings. The MB interpreted the revolution as a response to corruption and political monopolization by Mubarak and his associates, rather than a rejection of neoliberalism. However, this interpretation only captured one aspect of the multifaceted and intricate narrative.[83]

In response to expectations from its base, the MB reintroduced its Nahda Project, conceived by Shater fifteen years earlier, in the aftermath of the revolution. The project was the blueprint for aspiring 'Islamist technocrats [... with] impressive ideas on institutional reform, economic development, and urban renewal'.[84]

During an April 2011 lecture titled 'Features of Nahda: Gains of the Revolution and the Horizons for Development', Shater sought to clarify the essence of the Nahda Project and unveil his world view. He emphasized the profound significance of the Islamic reference, highlighting that it goes beyond a mere emotional or superficial term. Shater expressed that Islamism profoundly impacts all aspects of life and should be thoroughly understood as a substantial and fundamental matter, rather than a mere slogan. While indicating that the MB had not entirely abandoned Islamism and would not fully adopt a Turkish model, Shater provided a vague description of how to implement the Nahda Project. He acknowledged the lack of experience among the general public and stressed the need to educate people on various paths for social, economic, health, education and moral development.[85]

6.3 Cultivating an Islamic bourgeoisie

The establishment of two business associations, namely Namaa in Tunis and the Egyptian Business Development Association (EBDA) in Cairo, serves as a tangible outcome and verifiable impact resulting from the diffusion of ideas and collaboration between the AKP-Ennahda and AKP-MB. *Namaa*, meaning 'growth or development' in Arabic, was formed on 15 March 2011, just two weeks after Ennahda was legalized, as a non-profit association with the objective of facilitating connections and providing guidance to small- and medium-sized businesses, as well as attracting both domestic and foreign investors.[86]

In Cairo, three months prior to President Morsi assuming office in March 2012, Hassan Malek, who is Shater's business partner, established the EBDA (start' in Arabic). Both *Namaa* and EBDA had significant involvement from Turkey's MÜSİAD (Müslüman İşadamları Derneği), an organization founded as an alternative to Turkey's prominent secular business association, TÜSİAD (*Türkiye Sanayicileri ve İş İnsanları Derneği*).

Malek claimed publicly that he modelled EBDA on MÜSİAD.[87] In Turkey, while TÜSİAD was close to the established state elites and committed to preserving secular principles, MÜSİAD represented the Anatolian small- to medium-sized enterprises and had a close affinity with Islamist movements, especially the AKP's mother movement, *Milli Görüş*.[88] The role of MÜSİAD in the AKP's development should be clarified in order to appreciate the significance of the founding of EBDA in Egypt and *Namaa* in Tunisia. Following the postmodern coup of 28 February 1997, which toppled Erbakan's government and his *Refah Partisi*, the military attempted to limit Islamist business activities and their influence on the economy. While MÜSİAD was threatened with closure, its then chairman, Erol Yarar (1990–9) was tried in semi-military courts for inciting hatred.[89] At that time, therefore, 'the Islamic business elite found themselves at a crossroads: they could choose to support either closed-minded [conservative] Islamist political movements or open-minded modernist groups. Most chose the second option, providing financial and human resources for the establishment of the AKP',[90] which conveniently did not identify itself as an Islamist party but rather as a 'conservative democratic' one. The preference and support of 'Islamist capital' for the AKP over '*Milli Görüş*'s newly founded party *Saadet Partisi* (Felicity Party) was the most important component in the AKP's birth'.[91] The advent of the AKP witnessed the establishment of an ideological congruity between the conservative bourgeoisie and the emerging political entity, culminating in a novel alliance characterized by reciprocal reinforcement and advantageous collaboration.[92] This kind of symbiosis is not unique to Turkish Islamism. The business faction within Islamist movements, often led by small and medium-sized business owners, advocates for the elimination of anticompetitive practices, such as government-backed monopolies that prevailed in the economies of Tunisia and Egypt during the regimes of Ben Ali and Mubarak. Particularly in Egypt, religious entrepreneurs have exerted substantial influence within the Muslim Brotherhood.[93]

The common quest of MÜSİAD and the AKP required a gradual but crucial process: the reorganization of Turkey's political power structure. For this daunting task, the AKP relied on the social class that MÜSİAD represented, along with other tactics mentioned in Chapter 5. It is revealing how Ajami contextualized Turkey's 'neo-Islamic bourgeoisie' when unpacking the challenges faced by the Egyptian economy:

> The plain truth of it is that Egypt lacks the economic wherewithal to build a successful modern Islamic order, whatever that might mean. The Islamic Republic of Iran rests on oil, and even the moderate ascendancy of the AKP in Turkey is secured by prosperity stemming from the 'devout bourgeoisie' in the Anatolian hill towns. Egypt lies at the crossroads of the world, living off tourism, the Suez Canal, infusions of foreign aid, and remittances from Egyptians abroad.[94]

In this formulation, for the AKP, the Islamic bourgeoisie and its associations are as vital as oil is to the maintenance of Iran's regime. As a result, the main strategy that spread from the AKP to the MB and Ennahda was that of bringing together a loyal business class neglected by previous regimes.

Although MÜSİAD was established thanks to the neoliberal policies of the 1980s, its members had always claimed that wealth was distributed according to closeness to the secular state rather than the potential or quality of the business. As a result of globalization and Prime Minister Turgut Özal's liberalization policies, MÜSİAD companies were able to operate outside the government's reach. With the emergence of the AKP, the aspiration of the blending 'of Islam, capitalism, and democracy [. . .] reached its logical conclusion [and gave birth to] a new neo-Islamic bourgeoisie in Turkey'.[95] According to Cristofis, the transformation can be described as a 'bourgeois revolution', involving a profound reconfiguration of political power, economic capital and symbolic assets through democratic means. During this process, the bourgeoisie engaged in a struggle against the existing regime, receiving political backing from the marginalized classes in Anatolia and the inhabitants of economically disadvantaged regions on the peripheries of major urban centres.[96]

Tuğal, however, argues that the AKP's relationship with MÜSİAD in fact 'reinforced business–state interdependence, financialization, and speculative growth',[97] contrary to MÜSİAD's goals. What we see in this space is a common neoliberal agenda, not specific to Turkish polity, but applicable anywhere. Congruous with Foucault's governmentality framework, the state is not in retreat, but the government is expanded in such a way that it is restructured 'with techniques, shifting the regulatory competence of the state to "responsible" and "rational" individuals'.[98] In our case, these responsible and rational individuals are devout businessmen closely affiliated with the ruling elite, that is, the AKP.

Ayşe Buğra claims, in a similar vein, that a new conservative class has emerged thanks to significant capital accumulation. However, Buğra contends that this class's potential was not unleashed by the market-friendly policies of the AKP but, rather, 'with the help of a regulatory framework that has been continuously modified [by the AKP] to open more spaces for arbitrary government intervention in support of politically privileged entrepreneurs'.[99] There is indeed ample evidence that the AKP had channelled more resources into small- and medium-sized businesses through state banks to correct the imbalance that it saw between small MÜSİAD enterprises and large TÜSİAD companies.[100] Side by side with this strategy went increasing numbers of Muslim businessmen and the growth of the AKP's support base. Furthermore, the AKP's strategy of cultivating an Islamic bourgeoisie generated a climate in Turkey in which religious rituals such as praying five times a day and veiling became more relaxed and less puritan and were replaced by a 'business-oriented spirituality'.[101] In this climate, Islamist elites, groups and parties adjusted their goals and aspirations, adopting what Bayat refers to as post-Islamist tendencies such as dropping their 'comprehensive vision of Islam (including the goal of an Islamic state)'.[102]

When examining MÜSİAD's involvement in post-Uprising Tunisia and Egypt, Vannetzel and Yankaya employ the term 'intervene' rather than 'help', highlighting how MÜSİAD actively seized favourable opportunities to engage in the restructuring of business communities in both countries as part of its transnational community-building agenda.[103] The establishment of EBDA in Egypt and Namaa in Tunisia, introducing a novel business model,[104] was not an autonomous act or decision on the part of MÜSİAD but an element of the diffusion from the AKP to the MB and Ennahda. According to a senior Turkish diplomat who was present in Cairo at the time, the collaboration agreement with MÜSİAD was signed with Morsi in attendance, as EBDA was intended to serve as 'the smiling face of the Ikhwan, assuring the international system of their commitment to a liberal economy. Members of the Ikhwan who had established businesses in the Western countries were encouraged to join EBDA, and they responded accordingly.[105]

The composition of EBDA and the meetings of Malek and Shater with economic entities indicated a Machiavellian approach and an unwillingness to cut ties with the former regime. Before EBDA's foundation, Shater had liaised with fourteen investment managers from Europe, the United States and Africa in meetings arranged by 'the Egyptian bank EFG-Hermes, in which Mubarak's son Gamal had been a partner'.[106] Furthermore, EBDA organized 'reconciliation negotiations' with businessmen who had fled the country after facing corruption charges. These included Rachid Mohammed Rachid, former trade and industry minister under Nazif (2004–11), and Hussein Salem, Mubarak's friend, and a major player in a natural gas export deal with Israel.[107]

The foundation of the Tunisian Namaa was announced during a gathering of more than 500 Turkish, Tunisian and Libyan businessmen. Namaa, after signing an agreement with MÜSİAD, became its regional partner and assumed a position on the board of directors of the International Business Forum (IBF). In this role, Namaa was entrusted with organizing regional meetings in the Maghreb region.[108] According to Yankaya, the founding of Namaa represented the realization of the illusory Turkish model, whereby the principles of business action and social capital were diffused from the AKP to Tunisian business.[109]

The Namaa members also acknowledged their role in redefining Ennahda's economic approach, claiming that 'Tunisia can only follow a market economy path, not a socialist path. We want to apply the model of the Prophet Muhammad when he settled in Madinah. There were Jews and Christians. We want a free market without corruption. This is Islam'.[110] Interestingly, the Market of Madinah is an example frequently used by MÜSİAD as a symbol that purportedly sheds light on the economic vision of the Prophet Mohammad.

The Prophet is said to have established a marketplace in Bakh Zubair, a town in Madinah, where tradesmen were exempt from taxes and had no fixed stalls. Instead, they would set up their stalls on a first-come-first-served basis each morning.[111] Moreover, traders from all tribes were allowed to conduct business without discrimination. The Market of Madinah symbolizes a space where market rules operate freely.[112] It has been regarded as a utopian reference for Muslim entrepreneurs, characterized by communal solidarity, mutual compassion, tolerance and the protection of diversity.[113] Erol Yarar, the founding president of MÜSİAD stated in 2019 that the organization was established three decades ago with the aim of transforming the system. He emphasized the importance of recapturing the spirit of the Market of Madinah.[114]

In Ben Ali's Tunisia, the government used arbitrary rules to keep businesses from becoming involved in social or political movements. This was especially true for businesses outside the regime's clientelist network, such as those that did not join the UTICA (Union Tunisienne de l'Industrie, du Commerce et de l'Artisanat).[115] In this context, it is not surprising that businesspeople with ties to Ennahda had a weak presence in the private sector, while those with ties to the MB were able to keep their footing.[116] In June 2012, a MÜSİAD team went to Tunis and organized several meetings for *Namaa*. They introduced Namaa to the commerce section of the Turkish Embassy, and a dinner was organized, at which Ennahda leader Rachid Ghannouchi, the head of Namaa Mohammed Kochlaf, and the former deputy president of MÜSİAD discussed ways to strengthen collaboration between the two bodies.[117] Interestingly, on the same trip, MÜSİAD paid a visit to UTICA, where – according to the MÜSİAD report – Ali Nakai (UTICA's director of foreign relations 2011–18) asserted that UTICA was the most established and oldest business association and that it had been collaborating with Turkey's Union and Chambers of Commodity – TOBB (*Türkiye Odalar ve Borsacılar Derneği*).[118] TOBB may not be considered an autonomous organization and has been known to have ties to government.

However, it cannot be seen as organically linked to the AKP, as MÜSİAD is. TOBB is more centrist–right than Islamic. Therefore, it was important for UTICA, as the most prominent business association, to underline its existing collaboration with Turkish businesspeople through TOBB rather than MÜSİAD.

The economic network that MÜSİAD, *Namaa* and EBDA sought to construct after 2011 was a crucial part of the diffusion process. Namaa and EBDA – had they thrived like MÜSİAD and cultivated an Islamic bourgeoisie – would have been the cornerstones of the survival of Ennahda and the MB. MÜSİAD not only consolidated the Anatolian entrepreneur vote for the AKP but was instrumental in transferring money and power from the *ancien régime* to the AKP's base. Thus, the crux of the economic tactic was not only to preserve the neoliberal system but to change the actors that would benefit from it: the base of Ennahda and the MB. According to Cammett and Diwan, 'in the 1950s leaders such as Bourguiba and Nasser adopted an Atatürkian model of modernization in which the middle-class played a legitimizing role. Thus, for the Arab autocrats, losing their middle-class anchors was tantamount to becoming naked dictatorships with no operational narrative'.[119] In this sense, the strategy to create a bourgeoisie loyal to and dependent upon these Islamist actors was reverse mimicry of the founders of modern Turkey, Tunisia and Egypt.

The interdependence between the AKP and conservative businesses is undeniable. The AKP 'rapidly became a party of careerists who benefited from the vast selective incentives emanating from the party's control over government and municipalities'.[120] During the AKP era, the number of MÜSİAD branches in Turkey significantly increased, and the AKP progressively gained more votes in twenty-nine cities with a notable presence of MÜSİAD members. In these cities, the AKP received votes that were fifty times greater than its mother movement, *Milli Görüş*, represented by the Felicity Party – *Saadet Partisi*.[121] Its symbiotic partnership with MÜSİAD led the AKP to adopt democratic reforms until 2010, to secure 'their advantageous place in Turkey's changing economic system. As with other late-developing countries, Turkey's Islamic business elite have become contingent democrats to protect their material interests'.[122] Consistent with a post-Islamist framework, 'the AKP has absorbed Islamism into a neoliberal governance and one that is marked by national conservatism, free market globalization, limited pluralism, and the instrumentalization of religion'.[123]

Should MÜSİAD's undertakings in helping to establish *Namaa* in Tunisia and EBDA in Egypt be considered as activism in a bid to build an *ummah*? Vannetzel and Yankaya believe not, as the results in Tunisia and Egypt were divergent and reduced the expectation of a business *ummah*. In other words, even if the AKP and MÜSİAD leaders had intended to build a business *ummah*, this aspiration dissipated once it became evident that such a goal was unattainable. However, the empirical evidence presented in this book unmistakably demonstrates the diffusion of MÜSİAD's model and its role through training workshops for 'the importation process of MÜSİAD'.[124] Therefore, the initiation of *Namaa* and EBDA under MÜSİAD's mentorship can be interpreted as part of 'an economic advocacy network that seeks to densely exchange goods and capital as well as information and services and to bind actors with the sense of sharing common Islamic values. Rather than being part of the dominant "transnational capitalist class", its goal is to establish an alternative one with Islamic references'.[125]

Shortly after its establishment, EBDA witnessed a surge in membership, with numerous small enterprises eagerly joining its ranks. The association swiftly grew to encompass over 400 members, with an additional 1,000 companies eagerly awaiting admission.[126] Taking a cue from Erdogan's approach to organizing overseas visits, Morsi led a delegation of eighty businesspeople from EBDA on a trip to China in August 2012.[127] It is highly likely that, had the Morsi government remained in power for a similar duration as the AKP, a comparable clientelist relationship would have developed between the FJP and EBDA. Despite EBDA's rapid growth as a prominent business community with globally oriented political leaders well-versed in management techniques, it miscalculated the dynamics of the existing political class and the intricacies of party politics.[128] Furthermore, it exhibited a confrontational religious discourse towards any form of protest. As Haenni suggests, in Egypt, governance and pure pragmatism alone were insufficient since the country was not merely an enterprise.[129] Following the 2013 coup, the founders of EBDA, along with numerous members of the Muslim Brotherhood, were imprisoned, leading to the effective shutdown of EBDA.

Namaa, although overshadowed by UTICA, maintained its formal public presence and operated within the existing business structure until 2022. Driss, an executive member of Ennahda, acknowledged that *Namaa* did not achieve the same level of success as MÜSİAD due to UTICA's dominance in the private sector.[130] Nevertheless, *Namaa* made efforts to thrive and actively participated in MÜSİAD's business expos.[131] MÜSİAD continued its collaboration with Namaa and worked towards strengthening its presence in the African economy, up until the time of writing this book in 2022.

According to the French journalist Bonzon, *Namaa*'s underperformance cannot be solely attributed to UTICA's dominance over the private sector.

Bonzon argues that Ennahda's support base is heterogeneous, encompassing workers, the petty bourgeoisie, and students, while the AKP primarily cultivates its support from businessmen in central Anatolia. This distinction in their respective support bases may contribute to differences in the performance and influence of *Namaa* compared to MÜSİAD. 'In other words', says Bonzon, 'for Ennahda, 1 May [International Workers' Day] has a meaning; for the AKP, it does not'.[132] While this may be true, It is evident that the leadership of Ennahda does not adhere to socialist tendencies, as indicated by the response of the first Tunisian president, Moncef Marzouki (2011–13), when questioned by scholar Sami Zemni about the absence of economic reforms between 2011 and 2014. Marzouki attributed the lack of progress in economic reform primarily to Ennahda's resistance. He stated that Ennahda blocked social-democratic reform packages out of the belief that such measures would discourage international financial institutions and investors. Zemni claimed that 'Ennahda was an excellent student of Washington Consensus'.[133] This approach was supported by the United States and the EU, both of which advocated for Tunisia to maintain a high level of openness to global markets. Consequently, Tunisia adopted what was referred to as a '*nisf-nisf*' (half-half) policy, resulting in the absence of a robust economic reform programme.

In summary, there are two primary reasons why neither EBDA nor Namaa achieved the same level of success as MÜSİAD. First, as discussed in Chapters 2 and 3, there were notable divergences in the political structure and evolution of Islamism in Egypt, Tunisia and Turkey. Second, there were differences in the economic transformations that took place in these countries from the 1980s onwards. Turkish neoliberalization, as Tuğal posits, became a dominant ideology through a bottom-up process of Islamization. In contrast, Islamists in Egypt and Tunisia had a top-down relationship with their countries' corporatism and neoliberal opportunities.[134] Madi supports Tuğal's viewpoint, suggesting that capitalism and Islam have mutually transformed and invigorated each other within the Turkish context. Wealthy Turkish Muslims have actively embraced and internalized the surrounding capitalist culture, rather than pursuing an ascetic Weberian lifestyle.[135]

While both the Ben Ali and Mubarak regimes implemented neoliberal policies, there was no period of embourgeoisement among Islamist segments of society in Tunisia or Egypt. However, rather than focusing on the applicability of the AKP's tactics or the specific factors within Tunisia and Egypt's economic and political realms, it is crucial to emphasize the intentions of the political actors in the diffusion process. These intentions included widening their support base through cross-class alliances, making their Islamic base more prosperous and loyal through neoliberal policies, demonstrating allegiance to the free market aligned with the interests of their burgeoning bourgeoisie support,[136] and ultimately striving for success by any means necessary.

7

The new spirit of Islamism

Success rearranges the morphology of an ideology; it yields legitimacy and shapes identity. The pursuit of success alters our broad vision of value, and the illusion that success may be within reach and the myth of self-realization create tensions between our environment and our goals. These are neoliberal ways,[1] seen in the habits and minds of many who are influenced and constrained by the hegemonic practices of governments and transnational markets. Neoliberalism transcends mere economic ideas and functions as an all-encompassing ideology that seeps into the fabric of political and social arrangements.[2] Within the realm of neoliberalism, the retreat of government and the resulting space left to be filled by the market is not the sole consequence. Its most pervasive influence lies in its infiltration and proliferation within the mundane aspects of everyday life. This leads to the emergence of new ways of envisioning and conceptualizing life.[3] How have these new perspectives influenced Muslim and Islamist actors?

7.1 Islamist longing for success

Islamist politicians in positions of power were driven by aspirations for success for several reasons. First, there is a desire among young Muslims to achieve success, and some of these young individuals form the electorate for Islamist political movements. The second reason was elaborated by Foucault in a lecture from the 1980s: 'There will be either success or failure; success or failure, rather than legitimacy or illegitimacy, has now become the criterion of governmental action. So, success replaces legitimacy. [...] Success or failure, then, will replace the division between legitimacy and illegitimacy.'[4] Third, the debate in academia and the media on how Islamism failed contributed to the pursuit of success. Lastly, the discourse surrounding Islamism's perceived failure in academic and media circles has prompted Islamist actors to strive for success in order to counter these criticisms and prove the viability and effectiveness of their ideologies and strategies.

Olivier Roy's 1994 book *The Failure of Political Islam* has led, in the decades since, to a flurry of academic writing and polemic on the future of Islamism. In what he calls the sequel to *The Failure of Political Islam*, *Globalised Islam*, Roy continues his argument that Islamist movements had lost their revolutionary rigour and 'could not provide a blueprint for an Islamic state'.[5] The portrayal of Islamism by media pundits and scholars as 'fluctuating between cycles of success and failure, intertwined with hope and despair',[6] deepened the Islamists' hunger for success. According to Ali Bulaç, one of the prominent Islamist scholars in Turkey, Erbakan saw the aspiration to success as a trap:

> Following his removal from government in 1997, Erbakan delivered a speech to his followers in Bolu, where he expressed concerns about a dangerous concept he referred to as the 'Islamization of success'. According to Erbakan, this notion entailed Islamists attaining positions of power with the support of domestic and international forces. However, if they were to fail, they would face severe consequences and would be effectively excluded from any future power circles. This fear led Erbakan to maintain a cautious distance from the state for a period of time. It was during this period that the founders of the AKP realized that neither Erbakan's nor Al-Banna's perspective would enable them to assume and maintain power successfully.[7]

In hindsight, what Erbakan defined at the end of the 1990s as 'the success trap' finally devoured the MB in power. Bassiouni agrees: 'Having allowed Morsi to win the 2012 presidential election, the SCAF tested the Muslim Brotherhood's skills at the helm of the nation, with the relative certainty that it would be only a matter of time before it would fail to address the needs of the nation and become unpopular.'[8]

In contrast to Erbakan, the AKP's founders saw achieving success as a service to Islamism. Former deputy minister and AKP founder Beşir Atalay explains:

> Few Islamist parties in power have achieved significant success, particularly in terms of providing a strong economic vision. The AKP had become symbolic for the Muslim world, and we aim to spread this notion of success to other Islamist parties that share our tradition. We believe that by doing so, the perception of Islam will improve and prevent disengagement among young people, as seen in Iran. We want the world to recognize and say, 'Look at these Muslims! They have developed a thriving economy, ensured freedom for their people, and embraced

global openness.' However, it is unfortunate that Turkey's recent shift towards authoritarianism raises concerns about the future direction.⁹

In a similar vein, Ahmed Gaaloul, a member of the *shura* of Ennahda, sees the AKP's success as beneficial to all Islamist movements:

> Turkey is more developed and stronger than it was 25 years ago. That is the success story. And it is achieved by people who are inspired by the idea of Islam. This is beneficial to all Islamic-inspired parties and groups. The Turkish model has nothing to do with ideology. As a member of Nahda, I am inspired by Islam, but this inspiration does not guarantee that we will be able to put bread on people's tables. If my inspiration from Islam helps me fight corruption and poverty, then it is good. An Islamic party is successful not because it is an Islamic party but because it provides people with good economic solutions. In this context, Islam can be beneficial as it encompasses the fight against corruption and serving the people, which are integral aspects of worship.¹⁰

The perspectives of Atalay and Gaaloul offer two clues to what success means for Islamists, and especially for the actors involved in the diffusion process. The main task, it seems, is first to prove that the Islamist party in question is a legitimate actor capable of governing and then to assume power. The second task is staying in power. Accomplishing these goals is considered success from the perspective of Islamists. Moreover, success involves rectifying the reputation of Islam(ism). Ajmi Lourimi, a senior member of Ennahda, emphasized that Islamist movements in Sudan or Afghanistan were regarded as failures due to the negative image they portrayed of Islam. Conversely, Turkey's AKP is viewed as a success story because it proved that Islamist movements can exist without instilling fear or posing threats.¹¹

The head of Ennahda's political bureau, Noureddine Arbaoui, claimed, 'People can learn about their religion everywhere, from the internet, even from their phones. They do not need us for that anymore.'¹² This led Ennahda to shift its focus away from *dawa* after 2016, entrusting it to other entities that may lack formal Islamic training. Roy defines this process as 'post-Islamist Islamisation', which has 'nothing to do with the project of reconstructing society [through] state [power] and an all-encompassing Islamic ideology [but consists of] a cluster of individual practices that are used as a means of finding jobs, money, respect and self-esteem – the reference to Islam is everywhere and nowhere'.¹³

For Islamist leaders, success also serves as a means of seeking retribution. They present it as an expression of God's will, but it is also seen as a way to avenge years of repression and humiliation inflicted upon them by the West. In a notable example, President Erdoğan made a speech during his 2017 referendum campaign in Eskisehir, specifically addressing Turkey's immigrant population in Europe. He claimed that Europeans are accepting of Turks as low-skilled workers but resent Turks who own businesses or have successful careers: 'I ask that you send your children to the best schools possible. Drive the best cars. Live in the best houses. Have five children rather than three. This is the best answer to the hostilities you face there [in Europe].'[14]

In November 2021, an AKP MP named Mücahit Birinci faced criticism for wearing a Louis Vuitton scarf, during a period of severe currency devaluation and high inflation in Turkey. The price of the scarf, amounting to 330 GBP, exceeded the monthly minimum wage in the country. Birinci's response to the criticism reflected a sentiment shared among AKP members and potentially their electorate as well. He wrote on Twitter, 'I understand the main issue here! Who are we to wear such scarves ... The devout ... Who are we? Only a small, fanatical minority that once served the hegemonic mindset[15] has the right [to wear fancy clothes]. According to this fanatical minority, we, the pious and religious, are merely the doormen (*kapıcılar* in Turkish) of this country.'[16]

As Zadie Smith puts it, 'the forces of capital are pragmatic: capital does not bother itself with essentialisms. It transforms nobodies into somebodies – and vice versa – depending on where the labor is needed, and the profit can be made.'[17] The desire of Islamists to transform themselves from 'nobodies' to 'somebodies' is evident. This reflects the aspiration of Islamists to attain social and economic status, transcending their previous marginalization and asserting their presence in society.

Another important development is that Islamists – even those who assumed power through elections – witness a decline in their popular support. The academic consensus suggests that popular support for Islamism has reached its peak and is unlikely to increase further, as indicated by opinion surveys conducted primarily in Arab countries, which demonstrate a significant decline in support for religious parties and leaders.[18] Islamists face the challenge of satisfying the ever-changing needs of their base when the legitimizing effect of the Islamist discourse dissipates. The Islamists in question tacitly acknowledged, after decades of trial and error, that the benchmark for success was economic growth and the creation of electorally strong and loyal networks.

7.2 Post-Islamism and managerialism

The end of the Cold War marked the obsolescence of the transactional alliance between Western powers and Islamist movements in the Middle East, which was primarily based on the belief that Islamism would act as a barrier against the spread of communism. This shift was accompanied by an intellectual consensus, famously expressed in Fukuyama's essay 'The End of History' in 1989, that ideological debates had come to an end and that liberal democracy, characterized by a market or capitalist economy and an open competitive system, would prevail.[19] However, this consensus was short-lived as new ideological forces, notably Islamism, emerged soon after Fukuyama's proclamation.[20]

Consequently, the Western perception of the threat shifted from communism to Islamism, reflecting the evolving geopolitical landscape and the rise of Islamist movements as significant players on the global stage.

By the end of the twentieth century, a new order led by American interests emerged that triggered another struggle for all ideological entities, including the Islamists: 'the progress of a sort of rampant "recolonisation" [by] the global superpower'.[21] Undoubtedly, Al-Qaeda's attacks on New York and Washington DC in September 2001 and America's subsequent invasion of Afghanistan and Iraq were critical in how Islamist movements transformed their strategy and discourse over time and space – shifting 'between phases of confrontation and reconciliation and rejection and accommodation'.[22]

It is important to stress that, although the new world order constructed by the United States' soft and hard power in the Middle East informed Islamists' mobilization practices, the shifting phases of confrontation and accommodation were usually shaped by the stance of national governments towards the Islamist movements. Piscatori and Eickelman employ the market metaphor to explain the political praxis of Islamist groups. The price of the survival and authority of Islamist groups had to be negotiated with numerous actors: international actors, the national government, 'external patrons such as Saudi Arabia or Iran, other Islamist groups, and the masses or the target audiences from which they wish[ed] to attract sympathisers [. . .], masses whose religious and political formation they hope[d] to control'.[23] At critical junctures when international interest in and tension towards Islamist movements soared, such as after the attacks of 11 September, 'the artery of international relations hardened and the circle of conflict widened'.[24]

As a result of the changing dynamics in the Western powers' views of Islamists, the latter were obliged to change their strategy, goals and discourse, an imperative that other ideological movements escaped. However, the ideological reformation from the Cold War era to the post-Cold War era is not unique to Islamists.[25] Charles Tripp, in his seminal work on the evolution of the Islamic economy, explains how the changing human transactions around the globe influence Islamic imaginations and thoughts. He suggests that prudence is now measured by the success of individuals and institutions in their relations with the outside world, which, he claims, 'led to critical engagement with forms such as the violent rejectionism of *Al-Jama'at al-Islamiya* in Egypt or the acceptance of the free market and parliamentary republic in Turkey by the AKP'.[26]

To examine this change in strategy and goal, I choose to adopt the framework of post-Islamism. The post-Islamist world view indicates that certain underlying principles of Islamism, such as the establishment of an Islamic state, the negation of Western modernity and liberal institutions and a critical approach towards capitalism were abandoned. However, this does not mean that post-Islamist parties dropped all the values of Islamism; indeed, the AKP, Ennahda and the MB did not. Neither does it signify a historical end to Islamism but 'should be seen as the birth, out of a critical departure from Islamist experience, of a qualitatively different discourse and politics'.[27] Thus, it differs from other 'finalist prophecies', such as Daniel Bell's 'end of ideology'[28] or Fukuyama's 'end of history' theses 'to designate an ideological moment in the Cold War waged against the communist bloc, which in this perspective was the only ideological formation'.[29]

Post-Islamism does not denote the end of a historical or political period; rather, it describes a condition or project that the Islamists devised through trial-and-error processes. Similarly, 'a post-Islamist project is neither anti-Islamic, un-Islamic or secular'.[30]

For the purposes of the present chapter, I wish to underline the main contention of Bayat when referring to the historical significance of a new period in Islamist politics: 'While Islamism had its roots in Cold War politics, post-Islamist politics is shaped by the prevailing idioms of the post-Cold War period – the free market, civil society, non-violence and reform.'[31] The re-emergence of nationalism, combined with populism and the spread of Islamism in the aftermath of the Cold War, proved that ideologies multiply, wander into and interact in the worlds of other ideologies and are persistent. Again, such persistence does not imply that the features of ideologies are fixed; on the contrary, they are 'constantly being rewritten, not just reread, because [their] producers inherit that creative task from generation to generation, even from month to month, as the life span of ideology-formulating groups extends beyond that of their individual members'.[32]

7.2.1 What do Muslim youth want?

By the 1990s, Islamist movements in Egypt, especially the MB, found themselves in a contradictory position. Thanks to Nasser's educational policies, the number of high school and university graduates in Egypt had risen; however, they were jobless. The grievances of this unemployed but educated lumpen intelligentsia[33] were heard and mobilized by moderate Islamists and the MB. According to Wickham, it was self-interest that drew young people to Islamist organizations, which offered them support networks, an avenue for activism and a sense of purpose in life.[34]

Thus, on the one hand, the MB had to appeal to the workers and the lumpen intelligentsia, while also promoting 'the business interests of bankers, financiers, and entrepreneurs closer to the leadership of the Muslim Brothers. Yuppies of the "young generation" – some of them connected to Egypt's new small high-tech and telecommunications sectors – have embraced a new form [of doing politics and mobilization] of Islamism'.[35] During the mid-1990s, Qaradawi's television appearances revealed his recognition of the need to cater to the aspirations of young people and for that purpose 'a spirit shaped by realism should be injected'[36] to the Islamist project. When I met with Ghannouchi in December 2019, he articulated a similar conclusion, saying that 'both Turkish and Tunisian Islamism have begun to seek conciliation with reality rather than aiming to destroy reality [. . .] The reality I am talking about is Western realities'.[37] As seen, Islamists of our age, 'even as they seek to synthesise, adapt to or critique Western liberalism [and its institutions], [. . .] cannot exit its language and categories'.[38] Both Ghannouchi and Qaradawi believed that only by accepting 'the realities' could they give young people 'confidence that they can build a better future'.[39] What, though, are those realities?

In the context of Egypt, the processes of urbanization, Islamization and globalization have led to the fragmentation of the young generation. However, various social spaces such as 'coffee shops, college campuses, shopping malls, concert venues, *mulid* (the celebration of a saint's birth) festivals and street corners provided spaces for social interaction and active and passive networks, which led to the construction of youth identities and turned young people into social agents in both Egypt and Iran during the late 1990s'.[40] According to Olivier Roy, during that period, a new generation of bourgeois Islamists emerged who, owing to the diversification of the religious sphere and shifting geostrategic context, did not automatically locate themselves in the anti-Western camp with their more traditional elders.[41]

While Islam's role is overemphasized in Muslim societies, that of globalization is underestimated. Due to globalization and Westernization, the relationship between the Muslim and Islam has changed and the social authority of religion has faded.[42] In other words, it could be argued that politics has become less dependent on or subordinated to religion, although more empirical research is needed to validate this claim. Suffice it to say that neoliberal rationality views the state as a machine and believes that 'all governing is *for* markets and oriented by market principles'[43] which fundamentally alters values, moral codes and ideological goals.

This is where post-Islamist praxis begins. Mahdawi argues that a new metaphor/discourse/paradigm of post-Islamism has been introduced by ordinary people: 'as the younger generations demonstrated their commitment to a post-Islamist polity, the old guards were often trapped in their exclusivist and patriarchal Islamist discourse'.[44]

Post-Islamism includes 'the pursuit of the Islamic good life [. . . via] finding jobs, money, respect, and self-esteem [. . . which] thrives within the global free markets, consumption, and neoliberal circulation of capital'.[45] In this post-Islamist realm, the state's key position is replaced by 'an individualised piety, sense of private responsibility',[46] and 'the rising influence of conservative business figures' is indisputable, as demonstrated in Chapter 6. In other words, as Roy observes in citing Turkey's MÜSİAD,[47] 'post-Islamism means the privatisation of re-Islamisation, [which includes] the development of religious-minded middle-class entrepreneurs [who are] conservative in faith and beliefs, but modern in terms of business, [. . .] with a Weberian work ethic'.[48]

It is hardly surprising, then, that the advent of a new breed of self-trained Islamic preachers, such as Amr Khaled in Egypt and Abdullah Gymnastiar (Aa Gym) in Indonesia, coincided with the rise of neoliberalism in Muslim-majority countries. The prevalence of Khaled-like preachers over the traditional *ulama* is also part of the post-Islamist trend. While Egypt's orthodox Islamic *ulama* dismissed Khaled as unqualified to speak about Islam and accused him of diluting Islam's principles, he became extremely popular among the young in the 1990s. Khaled studied accounting at Cairo University before beginning to preach in private gatherings, where he gained notoriety. When he appeared on a television show in 2001 on Dream TV, an Egyptian satellite network, his broadcasting career and popularity skyrocketed, and his books, CDs and audio tapes sold in the millions.[49] Similar popular tele-preachers who followed in the footsteps of Amr Khaled are Khaled al-Gendy, Mustafa Hosni and Moez Masoud in Egypt,[50] Arifin Ilham, Jefri al-Bukhari and Yusuf Mansur (as well as Aa Gym) in Indonesia,[51] Cherif Haidara in Mali and the bestselling author of *Don't Be Sad* (*la tahzen*), Aaidh al-Qarni, in Saudi Arabia.[52]

What Khaled offered to devout middle-class Muslims via his television show *Lifemakers* (*suna'a al-hayat*) was a 'religious discourse carrying the values of the new spirit of capitalism: ambition, wealth, success, imagination, efficiency and concern for self'.[53] Wearing luxury fashion brands such as Hugo Boss, he commended his followers for pursuing the admirable values of modernity, such as hard work and efficiency.[54]

It is noteworthy that Khaled does not propose reformist ideas or create a new form of Islamic liberalism that diverges from Sunni orthodoxy[55] but, instead, encourages his followers to proactively seek personal success with a strong work ethic, to become a 'pious winner'.[56] According to Peter Mandaville, 'the vision contained in the work of Khaled, as well as the pro-West, pro-business orientation of new Islam epitomised in the AKP in Turkey, was decidedly friendly towards globalization, at least in its economic dimension'.[57]

7.2.2 Managerial awakening

Boltanski et al.'s *The New Spirit of Capitalism* provides an analysis of the evolution of capitalism from the late 1960s to the late 1990s. Their central argument suggests that capitalism is a seemingly absurd system in which workers have lost control over the fruits of their labour and the ability to pursue work without subordination, making it a process 'singularly lacking in justifications'[58] and explaining the loud and clear protests of May 1968. Throughout the 1980s, protests were suppressed until capitalism discovered a new means to be seen as a viable economic system in the eyes of the people. The ideology that justifies engagement with capitalism, according to Boltanski et al., is referred to as the spirit of capitalism. For Weber, the spirit of capitalism was the recognition of work (and, as previously stated, politics) as a religious duty, a vocation that provided workers, merchants and entrepreneurs with a normative drive. In essence, Protestantism had steered the spirit of capitalism. When Boltanski et al. compared the French management literature – the formulae offered to firms and organizations for their smooth operation – between 1959–69 and 1989–94, they discovered that the latter period had a distinct goal of 'creating meaning for shared goals where anyone can simultaneously develop their personal autonomy and contribute to the collective project', namely the survival of the capitalist system, as making profit was recognized as an insufficiently inspiring goal.[59] Managerialism was, thus, inserted into capitalist narratives, giving it a 'new spirit' and quelling opposition by providing workers with meaning and incentive.

Eyal et al. argue that managerialism, as a mentality, loomed over the transition of post-communist countries in the 1990s and that 'this mentality [where ideology and reality meet painfully] is not the exclusive property of CEOs; it is shared equally by all fractions [including] intellectuals and technocrats'.[60] They also argue that managerial mentality has the impetus to transform ideology.[61] Managerialism is designed to be a compilation of practical methods to 'improve the productivity of organisations as one improves the performance of a machine', but it also has a moral tone, 'taking into account not only personal aspirations to security and autonomy, but also the way these aspirations can be attached to a more general orientation to the common good'.[62] Chakravartty further suggests that the influence of the new management thinking, originating in Europe and North America during the 1980s and 1990s, extended to regions like India, 'where neoliberal economic reforms led to both economic growth led to economic growth alongside unprecedented suffering'.[63] Similarly, the MENA region experienced similar effects from these transformations.

The end of the 1990s also saw a surge of management books written by Islamist thinkers who, a decade earlier, had come to the United States from Iraq, Kuwait and Palestine for their studies. These individuals were exposed to managerial thought within the economics departments of American universities, which greatly influenced their perspectives. They subsequently produced pioneering works that sought to bridge the gap between their Islamic commitment and the field of management literature.[64] This so-called period of 'managerial awakening (sahwa idâriyya)', witnessed a convergence between Islamic values and the principles of management.[65] It is no coincidence that this 'managerial awakening' occurred when Islamism's attractiveness, vitality and sources of legitimacy had become depleted, 'even among its once-ardent supporters'.[66] This convergence can be seen as an attempt to reinvigorate and redefine the appeal of Islamism in a changing social and political landscape.

Qaradawi's book, *Religious Practices in Islam*, and the writings of former MB member Mohamed Abdel Gawad, Shaykh Mohamed al-Ghazali, Shaykh Mohamed Ahmed al-Râshid and Hisham Talib demonstrate an intersection between the self-management principles of American author Dale Carnegie,[67] capitalist concepts acquired from management science textbooks used in business schools[68] and Islamic concepts. These writings, which infused Islamic values into the discourse of American management, offered practical guidance for Muslims in their daily lives and endorsed the pursuit of success and happiness as legitimate goals. Islamic spiritual movements in Southeast Asia, particularly in Indonesia, melded business management practices and capitalist principles from popular life-coaching seminars with Muslim practice.[69] Consequently, 'the Islamic discourse embraced the modern business corporation as a model through which one could articulate specifically Islamic policies and objectives [and], in a quasi-Weberian twist, the spirit of Western corporate capitalism was absorbed into a system of Islamic ethics enriched by US-style managerialism and entrepreneurialism'.[70]

The Indonesian tele-preacher and entrepreneur Aa Gymnastair (aka Aa Gym) developed a brand called Management of the Heart (*Manajemen Qolbu* – MQ), blending Sufi ethics with Western self-help slogans, and presenting prosperity and piety as interconnected. Aa Gym not only broadcast a Sunday television show and a morning radio show but also provided MQ training programmes aimed at middle-class Muslims who worked in corporate firms.[71] Scholar Hoesterey, who interviewed Aa Gym at his home filled with translated books of American self-help gurus, observed that the MQ program encompassed not only managing hearts but also achieving success. 'Following decades of corruption and nepotism, Indonesians had renewed their faith in the possibilities of entrepreneurship and social mobility, of piety and prosperity. Aa Gym's self-help formulae for success gave a religious foundation and economic direction to these hopes, desires, and anxieties.'[72]

The prevalence of the self-help and management discourse, as well as the celebrity of the tele-preachers idolized by Muslim youth, can be seen as a 'cultural by-product of one of the many ruptures [that] have often been driven by the challenge of capitalism and contributed to a variety of social and cultural transformations – a pattern of modernization familiar around the world'.[73] In that sense, for example, the retreat of the state in Egypt due to economic liberalization policies coincided with the rise of figures like Amr Khaled and the self-help phenomenon in the 1990s.[74]

Bayat and Herrera highlight how the popularity of Amr Khaled and similar figures reflects the rejection of patronizing moral authority by Muslim youth. These devout young Muslims found themselves navigating between religious beliefs, popular culture and societal expectations, swinging 'back and forth from [the pop star] Amr Diab to Amr Khaled, from partying to prayers; and yet they felt the burden of a strong social control of their elders, teachers, and neighbours'.[75] A similar trend was observed among Iranian youth after the Iran-Iraq war, but Islamist leaders failed to recognize its significance. They dismissed these changes as strange behaviour, unaware that it was an attempt by the youth to integrate Islamic norms with their own interests and desires within the context of global neoliberalization.[76]

It is, therefore, neither strange nor shocking that contemporary Islamist parties which genuinely want to succeed will follow where society goes, particularly the young, whom they believe have lost their enthusiasm for Islamist politics. Bayat claims that change in the youth base of Ennahda and the MB continued after the Arab Uprisings: 'The trends of Muslim women taking off the hijab, or unmarried women leaving home to live on their own, did not appear to diminish. If anything, the desire for self-assertion and autonomy, albeit with associated tensions, seemed to amplify.'[77]

Listening to a self-help podcast while running appeals to young people who are seeking an alternative to traditional *ulama* and their guilt-inducing sermons. It also serves as a form of activism, allowing them to challenge and reject Western and/or secular 'discourses that stigmatise Islam or present it as an archaic religion'.[78] Malek Chennoufi, a member of Ennahda's youth wing, outlines the demands of her peers:

> Tunisian youth share similar aspirations to young people in other countries. They want economic stability and a decent standard of living. They want to be open to the world but also want the government to protect [Tunisia's] traditions. Young entrepreneurs need more encouragement and financial support to thrive.[79]

The Islamist leaders seemed to realize the disenchantment of the young with traditional religious authorities and attempted to connect with them through ad hoc, corporation-style solutions, such as organizing leadership workshops – as achieved by both the AKP and Ennahda. Nahdawi Nejmeddin Felhi elaborates:

> Parents now send their children to Ennahda because we provide them with assistance and training. We provide them with training in leadership skills, management, and teamwork. They dream of a better future, they are diverse in their thoughts, clothes, and ways of thinking. They aspire to be successful in their studies and to become future leaders. The dream is to achieve social and economic success and improve their country, as happens all over the world.[80]

Islamist parties not only adopt economic liberalism but also adapt their religious adherence according to a new global value system with a renewed spirit of capitalism. That value system, which prioritizes success and self-improvement, 'ultimately affects the way in which Islamists conceive the world'.[81] From the 2000s onwards, owing to the inevitable influence of global flows of money, people and ideas, Islamic economies engaged with secular, broader, economic governance methods and organizations.[82] A lax and laissez-faire attitude to the tourism sector, a liberal approach to economic policies and a pragmatic and malleable understanding of the morality of economic measures have become common among Islamist political parties.

7.2.3 Cheap Islamization

The AKP did not explicitly enforce an Islamization agenda until around 2010, instead promising economic growth and stability and passing democratic reforms as required by Turkey's EU accession process. Following the referendum-based passage of the 2010 constitutional reform package, which gave the AKP greater power over the judiciary, the party's policies took on an authoritarian tone, and a concomitant 'Islamization agenda' emerged. Nonetheless, it is crucial to understand exactly what the AKP's version of Islamization entails. How Islamist is AKP's Islamization?

First, Erdogan 'engaged in morality politics, by advocating the construction of a pious generation'.[83] Measures such as banning alcohol advertising, restricting alcohol sales,[84] and increasing the authority and budget[85] of the *Diyanet İşleri Başkanlığı* (Presidency of Religious Affairs) showcased the AKP's embrace of state-controlled religion for its own goals. The Diyanet, originally tasked with promoting Islam and supporting religious activities, became instrumentalized by the AKP to mobilize its electorate domestically and globally in countries such as Germany and Austria, where a sizeable Turkish diaspora exists. However, according to Mandaville, 'the increased power of Diyanet does not necessarily signify Islamization of the Turkish state but its deployment globally serves as an instrument of Turkish religious soft power'.[86] A watershed moment came when, in the summer of 2020, Erdoğan declared Hagia Sophia, the UNESCO-listed Byzantine Church, to be once again a mosque. The site had originally been declared a mosque following the Ottoman conquest of Istanbul in 1453 by the Ottoman Sultan Mehmet II but was designated a museum in 1924 by Atatürk after the foundation of modern Turkey, in a symbolic break with the past. Amid the international condemnation that followed the conversion of Hagia Sophia to a mosque by presidential order and Greece's reaction by declaring a day of mourning, Erdoğan led the first prayers, saying, 'This is Hagia Sophia breaking away from its chains of captivity. It was the greatest dream of our youth.'[87]

I consider these moves by the AKP to be 'piecemeal Islamization',[88] the 'banalization of Islamic referents'[89] or a 'cheap Islamization' strategy, all trademarks of post-Islamist Islamization. By cheap Islamization, Bayat means one 'resorting to the language of moral and cultural purity (e.g. calling for the banning of alcohol or "immoral" literature, or raising the issue of women's public appearance), appealing to identity politics', rather than aiming for the more 'costly projects' of establishing an Islamic state or economy, areas in which, as Islamists realized by the mid-1990s, 'they could not go very far'.[90] In a similar vein, Roy believes that because 'the AKP could not fulfil the Islamists' biggest promise about being against corruption, [Erdoğan] uses symbols as tools for consolidating the electorate. In that sense, what better symbol than converting the Hagia Sophia to a mosque? Erdoğan could not Islamize minds, so he is trying to Islamize stones. That is the punchline of the Hagia Sophia conversion'.[91]

According to Mümtazer Türköne, a scholar of Turkish nationalism and Islamism, the AKP's 'piecemeal Islamisation' and attempts to 'creat[e] a pious generation' backfired:

> Imam Hatip Schools are now more reactionary to Islamist politics than the students at regular schools. Many identify as deists because they witnessed corruption and authoritarianism flourishing under the guise of Islamist politics. Many of the mosques built by the AKP have no actual community; some mosques house homeless people and drug addicts.[92]

Even though Islamizing the society had backfired, could the AKP capture the state and subtly Islamize it? The answer to this question is complex. First, we need to ascertain what state capture means in the context of Turkey and the AKP. It is the gradual infiltration of 'pious cadres' into state institutions such as the police, the judiciary, ministries and public education[93] and the 'purge of secular cadres from the state'.[94] Since Turkey undertook a pro-secular nation-building process, the state capture in this sense may, Somer argues, 'be called an "Islamist project", that is, a revolutionary takeover of the state in the name of Islamization'.[95]

Tuğal agrees that this process 'can be taken as an instance of Islamic coercion'[96] since the secular cadres were replaced by devout cadres. However, I believe the 'Islamic' or devout qualities of the new cadres were of less importance to the AKP than their allegiance and loyalty to the party itself. Islamist parties are often accused of being wolves in sheep's clothing: if given the chance, they will Islamize the state and the rule of law. The AKP's authoritarian clientelist networks, mostly consisting of Muslim conservatives – and, more recently, nationalists – have been cited lately as a prime example of the Islamists' true intentions. However, the AKP's state capture and actions to stack institutions with loyalists do not necessarily relate to Islamic ideology or an Islamist project. As Kandil argues, 'What AKP's detractors complain about is hardly unique to Islamist movements: after all, few successful politicians could remain immune to the arrogance of power.'[97]

Rather than calling it Islamization, I prefer to refer to the AKP's transformation of human capital within state apparatuses as 'state capture' and its policies with Islamist referents as 'conservatism' similar to other groups in today's Europe. In this respect, it is noteworthy that, since 2011, the AKP has, through its control of the media and state resources, also marginalized and at times persecuted Islamist or initially pro-AKP intellectuals and politicians who became critical.[98]

Finally, it is essential to differentiate between the AKP's actions towards state capture in Turkey and the diffusion process that took place from 2011 to 2013. The AKP's undemocratic swerve, which was consolidated following the Gezi protests in 2013 and the attempted coup in 2016 in Turkey, should not obscure our analysis of the diffusion process. The findings of this research do not support the argument that there was a transnational Islamist project. Moreover, the diffusion process did not involve specific tactics for refashioning the judiciary, military or security apparatuses. The steps taken by the AKP to capture the state were vastly different from those suggested to Ennahda and the MB. The AKP's intention was to assist Ennahda and the MB in presenting themselves as 'normal' and legitimate political entities during critical moments. It is worth noting that, for the AKP, Ennahda and the Muslim Brotherhood, the criteria for appearing normal and legitimate had little to do with Islamist ideology.

8

Changing dynamics of the interplay

In retrospect, 2013 was a turning point for all involved in the diffusion process – the AKP, the MB and Ennahda. It was on the 28th of May when a modest assembly of environmental activists initiated a peaceful sit-in within Istanbul's Taksim Square, specifically taking root in Gezi Park. Their objective was to voice their opposition against the proposed demolition of the park, with intentions to reconstruct an Ottoman-era military barracks as part of the AKP's urban development strategy.

However, the plan to raze the park served as a tipping point for the protesters, intensifying the discontent that had been brewing due to the AKP's growing authoritarianism, the suppression of press freedom, and the implementation of development projects that disregarded environmental concerns, ultimately benefiting only a privileged pro-AKP minority. The Gezi protests swiftly spread throughout the country within a matter of days. Sustaining their vigour for a fortnight, they were eventually quelled, leaving a tragic toll in their wake. Twelve young lives were lost, and approximately 8,000 individuals found themselves wounded amid the tumultuous clashes.

On the 30th of June, as the Gezi protests were gradually subsiding in Turkey, a momentous event unfolded in Egypt. The government led by President Morsi was overthrown, and the military assumed control. In response to this abrupt shift in power, the MB orchestrated large-scale demonstrations, gathering crowds in Rabaa al-Adawiyya Square in Cairo. According to one of my interviewees present in Cairo during that time, there were claims that Erdogan, through an advisor, had urged the MB to engage in street protests as a means of counteracting the military's intervention. While I was unable to find conclusive evidence to substantiate this claim, the same source mentioned that the AKP had allegedly provided food aid to the protesters in Rabaa Square through Turkish Islamist NGOs.[1] Simultaneously, in Istanbul's Saraçhane district, Turkish Islamist associations organized mass prayers dedicated to expressing solidarity with the Morsi supporters who had encamped in Cairo's Rabaa Square for a duration of six weeks.² Rabaa Square would soon become the target of a violent raid by the Egyptian police on the 14th of August, resulting in a staggering loss of approximately 1,400 lives. In the subsequent days, hundreds of MB leaders were apprehended and detained by the authorities.³

Turkish graphic designer Saliha Eren, who had experience working on social media campaigns for the Arab Uprisings, closely followed the violent suppression of the Rabaa protesters in Egypt. Driven by her devout Muslim beliefs and empathy for Islamist circles, she endeavoured to express solidarity with the protesters by creating a powerful graphic symbol for the tragic event. Inspired by the iconic four-finger gesture adopted by the Egyptian demonstrators in Rabaa Square, she crafted a symbol showcasing four black fingers against a vibrant yellow backdrop. The color yellow symbolized Qubbat al-Shakhra, while black represented the city of Mecca.⁴ Remarkably, within a span of just twenty-four hours, the symbol had reached an astounding estimated audience of ninety million individuals through the platforms of Facebook and Twitter. 'I did not do it for personal gain or recognition. Very few people were aware that it was I who had created it.'⁵ Eren told me.

Eren and her friends launched a Twitter campaign using the symbol and the hashtag 'What is Rabaa' in Arabic, Turkish and English. The tweets included slogans highlighting the significance of Rabaa, such as the collapse of Western values, the resurgence of Muslims on the world stage, the birth of a new movement and the symbol of freedom.⁶ Although they did not have any direct contact with the AKP during the campaign, Turkish president Erdoğan observed the popularity of the four-finger gesture and started using it himself at his public gatherings.⁷ The yellow and black sign also gained traction among pro-Morsi protesters in Egypt.⁸

In the following weeks and months, sporadic protests took place in major Turkish cities against the Egyptian coup and the arrest of MB leaders.⁹ Reports emerged that President Erdoğan was deeply affected by the death of Esma Baltaggi, the daughter of MB leader Mohammad Baltaggi,¹⁰ and he publicly wept while reading Mohammad Baltaggi's letter to his deceased daughter on 23 August 2013, saying that 'he saw his own children in this letter'.¹¹

Erdoğan's emotional reaction highlighted his deep personal investment in the ousting of Morsi. His supporters also shared these sentiments, as evidenced by the uproar caused by a headline in *Hürriyet Daily* newspaper reporting Morsi's death sentence in 2015. The headline, which stated 'Death sentence for the president who assumed office with 52 per cent of the votes',¹² ignited controversy within AKP circles. Erdoğan interpreted Hürriyet's headline as a suggestion that he might face a similar fate. A few days later, during an AKP rally, he openly criticized *Hürriyet*'s parent company, Doğan Holding, stating, 'Have you seen how the Doğan Group reported Morsi's death sentence? Hey, Doğan Group, I don't care about you! If I come to the same end, *inshallah*, grant me martyrdom.'[13] Erdoğan's hypersensitivity towards the downfall of the Morsi government stemmed from his belief in a larger conspiracy to undermine his own government and its allies. He perceived both the Gezi protests and the Egyptian coup as part of this alleged grand plan orchestrated by Israel, Saudi Arabia and the United States. Consequently, the Gezi protests and the Egyptian military's actions against the Muslim Brotherhood intensified Erdoğan's sense of threat to his own position.[14]

'The Egyptian coup showed us that the West does not care about democracy and keeps silent in the face of a military dictatorship',[15] said a former AKP official. Three years later, Turkey experienced its own attempted coup on 15 July 2016, allegedly orchestrated by the Gülen movement, a former ally of Erdoğan. 'The resistance that we showed against the military coup on the night of 15 July was due to the lessons we had learned during Morsi's ousting', Eren claimed.[16] In the aftermath of the failed coup, Turkey witnessed an intensified crackdown on media, individual rights, the rule of law and academia, which had already been escalating since around 2010. As a result, as of 2022, Turkey has the highest number of imprisoned journalists globally,[17] and its democracy ranking has been steadily declining.[18] This environment prompted many intellectuals to leave Turkey, seeking refuge elsewhere.[19] Conversely, Turkey has become a safe haven for Egyptian Islamists fleeing the government of President Sisi.

8.1 Post-2013 period: Fear, isolation and activism

8.1.1 The MB – the AKP

Istanbul has emerged as a significant hub for the Muslim Brotherhood (MB) following the military coup in Egypt, serving as a venue for international conferences and meetings that help preserve the spirit of the organization.[20] Arab Scholarship and Expertise for Peace and Stability in the Middle East (MESBAR) claimed that 'many new Muslim Brotherhood institutions' headquarters are located in Istanbul'.[21] The historical animosity between the Saudi Kingdom and the MB, stemming from their rival claims to represent Sunni Islam in the region, may be a factor in these depictions of the relationship between the Turkish government and the MB, but they are not wholly unfounded.

Istanbul has served as a venue for several significant conferences and gatherings related to the Muslim Brotherhood (MB) and its affiliated groups. In July 2013, shortly after the removal of the Morsi government in Egypt, a conference was held in Istanbul, attended by Egyptian MB members and Ennahda's leader, Ghannouchi. Another conference took place in September 2013, where Egyptian MB leaders participated as representatives of the Parliamentary Union of Islamic Countries (PUIC).[22] In August 2014, opposition groups from Egypt, including former ministers of the Morsi government, announced the establishment of the 'Egyptian Revolutionary Council (ERC)' in Istanbul.[23]

A few months later, the MB's news site, Ikhwanweb, announced that 'the elected representatives of the Egyptian people, Egypt's legitimate parliamentarians, are holding parliamentary sessions in Istanbul's Bayrampaşa district.[24] Another conference, held in August 2015 in Istanbul and entitled The Conference for Countering Despotism and Bloodshed, drew criticism from Egyptian religious bodies affiliated with the government. The Fatwa Monitoring Observatory *Dar al-Iftaa* claimed that the conference demonstrated Turkey's hostility towards Egypt and its regional ambitions, while the deputy head of Al-Azhar expressed anger at the participants, accusing them of being tied to the MB.[25]

Meanwhile, gatherings in Istanbul continued without pause. In January 2016, former FJP lawmakers living in Turkey and elsewhere gathered in Istanbul to form 'The Exiled Egyptian Parliament'. Furthermore, Istanbul served as the venue for the MB's ninetieth anniversary celebration in April 2018. The event was attended by numerous MB leaders from different parts of the world, including Ibrahim Mounir, the deputy leader of the movement at that time, and Khaled Meshaal, the former head of the Hamas political bureau.[26]

Yusuf al-Qaradawi maintained his influential role even after the ousting of Morsi. While he became more vocal in his support for the Muslim Brotherhood, particularly after the Rabaa massacre, pressure from other Gulf states led to his departure from Al Jazeera Arabic's prime-time religious programme, al-Sharia wa-l-Ḥayah, effectively ending his seventeen-year run on the show.[27] However, he continued his activism and maintained a close relationship with Erdoğan until his death in 2022. One notable aspect of Qaradawi's involvement was his organization of the annual meetings of the International Union of Muslim Scholars (IUMS) in Istanbul. These gatherings provided a platform for significant Muslim Brotherhood members to meet with other Islamist groups and Islamic scholars. During these meetings, Qaradawi himself praised Erdoğan as a protector of Islam.[28] It is worth mentioning that although Erdoğan expressed support for the Morsi government and condemned the Sisi regime on multiple occasions, he never publicly acknowledged Turkey as a haven for exiled MB followers. Furthermore, he remained silent on the presence of the Muslim Brotherhood and the events hosted in Istanbul related to the group.

In addition to hosting conferences and facilitating meetings, Turkey played a crucial role in helping the MB maintain international visibility and bypass the repression of Egyptian president Sisi. Istanbul served as a primary base for the MB, allowing it to broadcast its message through sympathetic satellite networks.[29] One notable network was Al Sharq TV, owned by Ayman Nour, a former Egyptian parliamentarian who fled to Turkey after the 2013 military coup. Nour established the news channel in Istanbul's Tekstilkent, where it became known for providing Egyptians with alternative viewpoints and dissident opinions, much to the disapproval of President Sisi. Nour claimed that nine months before our meeting in his office, 'a group of Sisi's men came to the Al Sharq office and tried to hijack the live broadcast, but their attempt was averted by the channel's employees'.[30] Despite Nour's claim that Al Sharq does not propagate MB ideology, his team collaborated on specific issues with Al Watan, the MB channel in Istanbul. By 2018, Istanbul had become a hub for Arab-language television channels, with thirteen networks having their headquarters there. Among the most popular were Al Sharq, Al Watan and Mekameleen. Mekameleen, founded in 2014, featured Hamza Zawba, a former spokesperson of the FJP, as its anchor. These channels amassed a significant following on social media platforms, with Al Watan's video interaction rate surpassing that of Al Jazeera.[31]

According to Shaimaa Magued, who conducted interviews with anchors from the Muslim Brotherhood's (MB) television channels in Turkey, these channels adopted a confrontational anti-regime approach and a radical Islamic rhetoric.[32] They frequently employed incendiary rhetoric against the Egyptian military, calling for popular resistance and boycotts of President Sisi's supporters in the name of Islam.[33]

Turkey's harbouring of MB members prompted the Egyptian regime to undertake a public relations campaign against Turkey, worsening already strained relations with regional powers such as Saudi Arabia. While Saudi Arabia designated the MB a terrorist organization and banned all MB books,[34] the United Arab Emirates (UAE) froze its relations with Tunisia after Ennahda formed a government following the first election after the revolution in 2011, despite being Tunisia's second most important trading partner.

Saudi Arabia's stance regarding an MB government in power was no secret; indeed, according to a former AKP MP, the AKP had warned President Morsi about this. 'We said, make your first official visit to the Saudis, don't come to us [Turkey] first. Secure good relations with them to secure your place. He listened to us and made his first foreign visit to the Kingdom.'[35] However, as Tariq Al-Zomor observed, President Morsi's Saudi visits were far from fruitful:

> Dr Morsi told me that he aimed to mend ties with Saudi Arabia. I told him it is not that simple. But he didn't pay attention. However, the last time I spoke to him before the coup, his reaction was different. Saudis are not Muslims; they are Jews, he told me. It was around March 2013, and he realized that Saudis were, along with Israel, plotting against him.[36]

According to Abou Al Fadl, 'no country did more to undermine Morsi's regime and no government more openly celebrated his overthrow' than Saudi Arabia; adding 'the trail of money provides the best evidence'.[37] While the Saudi intelligence chief Prince Bandar bin Sultan went to Western capitals and campaigned for a military takeover in Egypt, 'the UAE, Kuwait and Saudi Arabia pledged money that far exceeds the aid Egypt receives from the US and the EU combined, in the event that the US and EU might attempt to punish the Egyptian army by cutting off aid'.[38] The MB's efforts to secure trade agreements with Turkey, China and India also caused tensions with wealthy generals within the Egyptian military, who emphasized the importance of maintaining commercial ties with Saudi Arabia, the UAE and Kuwait while being cautious about engaging with Turkey, Iran and China without US consent.[39] The intransigent positioning that placed Turkey and Qatar on one side and Saudi Arabia and the other Gulf Cooperation Council (GCC) countries on the other, started when the MB won the Egyptian elections in 2012, not after Morsi's fall. This alignment had far-reaching implications for various regional conflicts, such as the Syrian civil war, the Arab-Israeli conflict and the Libyan conflict.

The diffusion process between the AKP, the Egyptian MB and Ennahda during the post-2013 period can be seen as a form of 'transnational activism', distinct from the dynamics of the 2011–2013 period. While the aspiration for success remained, the survival imperative became dominant for the Islamists. However, it is important to clarify the concept of activism in this context. Recent scholarship challenges the notion that Islamic activism is solely contingent upon Islamic ideology and argues that 'Islamic activism is not sui generis'.[40] According to Çavdar, Islamist activism is a calculated pursuit of individual interests rather than a result of religious indoctrination. Islamists strategically and selectively use ideology, engaging in cost-benefit analysis and strategic calculation.[41]

According to rational choice theory, which posits that individuals act based on self-interest and the pursuit of maximum utility, one might expect Erdoğan to withdraw his support for the Egyptian MB following Sisi's takeover, as it would be counterproductive on multiple levels. However, although Erdoğan's political career has been archetypically that of a pragmatist, his actions do not always align with what is conventionally considered rational or in his self-interest. This apparent irrationality has been observed on various occasions.

One possible explanation for Erdoğan's continued support for the MB could be his desire to maintain his image as the protector of Muslims or the hope of the Islamic world, as suggested by figures like Qaradawi and Youssef Nada.[42] Additionally, hosting exiled MB members may resonate with his nationalist and conservative support base. Moreover, by providing a safe haven for MB dissidents, Erdoğan 'maintained leverage against Egypt and certain Gulf Cooperation Council countries'.[43] As the section on U-turns in this chapter will demonstrate, Erdogan's seemingly irrational behaviour of supporting the MB and provoking the Gulf countries after 2013 was transient and will have changed dramatically several years later.

8.1.2 Ennahda – the AKP

Regarding the coup in Egypt in 2013, Bedreddine Abdelkafi, a member of the executive bureau of Ennahda, stated, 'We have different realities in Tunisia than in Egypt, thank God, our military respects the will of the people.'[44] Unlike Egypt or neighbouring Algeria, where the state and the army were intricately entwined, Habib Bourguiba, the first president and founder of the Tunisian state, deliberately excluded the military from politics. The vice president of Ennahda, Noureddine Bhiri, claimed that the army meddling in politics is a red line for Tunisia. 'Bourguiba tried hard to build a military that does not interfere in politics. Even during the Ben Ali dictatorship, the military was not allowed to take hold.'[45] On the other hand, many of those within the Ennahda leadership believed that, in 2013 'there were exterior forces that tried to disrupt Tunisian society and all revolutions in the region at the time'.[46] According to one Nahdawi, Ahmed Gaaloul, who spent years in exile in the UK along with Ghannouchi and, after the revolution, became the Secretary of State in the Ministry of Youth, 'The old demons crawled back into our minds after the Egyptian coup'.[47]

The concerns expressed by the Nahdawis were not unfounded, as Tunisia experienced a series of political assassinations in 2013. Two prominent leftist politicians, Chokri Belaid and Mohamed Brahmi, were killed in separate incidents. The then Minister of the Interior Lofti Ben Jeddou had warned that 'the same gun' had killed both MPs, forcing Ennahda to cut all ties with Jihadi-Salafism and ban its most prominent group, Ansar al-Sharia.[48] These events triggered large-scale anti-Ennahda demonstrations, eventually leading to Ennahda's decision to step down and make way for a technocratic government in January 2014. Ennahda MP Sahbi Atig believes that these assassinations were orchestrated to create instability in Tunisia and provoke dissent within the revolutionary movement.

> We did not fear a military intervention like the one that occurred in Egypt. However, we were concerned that the hands – inside Tunisia and outside Tunisia – that plotted the assassinations would impede a democratic transition. Following discussions with leading social and political groups, we decided to step down so that a technocratic government could take over and continue with elections. It was a wise decision on our part.[49]

During the period encompassing the assassinations and Ennahda's withdrawal from power, a phase of bargaining unfolded in Tunisia. This juncture was crucial, as the success of the bargaining process and the relinquishing of power by one party were pivotal in avoiding a regression to authoritarianism.[50] Ennahda and the secular elites engaged in a 'bargained competition', aiming to negotiate their reintegration into the political order following the Uprisings.[51] Therefore, Ennahda's decision to voluntarily relinquish power had been, indeed, wise choice, setting Tunisia on a favourable trajectory. In contrast, At a similar critical juncture, the MB's failure to reach a national pact led to the Sisi regime's takeover in Egypt. However, while Ennahda's bargaining competition prevented disarray in Tunisia, it also led to 'the dilution of revolutionary demands and a reductionist form of pluralism that seemingly pitted Islamists against representatives of the old regime'.[52] There is some anecdotal evidence suggesting that the AKP, similar to the MB, warned of the consequences of not appeasing certain societal blocs and achieving consensus, but this research did not provide definitive information regarding whether the AKP advised Ennahda to step down during the 2013–14 bargaining period.

Starting in 2013, the Tunisian media began extensively criticizing Erdoğan's authoritarian practices and crackdowns on freedom, highlighting allegations of corruption investigations against him and the AKP. They argued that the myths of democratic rule and economic success had faded, suggesting that Erdoğan's failures would join those of other Islamists in the Middle East.[53] Erdoğan's personality also sparked controversy within Tunisian political circles. His display of the Rabaa sign (symbolizing support for the MB) alongside Tunisian president Beji Caid Essebsi in 2017 and the behaviour of his entourage at the Tunisian Parliament were perceived as arrogant and disrespectful.[54] Nevertheless, Ghannouchi maintained his close relations with Erdoğan, attending the latter's milestone events in Turkey in 2019[55] and participating in SETA symposiums, claiming that 'democracy and Islam are twins'[56] despite continued criticism from the leftist and secular media in Tunisia.[57]

Ghannouchi faced accusations of being manipulated by Erdoğan when he paid an unannounced visit to him, accompanied by his son-in-law Rafek Abdessalem, during Tunisia's government-forming period in 2019.[58] Some commentators argued that Ghannouchi, who had long theorized the compatibility of political Islam and democracy, took Erdoğan and his style as a model but failed to apply the lessons from Turkey's experience to Tunisia.[59]

Following President Saied's decision to sack the government and suspend parliament in July 2021, Ennahda, as the largest party in the Tunisian Parliament, faced a significant challenge. Ghannouchi's approach in dealing with President Saied's power grab has been described as a blend of the styles of Necmettin Erbakan and Recep Tayyip Erdoğan. Similar to how Erbakan, Erdoğan's mentor, yielded to the military intervention in Turkey in 1997, Ghannouchi avoided direct confrontation with Saied[60] but consistently criticized his actions as illegitimate and described them as a coup d'état.[61] Since then, Ennahda has experienced internal fractures, leading to bitter disputes among its members. Approximately 100 senior members, including former ministers, accused the party leadership and Ghannouchi of making mistakes that may have contributed to Saied's power grab. In September 2021, these senior members resigned from Ennahda, marking the most severe internal crisis for the party since its establishment in the 1980s.[62] Meanwhile, President Saied's popularity has remained around 72 per cent.[63] The deterioration of Tunisia's economy over the past decade and the mishandling of the Covid-19 pandemic have further boosted Saied's popularity but fuelled public distrust of Ennahda and its leader, Ghannouchi.

In November 2022, Ghannouchi appeared before a court in Sousse as part of an investigation into alleged money laundering and incitement to violence. The investigation, which began in June 2022, resulted in the freezing of bank accounts belonging to Ghannouchi, his son Moaz Ghannouchi and his son-in-law Rafek Abdeselam. Moaz Ghannouchi and Abdeselam had already left

Tunisia, while Rachid Ghannouchi was prohibited from leaving the country due to another investigation into the assassinations of Mohamed Brahmi and Chokri Belaid in 2013.

These investigations are part of a series of ongoing probes targeting Ghannouchi and members of Ennahda. One such case is the Instalingo case, initiated in October 2021, which alleges that Ennahda leaders planned an armed uprising against President Kais Saied through a company called Instalingo. The Instalingo case is also linked to another financial organization called Namaa, an association of Tunisian businessmen. As explained at length in Chapter 6, Namaa was AKP's brainchild, founded on the model of Turkey's MÜSİAD, with the assistance of Turkish businessmen close to the AKP. Namaa was outlawed in Tunisia in early 2022.

In December 2022, Abdel Karim Suleimani, a former Ennahda member and businessman, was detained for questioning regarding his involvement with Instalingo and Namaa.[64] The prosecutor alleges that Suleimani and others within Ennahda engaged in a money-laundering scheme, received foreign financial support, accumulated illicit wealth and potentially used some of the funds to send jihadists to Syria and Iraq. The Tunisian Ministry of Interior has provided limited information regarding these cases, and indictments are still pending.

According to sources at Tunisian radio news station Mosaique FM, the Namaa Association case, which implicates Ghannouchi, his family members and former prime minister Hamadi Jebali, is focused on investigating suspicious financial transactions that occurred after the January 2011 revolution. These transactions amount to approximately 30–35 million dollars and involve front companies.[65] There are also claims suggesting the involvement of a Qatari charity associated with the Emir of Qatar in this alleged scheme.[66] Reda Al-Radaoui, the head of the Tunisian Defense Authority, has stated that the Namaa Association, despite being established to promote foreign investment, was also engaged in facilitating the recruitment and transportation of individuals to conflict zones, particularly Syria. According to these sources, Namaa used foreign investment as a cover for its illicit activities.[67] It's intriguing that the link between the Namaa and the AKP has gone unnoticed by Tunisian news outlets. Aside from a passing mention of the cases against Ennahda without explanation, the Namaa case was almost non-existent in Turkish sources.

Financial corruption investigations are difficult to assess unless the prosecutor's reports and indictments are first reviewed. Without a comprehensive understanding of the evidence presented, it is not possible to draw definitive conclusions regarding the involvement of Namaa and Ennahda members in criminal activities.

Regarding the charges of 'inciting violence' and 'sending jihadists to foreign countries', it is important to consider Ennahda's history and character as an organization. Ennahda has historically distanced itself from such activities and has been involved in democratic processes and peaceful political engagement. Therefore, these charges appear inconsistent with Ennahda's known principles and practices.

Furthermore, Namaa had, since its founding, irritated Tunisia's established business elite by adopting a strategy similar to that of the MÜSİAD, which was to conduct its own business diplomacy in order to gradually access resources from the transnational network and impose itself as a trade broker in the international arena.[68]

Tunisia's president Kais Saied has been persecuting the opposition in ways that are straight out of the playbook of any authoritarian. Since sacking the government and suspending the parliament in June 2021, Saied has been targeting his opponents, particularly Ennahda. While Ennahda's relations with the AKP has been one of the reasons for this persecution, neither the AKP leaders nor its media outlets have shown any support for Ennahda.

8.2 Erdogan's U-turns vis-a-vis the MB

Around 2016, there were notable shifts in President Erdoğan's stance on the MB and Turkey's Middle Eastern policies in general. One significant change occurred in relation to the incident involving a Turkish flotilla attacked by Israel in 2010 while attempting to deliver aid to Gaza. Initially Erdogan was outraged against Israel, 'felt personally betrayed'.[69] However, following a rapprochement with Israel, his tone regarding the incident shifted, and he criticized the actions of İHH, asking if he was consulted before the Gaza mission. 'Did you ask me before going to Gaza?'[70] he asked rhetorically in the summer of 2016, six years after the incident, accusing the Islamist aid group of acting recklessly.

Another noteworthy change was observed in Erdoğan's views on the four-fingered symbol associated with the Rabaa massacre. Initially, the symbol was used by Erdoğan and the AKP to portray themselves as defenders of freedom, justice and legitimacy, particularly within the context of Islam. It signified their moral superiority and opposition to the oppression of Muslims worldwide and rejection of Western values.[71] The symbol served as a corporate identity[72] for Erdoğan and aimed to mobilize Muslim sentiment, both domestically and internationally.

However, following the attempted coup in Turkey in July 2016 and leading up to the 2017 constitutional referendum, in which Turkey transitioned to a presidential republic, Erdoğan reinterpreted the Rabaa symbol. He nationalized it, giving it a new meaning that aligned with the AKP's world view: one nation, one motherland, one flag, one state of a unified nation, motherland, flag and state. A brand-new meaning was given to the sign, separating it from its origins. In 2016, a bronze statue was made of Erdoğan's hand making the Rabaa sign, with the slogan '*Tek Millet, Tek Bayrak, Tek Vatan, Tek Devlet* (one nation, one motherland, one flag, one state)' written on it and distributed to everyone working in the parliament including visitors.[73] Erdoğan first ideologically abused the Rabaa massacre by inventing a modern-day myth, and then 'divorced [the] gesture from its original anchorage in the Egyptian context and denied connection with the Rabaa massacre' to consolidate his base at home and 'resume diplomatic relations with the Sisi government in Egypt'.[74]

In another example, Abdul Moneim Foutuh, an MB defector who was well known to AKP members, including Erdoğan, and who came fourth in Egypt's 2012 presidential elections with 17 per cent of the votes, took part in the protests against the coup in 2013 and was subsequently arrested in 2018. The MB spokesperson and Foutuh's family members[75] approached Erdoğan in the hope that he would condemn Foutuh's arrest. However, their efforts were met with silence from Erdoğan, indicating a lack of public support or condemnation from him regarding Foutuh's situation.[76]

Apart from Turkey's support for the MB and Saudi Arabia's support for Egypt's coup, relations between the two countries had grounded to a halt, both economically and diplomatically, following the murder of Saudi dissident journalist Jamal Khashoggi in Saudi Arabia's consulate in Istanbul in 2018. Turkish and US intelligence agencies implicated Saudi Crown Prince Muhammad Bin Salman (MBS) in the brutal killing, alleging that he had ordered it. President Erdoğan exerted international pressure on MBS and made the recordings public,[77] further straining the bilateral relationship. In response, Saudi Arabia initiated an unofficial boycott of Turkish exports, leading to a decline in the countries' foreign trade volume. While their trade had amounted to 5.2 billion USD in 2015, it decreased to 3.3 billion USD by 2019. This decline reflected the deepening economic and diplomatic rift between Turkey and Saudi Arabia.

After the media backlash over Jamal Khashoggi's murder, Saudi Crown Prince Muhammad Bin Salman retreated from the public eye and refrained from travelling outside of Saudi Arabia or granting interviews to non-Saudi media until March 2022. In an interview with The Atlantic, MBS expressed that the Khashoggi incident was the worst thing that happened to him and could have jeopardized his plans for reforming the country.[78] He claimed to have been 'hurt a lot'.[79]

A month after this interview, Turkey unexpectedly handed over the Khashoggi trial to Saudi Arabia, citing the Saudi authorities' refusal to extradite the suspects as the reason. Turkey stated that without the presence of the defendants, the Turkish courts could do little to proceed with the case.[80] However, in 2018, during a conference in Istanbul organized by the NGO 'League of Parliamentarians for Al-Quds', President Erdoğan asserted that the voice recordings related to the Khashoggi murder proved premeditation and warned that if Saudi Arabia failed to handle the case properly, Turkish courts would take action according to international law since the crime had occurred on Turkish soil. 'They [the Saudis] think we are stupid, they think the world is stupid', Erdoğan continued.[81]

Nevertheless, the Erdoğan of 2022 thought differently than the Erdoğan of 2018. What was behind this volte-face was clear to many: a month following his visit to Jeddah, Erdoğan invited MBS to Turkey, hoping these visits would lead to a 'major boost to bilateral ties as well as Turkey's deteriorating economy'.[82]

Following a period of strained relations that began with Turkey's support for the MB, a process of reconciliation between Turkey and the UAE commenced as well. From November 2021 to May 2022, Turkish president Erdoğan and UAE president Mohammad bin Zayed (MBZ) visited each other's countries on multiple occasions. These visits took place after nearly nine years of tense relations, during which various AKP officials and ministers, including the foreign affairs and interior ministers, accused MBZ of providing financial support for the attempted coup in Turkey on 15 July 2016.[83]

Turkey made efforts to improve relations with Egypt,[84] although reconciling with President Sisi proved to be more challenging than with MBS or MBZ. President Sisi continued to portray the Muslim Brotherhood (MB) as a malicious organization and presented himself as the saviour who rescued Egypt from their rule. The Egyptian state-controlled media also echoed this narrative. The popular Egyptian television series '*Al-Ikhtiar* (The Choice)' focused on the MB's short period of governance and their removal, becoming one of the most-watched shows in Egypt. The series promised to provide insights into what it described as Egypt's most dangerous 96 hours, highlighting Sisi's determination to save Egypt from the MB's dark path.[85]

AKP's conspicuous attempts to repair the damage caused by its support for the Islamist movements after the Uprisings raise the obvious question: Would the AKP government extradite MB members who live in Turkey? A senior but former MB member to whom I put this question told me that 'Erdoğan is pragmatic and does whatever he thinks is necessary for his country, such as making peace with Saudi Arabia, but he will not extradite the MB members because many of them are now Turkish citizens'.[86]

Hard on the heels of these interviews, at the end of April 2022, one of the primary MB television channels, Mekameleen, ceased broadcasting. Al Sharq TV, owned by Ayman Nour, followed suit and stopped broadcasting in Turkey.[87] In a written statement, the management of Mekameleen stated that 'it has decided to move the broadcast, studios, and all activities of the channel outside of Turkey, owing to the conditions that are not hidden from anyone and with the concern of continuing the mission of the channel to convey the whole truth. Our broadcasts from different parts of the world will be restarted'.[88]

On 21 November 2022, a photograph of Erdogan shaking hands with his Egyptian counterpart Abdel Fatah Al-Sisi at the World Cup in Qatar circulated widely. This meeting was notable considering the previous heated exchanges between the two leaders. Erdogan had repeatedly criticized Sisi, referring to him as a 'murderer' and 'putschist'[89] in relation to the Rabaa massacre and the death of Mohamed Morsi in prison. On the other hand, Sisi accused Erdogan of supporting the MB and attempting to destabilize the country. However, despite their past animosity, the two leaders were seen shaking hands with smiles in a high-profile international event like the World Cup. Following the photograph, Erdogan expressed his intention to meet with Sisi once the foreign ministers of both countries reach agreement on specific issues.[90] Two weeks prior to the handshake, the security teams of Turkey and Egypt held a meeting where they agreed not to take any actions that would jeopardize the security of their respective countries. This can be seen as a request from Egypt for Turkey to reconsider its policy in Libya referring to Turkey's preliminary deal with Libya's government in Tripoli in 2019, and Turkey asking Egypt to reassess its stance in the Eastern Mediterranean.[91]

Even though Egyptian presidency spokesperson Bassam Essam Rady stated on presidency's Facebook account that the handshake would be the beginning of developing bilateral relations,[92] Tariq Fahmy, a political scientist at the Cairo University, argues that 'there is still a long way to go and that Turkey needs to regain Egypt's trust and that there is no agreement between two countries on thorny issues, particularly Libya and the Mediterranean'.[93] Because, as explained in this chapter, the Eastern Mediterranean maritime dispute and the Libyan quagmire are not the only issues causing friction between Turkey and Egypt. Interestingly, the Turkish and Egyptian presidencies appear to have a tacit agreement not to bring up the 'other issue' that is the AKP's close ties to the MB.

Erdoğan's U-turn was perceived by the Arab media as a capitulation to Saudi Arabia and President Sisi of Egypt:

> Islamic principles and values rank low on the Turkish president's list of priorities. If Khashoggi had been alive, he might have handed him up to the Saudi authorities. What matters to him is to remain in the presidential palace and – to facilitate that – for the lira to recover and the Turkish economy to overcome the difficulties it currently faces owing to the failure of his policies. It is regrettable that some leaders of the Islamist movement still see him as the Caliph of the Muslims.[94]

Meanwhile, Turkish Islamists expressed their disappointment – albeit *sotto voce*. One of them stated that he 'cannot acquiesce Erdogan's handshake with the murderer Sisi. No and never! I despise Sisi and everything he stands for. I fully identify with Morsi and the values he represents. I feel very sad and wounded'.[95] Another confessed that he 'was devastated on behalf of the Muslim world'[96] after seeing the photo of the handshake. In September 2023, Erdoğan and Sisi held a side-meeting at the G20 Summit in India and discussed energy cooperation between Turkey and Egypt.

Erdogan's shift in attitude towards President Sisi of Egypt, as well as his efforts to mend relations with Saudi Arabia and the UAE, can primarily be attributed to his pragmatism and the utilitarian value these actions hold for maintaining his grip on power. The 2023 parliamentary and presidential elections in Turkey coincided with a challenging economic situation marked by soaring inflation and a devalued currency. In order to address the bleak economic prospects[97] that posed a threat to Erdogan's re-election, he pursued a strategy of breaking Turkey's regional isolation by seeking to re-establish economic ties with Saudi Arabia and the UAE. Erdogan's reconciliation with Sisi, MBZ and MBS can be best understood within the framework of realpolitik, as noted by Turkey expert Steven A Cook:

> The Turkish government has come to realize that its ability to impose its will on other regional powers, whether in the Eastern Mediterranean or in its support for Islamist movements across the Middle East, is not limitless. By reconciling with Saudi leaders, Erdogan aims to facilitate unimpeded flow of Turkish goods into the kingdom, explore the potential for new Saudi investments in Turkey,

and open up possibilities for currency swaps with Riyadh, in line with the actions taken by other Gulf governments.[98]

8.3 The current crisis, democracy and Islamism

The changing geopolitical dynamics which encompass the grounds that the AKP, the MB and Ennahda operate may lead us to conclude that we have on our hands three failures for various reasons. Two of the parties studied in this research have been ousted by coups: the MB in Egypt and Ennahda in Tunisia. Meanwhile, the AKP in Turkey, once hailed as an example of Muslim democracy, has become a pillar of illiberalism and the vehicle of a strongman spewing staunch anti-Western rhetoric. This is the convolution that this section must navigate through.

It is true that neither the research design nor the method employed in this book can explain why Ennahda and the MB were deposed or why the AKP became authoritarian. Exogenous factors such as the historical and domestic realities in each country regarding competing societal and political forces, as well as international trends, all contributed to current crisis some of which are not germane to the explanations I seek. Nonetheless, consideration of these issues is unavoidable. First and foremost, the aforementioned trajectory of events, including the failure of democracy and Erdogan's withdrawal of support from the MB and Ennahda when they no longer served his political agenda, aligns with the main argument of this book, which posits that the diffusion process between these actors was not primarily driven by democratic ideals or ideological alignment.

Can we, however, draw any conclusions about Islamists' stance towards democracy from this crisis-ridden picture? The first part of this penultimate section, then, will assess the nature of failures and then briefly apply the discussion of democracy and Islamism to the focus of this book.

The MB fell into disarray after the 2013 coup, suffering its greatest challenge since its founding in Cairo in 1928. Not only are the majority of the leaders now imprisoned in Egypt, but those members in exile members are separated by geography and political standing. Ennahda members have been persecuted since Tunisia president Kais Saeid took office in 2019 and suspended the parliament in 2021. The ousting of the MB in Egypt and Ennahda in Tunisia, as well as the rejection of their policies while in power – whether because they were authoritarian, too Islamist and therefore unappealing to secular and non-Muslim constituencies or incompetent in meeting the needs of their societies –

will undeniably have repercussions within these movements and other Islamist entities in the Muslim world. Similarly, the AKP's authoritarianism and recent turmoil in the Turkish economy will have detracted from the success story that many around the world accepted after the AKP came to power. Then, it can be denoted that we have three Islamist entities that managed to ascend to power but failed to govern, failed to integrate into existing domestic and international systems – however flawed they may be normatively – and failed to comply with democratic norms. Hence, the Islamist parties were tested in power and normatively vanquished. In other words, the Islamist movements that are the focus of this research attempted to follow in the AKP's footsteps to achieve success but failed to maintain power. This would be a hasty and superficial analysis – a masked *non sequitur* – of any political situation, let alone these complex developments.

I also do not consider crises as 'definitive and irrevocable' spaces in which only binary alternatives are permitted: 'success or failure, right or wrong, life or death, and finally, salvation or damnation'.[99] I prefer Koselleck's suggestion that crisis is 'an iterative periodizing concept'[100] whose guiding principle does not have to be progress,[101] as defined by modernization theory.

Mohammad Morsi's attempts to bestow 'himself and the Islamist-dominated assembly writing Egypt's new constitution, extraordinary new powers'[102] in 2012 were attributed to the despotic and totalitarian core of Islamism. Put another way, the argument went that any Islamist in power would put Islam's dogmas into practice; hence, an appropriation of state apparatus was inevitable.[103] However, retrospective analyses of Morsi's brief rule concluded that 'Morsi was no Mandela, but he was no autocrat either [. . .] and that Egypt under Morsi was undergoing a remarkably ordinary transition, neither wholly autocratic nor wholly democratic, falling almost exactly at the mean value of political transitions globally'.[104]

At this point, it is crucial to reflect on the limitations of the transitology framework that has been applied to the Arab Uprisings. This post-Cold War framework assumes that specific conditions, such as economic well-being, social pluralism and market-oriented economies, would naturally lead to a process of democratization.[105] However, this approach has been challenged by scholars like Carothers, who argue that it has yielded limited success in promoting democracy globally[106] whether in Latin America, the Balkans or Africa.

The democracy promotion community, often influenced by US policy advisers, has heavily relied on this transition paradigm and its institutional checklists. Yet, the reality is that few examples exist worldwide, including in

Latin America, the Balkans and Africa, where this paradigm has resulted in successful democratization and nation-building. It is important to recognize the diverse trajectories that have emerged from the Arab Uprisings, with different states taking unique paths that do not fit neatly into a binary framework of authoritarian restoration or democratization.[107] Therefore, it is essential to move beyond rigid paradigms and theories that fail to capture the complex dynamics and diverse outcomes of the post-Uprisings era. Exploring alternative approaches and contextual factors specific to each country's circumstances will provide a more comprehensive understanding of the complex processes at play.

The MB faced several challenges that contributed to its struggles in governing Egypt. First, it failed to effectively respond to the rapidly evolving economic and political landscape of the country. Second, its lack of experience in governance became evident, as it struggled to transition from an opposition movement to a ruling party. Third, the MB's approach remained rooted in protest and opposition tactics, which hindered its ability to effectively govern. Lastly, the organization was unable to restructure itself as a conventional political party, which further impeded its ability to adapt to the new political context.[108]

Attributing the MB's difficulties solely to Islamism would be oversimplifying the situation. It was true that the MB could not 'modify its ideology to adapt to Egypt's new environment after the January Uprisings' but this was partly 'because ideologies don't change overnight [but rather] take years, if not decades to be internalized within a movement's structure'.[109] This challenge is not unique to the MB but rather a common characteristic of ideological movements, as ideologies typically require significant time and internalization within the structure of a movement to undergo substantial changes.

In terms of consolidating the Islamist base, the AKP never had to compete with the Salafi whereas both Ennahda and the MB had to adapt their discourse and strategy in response to Salafi elements in their respective societies. Additionally, Egypt experienced increased sectarian tensions between Copts and Muslims following the fall of the regime, with apprehensions rising among Copts after Islamist actors, such as the MB, came to power. This exacerbated existing contention between the two communities, fuelled by a power vacuum and uncertainties surrounding the Islamist-led government. In comparison, neither Tunisia nor Turkey witnessed the same level of sectarian conflict escalating into violence. Finally, the MB's time in power was short-lived, making it challenging to assess definitively whether the symbols and tactics passed from the AKP to the MB would have been successful in the long term.

Two former Egyptian ministers, Yehia Hamed and Salah Abdel Maqsoud, deny that the Morsi government acted fast or recklessly. Wickham's interviews revealed a similar consensus within the MB: 'To be fair, all the Brotherhood and FJP leaders I interviewed stressed Morsi did invite several prominent secular and progressive Islamic leaders to join the government in various capacities, whether as vice presidents, as members of the President's Advisory Team or as cabinet ministers but virtually all of these overtures were rebuffed.'[110]

For Maqsoud, Morsi's presidency was too short to disrupt the regime in a way that would justify the secular and liberal fears:

> What did we do in eight months? Did we bring in *sharia* law? Did we force all women to wear the hijab? Did we cut off the hands of criminals? No, we did none of these. As the FJP, we opened our doors to everyone in Egypt. The FJP's deputy secretary-general was a Christian. There is a misunderstanding about the MB. We do not want to impose *sharia* by force. We would listen to the people to see if they want *sharia*. But secularists and the regime realized that if elections were to be free, they would never stand a chance against the Islamists. So, they collaborated with the army.[111]

In a similar vein, 'I want someone to cite one incident where Dr Morsi or his government has enacted any legislation that showed that the government is pro-religious people and against secular people. Please don't talk to me about fears of the future. They are imaginary,'[112] said former minister Hamed.

Hamed's view of the attitudes of the intelligentsia chimes with some of the academic writing on Egypt. For example, El Fadl asserts that 'Egypt's intelligentsia betrayed the revolution that they claimed to celebrate and support'[113] contending that 'the secularized intellectuals whether on the right or left adopted and promoted the claim that the Islamists were brought into power by the United States to implement an American agenda in the region'[114] and calling the Morsi government's legitimacy into question. Thus, the intelligentsia remained silent in the face of a military takeover in 2013.

Conversely, there is a valid argument that whatever the strategy adopted, the Morsi government was doomed to fail from the start: the *ancien régime* would never have let the MB rule the country. This is a view with which almost all Egyptian interviewees retrospectively agree. As to what triggered the military intervention, some pointed to closing the parliament, some to the denial of Shater's presidential nomination and some to the media furore that erupted following an Islamist attack in August 2012 on the Egyptian military's compound in the Sinai Peninsula, killing sixteen soldiers.

A similar conclusion can be drawn regarding Ennahda's downfall from government. It was not solely a result of its own shortcomings but was also influenced by President Saied's power grab, which affected Tunisian democratic institutions as a whole. It is important to remember that Ennahda took steps to address public concerns during its tenure, such as resigning from the government in 2014 in response to public outrage following the assassinations of leftist politicians. Additionally, the party declared in 2016 that it had transitioned from being an Islamist party to a Muslim democratic one, as discussed in the final section of Chapter 5. However, it is acknowledged by Ennahda's leaders that the party faced challenges in effectively governing and addressing Tunisia's long-standing economic issues. Nevertheless, these failures cannot be solely attributed to Ennahda's perceived incompetence or its Islamist character. The complex economic and governmental challenges faced by Tunisia are multifaceted and extend beyond the actions and ideology of a single political party.

The AKP's case is complex and cannot be easily categorized as a failure. Despite deviating from the model that once made it an example for other Islamist entities, the AKP continued to win elections and maintain power. However, significant changes took place in Turkey's political landscape, particularly through constitutional amendments in 2011 and 2017 that consolidated power in Erdoğan's hands. These changes undermined institutional checks and balances, leading to a more authoritarian governance structure.

Furthermore, the AKP experienced internal rifts, causing fragmentation among political actors associated with Islamism.

Erdoğan parted ways with senior members of the AKP who were intrinsic to its foundational ethos. Among them was the former president, Abdullah Gül, former prime minister and the brain behind Turkey's foreign policy during the Arab Uprisings, Ahmet Davutoğlu, and Ali Babacan, the former Minister of Economy who was trusted by the West and seen as implementing an appropriate financial regime in compliance with supranational financial institutions. Both Davutoğlu and Babacan have founded political parties – *Gelecek Partisi* (The Future Party) and *Deva Partisi* (The Democracy and Progress Party) respectively – and criticize Erdoğan's authoritarian and economic policies while highlighting corruption and injustice. The AKP has thus become an oligarchic party under Erdoğan, heedless of what constitutes and what violates legitimate political conduct. It also formed a transactional coalition with the ultra-nationalist party *Milliyetçi Hareket Partisi* (the MHP – The Nationalist Movement Party) and is filled with individuals who bind their political and economic well-being to that of Erdoğan. The current rhetoric of

Erdoğan and the AKP has both Islamist and hard-line nationalist undertones. Progress reports from the European Parliament and Commission cite the deterioration of press freedom and failure to fully meet the Copenhagen Criteria. In effect, we have witnessed the rise and fall of the Turkish model as observed through the transformation of the AKP during its tenure in power since 2002.

The AKP's authoritarian practices raise questions about the initial argument associating post-Islamism with democratic values.[115] Some critics argue that conceptualizations of post-Islamism, such as those by Roy and Bayat, are based on modernization theory and reflect the West's desires rather than the reality within Islamist movements. However, I disagree with these assertions. Neither Roy nor Bayat claim that Islamists fully embrace democracy, free speech and equal rights for women and minorities. They instead highlight a shift in the strategy and goals of Islamist politicians. Bayat also acknowledges the incoherence of the post-Islamist project and its ambivalence towards individual rights and liberties.[116] I view the post-Islamist paradigm as a dynamic and evolving concept, influenced by globalization and neoliberal governance. Its features are not fixed but subject to change and redefinition over time.

Furthermore, the AKP's shift towards authoritarianism cannot be solely attributed to its religious sensibilities. Secular governments, too, are capable of engaging in undemocratic behaviour, especially when bolstered by economic success, regional influence and weak opposition.[117] The AKP's authoritarianism does, therefore, negate the concept of post-Islamism but rather underscores the complex and challenging relationship between post-Islamist parties and democracy.

Bayat believes that compatibility between Islam and democracy is not a matter of philosophy but of politics:

> The pertinent question is not whether Islam and democracy are compatible (least of all because of the contested meanings attached to both Islam and democracy) but rather how and under what conditions Muslims can make their religion compatible with desired notions of democracy, how they can legitimise and popularise an inclusive reading of their doctrine in the same way that democrats have been struggling to broaden the narrow (white, male, propertied and merely liberal) notion of democracy.[118]

For Islamists democracy is a matter of debate and circumstance. However, the main factor here is not Islam. As Brumberg writes, 'For democracy to have any hope in the Arab world, it is not Islam that must be fixed, but politics itself.'[119]

On this matter, neither Islamists nor their secular but authoritarian counterparts have been able to demonstrate convincingly their democratic credentials.[120]

The governance patterns observed in the MENA region are not unique but rather part of a broader global trend. Similar dynamics can be observed in various political systems and regimes worldwide, where illiberal and authoritarian forms of rule have gained traction. The rise of illiberal populist parties and leaders in Europe, India, Russia and Latin America has fuelled discussions about a potential era of post-democracy.[121] The state-capturing strategies employed by the AKP and Erdogan in Turkey bear resemblance to those seen in other countries, such as Viktor Orban's Fidesz in Hungary or Jaroslaw Kaczynski's PiS in Poland.[122] This broader context highlights that the challenges to democracy and the rise of illiberalism extend beyond the Islamist context and are part of a global phenomenon. It emphasizes the need to analyse these trends in a comparative perspective, considering the shared characteristics and strategies employed by illiberal leaders across different regions.

The AKP cannot be seen as the sole representation of Islamism, despite its significant role within the broader journey of Islamism over the past 150 years. Different perspectives exist regarding the AKP's place in Turkish society. Secular factions view the AKP as the true face of Islamism, openly shaping the state and society in religious terms. On the other hand, some Islamists perceive the AKP's rule as a manifestation of neoliberal conservatism and a departure from the principles of Islamism. Similarly, interpreting the AKP's experience in power yields contrasting viewpoints. From one perspective, it can be seen as a success story if the main objective of Islamism is to attain and solidify state power. However, it is also viewed as a profound disappointment by those concerned about the AKP's adoption of authoritarian tools to suppress opponents and its embrace of neoliberal tactics that prioritize integration into the global system over justice and equality, which are fundamental aspects of Islamist politics.[123]

Critics, including Islamist theologian Kırbaşoğlu, argue that the AKP's main focus has become the preservation of the capitalist system to facilitate the unfair accumulation of wealth by President Erdoğan and his associates. 'This is against the core of Islam', he states, 'so, what is left of Islam or Islamism in the AKP?' he asks. 'Only ablution and prayer five times a day. Those are not enough even to qualify as Muslims.'[124]

Türköne suggests that the AKP missed a historic opportunity by transforming into a dictatorial regime, leading to a loss not only for Turkey's Islamist tradition but also for other Islamist movements worldwide that drew inspiration from the AKP model. Similar sentiments can be applied to the Muslim Brotherhood's experience in power, although it was never hailed as a model for other Islamist movements.

In conclusion, my intention has not been to make presuppositions about the inherent democratic or undemocratic nature of Islamist actors, nor to definitively determine the compatibility of Islam with democracy. Rather, I have sought to highlight the ideological flexibility of Islamism through its political evolution following the Arab Uprisings.

During this period, Islamism incorporated political elements influenced by Enlightenment values. In theory, there is no inherent obstacle to extending this borrowing to include democracy. However, the realization of such a synthesis depends on the dominance of democratic traditions to which Islamist movements must adapt themselves and their ideologies. Presently, this adaptation has not been fully realized in the political landscape of the Middle East and North Africa.[125] The complex relationship between Islamism and democracy remains an ongoing and evolving phenomenon, subject to various contextual factors and the interplay of political forces. By exploring the transformations and challenges faced by Islamist movements in power, I aim to shed light on the multifaceted nature of Islamism.

9

Conclusion

The sink, the cooker and Islamism

I have, in this book, told a story of two sets of relations between major Islamist movements/parties – the AKP – MB/FJP and the AKP – Ennahda – during and after the Arab Uprisings, and provided a snapshot of Islamist aspirations and ways of defining and overcoming crises. As structuralist Barrington Moore suggests, it is a utopian ideal of the social sciences to explain all questions arising from a topic. It is fruitless and 'dodges the main issue: what is worth knowing'[1] and what is possible to know. Thus, 'change is what requires explanation'.[2]

I endeavoured to elucidate the transformative evolution of Islamist objectives through a concentrated examination of the interconnections between the AKP-Ennahda and AKP-MB relationships. The primary focus of the research involved an assessment of the concept of success as a strategic objective for Islamists, investigating how the pursuit of success impacts the fundamental principles of Islamism as an ideological framework. Additionally, it explored the wider contextual framework encompassing the assimilation of neoliberal governance models into Islamist political frameworks. Furthermore, this study presented innovative empirical evidence concerning the ambitions and aims of Islamist actors who assumed power subsequent to enduring decades of repression.

Islamism emerged with the premise of addressing the multifaceted crises afflicting Muslim societies: the crisis of colonialism, the crisis of identity, the crisis of being left behind, and the crisis of post-colonial nation-building. Its central argument posited that Islam, as an all-encompassing divine system boasting a superior political model, cultural code, legal framework, and economic arrangement,[3] possessed the capacity to effectively tackle these challenges. Nonetheless, the quest for purely Islamic remedies to the contemporary political, economic and cultural exigencies proved inadequate and incomplete. This inadequacy was attributable to two primary factors: the dearth of innovative intellectual contributions from Islamist politicians and thinkers, and the pervasive influence of international dynamics and repressive regimes, which consistently impeded the natural flow of social and political life within the MENA region. The domestic and international affairs of Islamist movements and the reasons behind their success or failure are highly contentious and often politicized.[4]

In the aftermath of the downfall of regimes in Tunisia and Egypt, Turkey positioned itself as a natural leader for the MB and analogous Sunni Islamist movements in the Arab world. By demonstrating that a populist Sunni Islamist party could secure dominance through free elections, implement relatively successful economic policies and govern a significant regional power, Turkey sought to assert its leadership.[5] Erdoğan's recalibration of Turkey's foreign policy towards the MENA, along with the country's economic and developmental assistance to the MB and Ennahda, was primarily motivated by economic and military considerations. These geopolitical motives were intertwined with Turkey's energy dependency[6] and economic aspirations, rather than a concerted effort to establish an ideological-based order or spearhead Islamic activism. As evident from Erdoğan's subsequent attempts to disassociate his party from the predicaments arising from its support of the MB and Ennahda, the purported ideological common ground between the AKP, Ennahda and the Muslim Brotherhood was contingent upon its instrumental value.

Contrary to prevailing assumptions, contemporary Islamists perceive the concept of *ummah* through what could be termed a realist lens,[7] wherein Muslim solidarity assumes an emotional nature rather than serving as a determinant of foreign policy interests. It transforms into a 'loose universal Muslim consciousness'.[8] While it holds true that emotions can serve as a driving force for activism, it is worth noting that Muslims can be mobilized even by Islamist movements primarily focused on attaining power within specific national contexts, particularly when issues affecting Muslims in other countries are at stake.[9] However, this activism is also characterized by fragmentation along sectarian lines and is limited to national economic and political interests. This is exemplified by the notable 'inaction of countries such as Saudi Arabia, Iran, Pakistan, Turkey, Malaysia, and Indonesia in response to China's repressive measures against its Muslim Uyghur population'.[10]

Hence, the notion of *ummah* is redefined as a symbolic Muslim community that presents the potential for the establishment of a confederation or union comprising nation-states with Muslim-majority populations. Eickelman and Piscatori describe this redefinition as the localization of Muslim transnationalism, which does not lead to 'denationalization as one might assume from certain perspectives within transnational literature'.[11] On the contrary, within Muslim transnationalism, interactions across borders may actually reinforce states and local identities rather than undermine them.[12]

Both Ennahda and members of the Muslim Brotherhood who engaged with the AKP consistently emphasized their national and Islamist credentials. They asserted that their objective was to acquire practical knowledge and experience from the AKP, while highlighting that the close relationship forged after the 2011 uprisings was only possible because the AKP respected the sovereignty of Tunisia and Egypt, refraining from interfering in their domestic politics. Although ideological proximity served as the catalyst for the diffusion process between the parties involved, the driving forces behind this process were utilitarian calculations and the convergence of interests, specifically the desire to construct a success narrative by and for Islamists, rather than ideology or grand visions.

I argue that a new spirit of Islamism emerged from the 1990s until the aftermath of the Arab Uprisings, driven by the dual pressures of neoliberalism and internal crises within the Islamist movement. The Arab Uprisings served as a catalyst, crystallizing the disillusionment of young individuals with established ideologies such as secular liberalism, Marxism and traditional Islamism. The youth within the MB and Ennahda found it difficult to identify with their leaders and instead sought an alternative path – 'some form of post-Islamist third way – a more critical, open, and inclusive polity'.[13]

In the 1990s, capitalism, through the discourse of management, responded to critiques and was perceived as an egalitarian endeavour. It functioned as a tool for legitimizing a system undergoing a crisis. Conjointly, management discourse possessed a prescriptive nature, enabling it to rationalize profit-making as desirable and innovative.[14] By juxtaposing these two dimensions of managerialism with the diffusion process, I have attempted to demonstrate the interplay between them, which aimed to legitimize Islamist actors through a prescriptive formula, indicating a novel spirit in Islamist politics. The pursuit of success – defined in this study as 'winning elections', 'assuming power', 'staying in power', 'service to the people' and 'economic growth' – was depicted as a 'manageable' goal. This contribution to the existing literature sheds light on the evolving dynamics of Islamist politics.

Within the emerging paradigm of the new spirit of Islamism, two interconnected objectives have gained prominence: success and *sharriya* (legitimacy). This can be observed in the speeches and actions of prominent Islamist leaders. An illustrative example is the late Egyptian president,

Mohammad Morsi, who, in his final speech before the military coup in 2013, recurrently emphasized the concept of '*shariyya*' – 59 times within 45 minutes – as he asserted that the people were the ultimate source of authority. Morsi aimed to establish his legitimacy as the rightful holder of state power, asserting that the military did not possess such legitimacy.[15] The concept of legitimacy was also employed during pro-Morsi demonstrations in June 2013, where banners displayed slogans such as 'Legitimacy is a red line' and 'There is no alternative to legitimacy'. These slogans underscored the significance of legitimacy as a fundamental principle within the Islamist discourse and the determination of Islamist supporters to uphold it.

The emphasis on legitimacy by Islamist leaders highlights its crucial role as a cornerstone of their political claims and aspirations. It serves to establish their authority and to assert the will of the people as the basis for their legitimacy, reinforcing the importance of popular support and constitutional frameworks within the Islamist discourse.

Erdoğan also contextualizes all the major setbacks and challenges faced by his party, his power – and even to AKP's mother movement, *Milli Görüş* – within the legitimacy frame.

He asserts that those who advocated for the resignation of the legitimate government led by Necmettin Erbakan on 28 February 1997, eventually witnessed the triumph of the will of the people.[16]

In July 2008, when the AKP faced a close call, narrowly avoiding the closure of the party and the banning of its key figures from politics by a single vote within Turkey's highest court, Erdoğan repeatedly emphasized the strength derived from the people.

Erdoğan's emphasis on the concept of legitimacy, rooted in the will of the people, became particularly pronounced during discussions surrounding events such as the Gezi protests and corruption investigations against Erdoğan's family and cabinet on 17 December 2013. Pro-AKP columnists noted that Erdoğan recognized the importance of legitimacy within the Western framework of democracy, leading him to frequently stress the legitimacy of a government that obtains its mandate from democratic elections and the support of the people.[17] Furthermore, Erdoğan called on the West to defend democracy and voiced support for Egypt's Morsi government, describing it as 'an elected and legitimate administration'.[18]

Following the seizure of power by Tunisian president Kais Saied and the subsequent dissolution of parliament, a heated exchange regarding 'political legitimacy'[19] unfolded between Saied and Ghannouchi, among others.

Ghannouchi denounced Saied's actions as 'a coup against legitimacy', expressing opposition to the move. Riad Al-Shuaibi, a political adviser to Ennahda, asserted the party's commitment to peaceful protests aimed at restoring 'constitutional legitimacy'.[20] In response to President Saied's decision to prosecute members of the dissolved parliament, including Ghannouchi, for their alleged involvement in illegal meetings and conspiracy against the state, Ennahda released a written statement condemning the decision and stressing 'the legitimacy of the parliament'.[21]

Legitimacy has always held a crucial position within Islamist discourse, although its application and context have undergone transformations. At the turn of the twentieth century, Islamists perceived Western dominance and colonization as inherently illegitimate. Even after the departure of Western powers, the struggle persisted as newly formed nation-states adopted European models and were governed by secular authoritarian regimes supported by the West. Islamists viewed these regimes as remaining dependent on colonial powers and, as a result, fundamentally lacking legitimacy. Additionally, the perceived illegitimacy stemmed from these regimes' embrace of Western-style governance systems, which were considered man-made and based on nationalist, socialist or capitalist principles.

Prominent Islamist thinkers such as Qutb and Maududi advocated for the concept of 'hakimiyya Allah' or God's sovereignty, as they saw it as a remedy for Western materialism, which they viewed as a primary contaminant that enslaved individuals to their passions and consumerism while fostering competition and individualism. They believed that God's sovereignty would serve as a protective shield for society against the negative consequences of capitalism.[22] Qutb's Islamism rested upon three foundational pillars: the primacy of divine *sharia* over human law, the pursuit of social justice over materialism and the establishment of revolutionary Muslim societies in contrast to what he perceived as ignorant and pre-Islamic societies (*jahiliyya*).[23] These pillars highlight the core tenets of Qutb's Islamist ideology, emphasizing the dichotomy between divine law and human law, the pursuit of social justice against materialistic values and the vision of transforming Muslim societies through revolutionary means.[24] By advocating for God's sovereignty and these pillars, Islamists aimed to challenge the perceived illegitimacy of existing governing systems and promote an alternative framework based on Islamic principles.

By the beginning of the twenty-first century, there was a noticeable shift in how Islamists understood the concept of sovereignty for God. It began to be interpreted 'in the newly dominant terms of neoliberalism, as a form of economic or social management devoid of old-fashioned'.²⁵ What was previously attributed to the divine sphere was now being transferred to the realm of electoral politics. Being part of a 'manmade government' in a capitalist system or employing the concept of legitimacy within the framework of a majoritarian interpretation of democracy, where the ballot box is considered the primary source of legitimacy, was no longer questioned. An example of this transformation can be observed in the case of the Muslim Brotherhood. Their age-old slogan of 'Islam is the solution' was adapted to the new paradigm, as demonstrated by the FJP's (Freedom and Justice Party) official newspaper at the end of 2011. The slogan was modified to 'Elections are the solution (*al-intikhabat hiyya al-hal!*)',²⁶ reflecting the growing emphasis on the electoral process as the means to achieve their objectives.

This shift signifies a departure from the earlier Islamist discourse centred on divine sovereignty and the rejection of man-made systems. This evolution reflects the broader influence of neoliberal ideas and the incorporation of electoral processes within the Islamist framework.

To achieve their goals of crisis evasion and legitimacy, Islamist groups such as the MB, Ennahda and the AKP employed the conceptual frames of 'the Turkish model' and 'Muslim/conservative democracy'. These frames can be understood as picture frames that help focus attention by specifying what is relevant and what is not, delineating what is within the frame and what is outside of it in relation to the object of focus.²⁷ In this case, the frames of success through neoliberal policies and economic growth were in focus, while Islamist codes were pushed to the periphery.

The Islamists' repertoire of metaphors, symbols, narratives and rituals to define themselves, depict their rivals and allies, and identify the problems and solutions they proposed²⁸ seemed insufficient to tackle the challenges they faced, leading to their attempt to learn from the experiences of the AKP. In my view, the Islamist movements, particularly the AKP and Ennahda, have delegated their pursuit of 'capturing society' to civil society actors. The emphasis on tactical approaches for success among the Islamist actors examined in this research supports the notion that Islamism's repertoire of solutions, though potentially ambiguous, took a backseat. Additionally, one of the core activities of Islamism, namely preaching *dawa*, was outsourced and individualized through mediums such as television programmes and smartphone applications.

I argue that the absence of Islamist concepts to proactively address forthcoming challenges is a structural issue rather than a concealment of a covert intention to Islamize the state. The MB and Ennahda's efforts to be perceived as legitimate and 'normal' actors resulted in their transformation into political parties conforming to the neoliberal mould, where the state is viewed as a mere machine in a Hobbesian sense. The principle of parsimony underpins my argument here: Islamist entities respond to opportunities for power and success in a similar manner to other contemporary political parties across the ideological spectrum. There is nothing exceptional about their aspirations or methods when opportunities for power arise.

This book underscores that the primary impetus behind the transformation of contemporary Islamist parties lies in their pursuit of success, in other words, economic and political power. Drawing on the definition of capitalism by French historian Fernand Braudel, which includes a drive for both economic and political power along with the suppression of competition,[29] it becomes apparent that Islamists have become conventional capitalist agents.

Similarly, one feature shared by neoliberal systems worldwide is that the government becomes the business itself, with governance reduced to 'an exercise in the technical management of capital [thus ideologically founded politics appear dead], replaced by the politics of interest, entitlement, and identity – three counterpoints of a single triangle'.[30]

Within this triangle, political leaders serve as CEOs of a holding company responsible for governing the conduct of entrepreneurs, whose consumption is regarded as a form of production.[31] In this context, Islamist leaders have followed the well-trodden path and adopted the strategies employed by political leaders in neoliberal contexts. Their political interests, shaped by the surrounding opportunity structures, have compelled them to assume the role of 'CEOs of Islam', treating governance as a business enterprise. For instance, Ibrahim Mansi, an executive member of Jordan's Islamic Action Front (IAF), referred to the neoliberal AKP as the IAF's 'star' model, while the party's general secretary, Muhammad Awad al-Zayyid, stated that the party's primary slogan pledged to govern the country like a business.[32]

Prominent scholar of ideology Michael Freeden's morphological framework, which likens an ideology to a room, offers valuable insights into understanding ideological dynamics. By depicting a room, Freeden emphasizes the existence of non-negotiable core elements that distinguish one ideology from another. Just as a kitchen must have a cooker and a sink, ideologies possess central tenets that are intrinsic and defining. However, adjacent elements, similar to items borrowed from other rooms, can be incorporated into an ideology. True that a kitchen must have a cooker and a sink; however, it can borrow a table and a chair from the dining room or – if it is a contemporary open-plan kitchen that caters to the daily practicalities of its inhabitants – even a couch and television from the living room and perhaps a bookcase from the study. These borrowed items are the adjacent elements of the kitchen. The sink and cooker remain but may be covered. The priorities in the design of the kitchen may change, in that the table may be the centrepiece rather than the cooker, and the permeability with other rooms may continue or increase. These adjacent elements may not be non-negotiable, but they contribute to the overall ideological framework. Freeden proposes four key concepts, often referred to as the 4Ps, to illustrate the internal layout of ideologies: Priority, Proximity, Proportionality and Permeability. Priority refers to the shifting emphasis within an ideology, wherein certain elements take precedence over others.[33] Proximity highlights the interconnectedness of ideas and the borrowing of concepts from other ideologies. Proportionality relates to the relative weight and significance assigned to different conceptual components within an ideology, varying from one ideology to another. Finally, permeability underscores the extent to which ideas from other ideologies are incorporated or adapted. This framework can duly be applied to the analysis of Islamism.

Scholars of ideology, following Marx's perspective, have emphasized the demarcation between religion and ideology, contending that ideologies must be autonomous and separate from religious doctrines when formulating political projects.[34] This viewpoint is rooted in the emergence of ideologies as a modern phenomenon and Marx's stance on the relationship between religion and ideologies. On the other hand, Browers argues that the relationship between Islamism and the Quran as a source of inspiration should not be seen as fundamentally different from, for example, liberalism's relationship with the writings of John Stuart Mill or socialism's engagement with Marx's teachings. It is important to note that the Quran itself provides limited specific political programmes and maxims. The ideologization of the Quran requires significant effort, known as *ijtihad* or independent reasoning, by the *ulama*, resulting in the emergence of multiple interpretations and variants.[35] This is exactly why Islamism should be treated as a modern ideology similar to, for instance, nationalism. The faces, hues, strategies and short-term goals of Islamism may transform as this book attempted to demonstrate, but so do those of all the other macro-, thick-centred ideologies. In essence, the argument put forth is that Islamism should be treated as a modern ideology, subject to the same dynamics of transformation and adaptation as other macro-level ideologies.

According to Freeden's morphological framework, the core objective of Islamism is the Islamization of the state and society, although the prioritization of these objectives may vary among Islamists, and the definition of Islamization itself may evolve over time. Islamist parties, particularly following the Arab

Uprising, have moved away from the ideological absolutism of slogans like 'Islam is the solution' and have embraced a more pragmatic approach to politics.[36]

Ennahda's ideological revision after 2011, which involved redefining the role of Islam and asserting a cultural Islamic identity in their discourse,[37] aligns with the concept of post-Islamism proposed by Bayat. This supports Roy's argument that the unification of religion and politics, exemplified by the idealized Islamic State, is essentially an Islamic myth. In reality, the religious and political spheres remain autonomous.

Roy further suggests that the Islamization of the state and/or society should be understood in the context of modernization. During the Islamic revolution in Iran, for instance, modernization was equated with ethnocentricity and envisioned a linear progression from tradition to secular modernity. However, the understanding and pursuit of Islamization are influenced by the contemporary context and changing conceptions of modernity. The dichotomy between religion and secularism is no longer seen as a rigid binary, as societal shifts call for a more nuanced approach to the relationship between Islam and the state or society.[38]

The evolution of Islamist movements and the varied manifestations of their ideology in different national contexts highlight the dynamic and contradictory nature of Islamism.[39] Within an ideology, coherence can be flexible, and cores can be seen as quasi-contingent foundations that are structurally necessary but open to change in their contents.

There are certainly limits to the extent of the transformation of the core contents and the flexibility of coherence. As Heywood contends, 'there must be a point in which, by abandoning a particularly cherished principle or embracing a previously derided theory, an ideology loses its identity, or perhaps, is absorbed into a rival ideology. Could liberalism remain liberalism if it abandoned its commitment to liberty?'[40] The answer is no.

It would be an overstatement and incongruous to argue that Islamism is detached from its foundational element, Islam. However, the allegiance to Islam may vary in its nature, sometimes being primarily emotional and holding the central position within the ideology but potentially being set aside when designing political strategies.[41] If Islamism is defined as an ideology seeking to establish an Islamic order and a state based on *sharia* law and moral codes, we have observed a departure from these goals in the framework of post-Islamism. Yet an Islamist party or movement can abandon these objectives while remaining Islamist. The appeal and continued presence of Islamist parties in the post-Arab Uprising era, as noted by Bayat, demonstrate that Islamism has not collapsed but rather undergone a metamorphosis. Islamists abandoned their goals of an Islamist state because that 'road was blocked',[42] but they redeployed religious significations in other fields. However, this redeployment can result in a gradual dilution of the original essence of Islamism.[43] Ideological malleability is a decisive attribute that shapes the present political world, but it would also mould that certain ideology's future.[44] Islamism's malleability, the goals and the strategies of the Islamists are 'contingent on opportunity structures [. . .] and dynamics of their interaction with the state and other social and political actors',[45] similar to any other social and political movement.

The contention made here is not one of complete eradication of the core element of Islamism, namely the aspiration to Islamize both the state and society, but rather an assertion that it has diminished in prominence within the current historical context. The transformation of ideological concepts is deeply influenced by the interplay of conventions and the positioning of ideological actors vis-à-vis power dynamics.[46] Consequently, it comes as no surprise that the structure of Islamism has undergone rearrangement, whereby the core concepts pertaining to the Islamization of the state, legislature and subsequently society have been partially or entirely obscured, while the adjacent and peripheral concepts have undergone redefinition.

Using Freeden's kitchen analogy, I argue that the sink and the cooker are no longer the main attractions of 'the Islamist kitchen'. The inhabitants, for now, use the modern services of takeaway or deliveries. There is no cooking, no washing up. The dinner table, borrowed from the living or dining room, is now the centre of the action. The cooker and the sink are still there; if we look closely, we can make out their silhouettes and locations, but they are not in use as they were at the beginning of the twentieth century. The dinner table, in my depiction, represents the neoliberal mindset that rules almost every room in every house in every country. In this context, Islamists are not unique or different. They do not seek to rearrange the entire house nor possess an extensive repertoire of ideas, projects or strategies to do so. They do not position themselves in direct opposition to Western ideals or institutions; rather, they are seen as 'constituting a part of the West's ideological diversity'.[47] While they may not embrace the ideals of secularism, they devote little effort to actively combat them. Their priority lies in cultivating an image of success, even if it requires diluting Islamism's main credos. This emphasis on success serves to quiet the long-standing rumblings that Islamists have failed in their strategy and their attempt to construct an intellectually consistent and credible project.

Notes

Chapter 1

1. Talal Asad, *Secular Translations: Nation-State, Modern Self, and Calculative Reason*, Ruth Benedict Book Series (New York: Columbia University Press, 2019), 2.
2. Avi Spiegel, *Young Islam: The New Politics of Religion in Morocco and the Arab World*, Princeton Studies in Muslim Politics (Princeton: Princeton University Press, 2015).
3. Sean Chabot, 'Dialogue Matters: Beyond the Transmission Model of Transnational Diffusion between Social Movements', in *The Diffusion of Social Movements: Actors, Mechanisms, and Political Effects*, ed. Rebecca Kolins Givan, Kenneth M. Roberts and Sarah Anne Soule (Cambridge: Cambridge University Press, 2010), 100.
4. See Hazem Kandil, *Inside the Brotherhood* (Cambridge: Polity Press, 2015); Khalil al-Anani, *Inside the Muslim Brotherhood: Religion, Identity, and Politics* (New York: Oxford University Press, 2016); Joas Wagemakers, *The Muslim Brotherhood in Jordan* (Cambridge: Cambridge University Press, 2020); Spiegel, *Young Islam*; Anne Wolf, *Political Islam in Tunisia: The History of Ennahda* (London: Hurst & Company, 2017); Rory McCarthy, *Inside Tunisia's al-Nahda Between Politics and Preaching* (Cambridge: Cambridge University Press, 2018); Ceren Lord, *Religious Politics in Turkey: From the Birth of the Republic to the AKP* (Cambridge: Cambridge University Press, 2018); Victor J. Willi, *The Fourth Ordeal: A History of the Muslim Brotherhood in Egypt, 1968–2018* (Cambridge: Cambridge University Press, 2021).
5. A. Kadir Yildirim, *Muslim Democratic Parties in the Middle East*, Indiana Series in Middle East Studies (Bloomington: Indiana University Press, 2016); Quinn Mecham, 'Islamist Parties as Strategic Actors: Electoral Participation and its Consequences', in *Islamist Parties and Political Normalization in the Muslim World*, ed. Quinn Mecham and Julie Chernov Hwang (University of Pennsylvania Press, 2014); Sebnem Gumüşçu, *Democracy or Authoritarianism: Islamist Governments in Turkey, Egypt, and Tunisia* (Cambridge: Cambridge University Press, 2023).
6. Asef Bayat and Linda Herrera, *Global Middle East into the Twenty-First Century* (California: University of California Press, 2021), 4.
7. Maidul Islam, *Limits of Islamism: Jamaat-e-Islami in Contemporary India and Bangladesh* (Cambridge: Cambridge University Press, 2015), 70.
8. Mohammad Abdel Kader, 'Turkey's Relationship with the Muslim Brotherhood', *Al Arabiya*, 14 October 2013.

9. See examples of the discussion within opposition circles: Musa Özuğurlu, 'AKP'nin dış politikası, Suriye ve İhvan', *Sol Haber*, 26 March 2022; 'AKP sözcüsü Ömer Çelik Erdoğan ümmetçilik yapıyor eleştirilerine yanıt verdi', *Cumhuriyet*, 14 May 2021; Sabahattin Önkibar, 'Tayyip'in büyük paniği', *Aydınlık*, 2 December 2013; Erdal Atabek, 'Milletten ümmete geçerken', *Cumhuriyet*, 15 July 2019.
10. See examples from within Islamist and pro-AKP outlets: Murat Zelan, 'Erdoğan artık bizim değil', *Yeni Şafak*, 4 January 2018; 'Erdoğan ümmetin lideri', *Yeni Akit*, 12 August 2014; 'Ümmetin duası Erdoğan'la birlikte', *Yeni Şafak*, 23 June 2018.
11. Bassam Tibi, *Islamism and Islam* (New Haven and London: Yale University Press, 2012), 103.
12. Gilles Kepel, *Away from Chaos: The Middle East and the Challenge to the West* (New York: Columbia University Press, 2020), 161.
13. Gareth Jenkins, 'Islamism in Turkey', in *Routledge Handbook of Political Islam*, ed. Shahram Akbarzadeh (London: Routledge, 2012), 138.
14. Niall Ferguson, 'The Middle East's Next Dilemma', *Newsweek*, 19 June 2011.
15. Amir Taheri, 'Turkey and the neo-Ottoman Dream', *Middle East Spectator*, 5 August 2011.
16. See for more examples of such articles in Burcu Kaya Erdem, 'Adjustment of the Secular Islamist Role Model (Turkey) to the "Arab Spring": The Relationship between the Arab Uprisings and Turkey in the Turkish and World Press', *Islam and Christian–Muslim Relations* 23, no. 4 (2012): 446–9.
17. Dale F. Eickelman and James P. Piscatori, *Muslim Politics*, First edn, Princeton Studies in Muslim Politics (Princeton and Oxford: Princeton University Press, 1996), 163.
18. James P. Piscatori and Amin Saikal, *Islam beyond Borders: The Umma in World Politics* (Cambridge: Cambridge University Press, 2019), 27, 34.
19. Piscatori and Saikal, *Islam beyond Borders*, 1.
20. Aurélie Campana and Cédric Jourde, 'Islamism and Social Movements in North Africa, the Sahel and Beyond: Transregional and Local Perspectives', *Mediterranean Politics* 22, no. 1 (2017): 3–5.
21. S. Sayyid, *A Fundamental Fear: Eurocentrism and the Emergence of Islamism* (London: Zed Books, 2015), 31–51.
22. Olivier Roy, *Globalized Islam: The Search for a New Ummah* (New York: Columbia University Press, 2004), 70.
23. Roy, *Globalized Islam*, 58.
24. Olivier Roy, *The Failure of Political Islam* (London: I.B. Tauris, 1994), 201.
25. Larbi Sadiki, *Routledge Handbook of the Arab Spring: Rethinking Democratization* (London: Routledge, 2016).
26. See Fawaz A. Gerges, *Contentious Politics in the Middle East: Popular Resistance and Marginalised Activism beyond the Arab Uprisings* (Basingstoke: Palgrave

Macmillan, 2015); Lina Khatib and Ellen Lust, *Taking to the Streets: The Transformation of Arab Activism* (Baltimore: Johns Hopkins University Press, 2014).

27 Adam Roberts et al., *Civil Resistance in the Arab Spring: Triumphs and Disasters* (Oxford: Oxford University Press, 2016).

28 See John L. Esposito et al., *Islam and Democracy after the Arab Spring* (New York: Oxford University Press, 2016); Usaama al-Azami, Islam and the Arab Revolutions: The Ulama between Democracy and Autocracy (London: Hurst and Company, 2021); Ferran Izquierdo, John Etherington and Laura Feliu, *Political Islam in a Time of Revolt*, Islam and Nationalism (Basingstoke: Palgrave Macmillan, 2017); Eid Mohamed and Dalia Fahmy, *Arab Spring: Modernity, Identity and Change*, Critical Political Theory and Radical Practice (Basingstoke: Palgrave Macmillan, 2019); Robin B. Wright, *The Islamists Are Coming: Who They Really Are* (Washington, DC: Woodrow Wilson Center Press; United States Institute of Peace Press, 2012).

29 See McCarthy, *Inside Tunisia's al-Nahda*; Wolf, *Political Islam in Tunisia*.

30 Nouri Gana, *The Making of the Tunisian Revolution: Contexts, Architects, Prospects* (Edinburgh: Edinburgh University Press, 2013).

31 See Cihan Tuğal, *The Fall of the Turkish Model: How the Arab Uprisings Brought Down Islamic Liberalism* (Brooklyn: Verso, 2016). Alison Pargeter, *Return to the Shadows: The Muslim Brotherhood and An-Nahda since the Arab Spring* (London: Saqi, 2016).

32 Francesco Cavatorta and Lise Storm, *Political Parties in the Arab World [Electronic Resource]: Continuity and Change* (Edinburgh: Edinburgh University Press, 2018), 1–2.

33 Shadi Hamid, 'Political Party Development before and after the Arab Spring', in *Beyond the Arab Spring: The Evolving Ruling Bargain in the Middle East*, ed. Mehran Kamrava (New York: Oxford University Press, 2014), 132.

34 Michael Freeden, 'The Morphological Analysis of Ideology', in *The Oxford Handbook of Political İdeologies*, ed. Michael Freeden, Lyman Tower Sargent and Marc Stears (Oxford: Oxford University Press, 2015), 130.

35 Freeden, 'The Morphological Analysis of Ideology', 131.

36 Rebecca Kolins Givan, Kenneth M. Roberts and Sarah Anne Soule, eds., *The Diffusion of Social Movements: Actors, Mechanisms, and Political Effects* (Cambridge: Cambridge University Press, 2010), 2.

37 Givan, Roberts and Soule, *The Diffusion of Social Movements*.

38 Everett M. Rogers, *Diffusion of Innovations*, 5th edn (New York and London: Free Press, 2003).

39 Michael J. Willis, 'Morocco's Islamists and the Legislative Elections of 2002: The Strange Case of the Party that did not want to Win', *Mediterranean Politics* 9, no. 1 (2004): 53–81.

40 Nancy Bermeo, 'Democracy and the Lessons of Dictatorship', *Comparative Politics* 24, no. 3 (1992): 277.
41 Bermeo, 'Democracy and the Lessons of Dictatorship', 281.
42 John L. Esposito, Lily Zubaidah Rahim and Nāṣir Qubādzādah, *The Politics of Islamism: Diverging Visions and Trajectories*, Middle East Today (Basingstoke and Hampshire: Palgrave Macmillan, 2017), 15.
43 Feriha Perekli, 'The Applicability of the "Turkish Model" to Morocco: The Case of the Parti de la justice et du developpement (PJD)', *Insight Turkey* 14, no. 3 (2012): 95, 98.
44 Interview with a former foreign policy advisor to the AKP, Oxford, 19 February 2020.
45 Michael J. Willis, 'Evolution not Revolution? Morocco and the Arab Spring', in *Routledge Handbook of the Arab Spring: Rethinking Democratization*, ed. Larbi Sadiki (London: Routledge, 2016), 444.
46 Susanne Hoeber Rudolph, 'Introduction: Religion, States, and Transnational Civil Society', in *Transnational Religion and Fading States*, ed. Susanne Hoeber Rudolph and James P. Piscatori (Boulder: Westview Press, 1997), 36.
47 See Asef Bayat, *Post-Islamism: The Changing Faces of Political Islam* (New York: Oxford University Press, 2013); Wright, *The Islamists Are Coming*; Kamran Bokhari and Farid Senzai, *Political Islam in the Age of Democratization* (New York: Palgrave Macmillan, 2013); Yüksel Taşkın, 'Arap Baharı ve Türkiye'deki İslamcı çevrelere etkileri: Baharımızı kışa çevirtmeyeceğiz', *Birikim Dergisi*, July–August, no. 303–304 (2014); John L. Esposito, Tamara Sonn and John Obert Voll, *Islam and Democracy after the Arab Spring* (New York: Oxford University Press, 2016); Ali Bulaç, *Din ve Siyaset* (İstanbul: İnkilap Yayınevi, 2014); Jenny B. White, *Muslim Nationalism and the New Turks*, Princeton Studies in Muslim Politics (Princeton: Princeton University Press, 2013); Peter G. Mandaville, 'Post-Islamism as Neoliberalisation: New Social Movements in the Muslim World', in *Islam after Liberalism*, ed. Faisal Devji and Zaheer Kazmi (London: Hurst & Company, 2017); Tarek Chamkhi, 'Neo-Islamism in the Post-Arab Spring', *Contemporary Politics* 20, no. 4 (2014): 453–68; Tibi, *Islamism and Islam*; Tuğal, *The Fall of the Turkish Model*.
48 See Olivier Roy, 'The Myth of the Islamist Winter', *New Statesman* 141, no. 5136 (2012): 23–5.
49 Yohanan Benhaim and Kerem Öktem, 'The Rise and Fall of Turkey's Soft Power Discourse', *European Journal of Turkish Studies* 21 (2015): 9.
50 Michel Foucault, Michel Senellart and Graham Burchell, *The Birth of Biopolitics: Lectures at the Collège de France, 1978–79* (Houndmills, Basingstoke, Hampshire and New York: Palgrave Macmillan, 2008), 269.
51 Wendy Brown, *In the Ruins of Neoliberalism: The Rise of Antidemocratic Politics in the West*, The Wellek Library Lectures (New York: Columbia University Press, 2019), 19.
52 Sayyid, *A Fundamental Fear*, xxix.

53 Sayyid, *A Fundamental Fear*, xxx.
54 Andrew Bennett and Jeffrey T. Checkel, *Process Tracing: From Metaphor to Analytic Tool*, Strategies for Social Inquiry (Cambridge: Cambridge University Press, 2015), 7.
55 Alexander L. George and Andrew Bennett, *Case Studies and Theory Development in the Social Sciences*, BCSIA Studies in International Security (Cambridge, MA and London: MIT Press, 2005), 6.
56 T. M. J. Lenz, 'EU Normative Power and Regionalism: Ideational Diffusion and Its Limits', *Cooperation and Conflict* 48, no. 2 (2013): 222.
57 Glenn Adams et al., 'The Psychology of Neoliberalism and the Neoliberalism of Psychology', *Journal of Social Issues* 75, no. 1 (2019): 191.
58 Luc Boltanski, Eve Chiapello and Gregory Elliott, *The New Spirit of Capitalism*, New updated edn (London: Verso, 2018).
59 Bayat, *Post-Islamism*.

Chapter 2

1 Khalil Al-Anani, 'Upended Path: The Rise and Fall of Egypt's Muslim Brotherhood', *The Middle East Journal* 69, no. 4 (2015): 528.
2 Asef Bayat, 'Islamism and Social Movement Theory', *Third World Quarterly* 26, no. 6 (2005): 894.
3 Maidul Islam, *Limitism: Jamaat-e-Islami in Contemporary India and Bangladesh's of Islam* (Cambridge: Cambridge University Press, 2015), 71.
4 Richard C. Martin and Abbas Barzegar, *Islamism: Contested Perspectives on Political Islam* (Stanford: Stanford University Press, 2010), 11.
5 Joel Beinin and Joe Stork, 'On the Modernity, Historical Specificity, and International Context of Political Islam', in *Political Islam: Essays from Middle East Report*, ed. Joel Beinin and Joe Stork (London: Tauris, 1997), 8.
6 Jocelyne Cesari, 'Political Islam: More than Islamism', *Religions* 12, no. 5 (2021): 2–4.
7 Yusuf Al-Qaradawi, *Islamic Awakening between Rejection and Extremism* (International Institute of Islamic Thought, 2007).
8 Abdel Salam Sidahmed and Anoushiravan Ehteshami, *Islamic Fundamentalism*, Twentieth Century Religious Thought (Boulder: Westview Press, 1996), 21.
9 François Burgat, 'From National Struggle to the Disillusionments of "Recolonization": The Triple Temporality of Islamism', in *Political Islam: A Critical Reader*, ed. Frederic Volpi (London: Routledge, 2011), 34.
10 Nazih N. M. Ayubi, *Political Islam: Religion and Politics in the Arab World* (London: Routledge, 1991), 130, 39.
11 Pargeter, *Return to the Shadows*, 17–19.

12 Annette Ranko and Justyna Nedza, 'Crossing the Ideological Divide? Egypt's Salafists and the Muslim Brotherhood after the Arab Spring', *Studies in Conflict and Terrorism* 39, no. 6 (2016): 528.
13 Alison Pargeter, *The Muslim Brotherhood: From Opposition to Power* (London: Saqi, 2013), 47.
14 al-Anani, *Inside the Muslim Brotherhood*, 7.
15 Chris Harnisch and Quinn Mecham, 'Democratic Ideology in Islamist Opposition? The Muslim Brotherhood's "Civil State"', *Middle Eastern Studies* 45, no. 2 (2009): 191.
16 Harnisch and Mecham, 'Democratic Ideology in Islamist Opposition?', 193.
17 Harnisch and Mecham, 'Democratic Ideology in Islamist Opposition?', 202.
18 Carrie Rosefsky Wickham, *The Muslim Brotherhood: Evolution of an Islamist Movement* (Princeton: Princeton University, 2013), 275.
19 Adel Abdel Ghafar Ghafar, Bill Hess, *Islamist Parties in North Africa: A Comparative Analysis of Morocco, Tunisia and Egypt* (Brookings Institution, June 2018), 7.
20 Maria Claret-Campana and Athina Lampridi-Kemou, 'Islamist Forces in Contemporary Egypt: The End of Conventional Dualities', in *Political Islam in a Time of Revolt*, ed. Ferran Izquierdo, John Etherington and Laura Feliu (Basingstoke: Palgrave Macmillan, 2017), 131.
21 Noha Mellor, *Voice of the Muslim Brotherhood: Da'wa, Discourse, and Political Communication* (London: Routledge, 2017), 183–7.
22 Tarek Osman, *Egypt on the Brink: From Nasser to the Muslim Brotherhood*, Updated edn (New Haven: Yale University Press, 2013), 118.
23 Kamal Helbawy, 'The Muslim Brotherhood in Egypt: Historical Evolution and Future Prospects', in *Political Islam: Context versus Ideology*, ed. Khalid Haruub, SOAS Middle East Issues (London: Saqi, 2010), 85.
24 Bayat, *Post-Islamism*, 25.
25 Asef Bayat, 'Arab Revolts: Islamists Aren't Coming!' *Insight Turkey* 13, no. 2 (2011): 9–14.
26 Wickham, *The Muslim Brotherhood*, 280.
27 Kenneth Perkins, 'Playing the Islamic Card: The Use and Abuse of Religion in Tunisian Politics', in *The Making of the Tunisian Revolution*, ed. Nouri Gana (Edinburgh University Press, 2013), 61.
28 Michael J. Willis, *Politics and Power in the Maghreb: Algeria, Tunisia and Morocco from Independence to the Arab Spring* (London: Hurst, 2012), 156.
29 Sayida Ounissi, 'Ennahda from Within: Islamists or "Muslim Democrats"?' in *Rethinking Political Islam*, ed. Shadi Hamid and William F. McCants (New York: Oxford University Press, 2017), 231.
30 Wolf, *Political Islam in Tunisia*, 50.
31 François Burgat, *Face to Face with Political Islam* (London: I.B. Tauris, 2003), 29.
32 Willis, *Politics and Power in the Maghreb*, 166.
33 Wolf, *Political Islam in Tunisia*, 97.

34 McCarthy, *Inside Tunisia's al-Nahda*, 102.
35 Salwa Ismail, *Rethinking Islamist Politics: Culture, the State and Islamism* (London New York: I.B. Tauris, 2006), 138.
36 McCarthy, *Inside Tunisia's al-Nahda*, 120.
37 McCarthy, *Inside Tunisia's al-Nahda*, 104.
38 McCarthy, *Inside Tunisia's al-Nahda*, 120.
39 Monica L. Marks, *Convince, Coerce, or Compromise? Ennahda's Approach to Tunisia's Constitution*, Brookings Doha Center Analysis Paper (February 2014), 2.
40 The role that ijtihads play in the malleability of Islamism as an ideology can be explained like this: 'the distinction between the core and dependent variables, the stable and the flexible constituents of Islam in which [...] duties towards God are classified as part of the immutable core of Islam, while duties towards men – with the exception of a limited number of issues definitively laid down in the Koran Sunna – are subject to change and re-definition through *ijtihad*', in Gudrun Kramer, *Visions of an Islamic Republic: Good Governance According to the Islamists*, ed. Frederic Volpi, Political Islam: A Critical Reader (London: Routledge, 2011), 88–9.
41 Interview with Beşir Atalay, Ankara, 2 August 2019.
42 Mümtazer Türköne, *Doğum ile Ölüm arasında İslamcılık* (İstanbul: Kapı Yayınları, 2012), 171.
43 Wolf, *Political Islam in Tunisia*, 4.
44 Rory McCarthy, 'When Islamists Lose: The Politicization of Tunisia's al-Nahda Movement', *Middle East Journal* 72 (2018): 19.
45 Interview with Rachid Ghannouchi, Tunis, 20 December 2019.
46 Fikret Adaman, Murat Arsel and Bengi Akbulut, 'Neoliberal Developmentalism, Authoritarian Populism, and Extractivism in the Countryside: The Soma Mining Disaster in Turkey', *The Journal of Peasant Studies* 46, no. 3 (2019): 520.
47 Izak Atiyas, Ozan Bakış and Esra Çeviker Gürakar, 'Anatolian Tigers and the Emergence of the Devout Bourgeoisie in the Turkish Manufacturing Industry', in *Crony Capitalism in the Middle East: Business and Politics from Liberalization to the Arab Spring*, ed. Ishac Diwan, M. Adeel Malik and Izak Atiyas (Oxford: Oxford University Press, 2019), 94.
48 Yael Navaro-Yashin, 'The Market for Identities: Secularism, Islamism, Commodities', in *Fragments of Culture: the Everyday of Modern Turkey*, ed. Deniz Kandiyoti and Ayşe Saktanber (London: I.B. Tauris, 2002), 223.
49 Ahmet Insel, 'The AKP and Normalizing Democracy in Turkey', *The South Atlantic Quarterly* 102, no. 2–3 (2003): 296.
50 In Turkey the incidents that led to the fall of Erbakan's government are referred to as a postmodern coup because although there was no military takeover, Erbakan was removed due to his clash with the military.
51 Yael Navaro-Yashin, *Faces of the State: Secularism and Public Life in Turkey* (Princeton and Oxford: Princeton University Press, 2002), 249.

52 Tuğal, *The Fall of the Turkish Model*, 25.
53 Tuğal, *The Fall of the Turkish Model*, 25–7.
54 Interview with Beşir Atalay, Ankara, 2 August 2019.
55 After Erdogan's triumph in the 2023 election, Kalın assumes the role of the newly appointed head of intelligence.
56 İbrahim Kalın, 'The AK Party in Turkey', in *The Oxford Handbook of Islam and Politics*, ed. John L. Esposito and Emad Eldin Shahin (Oxford: Oxford University Press, 2013), 426.
57 Bulaç, *Din ve Siyaset*, 172.
58 Lord, *Religious Politics in Turkey*, 243.

Chapter 3

1 Givan, Roberts and Soule, *The Diffusion of Social Movements*, 3.
2 I employ Herbert A. Simmons' definition of bounded rationality which takes into account the limitations of the decision-making actor both in terms of knowledge and computational capacity. See H. A. Simon, 'Bounded Rationality', in *Utility and Probability*, ed. M. Milgate, J. Eatwell and P. Newman (London: Palgrave Macmillan, 1990), 15.
3 Daniel Kahneman and Shane Frederick, 'Representativeness Revisited: Attribute Substitution in Intuitive Judgment', in Thomas Gilovich and Dale W. Griffin, *Heuristics and Biases: The Psychology of Intuitive Judgment* (Cambridge: Cambridge University Press, 2002), 53.
4 Chabot, 'Dialogue Matters', 100.
5 Both are considered terrorist organizations by the Turkish government.
6 Hamza Türkmen, *İslami Mücadelenin Yeni Dili* (İstanbul: Ekin Yayınları, 2013), 145.
7 Türkmen, *İslami Mücadelenin Yeni Dili*, 140.
8 Türkmen, *İslami Mücadelenin Yeni Dili*, 148.
9 Türkmen, *İslami Mücadelenin Yeni Dili*, 149.
10 Nureddin Şirin, 'Erbakan adı altında Erbakan Hocayı Bitirme Operasyonu', *Tevhid Haber*, 19 July 2010.
11 Maryam Ben Salem, '"God Loves the Rich": The Economic Policy of Ennahda: Liberalism in the Service of Social Solidarity', *Politics & Religion* 13, no. 4 (2020): 701.
12 İsmail Kara, *Cumhuriyet Türkiye'sinde Bir Mesele Olarak İslam 2* (İstanbul: Dergah Yayınları, 2019), 508.
13 Kara, *Cumhuriyet Türkiye'sinde Bir Mesele Olarak İslam 2*, 503–7.
14 Kara, *Cumhuriyet Türkiye'sinde Bir Mesele Olarak İslam 2*, 534–5.
15 Necip Fazıl Kısakürek, *Türkiye'nin Manzarası* (İstanbul: Büyük Doğu Yayınları, 1985), 134–5.

16 Mehmed Kırkıncı, *Hayatım-Hatıralarım* (İstanbul: Zafer Yayınları, 2004), 328–9.
17 Emeti Saruhan, Interview with İhsan Süreyya Sırma, 'İhvan siyaseti Erbakan Hoca'dan öğrendi', *Yeni Şafak*, 1 September 2013.
18 Necip Yavuzer, 'Siyasi Arenada Müslümanlar Erbakan'ı Ne Kadar Tanıdı', *İslami Analiz*, 28 February 2017.
19 Dina Shehata, *Islamists and Secularist in Egypt: Opposition, Conflict, and Cooperation* (New York: Routledge, 2009), 87.
20 Raşid El Gannuşi, *İslam Devletinde Kamusal Vatandaşlık Hakları* (İstanbul: Birleşik Yayıncılık, 1996). A later publication has a slightly different name: Raşid El Gannuşi, *İslam Devletinde Kamusal Özgürlükler* (İstanbul: Mana Yayınları, 2012).
21 Raşid El Gannuşi, *Laiklik ve Sivil Toplum* (İstanbul: Mana Yayınları, 2010); Raşid Gannuşi, *Kur'an ve Yaşam Arasında Kadın* (İstanbul: Mana Yayınları, 2011).
22 Interview with Rachid Ghannouchi, Tunis, 20 December 2019.
23 Mehmet Metiner, *Yemyeşil Şeriat Bembeyaz Demokrasi* (Istanbul: Doğan Kitap, 2004). Cited in Müyesser Yıldız, 'Erdoğan aslına mı rücu etti', *Oda TV*, 13 July 2020.
24 Interview with Rachid Ghannouchi, Tunis, 20 December 2019.
25 Recai Kutan, 'Necmettin Erbakan'ı ve 28 Şubat'ı iyi anlamak-1', *Milli Gazete*, 27 February 2020.
26 Joel Campagna, 'From Accomodation to Confrontation: The Muslim Brotherhood in the Mubarak Years', *Journal of International Affairs* 50, no. 1 (1996): 278–304.
27 'Dünyanın lideri', *Milli Gazete*, 11 April 2014.
28 William M. Hale, *Turkish Foreign Policy, 1774–2000* (London: Frank Cass, 2000), 304.
29 Muhammed Nabil Helmy, 'Amr Musa'nın Hatıralarında Arap Siyaseti', *Şarkul Avsat*, 21 September 2017.
30 'a'laqat al-ikhwan al-muslimin bi'turkiya', Ikhwanwiki.
31 'a'laqat al-ikhwan al-muslimin bi'turkiya', Ikhwanwiki.
32 Interview with Rachid Ghannouchi, Tunis, 20 December 2019.
33 Ezgi Başaran, Interview with Necmettin Erbakan, 'Zekamı ölçmeye makina dayanmaz', *Radikal*, 2 January 2011.
34 Ezgi Başaran, *Frontline Turkey: The Conflict at the Heart of the Middle East* (London: I.B. Tauris, 2017), 58.
35 Mehdi Ben Hamida, 'al-islam al-siyasi: al-tajribat al-turkyiat wa'ltajribat al-tunisiyat?', *Al Hiwar*, 6 April 2014.
36 'Erbakan'ın cenazesine kimler katılacak', *Takvim*, 28 February 2011.
37 Tobias Böhmelt et al., 'Party Policy Diffusion', *American Political Science Review* 110, no. 2 (2016): 399.
38 Böhmelt et al., 'Party Policy Diffusion', 398–9.
39 Pietro Marzo, 'Critical Junctures, Path Dependence and Al-Nahda's Contribution to the Tunisian Transition to Democracy', *The Journal of North African Studies* 24, no. 6 (2019): 917.

40 Böhmelt et al., 'Party Policy Diffusion', 400.
41 Böhmelt et al., 'Party Policy Diffusion', 401.
42 Daniel Rodgers, 'Bearing Tales: Networks and Narratives in Social Policy Transfer', *Journal of Global History* 9, no. 2 (2014): 308.
43 Ihsan Dağı, 'Post-Islamism a la Turca', in *Post-Islamism: The Changing Faces of Political Islam*, ed. Asef Bayat (New York: Oxford University Press, 2013), 71–2.
44 Cihan Tuğal, 'Religious Politics, Hegemony, and the Market Economy: Parties in the Making of Turkey's Liberal-Conservative Bloc and Egypt's Diffuse Islamization', in *Building Blocs: How Parties Organize Society*, ed. Cedric De Leon, Desai Manali and Cihan Tuğal (Palo Alto: Stanford University Press, 2015), 88.
45 Mona El-Ghobashy, 'The Metamorphosis of the Egyptian Muslim Brothers', *International Journal of Middle East Studies* 37, no. 3 (2005): 391.
46 Aron Buzogány, 'Illiberal Democracy in Hungary: Authoritarian Diffusion or Domestic Causation?' *Democratization: Clusters of Authoritarian Diffusion and Cooperation: The Role of Interests vs. Ideology?* 24, no. 7 (2017): 1310.
47 Doug McAdam, J. McCarthy and M. Zald, 'Introduction: Opportunities, Mobilizing Structures, and Framing Processes – Toward a Synthetic, Comparative Perspective on Social Movements', in *Comparative Perspectives on Social Movements: Political Opportunities, Mobilizing Structures, and Cultural Framing*, ed. Doug McAdam, J. McCarthy and M. Zald (Cambridge: Cambridge University Press, 1996), 6.
48 Vivien A. Schmidt, 'Taking Ideas and Discourse Seriously: Explaining Change through Discursive Institutionalism as the Fourth "New Institutionalism"', *The European Political Science Review* 2, no. 1 (2010): 3.
49 McAdam et al., 'Introduction: Opportunities, Mobilizing Structures, and Framing Processes', 16.
50 Justin A. Hoyle, 'A Matter of Framing: Explaining the Failure of Post-Islamist Social Movements in the Arab Spring', *Digest of Middle East Studies* 25, no. 2 (2016): 204.
51 Sidney G. Tarrow, *The New Transnational Activism*, Cambridge Studies in Contentious Politics (New York and Cambridge: Cambridge University Press, 2005), 63.
52 David A. Snow and Scott C. Byrd, 'Ideology, Framing Processes, and Islamic Terrorist Movements', *Mobilization (San Diego, Calif.)* 12, no. 2 (2007): 124.
53 Snow and Byrd, 'Ideology, Framing Processes, and Islamic Terrorist Movements', 126.
54 Kevin Gillan, 'Understanding Meaning in Movements: A Hermeneutic Approach to Frames and Ideologies', *Social Movement Studies* 7, no. 3 (2008): 248.
55 David A. Snow, 'Framing Processes, Ideology, and Discursive Fields', in *Blackwell Companion to Social Movements*, ed. David A. Snow, Sarah Anne Soule and Hanspeter Kriesi (Malden: Blackwell, 2004), 399.

56 Gillan, 'Understanding Meaning in Movements', 257.
57 Snow and Byrd, 'Ideology, Framing Processes, and Islamic Terrorist Movements', 130.
58 Gillan, 'Understanding Meaning in Movements', 258.
59 J. L. Esposito, Lily Zubaidah Rahim and Naser Ghobazadeh (eds), 'Transformations', in *The Politics of Islamism: Diverging Visions and Trajectories* (Basingstoke, Hampshire: Palgrave Macmillan, 2017), 270.
60 Interview with Yehia Hamed, Istanbul, 30 July 2018 and interview with Fethi Ayadi, Tunis, 18 November 2019.
61 Yalçın Akdoğan, *AK Parti ve Muhafazakar Demokrasi* (İstanbul: Alfa Yayınları, 2004).
62 Yüksel Taşkın, 'Hegemonizing Conservative Democracy and the Problems of Democratization in Turkey: Conservatism Without Democrats?' *Turkish Studies* 14, no. 2 (2013): 294.
63 '2023 Siyasi Vizyon: Muhafazakâr Demokrat Siyasi Kimlik', AK Parti.
64 Esposito, Sonn and Voll, *Islam and Democracy*, 37.
65 Taşkın, 'Hegemonizing Conservative Democracy and the Problems of Democratization in Turkey', 294.
66 Interview with Ali Bulaç, İstanbul, 20 December 2021.
67 Bayat, *Post-Islamism*, 9.
68 Bayat, 'Arab Revolts: Islamists Aren't Coming!' 13.
69 Seyla Benhabib, 'The New Legitimation Crises of Arab States and Turkey', *Philosophy & Social Criticism* 40, no. 4–5 (2014): 351.
70 Faisal Devji and Zaheer Kazmi, *Islam after Liberalism* (London: Hurst & Company, 2017), 9.
71 Saad Eddin Ibrahim, 'Toward Muslim Democracies', *Journal of Democracy* 18, no. 2 (2007): 9.
72 Rachid Ghannouchi, *al-huriyyat al- 'ammah fi al-dawla al-islamiyya* (Beirut: Markaz Dirasat Al-Arabiyya, 1993).
73 Nazek Jawad, 'Democracy in Modern Islamic Thought', *British Journal of Middle Eastern Studies* 40, no. 3 (2013): 327.
74 Azzam Tamimi, *Rachid Ghannouchi: A Democrat within Islamism* (Oxford and New York: Oxford University Press, 2001), 198.
75 Tamimi, *Rachid Ghannouchi: A Democrat within Islamism*, 198.
76 Tamimi, *Rachid Ghannouchi: A Democrat within Islamism*, 198.
77 Jawad, 'Democracy in Modern Islamic Thought', 328.
78 Interview with Ali Larayedh, Tunis, 18 November 2019.
79 Interview with Rafek Abdesselam, Tunis, 20 December 2019.
80 Interview with Maha Somrani, telephone, 8 May 2020.
81 Interview with Khalil Amiri, telephone, 23 December 2019.

82 More explanations on this period and how the AKP advised Ennahda on this issue are included in Chapter 5.
83 Assia Atrous, 'Erdogan... lam taeud al-namudhaj al-matlub', *Assabah*, 6 October 2012.
84 Interview with Oussama Sagheir, telephone, 12 November 2019.
85 Derya Göçer and Marc Herzog, 'Turkey and the Arab Uprisings', in *Routledge Handbook of the Arab Spring: Rethinking Democratization*, ed. Larbi Sadiki (London: Routledge, 2016), 509.
86 Tuğal, *The Fall of the Turkish Model*, 4.
87 Tuğal, *The Fall of the Turkish Model*, 4.
88 Fatima Sajjad and Umbreen Javaid, 'The Civilizational Rift and the Idea of the Turkish Model: A Case Study (2002-2014)', *Journal of Political Studies* 23, no. 1 (2016): 138.
89 Sajjad and Javaid, 'The Civilizational Rift and the Idea of the Turkish Model', 141.
90 Sajjad and Javaid, 'The Civilizational Rift and the Idea of the Turkish Model', 143.
91 McCarthy, 'When Islamists Lose', 370.
92 Anne Wolf, 'An Islamist "Renaissance"? Religion and Politics in Post-revolutionary Tunisia', *The Journal of North African Studies* 18, no. 4 (2013): 560.
93 Monica Marks, 'Tunisia's Islamists and the "Turkish Model"', *Journal of Democracy* 28, no. 1 (2017): 2.
94 Interview with Abdelkarim Harouni, Tunis, 19 December 2019.
95 Interview with Naofel Jamali, Tunis, 12 November 2019.
96 Interview with Meherzia Labidi, Tunis, 16 November 2019.
97 'Kapatma kararı Washington'da tartışıldı', *Habertürk*, 16 May 2008.
98 Harnisch and Mecham, 'Democratic Ideology in Islamist Opposition?', 195.
99 'Egypt's Muslim Brotherhood and the AKP in Turkey', Ikhwanweb, 29 August 2008.
100 Interview with Amr Darrag, İstanbul, 18 July 2018.
101 Nathan J. Brown, 'When Victory Becomes an Option: Egypt's Muslim Brotherhood Confronts Success', Carnegie Endowment for International Peace (2012): 14.
102 Hesham Al-Awadi, *The Muslim Brothers in Pursuit of Legitimacy: Power and Political Islam in Egypt under Mubarak* (London: I.B. Tauris, 2014), 164.
103 Wickham, *The Muslim Brotherhood*, 281.
104 Hesham Sallam, 'Obsessed with Turkish Models in Egypt', *Jadaliyya*, 30 June 2013.
105 Willi, *The Fourth Ordeal*, 259.
106 'Egypt: FJP Launches Official Party Newspaper', *Ikhwanweb*, 22 October 2011. Also see the first page of the newspaper in Appendix Figure 1.
107 'Frequently Asked Questions', FJP Online, cited in Marie Vannetzel, 'Confronting the Transition to Legality', in *Egypt's Revolutions: Politics, Religion, and Social Movements*, ed. Bernard Rougier and Stéphane Lacroix (Basingstoke: Palgrave Macmillan, 2016), 47.
108 Willi, *The Fourth Ordeal*, 256.

109 Tobias Schumacher, 'The European Union and Democracy Promotion', in *Routledge Handbook of the Arab Spring: Rethinking Democratization*, ed. Larbi Sadiki (London: Routledge, 2016), 560.

110 Raoudha Ben Othman, 'European Union Democracy Promotion in Tunisia', in *Routledge Handbook of the Arab Spring: Rethinking Democratization*, ed. Larbi Sadiki (London: Routledge, 2016), 603.

111 Benhaim and Öktem, 'The Rise and Fall of Turkey's Soft Power Discourse', 6.

112 Halit Mustafa Tagma, Elif Kalaycioglu and Emel Akcali, '"Taming" Arab Social Movements: Exporting Neoliberal Governmentality', *Security Dialogue* 44, nos. 5–6 (2013): 376.

113 Jörg Huffschmid, *Economic Policy for a Social Europe: A Critique of Neo-liberalism and Proposals for Alternatives* (Basingstoke: Palgrave Macmillan, 2005), 24.

114 Zsuzsa Ferge, 'European Integration and the Reform of Social Security in the Accession Countries', *European Journal of Social Quality* 3, no. 1/2 (2001): 14.

115 Ferge, 'European Integration', 16.

116 Ferge, 'European Integration', 19.

117 Ferge, 'European Integration', 20.

118 T. M. J. Lenz and Kalypso Nicolaidis, 'EU-topia? A Critique of the European Union as a Model', *Culture, Practice & Europeanization* 4, no. 2 (2019): 92–5.

119 Menderes Çınar, 'From Moderation to De-moderation: Democratic Backsliding of the AKP in Turkey', in *The Politics of Islamism: Diverging Visions and Trajectories*, ed. J. L. Esposito, Lily Zubaidah Rahim and Naser Ghobazadeh (Basingstoke, Hampshire: Palgrave Macmillan, 2017), 148.

120 Roy, *Globalized Islam*, 70.

121 Roy, *Globalized Islam*, 75.

122 Huffschmid, *Economic Policy for a Social Europe*, 3.

123 David Harvey, *A Brief History of Neoliberalism* (Oxford: Oxford University Press, 2005), 163.

124 Emel Akçalı, 'Introduction: Neoliberal Governmentality and the Future of the State in the Middle East and North Africa', in *Neoliberal Governmentality and the Future of the State in the Middle East and North Africa*, ed. Emel Akçalı (Basingstoke, Hampshire: Palgrave Macmillan, 2015), 3.

125 Aktas, 'The Rise and the Fall of the Turkish Economic Success Story under AKP (JDP)', *Dynamics of Muslim Life* 11, no. 2 (2017): 176–7.

126 Raymond A. Hinnebusch, 'Political Parties in MENA: Their Functions and Development', *British Journal of Middle Eastern Studies: Political Parties in the Middle East: Historical Trajectories and Future Prospects* 44, no. 2 (2017): 172.

127 Elisabeth Gidengil and Ekrem Karakoç, 'Which Matters More in the Electoral Success of Islamist (successor) Parties – Religion or Performance? The Turkish Case', *Party Politics* 22, no. 3 (2016): 326, 35.

128 Interview with Rachid Ghannouchi, Tunis, 20 December 2019.

Chapter 4

1. Kemal Kirişci, 'The Transformation of Turkish Foreign Policy: The Rise of the Trading State', *New Perspectives on Turkey* 40 (2009): 29–56.
2. 'Recep Tayyip Erdoğan Storms Out of Davos after Clash with Israeli President over Gaza', *The Guardian*, 30 January 2009.
3. Interview with Ali Larayedh, Tunis, 18 November 2019.
4. Interview with Ajmi Lourimi, Tunis, 18 November 2019.
5. 'İstanbul'da Filistin konferansı', *Hürriyet*, 23 May 2009.
6. Interview with Bassem Khafagi, İstanbul, 31 July 2018.
7. Mensur Akgün, Sabiha Senyücel Gündoğar, Jonathan Levack and Gökçe Perçinoğlu, 'The Perception of Turkey in the Middle East 2010', TESEV Foreign Policy Programme, İstanbul, February 2011, 7.
8. Çınar, 'From Moderation to De-moderation: Democratic Backsliding of the AKP in Turkye', 149.
9. TBMM 37th Assembly *minutes*, 14 December 2011.
10. Richard Falk, 'Turkey's Brilliant Statecraft: The Achievement of Ahmet Davutoğlu', *Foreign Policy Journal*, 19 November 2011.
11. Kubilay Arin, 'Turkish Think Tanks, the AKP's Policy Network from Neo-Gramscian and Neo-Ottoman Angles', *Center for Turkish Studies Occasional Paper Series*, Book 4, 2015.
12. Interview with Ahmet Davutoğlu, Ankara, 20 August 2019.
13. 'Erdoğan ısrarlı: Kriz teğet geçecek', *Big Para Hürriyet*, 3 April 2009.
14. Tuğal, 'Religious Politics', 119.
15. Interview with high-level Turkish bureaucrat 2.
16. Interview with Metin Turan, İstanbul, 25 July 2018.
17. Mustafa Al-Labbad, 'Egypt and Turkey: Future Horizons', *Ahram*, 19 September 2011.
18. 'İşte Türkiye'nin Mısır'a yaptığı yardım', *Vatan*, 5 July 2013.
19. Doga Ulas Eralp, *Turkey as a Mediator: Stories of Failure and Success* (Pennsylvania: Lexington Book, 2016), 45.
20. 'Erdogan Mursi görüşmesi sona erdi', *Habertürk*, 30 September 2012.
21. Interview with former AKP MP 2.
22. Alper Y. Dede, 'The Arab Uprisings: Debating the Turkish Model', *Insight Turkey* 13, Issue 2 (2011): 26.
23. Uğur Ergan, 'Tarihi ziyaret için yoğun güvenlik', *Hürriyet*, 19 November 2012.
24. 'Erdoğan'dan Mübarek'e: Halka kulak ver', *CNN Turk*, 2 February 2011.
25. 'İstanbul Mısır Konsolosluğu önünde eylem', *CNN Turk*, 3 February 2011.
26. 'Mısır'dan bir kez daha 'Bize karışmayın!', *Oda TV*, 8 February 2011.
27. 'Merhaba to Cairo Mr. Gul', *Egyptian Chronicles*, 4 March 2011.
28. Interview with Mehmet Akif Ersoy, Istanbul, 23 July 2018.
29. Interview with Mehmet Akif Ersoy, Istanbul, 23 July 2018.

30 Appendix, Figure 2.
31 Tülay Karadeniz and Yasmin Saleh, 'Turkish PM Throws Weight behind Arab Cause', *Reuters*, 13 September 2011.
32 'Erdoğan Mısır'da sevinç gösterileriyle karşılandı', *BBC Türkçe*, 13 September 2011.
33 Appendix Figure 3.
34 Steven Cook, 'Egypt and Turkey: Nightmares', *CFR Blog*, 25 November 2013.
35 'Al'ashrt masa'a', YouTube.
36 'Laiklik her dine eşit mesafede', *Hürriyet*, 15 September 2011.
37 Interview with Ayman Nour, Istanbul, 16 July 2018.
38 Brown, 'When Victory Becomes an Option', 15.
39 'Laiklik mesajı Müslüman Kardeşler'i çok kızdırdı', *Vatan*, 15 September 2011.
40 Interview with high-level bureaucrat 1.
41 The first source is a person close to the Al Banna family, whom I had met in the winter of 2017 in the UK. The second source is the former Cairo correspondent of Turkey's news agency, Anadolu Ajansı (AA), Metin Turan. The third source is journalist Can Dündar's 6 July 2013 interview with Saif Al-Islam Al-Banna, in which Banna mentions Erdoğan sitting in the exact place where Dündar was.
42 Kandil, *Inside the Brotherhood*, 536.
43 Wickham, *The Muslim Brotherhood*, 256.
44 Brown, 'When Victory Becomes an Option', 6.
45 Interview with Amr Darrag, İstanbul, 18 July 2018.
46 Pargeter, *Return to the Shadows*, 42.
47 'İHH Başkanı Fehmi Bülent Yıldırım, AKP'nin Mısır ve Suriye politikalarını eleştirdi', *Oda TV*, 23 January 2015.
48 Interview, Istanbul, April 2022.
49 Interview with Wadah Khanfar, London, 6 December 2018.
50 Interview with former AKP MP 2, 3 August 2018.
51 Eralp, *Turkey as a Mediator*, 45.
52 Interview with Ahmet Davutoğlu, İstanbul, 20 August 2019.
53 'Kongrede ağır konuklar', *IHA*, 30 September 2012.
54 'Mısır Cumhurbaşkanı Muhammed Mursi Ak Parti 4. Kongresine katıldı', *YouTube*, 30 September 2012.
55 'Mursi AKP'nin mitinginde', *Cumhuriyet*, 17 May 2015.
56 'Erdoğan Tunus'ta sloganlarla karşılandı', *Al Jazeera Türk*, 20 September 2011.
57 'Turkey's Erdogan Makes a Case for Islam and Democracy in Tunisia', *France 24*, 15 September 2011.
58 'Turkey's Erdogan Makes a Case for Islam and Democracy in Tunisia'.
59 'Bir Müslüman laik ülke yönetebilir', *Hürriyet*, 16 September 2011.
60 Interview with Ajmi Lourimi, Tunis, 18 November 2019.
61 Interview with Lotfi Zitoun, telephone, 14 May 2020.
62 Interview with Sayyida Ounnisi, telephone, 11 May 2020.

63 Arienne Bonzon, 'Turquie- Tunisie, la filiation de l'AKP', *Slate*, 3 February 2011.
64 'An al-awan ki yagharaf al-al'amaghniyyun an li-tunis awladaan kathir', *Al Manar*, 26 October 2011.
65 Rory McCarthy, 'Al-Nahda: From Preaching Circles to Politics', *The Middle East in London* 14, no. 1 (2018): 374.
66 Interview with Beşir Atalay, Ankara, 2 August 2019.
67 Emma C. Murphy, 'The Tunisian Elections of October 2011: A Democratic Consensus', *The Journal of North African Studies* 18, no. 2 (2013): 238.
68 Interview with Beşir Atalay, Ankara, 2 August 2019.
69 Murphy, 'The Tunisian Elections of October 2011', 240.
70 Tuğal, *The Fall of the Turkish Model*, 177.
71 İpek Yezdani, 'No Need for Secularism in Tunisia: Ghannouchi', *Hurriyet Daily News*, 24 December 2011.
72 Dış politika kronolojisi, *Türkiye Cumhuriyeti Dışişleri Bakanlığı*, January 2012.
73 'SETA Panel: Arap Baharı, Tunus ve Türkiye', *SETA*, 11 January 2012.
74 'SETA Panel: Arap Baharı, Tunus ve Türkiye'.
75 Interview with Ajmi Lourimi, Tunis, 18 November 2019.
76 Fuad Ferhavi, 'Abdullah Gül'ün Tunus Ziyareti: Ekonomik Öncelik ve Bölgesel Eksen İhtiyacı', *USAK Analiz*, 19 (2012): 4.
77 'Cumhurbaşkanı Gül Tunus'ta', *Anadolu Ajansı*, 9 March 2012.
78 'Türkiye ile Tunus arasında yeni iş birliği anlaşması', *Haber 7*, 17 July 2012.
79 Interview with Ali Larayedh, Tunis, 18 November 2019.
80 Interview with Meherzia Labidi, Tunis, 12 November 2019.
81 Interview with Fethi Ayadi, Tunis, 18 November 2019.
82 Wolf, *Political Islam in Tunisia*, 144.
83 Wolf, *Political Islam in Tunisia*, 150.
84 Wolf, *Political Islam in Tunisia*, 166.
85 Interview with Fethi Ayadi, Tunis, 18 November 2019.
86 Abd El Jalil Tamimi, 'ziyarat erdogan li Tounes wa al mawakef al baessa li bathi al kiadat al siyassiya', *Hakaek*, 20 December 2017.
87 Wolf, 'An Islamist "Renaissance"?', 568.
88 Rodgers, 'Bearing Tales', 308.
89 May Darwich, 'Creating the Enemy, Constructing the Threat: The Diffusion of Repression against the Muslim Brotherhood in the Middle East', *Democratization: Clusters of Authoritarian Diffusion and Cooperation: The Role of Interests vs. Ideology?* 24, no. 7 (2017): 1392.
90 Interview with Takouo Lassoued, telephone, 7 May 2020.
91 Francesco Cavatorta and Fabio Merone, 'Moderation through Exclusion? The Journey of the Tunisian Ennahda from Fundamentalist to Conservative Party', *Democratization* 20, no. 5 (2013): 860.

92 Marzo, 'Critical Junctures', 925.
93 Interview with Amr Darrag, İstanbul, 18 July 2018.
94 Bülent Aras, 'The Davutoğlu Era in Turkish Foreign Policy', *Insight Turkey* 11, no. 3 (2009): 127.
95 Aras, 'The Davutoğlu Era in Turkish Foreign Policy', 135.
96 Interview with Ahmed Gaaloul, Tunis, 18 December 2019.
97 Jackie Smith, 'Transnational Processes and Movements', in *The Blackwell Companion to Social Movements*, ed. David A. Snow, Sarah Anne Soule and Hanspeter Kriesi (Malden: Blackwell, 2004), 323.
98 Interview with Sayyida Ounnisi, telephone, 11 May 2020.
99 Interview with Oussama Sagheir, telephone, 12 November 2019.
100 Interview with Nidhal Gharbi, Tunis, 7 May 2020.
101 Interview with Nejmeddine Felhi, Tunis, 19 December 2019.
102 Interview with Talip Küçükcan, İstanbul, 12 July 2018.
103 Interview with Amr Darrag, İstanbul, 18 July 2018.
104 Nancy Bermeo, 'Democracy and the Lessons of Dictatorship', 286.
105 Interview with Talip Küçükcan, İstanbul, 12 July 2018.
106 Talip Küçükcan was a columnist for *Sabah Daily*, as was the former director of SETA, Fahrettin Altun. Another former director, Taha Özhan, was a columnist for the *Daily Star*.
107 Benhaim and Öktem, 'The Rise and Fall of Turkey's Soft Power Discourse', 13.
108 Cited in Benhaim and Öktem, 'The Rise and Fall of Turkey's Soft Power Discourse', 18.
109 'Türkiye'nin hikayesini dünyaya anlatıyor', *Haber 7*, 31 January 2013.
110 Kamal Ben Younes, 'mustashar rayiys al-hukumat al-turkiat: hakdha nanzur 'iilaa mustaqbal ealaqatina mae tunis wasuria warusia', *Assabah*, 5 June 2014.
111 'Tunisie - La nouvelle zone industrielle pilote à Ennahli créera 25 mille emplois', *Rekrute*, 25 February 2013.
112 'Israel Mulls Crackdown on Turkey's Aid Activity in Jerusalem: Report', *I24 News*, 7 July 2018.
113 Interview with Mehmet Akif Ersoy, Istanbul, 23 July 2018.
114 Interview with high-level Turkish bureaucrat 2, 1 August 2018.
115 Givan, Roberts and Soule, *The Diffusion of Social Movements*, 3.
116 Givan, Roberts and Soule, *The Diffusion of Social Movements*, 13.
117 Piscatori and Saikal, *Islam beyond Borders*, 163.
118 Givan, Roberts and Soule, *The Diffusion of Social Movements*, 12.
119 Usaama al-Azami, 'Abdullāh bin Bayyah and the Arab Revolutions: Counter-revolutionary Neo-traditionalism's Ideological Struggle against Islamism', *The Muslim world (Hartford)* 109, no. 3 (2019): 352.

120 Fabio Merone, 'Politicians or Preachers? What Ennahda's Transformation Mean for Tunisia', Carnegie Endowment, January 2019, 4.
121 Interview with Ajmi Lourimi, Tunis, 18 November 2019.
122 'Erdoğan ile Karadavi'nin fotoğrafı yayınlandı', *Yeni Akit*, 20 May 2015.
123 Shaul Bartal, 'Sheikh Qaradawi and the Internal Palestinian Struggle Issues Preventing Reconciliation between Fatah and Hamas and the Influence of the Qaradāwi Era over the Struggle Between the Organizations', *Middle Eastern Studies* 51, no. 4 (2015): 585.
124 al-Azami, 'Abdullāh bin Bayyah and the Arab Revolutions', 346.
125 *al-hurriya wal 'adala*, 29 October 2011, 11, cited in Mellor, *Voice of the Muslim Brotherhood*, 196.
126 Bartal, 'Sheikh Qaradawi and the Internal Palestinian Struggle', 594.
127 Da Ta Banu, 'Constructing the "Arab Spring": News Discourses in Turkish Newspapers', *Global Media Journal* 6, no. 2 (2013): 26.
128 Kadir A. Yıldırım, 'The New Guardians of Religion: Islam and Authority in the Middle East', Baker Institute for Public Policy, March 2019, 18–20.
129 The respondents were given a list of 82 individuals and asked, 'Which of the religious leaders below do you approve of? Please select all that apply.'
130 'İslam dünyasına birkaç Erdoğan lazım', *Yeni Şafak*, 25 June 2010.
131 See 'Dünya Müslüman Alimler Birliği'nin 5. Genel Kurulu İstanbul'da yapıldı', *TRT*, 4 November 2018 and 'Karadavi: Erdoğan İslam için bir umuttur', *Sabah*, 24 April 2016.
132 'Karadavi kararına sert tepki', *Milli Gazete*, 8 December 2014.
133 'Karadavi kararına sert tepki', *Milli Gazete*, 8 December 2014.
134 Tarrow, *The New Transnational Activism*, 106.
135 Tarrow, *The New Transnational Activism*, 105.
136 Sam Cherribi, *Fridays of Rage: Al Jazeera, the Arab Spring, and Political Islam* (New York: Oxford University Press, 2017), 244.
137 Cherribi, *Fridays of Rage*, 245.
138 Wadah Khanfar, 'These Are Crucial Times in Egypt's Transition to Democracy', *Guardian*, 20 May 2012.
139 Wadah Khanfar, 'Al-Jazeera gave Arab Youth a Voice; Gulf Regimes must not Silence It', *Guardian*, 26 June 2017.
140 Birol Başkan, *Turkey and Qatar in the Tangled Geopolitics of the Middle East* (New York: Palgrave Macmillan, 2016), 76.
141 Hakan Albayrak, 'Vaddah', *Yeni Şafak*, 24 September 2011.
142 'Al-Sharq Forum Konferansı İstanbul'da başladı', *Haberler*, 18 March 2017 and 'Ortadoğu ve güvenlik diyalogu: Gençlik Perspektifi Konferansı', *Milliyet*, 26 June 2018, and 'Breaking the Cycle of Crisis in the MENA', *YouTube – Al Sharq Strategic Research Channel*, 9 November 2016.

Chapter 5

1. François Burgat, 'Islam and Islamist Politics in the Arab World: Old Theories, New Facts?', in *Islamist Politics in the Middle East: Movements and Change*, ed. Samer S. Shehata (Abingdon, Oxon and New York: Routledge, 2011), 24.
2. Interview with Sayida Ounissi, telephone, 11 May 2020.
3. Chabot, 'Dialogue Matters', 102.
4. André Bank, 'The Study of Authoritarian Diffusion and Cooperation: Comparative Lessons on Interests versus Ideology, Nowadays and in History', *Democratization: Clusters of Authoritarian Diffusion and Cooperation: The Role of Interests vs. Ideology?* 24, no. 7 (2017): 1348.
5. Tanja A. Börzel and Thomas Risse, 'From Europeanisation to Diffusion: Introduction', *West European Politics* 35, no. 1 (2012): 7.
6. Bennett and Checkel, *Process Tracing*, 7.
7. Börzel and Risse, 'From Europeanisation', 9.
8. Börzel and Risse, 'From Europeanisation', 9.
9. S. K. Das, *Making the Poor Free?* (Delhi: Oxford University Press, 2015), 1.
10. Jonathan Joseph, *The Social in the Global: Social Theory, Governmentality and Global Politics*, Cambridge Studies in International Relations 122 (Cambridge: Cambridge University Press, 2012), 3–4.
11. Arjen Boin, Allan McConnell and Paul Hart, *Governing after Crisis: The Politics of Investigation, Accountability and Learning*, Cambridge Core (Cambridge: Cambridge University Press, 2008), 25.
12. Christopher J. O'Donnell, *Productivity and Efficiency Analysis: An Economic Approach to Measuring and Explaining Managerial Performance* (Singapore: Springer, 2018), 1–54.
13. Raymond Hinnebusch, 'Introduction: Understanding the Consequences of the Arab Uprisings – Starting Points and Divergent Trajectories', *Democratization: From Arab Spring to Arab Winter: Explaining the Limits of Post-uprising Democratisation – Guest Editor: Raymond Hinnebusch* 22, no. 2 (2015): 206.
14. Walter Armbrust, *Martyrs and Tricksters: An Ethnography of the Egyptian Revolution*, Princeton Studies in Muslim Politics 75 (Princeton: Princeton University Press, 2019), 10.
15. Boin, McConnell and Hart, *Governing after Crisis*, 3.
16. Interview with Beşir Atalay, Ankara, 2 August 2019.
17. Murat Somer, 'When Is Normalization Also Democratization? Islamist Political Parties, The Turkish Case and the Future of Muslim Polities', in *Islamist Parties and Political Normalization in the Muslim World*, ed. Julie Chernov and Hwang Quinn Mecham (Philadelphia: University of Pennsylvania Press, 2014), 42.

18 US Embassy (Tunis) cable to State Department, 06TUNIS2298, 'An-Nahda Leader Jebali: Moderate Islamism Is the Future', Confidential//Noforn, 6 September 2006 cited in Wolf, 'An Islamist "Renaissance"?', 567.
19 Quinn Mecham and Julie Chernow Hwag, 'The New Dynamism of Islamist Parties', in *Islamist Parties and Political Normalization in the Muslim World*, ed. Quinn Mecham and Julie Chernov Hwang (Philadelphia: University of Pennsylvania Press, 2014), 180.
20 Quinn Mecham, 'Islamist Parties and Foreign Policy in North Africa: Bridging İdeology and Pragmatism', *The Journal of North African Studies* 24, no. 4 (2019): 656.
21 Max Weber, *Political Writings* (New York: Cambridge University Press, 1994), 350.
22 Weber, *Political Writings*, 341.
23 'Cumhurbaşkanı: Türkiye'nin yeni ve sivil bir Anayasa'yı tartışması değişen şartların kaçınılmaz gereğidir', *Anadolu Ajansı*, 24 March 2020.
24 AK Parti Teşkilatları, AKP.
25 'Cumhurbaşkanı: Türkiye'nin yeni ve sivil bir Anayasa'yı tartışması', *Anadolu Ajansı*.
26 Interview with Mohammed Ali Azaeiz, Tunis, 18 November 2019.
27 Wickham, *The Muslim Brotherhood*, 296.
28 Brown, 'When Victory Becomes an Option', 18.
29 Interview with Amr Darrag, Istanbul, 18 July 2018.
30 McCarthy, 'When Islamists Lose', 369.
31 Interview with a Nahdawi, London, 2019.
32 Charles Kurzman and Ijlal Naqvi, 'Do Muslims Vote Islamic?', *Journal of Democracy* 21, no. 2 (2010): 50–1.
33 Kurzman and Naqvi, 'Do Muslims Vote Islamic', 52.
34 Kurzman and Naqvi, 'Do Muslims Vote Islamic', 54, 55.
35 Kurzman and Naqvi, 'Do Muslims Vote Islamic', 57, 59.
36 Interview with Abdelkarim Harouni, Tunis, 19 December 2019.
37 Interview with Moussa Ben Ahmed, Tunis, 20 November 2019.
38 Interview with Fethi Ayadi, Tunis, 18 November 2019.
39 Interview with Nidhal Gharbi, Tunis, 7 May 2020.
40 Fouad Ajami, 'The Arab Spring at One: A Year of Living Dangerously', *Foreign Affairs* 91, no. 2 (2012): 63.
41 Samer S. Shehata, 'Political Da'wa: Understanding the Muslim Brotherhood's Participation in Semi-authoritarian Elections', in *Islamist Politics in the Middle East: Movements and Change*, ed. Samer S. Shehata (Abingdon, Oxon and New York: Routledge, 2011), 121.
42 Shehata, 'Political Da'wa', 133.
43 Shehata, 'Political Da'wa', 133.
44 Interview with former AKP MP 1, Ankara, 24 July 2018.

45 Interview with former AKP MP 1, Ankara, 24 July 2018.
46 For example, during the Kurdish peace process, which commenced in late 2012, the AKP conducted polls almost every month. In fact, the Kurdish party HDP's then leader, Selahattin Demirtaş, declared that it was primarily because the AKP polls revealed a rise in votes for the Kurdish HDP and a decrease in those for the AKP that Erdoğan decided to halt the peace process. See Ezgi Başaran, 'HDP co-chair Demirtaş reveals details of peace process', *Hürriyet Daily News*, 28 July 2015.
47 Interview with former AKP MP 1, Ankara, 24 July 2018.
48 Appendix, Figure 4.
49 Interview with former AKP MP 2, 3 August 2018.
50 Interview with Metin Turan, İstanbul, 25 July 2018.
51 Interview with Yehia Hamed, Istanbul, 30 July 2018.
52 Interview with Talip Küçükcan, İstanbul, 12 July 2018.
53 Interview with Noureddine Arboui, Tunis, 20 December 2019.
54 Interview with a Nahdawi, London, October 2019.
55 Interview with Ajmi Lourimi, Tunis, 18 November 2019.
56 Interview with Rabeb ben Lotaief, Tunis, 18 November 2019.
57 Interview with Bechir Yousifi, Tunis, telephone, 7 May 2020.
58 Interview with Mohammed Ali Azaiez, Tunis, 18 November 2018.
59 Tobias Böhmelt et al., 'Party Policy Diffusion', 400.
60 Asef Bayat, 'Activism and Social Development in the Middle East', *The International Journal of Middle East Studies* 34, no. 1 (2002): 11.
61 Melani Cammett and Pauline Jones Luong, 'Is There an Islamist Political Advantage?', *Annual Review of Political Science (Palo Alto, Calif.)* 17 (2014): 201.
62 Cammett and Luong, 'Is There an Islamist Political Advantage?', 202.
63 Yusuf El-Karadavi, 'Türkiye'nin yeniden İslam dünyasının merkezi olması için dua ediyoruz', *Sabah*, 4 November 2018.
64 Tuğal, 'Religious Politics', 91.
65 Tuğal, 'Religious Politics', 100.
66 Ihsan Dağı, 'Post-Islamism a la Turca', 90.
67 Interview with Boutheina Ben Yaghlane, telephone, 21 May 2020.
68 Interview with Adel Ben Amor, telephone, 18 May 2020.
69 Jenny B. White, 'Islamist Social Networks and Social Welfare Services in Turkey', in *Islamist Politics in the Middle East: Movements and Change*, ed. Samer S. Shehata (Abingdon, Oxon and New York: Routledge, 2011), 61.
70 Melissa Marschall, Marwa Shalaby and Saadet Konak Unal, 'Municipal Service Delivery, Identity Politics and Islamist Parties in Turkey', POMEP Studies (September 2017), 32. https://pomeps.org/municipal-service-delivery-identity-politics-and-islamist-parties-in-turkey.
71 Interview with Wadah Khanfar, London, 6 December 2018.

72 Interview with Mesut Özcan, Ankara, 24 July 2018.
73 Interview with Mohamed Hgazy, telephone, 9 May 2020.
74 Interview with Yehia Hamed, Istanbul, 30 July 2018.
75 Interview with a former AKP MP 1, Ankara, 24 July 2018.
76 'Türkiye'den Mısır'a 150 adet çöp kamyonu', *Hürriyet*, 28 May 2013.
77 Interview with a Turkish bureacrat, Istanbul, 30 July 2018.
78 Interview with former AKP MP 1, Ankara, 24 July 2018.
79 See Erdoğan's rally in İzmir to promote AKP's candidate before March 2019 local elections: 'CHP yolsuzluk ve çöp demek', *Hürriyet*, 6 January 2019.
80 'AK Parti'nin yeni reklam filmi: Gönül adamı Recep Tayyip Erdoğan', *Takvim*, 11 January 2019.
81 Mehran Kamrava, 'The Rise and Fall of Ruling Bargains in the Middle East', in *Beyond the Arab Spring: The Evolving Ruling Bargain in the Middle East*, ed. Mehran Kamrava (New York: Oxford University Press, 2014), 17.
82 İbrahim Karagül, 'Başbakan Davutoğlu ve Yeni Türkiye Devrimi', *Yeni Şafak*, 22 August 2014.
83 Roy, 'The Myth of the Islamist Winter'.
84 Gary King, Robert O. Keohane and Sidney Verba, *Designing Social Inquiry: Scientific Inference in Qualitative Research* (Princeton: Princeton University Press, 1994), 8–9.
85 Bennett and Checkel, *Process Tracing*, 7.
86 Clayton Roberts, *The Logic of Historical Explanation* (University Park: Pennsylvania State University Press, 1996), 66.
87 Vannetzel, 'Confronting the Transition to Legality', 43.
88 Al-Anani, 'Upended Path', 533.
89 'Ikhwan misr hal', *Al-Madina*, 8 April 2011.
90 Interview with former AKP MP 1, Ankara, 24 July 2018.
91 David D. Kirkpatrick, 'Blow to Transition as Court Dissolves Egypt's Parliament', *New York Times*, 12 June 2012.
92 Interview with former AKP MP 1, Ankara, 24 July 2018.
93 Asef Bayat, 'The Arab Spring and its Surprises', *Development and Change* 44, no. 3 (2013): 591.
94 Shadi Hamid, *Temptations of Power: Islamists and Illiberal Democracy in a New Middle East* (New York and Oxford: Oxford University Press, 2014), 156.
95 Wickham, *The Muslim Brotherhood*, 269.
96 Wickham, *The Muslim Brotherhood*, 270.
97 M. Cherif Bassiouni, *Chronicles of the Egyptian Revolution and its Aftermath: 2011–2016* (Cambridge and New York: Cambridge University Press, 2017), 124.
98 Mohamed Younis, 'Egyptians' Views of Government Crashed before the Overthrow', *Gallup*, 1 August 2013.
99 Interview with senior Turkish diplomat 2, telephone, 1 August 2018.

100 Bassiouni, *Chronicles of the Egyptian Revolution and its Aftermath: 2011–2016*, 125.
101 Tuğal, 'Religious Politics', 97.
102 'Erdoğan: Rüku ve secde dışında eğilmedik', *Haber 7*, 28 February 2012.
103 'Diklenmeden… Dik durduk, sonucu aldık', *Star*, 23 March 2013.
104 Interview with Beşir Atalay, Ankara, 2 August 2019.
105 Aktas, 'The Rise and the Fall of the Turkish Economic Success Story under AKP (JDP)', 176.
106 Aslı Ü. Bali, 'A Turkish Model for the Arab Spring?', *Middle East Law and Governance* 3, Issue 1–2 (2011): 30.
107 Interview with Talip Küçükcan, İstanbul, 12 July 2018.
108 Interview with Mesut Özcan, Ankara, 24 July 2018.
109 Wickham, *The Muslim Brotherhood*, 296.
110 Hamid, *Temptations of Power*, 144, 83.
111 Brown, 'When Victory Becomes an Option', 18.
112 Interview with Ahmet Davutoğlu, İstanbul, 20 August 2019.
113 Interview with former AKP MP 1, Ankara, 24 July 2018.
114 Khaled Abou El Fadl, 'Egypt's Secularized Intelligentsia and the Guardians of Truth', in *Egypt and the Contradictions of Liberalism: Illiberal Intelligentsia and the Future of Egyptian Democracy*, ed. Dalia Fahmy and Daanish Faruqi (Oxford: OneWorld, 2017).
115 Ricardo René Laremont, 'Moving Past Revolution and Revolt: Transitions to Democracy in North Africa', in *Revolution, Revolt and Reform in North Africa: The Arab Spring and Beyond*, ed. Ricardo René Laremont (Abingdon, Oxon and New York: Routledge 2014), 151.
116 Laremont, 'Moving Past Revolution and Revolt', 149.
117 Interview with Tariq Al-Zomor, Istanbul, 6 August 2018.
118 Pargeter, *Return to the Shadows*, 28.
119 Interview with Salah Abdel Maqsoud, Istanbul, 1 August 2018.
120 Robert Springborg, *Egypt* (Cambridge: Polity, 2018), 135.
121 Hazem Kandil, *The Power Triangle: Military, Security, and Politics in Regime Change* (New York: Oxford University Press, 2016), 17.
122 'MİT Müsteşarı Hakan Fidan'a özel görev', *Milli Gazete*, 30 September 2013.
123 'MİT Müsteşarı Mursi'yi uyarmış', *Sabah*, 23 August 2013.
124 Gidengil and Karakoç, 'Which Matters More in the Electoral Success of Islamist (Successor) Parties', 334.
125 Interview with Zeinab Brahmi, Tunis, 19 December 2019.
126 Interview with Ridha Driss, Tunis, 18 November 2019.
127 Marzo, 'Critical Junctures', 921.
128 Interview with Ajmi Lourimi, Tunis, 18 November 2019.
129 Leonardo Morlino, *Democracy between Consolidation and Crisis: Parties, Groups, and Citizens in Southern Europe* (Oxford: Oxford University Press, 1998), 339.

130 Interview with Moussa Ben Ahmed, Tunis, 20 November 2019.
131 Interview with Sayyida Ounnisi, telephone, 11 May 2020.
132 Interview with Lotfi Ziotun, telephone, 14 May 2020.
133 Bülent Karaatlı, *Arap Baharı'nda Farklı Bir Ülke: Tunus* (Ankara: Nobel Yayınları, 2018), 213–14.
134 Antonio Gramsci, Quintin Hoare and Geoffrey Nowell-Smith, *Selections from the Prison Notebooks of Antonio Gramsci* (London: Lawrence & Wishart, 1971).

Chapter 6

1 Anoushiravan Ehteshami, 'Islam as a Political Force in International Politics', in *Islam in World Politics*, ed. Nelly Lahoud and Anthony H. Johns (London: Routledge, 2005), 32.
2 Tarek E. Masoud, *Counting Islam: Religion, Class, and Elections in Egypt*, Problems of International Politics (New York: Cambridge University Press, 2014), 208.
3 Antony Shadid, 'In One Slice of Egypt, Daily Woes Top Religion', *New York Times*, 15 February 2011.
4 M. Abdelrahman, 'A Hierarchy of Struggles? The "Economic" and the "Political" in Egypt's Revolution', *Review of African Political Economy* 39, no. 134 (2012): 616.
5 Mona Atia, 'A Way to Paradise: Pious Neoliberalism, Islam, and Faith-Based Development', *Annals of the Association of American Geographers* 102, no. 4 (2012): 814, www.jstor.org/stable/23275509.
6 Nader Habibi, 'The Economic Agendas and Expected Economic Policies of Islamists in Egypt and Tunisia', Crown Center for Middle East Studies (2012), 2–3.
7 Francesco Cavatorta and Samir Amghar, 'Symposium—Islamism, Islamist Parties, and Economic Policy-Making in the Neo-Liberal Age', *Politics & Religion* 13, no. 4 (2020): 686.
8 'La revanche des arabes', *Le Monde*, 24 February 2011.
9 Olivier Roy, 'The Myth of the Islamist Winter', 25.
10 Walter Armbrust, 'The Revolution against Neoliberalism', in *The Dawn of the Arab Uprisings: End of an Old Order?*, ed. Haddad Bassam, Rosie Bsheer, Ziad Abu-Rish and Roger Owen (London: Pluto Press, 2012), 114.
11 Armbrust, 'The Revolution against Neoliberalism', 115.
12 Akçali, 'Introduction', 2.
13 Adam Hanieh, *Egypt's 'Orderly Economic Transition': Accelerated Structural Adjustment under a Democratic Veneer?*, Centre for Development Policy and Research (SOAS, University of London, July 2011).
14 'Remarks at the Opening Press Conference World Bank Group President Robert B. Zoellick', *World Bank*, 11 April 2011.

15 Gil Eyal, I. Szelényi and E. Townsley, 'The Theory of Post-communist Managerialism', *New Left Review*, no. 222 (1997): 70.
16 Maxime Rodinson, *Islam and Capitalism* (London: Allen Lane, 1974), 155.
17 Mustafa Al-Siba'i, *ishtirakiyat al-islam*, 2nd edn (Damascus: Mu'assasat al-Matba'at Al-'Arabiyah, 1960).
18 Khalil al-Anani, 'Devout Neoliberalism?! Explaining Egypt's Muslim Brotherhood's Socio-Economic Perspective and Policies', *Politics and Religion* 13, no. 4 (2020): 752.
19 Habibi, *The Economic Agendas and Expected Economic Policies of Islamists in Egypt and Tunisia*, 3.
20 Lena Rethel, 'Corporate Islam, Global Capitalism and the Performance of Economic Moralities', *New Political Economy* 24, no. 3 (2019): 351.
21 Ibrahim Saif and Mohammed Abu Rumman, 'The Economic Agenda of the Islamist Parties', Carnegie Endowment Middle East Center (2012), 5.
22 Margherita Picchi, 'Islam as the Third Way: Sayyid Quṭb's Socio-Economic Thought and Nasserism', *Oriente Moderno* 97, no. 1 (2017): 186.
23 Picchi, 'Islam as the Third Way' 188.
24 Picchi, 'Islam as the Third Way' 189.
25 Rethel, 'Corporate Islam, Global Capitalism and the Performance of Economic Moralities', 351.
26 Tagma, Kalaycioglu and Akcali, '"Taming" Arab Social Movements', 379.
27 Cavatorta and Amghar, 'Symposium—Islamism, Islamist Parties, and Economic Policy-Making in the Neo-Liberal Age', 689.
28 Al-Anani, 'Devout Neoliberalism?!', 753.
29 Samir Amin, 'Political Islam in the Service of Imperialism', *Monthly Review* 59, no. 7 (2007): 2–3.
30 Étienne Balibar, 'Absolute Capitalism', in *Mutant Neoliberalism: Market Rule and Political Rupture*, ed. William Callison and Zachary Manfredi (New York: Fordham University Press, 2019), 260.
31 Francesco Cavatorta, 'The Convergence of Governance: Upgrading Authoritarianism in the Arab World and Downgrading Democracy Elsewhere?', *Middle East Critique: The Future of Middle Eastern Political Rule through Lenses of the Past: Revisiting the (first) Era of Post-Democratization* 19, no. 3 (2010): 228.
32 Sarah Babb, *Managing Mexico: Economists from Nationalism to Neoliberalism* (Princeton: Princeton University Press, 2018), 2.
33 Harvey, *A Brief History of Neoliberalism*, 156.
34 Atia, '"A Way to Paradise"', 81.
35 Atia, '"A Way to Paradise"', 814.
36 Edward Webb, 'Changing the Player, Not the Game. Ennahda's Homo İslamicus', *ASPJ Africa & Francophonie* 5, no. 1 (2014): 4.

37　Cavatorta and Amghar, 'Symposium—Islamism, Islamist Parties, and Economic Policy-Making in the Neo-Liberal Age', 691.
38　Aihwa Ong, *Neoliberalism as Exception [Electronic Resource]: Mutations in Citizenship and Sovereignty* (Durham: Duke University Press, 2006), 13.
39　Joel Beinin, 'Political Islam and the New Global Economy: The Political Economy of an Egyptian Social Movement', *The New Centennial Review* 5, no. 1 (2005): 163.
40　Adams et al., 'The Psychology of Neoliberalism and the Neoliberalism of Psychology', 194.
41　Jason Hackworth, 'Religious Neoliberalism(s)', in *Faith Based, Religious Neoliberalism and the Politics of Welfare in the United States* (Athens: University of Georgia Press, 2012), 40.
42　Jean Comaroff and John L. Comaroff, *Millennial Capitalism and the Culture of Neoliberalism* (Durham: Duke University Press, 2001), 23.
43　Hackworth, 'Religious Neoliberalism(s)', 45.
44　Harvey, *A Brief History of Neoliberalism*, 157.
45　Tuğal, *The Fall of the Turkish Model*, 41.
46　Hamid, 'Political Party Development Before and After the Arab Spring', 146.
47　Ishac Diwan, Philip Keefer and Marc Schiffbauer, 'Crony Capitalism in Egypt', in *Crony Capitalism in the Middle East: Business and Politics from Liberalization to the Arab Spring*, ed. Ishac Diwan, M. Adeel Malik and Izak Atiyas (Oxford: Oxford University Press, 2019), 68.
48　Diwan et al., 'Crony Capitalism in Egypt', 85.
49　Interview with Walid by Hazem Kandil, Cairo, 27 March 2013, cited in Kandil, *Inside the Brotherhood*, 114.
50　Unpublished document cited in Kandil, *Inside the Brotherhood*, 112.
51　Kandil, *Inside the Brotherhood*, 112.
52　'mubadara jamaa'a al-Ikhwan al-muslimin lil-ıslaah al-dahili fi misr', *Al Jazeera*, 16 May 2005.
53　Tuğal, 'Religious Politics', 11.
54　Mathieu Rousselin, 'In the Name of Allah and of the Market: The Capitalist Leanings of Tunisian Islamists', *Science & Society* 80, no. 2 (2016): 211.
55　Ben Salem, '"God Loves the Rich"', 706.
56　Ben Salem, '"God Loves the Rich"', 712.
57　Larbi Sadiki, 'Tunisia's Ennahda: Islamists Turning the Learning Curve of Democracy and Civic Habituation', in *The Politics of Islamism: Diverging Visions and Trajectories*, ed. J. L. Esposito, Lily Zubaidah Rahim and Naser Ghobazadeh (Basingstoke, Hampshire: Palgrave Macmillan, 2017), 109.
58　Rousselin, 'In the Name of Allah and of the Market', 208–9.
59　Yıldız Atasoy, *Islam's Marriage with Neoliberalism: State Transformation in Turkey* (London: Palgrave Macmillan, 2009), 109.

60 Rachid Ghannouchi, 'huwl ishkaliya al-barnamaj al-iqtisadi lida al-islamiyyin', *Al Jazeera*, 29 April 2011.
61 'Ennahda Movement Programme for Freedom, Justice, and Development in Tunisia', *Issuu – Ennahda Electoral Programme* (English), 2 October 2011.
62 Habibi, *The Economic Agendas and Expected Economic Policies of Islamists in Egypt and Tunisia*, 5.
63 Ben Salem, '"God Loves the Rich"', 704.
64 Brown, 'When Victory Becomes an Option', 15–16.
65 Rousselin, 'In the Name of Allah and of the Market', 204.
66 Dilek Yankaya, 'Du cadre d'action collective au programme partisan: ancrages patronaux des islamismes en Turquie et en Tunisie', *L'année du Maghreb* (2020).
67 Interview with Amr Darrag, Istanbul, 18 July 2018.
68 Interview with Ridha Driss, Tunis, 18 November 2019.
69 Interview with Amr Darrag, Istanbul, 18 July 2018.
70 Interview with senior Turkish bureaucrat 1.
71 Ziya Öniş, 'The Political Economy of Turkey's Justice and Development Party', in *The Emergence Ofa New Turkey: Islam, Democracy, and the Emergence Oft He Ak Parti*, ed. Hakan Yavuz (Salt Lake City: University of Utah Press, 2006), 208.
72 'Brotherhood asks Al-Azhar to Issue a Fatwa on IMF Loan', *Egypt Independent*, 29 August 2012.
73 Interview with former AKP MP 2.
74 Pargeter, *Return to the Shadows*, 65.
75 David Kirkpatrick, 'Keeper of Islamic Flame Rises as Egypt's New Decisive Voice', *New York Times*, 12 March 2012.
76 Bernard Rougier and Stéphane Lacroix, *Egypt's Revolutions* (Place of publication not identified: Palgrave Macmillan US, 2016), 266.
77 Willi, *The Fourth Ordeal*, 145.
78 Roy, 'The Myth of the Islamist Winter', 24.
79 Babb, *Managing Mexico*, 1.
80 'İstikbal mobilya Kahire'de', *Yeni Şafak*, 5 May 2003.
81 'Sarar Mısır'da mağaza açtı', *Hürriyet*, 3 December 2005.
82 Angela Joya, 'Neoliberalism, the State and Economic Policy Outcomes in the Post-Arab Uprisings: The Case of Egypt', *Mediterranean Politics* 22, no. 3 (2017): 346.
83 Joya, 'Neoliberalism, the State and Economic Policy Outcomes in the Post-Arab Uprisings', 348.
84 Hamid, *Temptations of Power*, 177.
85 'Khairat al-Shater', Hudson Institute, 10 April 2012.
86 'jama'a namaa tunisie', *Assiyasi Net*, 15 March 2011.
87 Marroushi, Nadine, 'Brotherhood Businessman urges Business to Play Role in Development', *Egypt Independent*, 15 April 2012.

88 Öniş, 'The Political Economy of Turkey's Justice and Development Party', 221.
89 '28 Şubat siyasi değildi', *Anadolu Ajansı*, 20 April 2012.
90 Filiz Başkan, 'The Rising Islamic Business Elite and Democratization in Turkey', *Journal of Balkan and Near Eastern Studies* 12, no. 4 (2010): 416.
91 A. Ekber Doğan and Yasin Durak, 'İslami Burjuvazinin Yükselişi ve Neoliberalizmin Toplumsallaştırılması: İki dindar şehrin başarı hikayesinin perde arkası', in *'Yeni Türkiye'ye Varan Yol*, ed. İsmet Akça, Bekmen Ahmet and Özden Barış Alp (İstanbul: İletişim Yayınları, 2018), 304.
92 Gamze Çavdar, 'Islamist New Thinking in Turkey: A Model for Political Learning?', *Political Science Quarterly* 121, no. 3 (2006): 484.
93 Habibi, *The Economic Agendas and Expected Economic Policies of Islamists in Egypt and Tunisia*, 4.
94 Ajami, 'The Arab Spring at One', 63.
95 Ozlem Madi, 'From Islamic Radicalism to Islamic Capitalism: The Promises and Predicaments of Turkish-Islamic Entrepreneurship in a Capitalist System', *Middle Eastern Studies* 50, no. 1 (2014): 148.
96 Nikos Christofis, 'The AKP's "Yeni Turkiye": Challenging the Kemalist Narrative?', *Mediterranean Quarterly: A Journal of Global Issues* 29, no. 3 (2018): 14.
97 Tuğal, *The Fall of the Turkish Model*, 204.
98 Das, *Making the Poor Free?*, 6.
99 Ayşe Buğra, 'The Truth', *Open Democracy*, 25 August 2014.
100 Öniş, 'The Political Economy of Turkey's Justice and Development Party', 217.
101 Tuğal, 'Religious Politics', 99.
102 Tuğal, 'Religious Politics', 100.
103 Marie Vannetzel and Dilek Yankaya, 'Crafting a Business Umma? Transnational Networks of "Islamic Businessmen" after the Arab Spring', *Mediterranean Politics* 24, no. 3 (2019): 297.
104 Vannetzel and Yankaya, 'Crafting a Business Umma?'.
105 Interview with senior Turkish diplomat 1, Skype, 31 July 2018.
106 Wael Gamal, 'Lost Capital: The Egyptian Muslim Brotherhood's Neoliberal Transformation', Carnegie Endowment Middle East Center (2019), 3.
107 Gamal, 'Lost Capital', 4.
108 Yankaya, 'Du cadre d'action collective au programme partisan'.
109 Yankaya, 'Du cadre d'action collective au programme partisan'..
110 Interview with a Tunisian businessman by Dilek Yankaya in April 2018 in 'Du cadre d'action collective au programme partisan'.
111 M. J. Kister, 'Peygamberi'in Pazarı', *Cumhuriyet Üniversitesi İlahiyat Fakültesi Dergisi* 6, no. 2 (2002): 26.
112 'The Prophetic Economy – How an Islamic Economy was Born', *Islamic Finance Guru*, 6 April 2020.

113 Sadiki, 'Tunisia's Ennahda: Islamists Turning the Learning Curve of Democracy and Civic Habituation', 94. Also see prominent Turkish Islamist Ali Bulaç's recent work: Ali Bulaç, *Medine Sözleşmesi* (İstanbul: Çıra Yayınları, 2020).
114 'Ekonomik güç bilgiye sahip olanın elinde toplanıyor', MÜSİAD, 8 November 2019.
115 Vannetzel and Yankaya, 'Crafting a Business Umma?', 298.
116 Vannetzel and Yankaya, 'Crafting a Business Umma?', 299.
117 MÜSİAD Fuar Tanıtım Raporu: Tunus ve Fas, 24–28 June 2012, 4.
118 MÜSİAD Fuar Tanıtım Raporu: Tunus ve Fas, 24–28 June 2012, 9.
119 Melani and Ishac Diwan Cammett, *The Political Economy of the Arab Uprisings* (Boulder: Westview Press, 2014), 19.
120 Güneş Murat Tezcür, *Muslim Reformers in Iran and Turkey: The Paradox of Moderation*, 1st edn (Austin: University of Texas Press, 2010), 46.
121 See Table 2 in Başkan, 'The Rising Islamic Business Elite and Democratization in Turkey', 411.
122 Başkan, 'The Rising Islamic Business Elite and Democratization in Turkey', 409.
123 Bayat, *Post-Islamism*, 11.
124 Vannetzel and Yankaya, 'Crafting a Business Umma?', 304.
125 Vannetzel and Yankaya, 'Crafting a Business Umma?', 291, 94.
126 Marwa Awad, 'Islamist Businessman', *Reuters*, 17 October 2012.
127 Awad, 'Islamist Businessman'.
128 Patrick Haenni, 'The Reasons for the Muslim Brotherhood's Failure in Power', in *Egypt's Revolutions*, ed. Bernard Rougier and Stéphane Lacroix (New York: Palgrave Macmillan, 2016), 28.
129 Haenni, 'The Reasons for the Muslim Brotherhood's Failure in Power', 35.
130 Interview with Ridha Driss, Tunis, 18 November 2019.
131 See Namaa's Facebook page.
132 Bonzon, 'Turquie–Tunisie, la filiation de l'AKP'.
133 Sami Zemni's talk entitled 'The Trajectory of the Tunisian Revolution: Between Continuities and Disjunctures', *The Middle East Centre, St Antony's College*, 18 November 2020.
134 Tuğal, *The Fall of the Turkish Model*, 50, 51, 55.
135 Madi, 'From Islamic Radicalism to Islamic Capitalism', 158.
136 Tuğal, 'Religious Politics', 97.

Chapter 7

1 Adams et al., 'The Psychology of Neoliberalism and the Neoliberalism of Psychology', 197.

2. See Stephanie Lee Mudge, 'What is Neo-liberalism?', *Socio-economic Review* 6, no. 4 (2008): 703–31; Rachel S. Turner, 'Neo-Liberal Constitutionalism: Ideology, Government and the Rule of Law', *Journal of Politics and Law (Toronto)* 1, no. 2 (2008): 47–55; Harvey, *A Brief History of Neoliberalism*.
3. Niamh Stephenson and Dimitris Papadopoulos, 'Exit from the Regime of Life Control: Biopolitics, Anticipatory Risk and the Excess of Experience', *Somatechnics* 1, no. 2 (2011): 418.
4. Foucault, Senellart and Burchell, *The Birth of Biopolitics: Lectures at the Collège de France, 1978–79*, 16.
5. Roy, *Globalized Islam*, 1.
6. J. L. Esposito, Lily Zubaidah Rahim and Naser Ghobazadeh, 'Introduction: Theological Contestations and Political Coalition-Building', in *The Politics of Islamism: Diverging Visions and Trajectories*, ed. J. L. Esposito, Lily Zubaidah Rahim and Naser Ghobazadeh (Basingstoke, Hampshire: Palgrave Macmillan, 2015), 2.
7. Interview with Ali Bulaç, 20 December 2021, Istanbul.
8. M. Cherif Bassiouni, 'Egypt's Unfinished Revolution', in *Civil Resistance in the Arab Spring: Triumphs and Disasters*, ed. Adam Roberts et al. (Oxford: Oxford University Press, 2016), 64.
9. Interview with Beşir Atalay, Ankara, 2 August 2019.
10. Interview with Ahmed Gaaloul, Tunis, 18 December 2019.
11. Interview with Ajmi Lourimi, Tunis, 18 November 2019.
12. Interview with Noureddine Arbaoui, Tunis, 20 December 2019.
13. Roy, *Globalized Islam*, 98.
14. 'Erdoğan'dan Avrupa'daki Türklere: 3 değil 5 çocuk yapın', *Al Jazeera*, 17 March 2017.
15. By 'crazed minority' with a 'hegemonic mindset', Binici crudely refers to Turkey's secular strata.
16. 'AKP'li Mücahit Birinci: Hay atkı kadar başınıza taş düşsün', *Cumhuriyet*, 22 November 2021.
17. Zadie Smith, 'Introduction', in *Recitatif*, ed. Toni Morrison (London: Vintage, 2022), xxxvi.
18. Cesari, 'Political Islam: More than Islamism', 1.
19. Francis Fukuyama, 'The End of History?', *The National Interest* 16 (1989): 3–18.
20. Andrew Heywood, *Political İdeologies: An İntroduction* (London: Palgrave, 2017), 326.
21. Volpi, *Political Islam*, 30.
22. Sadiki, 'Tunisia's Ennahda: Islamists Turning the Learning Curve of Democracy and Civic Habituation', 118.
23. Dale F. Eickelman and James P. Piscatori, *Muslim Politics*, 2nd edn, Princeton Studies in Muslim Politics (Princeton and Oxford: Princeton University Press, 2004), 132.

24 Ehteshami, 'Islam as a Political Force in İnternational Politics', 34.
25 For example, at the beginning of the 2000s, the Italian left, despite reluctant attempts to depart from the Cold War paradigm and 'flirt[ing] more than others with the "end of ideology" argument', realized the need to adapt their discourse to shifting public opinion. See Elisabetta Brighi and Lilia Giugni, 'Foreign Policy and the Ideology of Post-ideology: The Case of Matteo Renzi's Partito Democratico', *The International Spectator* 51, no. 1 (2016): 19–20.
26 Charles Tripp, *Islam and the Moral Economy: The Challenge of Capitalism* (Cambridge: Cambridge University Press, 2006), 11, 9.
27 Bayat, *Post-Islamism*, 28.
28 Daniel Bell, *The End of Ideology: On the Exhaustion of Political Ideas in the Fifties* (Glencoe: Free Press, 1960).
29 Aziz Azmah, *Islams and Modernities*, 22.
30 Bayat, *Post-Islamism*, 8.
31 Bayat, 'The Arab Spring and its Surprises', 599.
32 Michael Freeden, 'Confronting the Chimera of a "Post-ideological" Age', *Critical Review of International Social and Political Philosophy* 8, no. 2 (2005): 255.
33 Carrie Rosefsky Wickham, *Mobilizing Islam: Religion, Activism, and Political Change in Egypt* (New York and Chichester: Columbia University Press, 2003), 36–62.
34 Wickham, *Mobilizing Islam*, 151.
35 Beinin, 'Political Islam and the New Global Economy', 135.
36 Raymond William Baker, *Islam without Fear: Egypt and the New Islamists* (Cambridge, MA and London: Harvard University Press, 2003), 216.
37 Interview with Rachid Ghannouchi, Tunis, 20 December 2019.
38 Devji and Kazmi, *Islam after Liberalism*, 9.
39 Baker, *Islam without Fear: Egypt and the New Islamists*, 216.
40 Asef Bayat and Linda Herrera, *Being Young and Muslim: New Cultural Politics in the Global South and North* (New York and Oxford: Oxford University Press, 2010), 41.
41 Roy, 'The Myth of the Islamist Winter', 25.
42 Roy, *Globalized Islam*, 14, 22.
43 Brown, *In the Ruins of Neoliberalism*, 20.
44 Mojtaba Mahdavi, 'Whither Post-Islamism: Revisiting the Discourse/Movement After the Arab Spring', in *Arab Spring: Modernity, Identity and Change*, ed. Eid Mohamed and Dalia Fahmy (Basingstoke: Palgrave Macmillan, 2019), 16, 26.
45 Mandaville, 'Post-Islamism as Neoliberalisation', 288.
46 Robbert A. F. L. Woltering, 'Post-Islamism in Distress? A Critical Evaluation of the Theory in Islamist-Dominated Egypt', *Die Welt des Islams* 54, no. 1 (2014): 109.
47 Roy, *Globalized Islam*, 97.
48 Roy, *Globalized Islam*, 97.

49　Shaimaa El Naggar, 'The Discursive Construction of Muslim Identities by Contemporary Muslim Televangelists in the West' (ProQuest Dissertations Publishing, 2016), 15.
50　Al-Sayed Zaied, 'Da'wa for Dollars: A New Way of Muslim Televangelist', *Arab Insight* 1, no. 3 (2008): 23–4.
51　Ahmad Najib Burhani, 'Muslim Televangelists in the Making: Conversion Narratives and the Construction of Religious Authority', *The Muslim World: A Quarterly Review of History, Culture, Religions & The Christian Mission in Islamdom* 110, no. 2 (2020): 154.
52　James Bourk Hoesterey, *Rebranding Islam: Piety, Prosperity, and a Self-help Guru*, Studies of the Walter H. Shorenstein Asia-Pacific Research Center (Stanford: Stanford University Press, 2016), 11.
53　Husam Tammam and Patrick Haenni, 'Au diable les loosers! Le succès et l'achievement, nouvelles valeurs islamiques en Égypte', *Mouvements (Paris, France: 1998)* no. 36, no. 6 (2004): 44.
54　Sebnem Gumuscu, 'Class, Status, and Party: The Changing Face of Political Islam in Turkey and Egypt', *Comparative Political Studies* 43, no. 7 (2010): 851.
55　Peter G. Mandaville, *Islam and Politics*, Third edn (London: Routledge, 2020), 291.
56　Haenni and Tammam, 'Penser dans l'au-delà de l'islamisme', *Revue des mondes musulmans et de la Méditerranée* 123 (2008): 179–201.
57　Mandaville, *Islam and Politics*, 292.
58　Boltanski, Chiapello and Elliott, *The New Spirit of Capitalism*, 7.
59　Boltanski, Chiapello and Elliott, *The New Spirit of Capitalism*, 63.
60　Eyal et al., 'The Theory of Post-communist Managerialism', 86.
61　Eyal et al., 'The Theory of Post-communist Managerialism', 87.
62　Boltanski, Chiapello and Elliott, *The New Spirit of Capitalism*, 55.
63　Paula Chakravartty and Sreela Sarkar, 'Entrepreneurial Justice: The New Spirit of Capitalism in Emergent India', *Popular Communication* 11, no. 1 (2013): 60.
64　Tammam and Haenni, 'Au diable les loosers', 45.
65　Bernard Pras, 'Management et islam: Vers une convergence de valeurs', *Revue Française de Gestion* 33, no. 171 (2007): 92–3.
66　Asef Bayat, 'The Coming of a Post-Islamist Society', *Critique: Critical Middle Eastern Studies*, no. 9 (1996): 45.
67　Tammam and Haenni, 'Au diable les loosers', 45–6.
68　Willi, *The Fourth Ordeal*, 157.
69　Florence Bergeaud-Blackler, Johan Fischer and John Lever, 'Introduction: Studying the Politics of Global Halal Markets', in *Halal Matters: Islam, Politics and Markets in Global Perspective*, ed. Florence Bergeaud-Blackler, John Lever and Johan Fischer (London: Routledge, 2015), 8.
70　Willi, *The Fourth Ordeal*, 158.

71 Hoesterey, *Rebranding Islam*, 1, 3, 10.
72 Hoesterey, *Rebranding Islam*, 12.
73 Jeffrey T. Kenney, 'Selling Success, Nurturing the Self: Self-Help Literature, Capitalist Values, and the Sacralization of Subjective Life in Egypt', *The International Journal of Middle East Studies* 47, no. 4 (2015): 664.
74 Kenney, 'Selling Success, Nurturing the Self', 672.
75 Bayat and Herrera, *Being Young and Muslim*, 46.
76 Bayat and Herrera, *Being Young and Muslim*, 20.
77 Asef Bayat, *Revolutionary Life: The Everyday of the Arab Spring* (Cambridge, MA: Harvard University Press, 2021), 241.
78 Amel Boubekeur, 'Post-Islamist Culture: A New Form of Mobilization?', *History of Religions* 47, no. 1 (2007): 77–9.
79 Interview with Malek Chennoufi, telephone, 6 May 2020.
80 Interview with Nejmeddine Felhi, Tunis, 19 December 2019.
81 Cavatorta and Amghar, 'Symposium – Islamism, Islamist Parties, and Economic Policy-Making in the Neo-Liberal Age', 691.
82 Rethel, 'Corporate Islam, Global Capitalism and the Performance of Economic Moralities', 352–4.
83 Esen Kirdiş and Amina Drhimeur, 'The Rise of Populism? Comparing Incumbent Pro-Islamic Parties in Turkey and Morocco', *Turkish Studies* 17, Issue 4 (2016): 604.
84 T.C. Resmi Gazete, *Sayı 28674*, 11 June 2013.
85 Mustafa, Çakır, 'Diyanet İşleri Başkanlığı'nın bütçesi çok sayıda bakanlığı ve idareyi geride bıraktı', *Cumhuriyet*, 15 September 2021.
86 Mandaville, *Islam and Politics*, 178.
87 Bethan McKernan, 'Erdoğan Leads First Prayers at Hagia Sophia Museum Reverted to a Mosque', *Guardian*, 24 July 2020.
88 Volpi, *Political Islam*, 4.
89 Ismail, *Rethinking Islamist Politics*, 172.
90 Asef Bayat, *Making Islam Democratic: Social Movements and the Post-Islamist Turn*, Stanford Studies in Middle Eastern and Islamic Societies and Cultures (Stanford: Stanford University Press, 2007), 9.
91 Ezgi Başaran 'Erdoğan could not Islamize Minds, so He is Islamizing the Stones', *Duvar English*, 21 July 2020.
92 Interview with Mümtazer Türköne, Istanbul, 17 December 2021.
93 Tuğal, 'Religious Politics', 99.
94 Tuğal, 'Religious Politics', 99.
95 Murat Somer, 'Conquering versus Democratizing the State: Political Islamists and Fourth Wave Democratization in Turkey and Tunisia', *Democratization* 24, no. 6 (2017): 1028.
96 Tuğal, 'Religious Politics', 99.

97 Kandil, *Inside the Brotherhood*, 171.
98 Talha Köseoğlu, 'Islamists and the State: Changing Discourses on the State, Civil Society and Democracy in Turkey', *Turkish Studies* 20, no. 3 (2019): 342.

Chapter 8

1 Interview with a Turkish journalist, Istanbul, 7 August 2018.
2 'Saraçhane'de Mısır nöbeti sürüyor', *Genç Dergi*, 29 July 2013.
3 'Rabaa: The Massacre that Ended the Arab Spring', *Middle East Eye*, 14 August 2018.
4 Appendix, Figure 5.
5 Interview with Saliha Eren, Istanbul, 12 July 2018.
6 Appendix, Figure 6.
7 'Rabia işaretiyle Arap dünyasına umut oldu', *Sabah*, 19 August 2013.
8 Appendix, Figure 7.
9 'İdam kararları Mısır Konsolosluğu önünde protesto edildi', *İHH*, 29 April 2013.
10 'Başbakan şehit Esma için ağladı', *Milliyet*, 21 August 2013.
11 'Erdoğan'ı ağlatan mektup', *Hürriyet*, 23 August 2013.
12 'İşte o utanç manşetleri', *Sabah*, 4 October 2015.
13 'Erdoğan: Ben Mursi'nin akıbetine uğrarsam . . .', *T24*, 17 May 2015.
14 Interview with Behlül Özkan, Istanbul, 17 July 2018.
15 Interview with former AKP MP 2.
16 Interview with Saliha Eren, Istanbul, 12 July 2018.
17 See Committee to Protect Journalists (CPJ) report on Turkey.
18 '2018 Democracy Index', *Bianet*, 9 January 2019.
19 Mark Lowen, 'Turkey Brain Drain: Crackdown Pushes Intellectuals Out', *BBC*, 28 December 2017.
20 Kader, 'Turkey's Relationship with the Muslim Brotherhood'.
21 'The Muslim Brotherhood', *MESBAR*, 13 December 2018.
22 'The Muslim Brotherhood', *MESBAR*.
23 İpek Yezdani, 'Egyptian Opposition Establishes Revolutionary Council in Istanbul', *Hurriyet Daily News*, 9 August 2014.
24 'Egyptian Parliament', *Ikhwanweb*, 19 December 2014.
25 Sonia Farid, 'The Brotherhood's Istanbul Conference: Turkey's Message to Egypt', *Al Arabiya*, 18 August 2015.
26 'Muslim Brotherhood Celebrates 90 years of Giving', *Middle East Monitor*, 2 April 2018.
27 al-Azami, 'Abdullah bin Bayyah and the Arab Revolutions', 352–3.
28 'Karadavi: Erdoğan İslam için umuttur', *Sabah*, 24 April 2016.

29 Eric Trager, *Arab Fall: How the Muslim Brotherhood Won and Lost Egypt in 891 Days* (Washington, DC: Georgetown University Press, 2016), 233.
30 Interview with Ayman Nour, Istanbul, 16 July 2018.
31 Murat Sofuoğlu, 'Istanbul: A Haven for Egyptian Journalists in Exile', *TRT World*, 31 March 2018.
32 Shaimaa Magued, 'The Egyptian Muslim Brotherhood's Transnational Advocacy in Turkey: A New Means of Political Participation', *British Journal of Middle Eastern Studies* 45, no. 3 (2018): 480–97.
33 Mokhtar Awad and Nathan Brown, 'Mutual Escalation in Egypt', *Washington Post*, 9 February 2015.
34 Stephane Lacroix, 'Saudi Arabia's Muslim Brotherhood Predicament', *Washington Post*, 20 March 2014.
35 Interview with former AKP MP 1.
36 Interview with Tariq Al-Zomor, Istanbul, 6 August 2018.
37 Khaled Abou El Fadl, 'Failure of a Revolution: The Military, Secular Intelligentsia and Religion in Egypt's Pseudo-Secular State', in *Routledge Handbook of the Arab Spring: Rethinking Democratization*, ed. Larbi Sadiki (London: Routledge, 2016), 265.
38 El Fadl, 'Failure of a Revolution', 265.
39 El Fadl, 'Failure of a Revolution', 266.
40 Quintan Wiktorowicz, 'Islamic Activism and Social Movement Theory', in *Islamic Activism: A Social Movement Theory Approach*, ed. Quintan Wiktorowicz, Indiana Series in Middle East Studies (Bloomington: Indiana University Press, 2004), 3.
41 Gamze Çavdar, 'Islamist Rationality: An Assessment of the Rational Choice Approach', *Politics & Religion* 5, no. 3 (2012): 585.
42 'Müslüman Kardeşler: Türkiye İslam dünyasının umudu', *Sabah*, 12 May 2018.
43 Krishnadev Calamur, 'The Irony of Turkey's Crusade for a Missing Journalist', *Atlantic*, 15 October 2018.
44 Interview with Bedreddine Abdelkefi, telephone, 13 May 2020.
45 Interview with Noureddinne Bhiri, telephone, 18 May 2020.
46 Interview with Bedreddine Abdelkefi, telephone, 13 May 2020.
47 Interview with Ahmed Gaaoul, Tunis, 18 December 2019.
48 Marzo, 'Critical Junctures', 923.
49 Interview with Sahbi Atig, telephone, 19 May 2020.
50 Marzo, 'Critical Junctures', 919.
51 Amel Boubekeur, 'Islamists, Secularists and Old Regime Elites in Tunisia: Bargained Competition', *Mediterranean Politics* 21, no. 1 (2016): 108.
52 Boubekeur, 'Islamists, Secularists and Old Regime Elites', 109.
53 Aroua Kooli, 'usturat Erdogan ..antht?! allaenat alsuwriat tutariduh', *Assbah*, 31 March 2014.

54 Zied Krichan, 'min alqayimat alswda' 'iilaa nsf tabrir alqarar al'iimaratii 'iilaa al'iishkalat albrutukuliat fi ziarat ardughan: fi daef al'ada' altuwnisii alrasmi', *Le Maghreb*, 28 December 2017. Also see Hassen Ayadi, 'recep tayyip erdogan isatadif maktab majlis al-nuwwab fi qasr qartajan: min aldayf wa min al-madif?', *Le Maghreb*, 28 December 2017.
55 'Büyük Çamlıca Camii'ne Görkemli Açılış', *Hürriyet*, 3 May 2019.
56 'Tunus Nahda Lideri Gannuşi: İslam ile demokrasinin ikiz olduğuna inanıyoruz', *SETA*, 26 February 2019.
57 'liqaa' al Ghannouchi Erdogan bitathir jadlan wa as'an fi tunis', *Bawabaa*, 22 October 2019.
58 'Al Ghannouchi yabhath 'an al-d'am min rafiq al-fikr Erdogan', *Al Marjie*, 22 October 2019.
59 Hamza Alyan, 'ayn al-ghannouchi wa ikhwan tunis min tajribat erdogan?', *Al Jarida*, 8 February 2021.
60 Ahmed Al-Sharif, 'al-ghannouchi 'alaa kuhtaa erbakan', *Al Omah*, 1 August 2021.
61 Majed Azzam, 'al-ghannouchi beyn namudhaji erbakan wa erdogan', *Arabi 21*, 26 August 2021.
62 Tarek Amara, 'More than 100 Officials from Tunisia's Islamist Ennahda Party Resigned amid Crisis', *Reuters*, 25 September 2021.
63 'tunisiyun ya'tabirun d'awha al-ghannouchi li intihabat mabkura munawrah lil harub', *Al-Ghad*, 4 December 2021.
64 'Tunisia: Authorities Arrest Ennahda Leaders on Charges of Money Laundering', *Middle East Monitor*, 6 January 2023.
65 'tunis… tawqif qiadiun sabiq fi haraka Ennahda bi tuhmat ghasil al'amwal', *Al Watan News*, 31 December 2022.
66 Mohamed Yassine Jelasi, 'Financement illicite d'Ennahda: Namaa Tunisie, Ooredoo et le Qatar', *Nawaat*, 14 February 2022.
67 'Abdel Karim Suleiman . . . al fasad yafuku shafra "lighaz" ikhwan tunis', *Al Ain*, 11 January 2023.
68 Dilek Yankaya, 'Le Commerce Exterieur Comme Strategie d'Integration a l'etat. Le Parcours d'Obstacles d'une Assosication Patonale Issue du Mouvemant Islamiste en Tunisie', *Mondes en Développement*, vol. 50-2022/2, issue 198, 99.
69 Ian Traynor, 'Gaza Flotilla Raid Draws Furious Response from Turkey's Prime Minister', *Guardian*, 1 June 2010.
70 'Erdoğan'dan Mavi Marmara fırçası: Giderken bana mı sordunuz?', *Sözcü*, 30 June 2016.
71 Pierre Hecker, 'The "Arab Spring" and the End of Turkish Democracy', in *Arab Spring: Modernity, Identity and Change*, ed. Eid Mohamed and Dalia Fahmy (Basingstoke: Palgrave Macmillan, 2019), 69.
72 Hecker, 'The "Arab Spring" and the End of Turkish Democracy', 71.
73 'Milletvekillerine Erdoğan'ın masasında da bulunan 'Rabia heykeli' dağıtıldı', *T24*, 4 May 2016.

74 Hecker, 'The "Arab Spring" and the End of Turkish Democracy', 75.
75 'Abu Al-Futuh rahin ala'etqal . . . misr aydan', *Al Jazeera*, 7 July 2018.
76 François Burgat and Bjorn Olaj Otvik, 'an 'abd al-moneim al-futh', *Al Jadid al-Araby*, 4 July 2018.
77 Bethan McKernan, 'Appalling Khashoggi Shocked Saudi İntelligence- Erdoğan', *Guardian*, 13 November 2018.
78 Graeme Wood, 'Absolute Power', *Atlantic*, 3 March 2022.
79 Wood, 'Absolute Power'.
80 'Khashoggi: Anger as Turkish Court Halts Murder Trial', *BBC*, 7 April 2022.
81 'Cumhurbaşkanı Erdoğan, kan donduran o cümleyi ilk kez paylaştı', *Hürriyet*, 14 December 2018.
82 Kozok, Fırat and Selcan Hacaoglu, 'Erdogan Invites Saudi Crown Prince as Turkey Seeks Investment', *Bloomberg*, 23 May 2022.
83 '15 Temmuz'u BAE finanse etti iddiası', *Gazete Duvar*, 12 June 2017; 'BAE'yi FETÖ'nün finansörü olarak gösteriyorlardı: Erdoğan'ın BAE için dikkat çeken mesajı', *Cumhuriyet*, 16 February 2022.
84 'Dışişleri Bakanı Mevlüt Çavuşoğlu: Mısır'la ilişkiler düzelir, düzelmesi de gerekir', *Anadolu Ajansı*, 14 April 2022.
85 Mounir, Ghufrane, 'Al-Iktiyar 3: Why an Egyptian Ramadan Drama is Provoking Anger', *Middle East Eye*, 8 April 2022.
86 Interview with a senior former MB member, 7 April 2022.
87 'li madha kharaj al'amir bin salman alrrabh al'akbar wal' islam alsiyasi alkhasir al'abraz min ziyarat 'Erdogan lil Saudia? Wa madha yani tazamun al-ziyarat mae 'iighlaq qanaa 'mekameleen' al'ikhwani?', *Rai Al-Youm*, 30 April 2022.
88 'Müslüman Kardeşler'in yayın organından Türkiye kararı: Yayınlarını durdu', *Cumhuriyet*, 30 April 2022.
89 'Türkiye-Mısır yakınlaşması: Dokuz yılda 'Katil Sisi'den 'Sayın Sisi'ye nasıl gelindi?', *BBC Türkçe*, 12 December 2022.
90 'Erdogan Says Turkish, Egyptian Ministers to Meet in Process of Building Ties', *Reuters*, 27 November 2022.
91 'baed musafahat al-sisi . . . al-rais al-turki yuelin "talabah al wahida" min misr', *Al Hurra*, 21 November 2022.
92 Spokesman of the Egyptian Presidency, Facebook, 21 November 2022.
93 'baed musafahat al-sisi wa erdogan ma mustaqbal alaqat misr wa turkia?', *Al Sharq al-Awsat*, 22 November 2022.
94 Abdel Bari Atwan, 'Erdogan Capitulates to MBS', *Rai Al-Youm*, 2 April 2022.
95 İsmail Kılıçaslan, 'İki meselenin peşinde', *Yeni Şafak*, 22 November 2022.
96 Ali Karahasanoğlu, 'Yazıklar olsun bize! Keşke o fotoyu görmeseydim', *Yeni Akit*, 21 November 2022.
97 Ben Hubbard, 'Skyrocketing Prices in Turkey Hurt Families and Tarnish Erdogan', *New York Times*, 5 December 2022.

98 Steven A. Cook, 'Why Turkey is Resetting Relations with Saudi Arabia', Council on Foreign Relations, 4 May 2022.
99 Reinhart Koselleck, *The Practice of Conceptual History: Timing History, Spacing Concepts* (Stanford: Stanford University Press, 2002), 237.
100 Koselleck, *The Practice of Conceptual History*, 240.
101 Koselleck, *The Practice of Conceptual History*, 243.
102 Peter Beaumont, 'Morsi Power Grab Angers Egypt Opposition Groups', *Guardian*, 23 November 2012.
103 Joel Beinin and Joe Stork, *Political Islam: Essays from Middle East Report* (London: Tauris, 1997), 35.
104 Shadi Hamid and Meredith Wheeler, 'Was Mohammed Morsi an Autocrat?', *Atlantic*, 31 March 2014.
105 Samuel P. Huntington, 'Will More Countries Become Democratic?', *Political Science Quarterly* 131, no. 2 (2016): 261.
106 Thomas Carothers, 'The End of the Transition Paradigm', *Journal of Democracy* 13, no. 1 (2002): 18.
107 Hinnebusch, 'Introduction: Understanding the Consequences of the Arab Uprisings – Starting Points and Divergent Trajectories', 205–6.
108 Khalil Al-Anani, 'The "Anguish" of the Muslim Brotherhood', in *Routledge Handbook of the Arab Spring : Rethinking Democratization*, ed. Larbi Sadiki (London: Routledge, 2016), 235.
109 Al-Anani, 'The "Anguish"', 235.
110 Wickham, *The Muslim Brotherhood*, 305.
111 Interview with Salah Abdel Maqsoud, Istanbul, 1 August 2018.
112 Interview with Yehia Hamed, Istanbul, 30 July 2018.
113 Khaled Abou El Fadl, 'Egypt's Secularized Intelligentsia and the Guardians of Truth', *The Search For Beauty*, 15 January 2017. https://www.searchforbeauty.org/2017/01/15/egypt-s-secularized-intelligentsia-and-the-guardians-of-truth-by-khaled-abou-el-fadl/.
114 El Fadl, 'Egypt's Secularized Intelligentsia and the Guardians of Truth'.
115 Bayat, 'The Coming of a Post-Islamist Society', 45.
116 Bayat, 'The Coming of a Post-Islamist Society', 45.
117 Bayat, *Post-Islamism*, 12.
118 Bayat, *Making Islam Democratic*, 5.
119 Daniel Brumberg, 'Authoritarian Legacies and Reform Strategies in the Arab World', in *Political Liberalization & Democratization in the Arab World*, ed. Rex Brynen, Bahgat Korany and Paul Noble (Boulder and London: Lynne Rienner, 1995), 98.
120 Beinin and Stork, *Political Islam*, 22.
121 Cavatorta, 'The Convergence of Governance: Upgrading Authoritarianism in the Arab World and Downgrading Democracy Elsewhere?', 217.

122 See Anne Applebaum, *Twilight of Democracy: The Failure of Politics and the Parting of Friends* (London: Allen Lane, 2020).
123 Tanıl Bora and Kerem Ünüvar, 'İslamcılık ve AKP: Mazeret ve kibir', *Birikim Dergisi*, July–August, no. 303–4 (2014): 16.
124 Bayram Koca, 'M. Hayri Kırbaşoğlu ile söyleşi: İslam, sol ve AKP', *Birikim Dergisi*, July–August, no. 303–4 (2014): 184–5.
125 Sidahmed and Ehteshami, *Islamic Fundamentalism*, 26.

Chapter 9

1 Barrington Moore, *Social Origins of Dictatorship and Democracy [Electronic Resource]: Lord and Peasant in the Making of the Modern World* (Boston: Beacon Press, 1993), 489.
2 Moore, *Social Origins of Dictatorship and Democracy*, 486.
3 Bayat, *Making Islam Democratic*, 7.
4 Shehata, 'Introduction', in *Islamist Politics in the Middle East: Movements and Change*, ed. Samer S. Shehata (Routledge, 2011), 1.
5 F. Gregory Gause, 'The Price of Order: Settling for Less in the Middle East', *Foreign Affairs* 101, no. 2 (2022): 10–14, 16–21.
6 Helen Thompson, *Disorder: Hard Times in the 21st Century* (Oxford: Oxford University Press, 2022), 270.
7 Al-Kadi, 'Between Foreign Policy and the Umma: The Muslim Brotherhood in Egypt and Jordan', *The Muslim world (Hartford)* 109, no. 3 (2019): 260.
8 Sadiki, 'Tunisia's Ennahda: Islamists Turning the Learning Curve of Democracy and Civic Habituation', 95.
9 Andrew F. March, 'Political Islam: Theory', *Annual Review of Political Science* 18, no. 1 (2015): 105.
10 Piscatori and Saikal, *Islam beyond Borders*, 9.
11 Eickelman and Piscatori, *Muslim Politics*, 150.
12 André Bank and Roy Karadag, 'The "Ankara Moment": The Politics of Turkey's Regional Power in the Middle East, 2007–11', *Third World Quarterly* 34, no. 2 (2013): 155.
13 Bayat, *Revolutionary Life*, 103.
14 Tammam and Haenni, 'Au diable les loosers'.
15 'al-rais mursi astakhdim mustalah 'shariyatan' 59 maratan', *Al Arabiya*, 3 July 2013.
16 'Bu millet 28 Şubatların değil, kendi iradesinin bin yıl süreceğini eline geçen her fırsatta göstermiştir', *Türkiye Cumhuriyeti Cumhurbaşkanlığı*, 28 February 2015.
17 Nick Tatterstall and Daren Butler, 'Turkey Dismisses Corruption case that has Dogged PM Erdogan', *Reuters*, 2 May 2014.

18 Yusuf Selman İnanç, 'Avrupa Erdoğan'ı anladı mı?', *Sabah*, 24 January 2014.
19 'al-shariyya al-siyasati tusheil siraean bayn kais saeid wa rachid al-ghannouchi', *Attounisiyoun*, 29 April 2022.
20 'mustashar al-ghannouchci:mutamasikun bi'leawdat 'iilaa al-shariyya al-dusturiya', *Afrigate News*, 10 January 2022.
21 'ennahda tarfud muhakamat zaeimiha rachid al-ghannouchi wa tawkid 'alaa shariyya', *Business News Arabi*, 4 April 2022.
22 Shahram Akbarzadeh, 'The Paradox of Political Islam', in *Routledge Handbook of Political Islam*, ed. Shahram Akbarzadeh (London: Routledge, 2012), 5–7.
23 Michaelle L. Browers, 'Islamic Political Ideologies', in *The Oxford Handbook of Political Ideologies*, ed. Michael Freeden, Lyman Tower Sargent and Marc Stears (Oxford: Oxford University Press, 2015), 632.
24 S. Qutb, *Al-Mustaqbal li Hadha al-Din* (Cairo: Maktabat Wahda, 1965), 32–5. cited in Moussalli, 'Sayyid Qutb: Founder of Radical Islamic Political Ideology', in *Routledge Handbook of Political Islam*, ed. Shahram Akbarzadeh (London: Routledge, 2012), 15.
25 Devji and Kazmi, *Islam after Liberalism*, 7.
26 In 'al-hurriyya wa-l- 'adala', 22 November 2011, cited in Neil Ketchley, *Egypt in Time of Revolution: Contentious Politics and the Arab Spring* (Cambridge: Cambridge University Press, 2017), 78.
27 Snow, 'Framing Processes, Ideology, and Discursive Fields', 384.
28 Aurélie Campana and Cédric Jourde, *Islamism and Social Movements in North Africa, the Sahel and Beyond: Transregional and Local Perspectives*, Routledge Studies in Mediterranean Politics; 7 (London and New York: Routledge, 2018), 4.
29 Martin Hellwig, '"Capitalism: What has Gone Wrong?": Who Went Wrong? Capitalism? The Market Economy? Governments? "Neoliberal" Economics?' *Oxford Review of Economic Policy* 37, no. 4 (2021): 665.
30 John Comaroff, 'The End of Neoliberalism?: What Is Left of the Left', *The Annals of the American Academy of Political and Social Science* 637, no. 1 (2011): 146.
31 Foucault, Senellart and Burchell, *The Birth of Biopolitics: Lectures at the Collège de France, 1978–79*, 226.
32 Powers, '"Run the Country like a Business?" The Economics of Jordan's Islamic Action Front', *Critical Research on Religion* 7, no. 1 (2019): 38–57.
33 Freeden, 'The Morphological Analysis of Ideology', 134.
34 Michaelle L. Browers, 'The Secular Bias in Ideology Studies and the Case of Islamism', *Journal of Political Ideologies* 10, no. 1 (2005): 79.
35 Browers, 'The Secular Bias in Ideology Studies and the Case of Islamism', 86.
36 Browers, 'The Secular Bias in Ideology Studies and the Case of Islamism'.
37 McCarthy, *Inside Tunisia's al-Nahda*, 173.
38 Roy, *Globalized Islam*, 19.

39 Akbarzadeh, 'The Paradox of Political Islam', 1.
40 Heywood, *Political Ideologies*, 13.
41 Michael Freeden, 'Editorial: Fundaments and Foundations in Ideologies', *Journal of Political Ideologies* 10, no. 1 (2005): 7.
42 Ismail, *Rethinking Islamist Politics*, 161.
43 Ismail, *Rethinking Islamist Politics*.
44 Michael Freeden, *Ideologies and Political Theory: A Conceptual Approach*, Ebook Central (Oxford and New York: Clarendon Press; Oxford University Press, 1996), 111.
45 Ismail, *Rethinking Islamist Politics*, 176.
46 Quentin Skinner, 'Some Problems in the Analysis of Political Thought and Action', *Political Theory* 2, no. 3 (1974): 292–300, cited in Jonathan Leader Maynard, 'A Map of the Field of Ideological Analysis', *Journal of Political Ideologies* 18, no. 3 (2013): 303.
47 Sami Zubaida, *Beyond Islam: A New Understanding of the Middle East*, Library of Modern Middle East Studies; 84 (London: I.B. Tauris, 2011), 114.

Bibliography

Abdelrahman, Maha M. 'A Hierarchy of Struggles? The "Economic" and the "Political" in Egypt's Revolution'. *Review of African Political Economy* 39, no. 134 (2012): 614–28.

Abdelrahman, Maha M. *Egypt's Long Revolution: Protest Movements and Uprisings*. London: Routledge, 2014.

Abrahamian, Ervand. *The Coup: 1953, the Cia, and the Roots of Modern U.S.-Iranian Relations*. New York: The New Press, 2015.

Adaman, Fikret, Murat Arsel and Bengi Akbulut, 'Neoliberal Developmentalism, Authoritarian Populism, and Extractivism in the Countryside: The Soma Mining Disaster in Turkey'. *The Journal of Peasant Studies* 46, no. 3 (2019): 514–36.

Adams, Glenn, Sara Estrada-Villalta, Daniel Sullivan and Hazel Rose Markus. 'The Psychology of Neoliberalism and the Neoliberalism of Psychology'. *Journal of Social Issues* 75, no. 1 (2019): 189–216.

Adas, Emin Baki. 'The Making of Entrepreneurial Islam and the Islamic Spirit of Capitalism'. *Journal for Cultural Research* 10, no. 2 (2006): 113–37.

Adly, Amr. 'Between Social Populism and Pragmatic Conservatism'. In *Egypt's Revolutions: Politics, Religion, and Social Movements*, edited by Bernard Rougier and Stephane Lacroix, 61–80. Basingstoke: Palgrave Macmillan, 2016.

Ahmed, Huda Hadi and Al-Suwaidani Hamid Mohammed Taha. 'Al-Siyasa Al-Turkia Tujah Afriqia Fi 'Ahd Hizb Al-'Adala Wa Al-Tanmiya'. *College of Education for Women* 30, no. 4 (2019): 153–65.

Ajami, Fouad. 'The Arab Spring at One: A Year of Living Dangerously'. *Foreign Affairs* 91, no. 2 (2012): 56–65.

Akbarzadeh, Shahram. 'The Paradox of Political Islam'. In *Routledge Handbook of Political Islam*, edited by Shahram Akbarzadeh, 1–8. London: Routledge, 2012.

Akçalı, Emel. 'Introduction: Neoliberal Governmentality and the Future of the State in the Middle East and North Africa'. In *Neoliberal Governmentality and the Future of the State in the Middle East and North Africa*, edited by Emel Akçali, 1–14. Basingstoke, Hampshire: Palgrave Macmillan, 2015.

Akdoğan, Yalçın. *AK Parti ve Muhafazakar Demokrasi*. İstanbul: Alfa Yayınları, 2004.

Aktas, Elvan. 'The Rise and the Fall of the Turkish Economic Success Story under Akp (JDP)'. *Dynamics of Muslim Life* 11, no. 2 (2017): 171–83.

Al-Affendi, Abdelwahab. 'Umma, State and Movement: Events That Shaped the Modern Debate'. In *Political Islam: Context versus Ideology*, edited by Khalid Harub, 20–37. SOAS Middle East issues. London: Saqi, 2010.

Al-Anani, Khalil. 'Devout Neoliberalism?! Explaining Egypt's Muslim Brotherhood's Socio-Economic Perspective and Policies'. *Politics and Religion* 13, no. 4 (2020): 748–67.

Al-Anani, Khalil. *Inside the Muslim Brotherhood: Religion, Identity, and Politics*. New York: Oxford University Press, 2016.

Al-Anani, Khalil. 'The "Anguish" of the Muslim Brotherhood'. In *Routledge Handbook of the Arab Spring: Rethinking Democratization*, edited by Larbi Sadiki, 227–39. London: Routledge, 2016.

Al-Anani, Khalil. 'Upended Path: The Rise and Fall of Egypt's Muslim Brotherhood'. *The Middle East Journal* 69, no. 4 (2015): 527–43.

Al-Awadi, Hesham. *The Muslim Brothers in Pursuit of Legitimacy: Power and Political Islam in Egypt under Mubarak*. London: I.B. Tauris, 2014.

Al-Azami, Usaama. 'Abdullah Bin Bayyah and the Arab Revolutions: Counter-Revolutionary Neo-Traditionalism's Ideological Struggle against Islamism'. *The Muslim World (Hartford)* 109, no. 3 (2019): 343–61.

Al-Azami, Usaama. 'Locating Hakimiyya in Global History: The Concept of Sovereignty in Premodern Islam and Its Reception after Mawdūdī and Quṭb'. *Journal of the Royal Asiatic Society*, Series 3 (2021): 1 of 22.

Al-Ghannouchi, Rachid. *al-huriyyat al- 'ammah fi al-dawla al-islamiyya*. Beirut: Markaz Dirasat Al-Arabiyya, 1993.

Al-Kadi, Alia. 'Between Foreign Policy and the Umma: The Muslim Brotherhood in Egypt and Jordan'. *The Muslim World (Hartford)* 109, no. 3 (2019): 240–60.

Al-Qaradawi, Yusuf. *Islamic Awakening between Rejection and Extremism*. London: International Institute of Islamic Thought, 2007.

Al-Rodhan, Nayef R. F., Graeme P. Herd and Lisa Watanabe. *Critical Turning Points in the Middle East: 1915–2015*. New York: Palgrave Macmillan, 2013.

Al-Siba'i, Mustafa. *Ishtirakiyat Al-Islam*. 2nd edn. Damascus: Mu'assasat al-Matba'at Al-'Arabiyah, 1960.

Alterman, Jon B. 'Free Markets, Free Muslims'. *Foreign Affairs* 88, no. 6 (2009): 141–5.

Altuntaş-Çakır, Ravza. 'Umma: A Modern Turkish Approach'. *The Muslim World* 109, no. 3 (2019): 289–307.

Amin, Samir. 'Political Islam in the Service of Imperialism'. *Monthly Review* 59, no. 7 (2007): 1–19.

Applebaum, Anne. *Twilight of Democracy: The Failure of Politics and the Parting of Friends*. London: Allen Lane, 2020.

Aras, Bülent. 'The Davutoğlu Era in Turkish Foreign Policy'. *Insight Turkey* 11, no. 3 (2009): 127–42.

Armbrust, Walter. *Martyrs and Tricksters: An Ethnography of the Egyptian Revolution*. Princeton Studies in Muslim Politics; 75. Princeton: Princeton University Press, 2019.

Armbrust, Walter. 'The Revolution against Neoliberalism'. In *The Dawn of the Arab Uprisings: End of an Old Order?*, edited by Bassam Haddad, Rosie Bsheer and Abu-Rish Ziad, foreword by Roger Owen, 113–23. London: Pluto Press, 2012.

Asad, Talal. *Secular Translations: Nation-State, Modern Self, and Calculative Reason.* Ruth Benedict Book Series. New York: Columbia University Press, 2019.

Atasoy, Yıldız. *Islam's Marriage with Neoliberalism: State Transformation in Turkey.* London: Palgrave Macmillan UK; Imprint: Palgrave Macmillan, 2009.

Atia, Mona. '"A Way to Paradise": Pious Neoliberalism, Islam, and Faith-Based Development'. *Annals of the Association of American Geographers* 102, no. 4 (2012): 808–27.

Atiyas, Izak, Ozan Bakış and Esra Çeviker Gürakar, 'Anatolian Tigers and the Emergence of the Devout Bourgeoisie in the Turkish Manufacturing Industry'. In *Crony capitalism in the Middle East: Business and Politics from Liberalization to the Arab Spring*, edited by Ishac Diwan, Adeel Malik and Izak Atiyas, 94. Oxford: Oxford University Press, 2019.

Ayoob, Mohammed. 'Political Islam: Image and Reality'. *World Policy Journal* 21, no. 3 (2004): 1–14.

Ayubi, Nazih N. M. *Political Islam: Religion and Politics in the Arab World*. London: Routledge, 1991.

Azmah, Aziz. *Islams and Modernities*. 3rd edn. London: Verso, 2009.

Babb, Sarah. *Managing Mexico: Economists from Nationalism to Neoliberalism.* Princeton: Princeton University Press, 2018.

Baker, Raymond William. *Islam without Fear: Egypt and the New Islamists*. Cambridge, MA and London: Harvard University Press, 2003.

Bali, Aslı Ü., 'A Turkish Model for the Arab Spring?', *Middle East Law and Governance* 3, Issue 1–2 (2011): 24–42.

Balibar, Étienne. 'Absolute Capitalism'. In *Mutant Neoliberalism: Market Rule and Political Rupture*, edited by William Callison and Zachary Manfredi, 269–90. New York: Fordham University Press, 2019.

Balkan, Neşecan, Erol Balkan and Ahmet Öncü. *The Neoliberal Landscape and the Rise of Islamist Capital in Turkey*. New York and Oxford: Berghahn Books, 2015.

Bank, Andre. 'The Study of Authoritarian Diffusion and Cooperation: Comparative Lessons on Interests versus Ideology, Nowadays and in History'. *Democratization: Clusters of Authoritarian Diffusion and Cooperation: The Role of Interests vs. Ideology?* 24, no. 7 (2017): 1345–57.

Bank, Andre and Roy Karadag. 'The "Ankara Moment": The Politics of Turkey's Regional Power in the Middle East, 2007–11'. *Third World Quarterly* 34, no. 2 (2013): 287–304.

Banu, Da Ta. 'Constructing the "Arab Spring": News Discourses in Turkish Newspapers'. *Global Media Journal* 6, no. 2 (2013): 19–33.

Bartal, Shaul. 'Sheikh Qaradawi and the Internal Palestinian Struggle Issues Preventing Reconciliation between Fatah and Hamas and the Influence of the Qaradāwi Era over the Struggle between the Organizations'. *Middle Eastern Studies* 51, no. 4 (2015): 585–99.

Başaran, Ezgi. *Frontline Turkey: The Conflict at the Heart of the Middle East*. London: I.B. Tauris, 2017.

Başkan, Filiz. 'The Rising Islamic Business Elite and Democratization in Turkey'. *Journal of Balkan and Near Eastern Studies* 12, no. 4 (2010): 399–416.
Bassiouni, M. Cherif. *Chronicles of the Egyptian Revolution and Its Aftermath: 2011–2016*. Cambridge and New York: Cambridge University Press, 2017.
Bassiouni, M. Cherif. 'Egypt's Unfinished Revolution'. In *Civil Resistance in the Arab Spring: Triumphs and Disasters*, edited by Adam Roberts, Michael J. Willis, Rory McCarthy and Timothy Garton Ash, 53–87. Oxford: Oxford University Press, 2016.
Bayat, Asef. 'Activism and Social Development in the Middle East'. *International Journal of Middle East Studies* 34, no. 1 (2002): 1–28.
Bayat, Asef. 'Arab Revolts: Islamists Aren't Coming!' *Insight Turkey* 13, no. 2 (2011): 9–14.
Bayat, Asef. 'Islamism and Social Movement Theory'. *Third World Quarterly* 26, no. 6 (2005): 891–908.
Bayat, Asef. *Life as Politics: How Ordinary People Change the Middle East*. Second edn. Stanford: Stanford University Press, 2013.
Bayat, Asef. *Making Islam Democratic: Social Movements and the Post-Islamist Turn*. Stanford Studies in Middle Eastern and Islamic Societies and Cultures. Stanford: Stanford University Press, 2007.
Bayat, Asef. 'Plebeians of the Arab Spring'. *Current Anthropology* 56 (2015): 33–43.
Bayat, Asef. *Post-Islamism: The Changing Faces of Political Islam*. New York: Oxford University Press, 2013.
Bayat, Asef. *Revolution without Revolutionaries: Making Sense of the Arab Spring*. Stanford Studies in Middle Eastern and Islamic Societies and Cultures. Stanford: Stanford University Press, 2017.
Bayat, Asef. *Revolutionary Life: The Everyday of the Arab Spring*. Cambridge, MA: Harvard University Press, 2021.
Bayat, Asef. 'The Arab Spring and Its Surprises'. *Development and Change* 44, no. 3 (2013): 587–601.
Bayat, Asef. 'The Coming of a Post-Islamist Society'. *Critique: Critical Middle Eastern Studies*, no. 9 (1996): 43–52.
Bayat, Asef and Linda Herrera. *Being Young and Muslim: New Cultural Politics in the Global South and North*. New York and Oxford: Oxford University Press, 2010.
Beinin, Joel. 'Political Islam and the New Global Economy: The Political Economy of an Egyptian Social Movement'. *The New Centennial Review* 5, no. 1 (2005): 111–39.
Beinin, Joel and Joe Stork. 'On the Modernity, Historical Specificity, and International Context of Political Islam'. In *Political Islam: Essays from Middle East Report*, edited by Joel Beinin and Joe Stork. London: Tauris, 1997.
Beinin, Joel and Joe Stork. *Political Islam: Essays from Middle East Report*. London: Tauris, 1997.
Bell, Daniel. *The End of Ideology: On the Exhaustion of Political Ideas in the Fifties*. Glencoe: Free Press, 1960.

Ben Othman, Raoudha. 'European Union Democracy Promotion in Tunisia'. In *Routledge Handbook of the Arab Spring: Rethinking Democratization*, edited by Larbi Sadiki, 559–73. London: Routledge, 2016.

Ben Salem, Maryam. '"God Loves the Rich". The Economic Policy of Ennahda: Liberalism in the Service of Social Solidarity'. *Politics & Religion* 13, no. 4 (2020): 695–718.

Benhabib, Seyla. 'The New Legitimation Crises of Arab States and Turkey'. *Philosophy & Social Criticism* 40, no. 4–5 (2014): 349–58.

Benhaim, Yohanan and Kerem Öktem, 'The Rise and Fall of Turkey's Soft Power Discourse'. *European Journal of Turkish Studies* 21 (2015): 1–25.

Bennett, Andrew and Jeffrey T. Checkel. *Process Tracing: From Metaphor to Analytic Tool*. Strategies for Social Inquiry. Cambridge: Cambridge University Press, 2015.

Bergeaud-Blackler, Florence, Johan Fischer and John Lever. 'Introduction: Studying the Politics of Global Halal Markets'. In *Halal Matters: Islam, Politics and Markets in Global Perspective*, edited by Florence Bergeaud-Blackler, John Lever and Johan Fischer, 1–18. London: Routledge, 2015.

Bermeo, Nancy. 'Democracy and the Lessons of Dictatorship'. *Journal Comparative Politics* 24, no. 3 (1992): 273–91.

Bockman, Johanna and Gil Eyal. 'Eastern Europe as a Laboratory for Economic Knowledge: The Transnational Roots of Neoliberalism'. *American Journal of Sociology* 108, no. 2 (2002): 310–52.

Bogaert, Koenraad. 'Contextualizing the Arab Revolts: The Politics behind Three Decades of Neoliberalism in the Arab World'. *Middle East Critique* 22, no. 3 (2013): 213–34.

Böhmelt, Tobias, Lawrence Ezrow, Roni Lehrer and Hugh Ward. 'Party Policy Diffusion'. *American Political Science Review* 110, no. 2 (2016): 397–410.

Boin, Arjen, Allan McConnell and Paul't Hart. *Governing after Crisis: The Politics of Investigation, Accountability and Learning*. Cambridge Core. Cambridge: Cambridge University Press, 2008.

Bokhari, Kamran and Farid Senzai, *Political Islam in the Age of Democratization*. New York: Palgrave Macmillan, 2013.

Boltanski, Luc, Eve Chiapello and Gregory Elliott. *The New Spirit of Capitalism*. New updated edn. London: Verso, 2018.

Bora, Tanıl and Kerem Ünüvar. 'İslamcılık Ve Akp: Mazeret Ve Kibir'. *Birikim Dergisi* July–August, no. 303–4 (2014): 14–18.

Borg, Stefan. 'The Arab Uprisings, the Liberal Civilizing Narrative and the Problem of Orientalism'. *Middle East Critique* 25, no. 3 (2016): 211–27.

Börzel, Tanja A. and Thomas Risse. 'From Europeanisation to Diffusion: Introduction'. *West European Politics* 35, no. 1 (2012): 1–19.

Boubekeur, Amel. 'Islamists, Secularists and Old Regime Elites in Tunisia: Bargained Competition'. *Mediterranean Politics* 21, no. 1 (2016): 107–27.

Boubekeur, Amel. 'Post-Islamist Culture: A New Form of Mobilization?'. *History of Religions* 47, no. 1 (2007): 75–94.

Brenner, Neil, Jamie Peck and N. I. K. Theodore. 'Variegated Neoliberalization: Geographies, Modalities, Pathways'. *Global Networks* 10, no. 2 (2010): 182–222.

Brighi, Elisabetta and Lilia Giugni. 'Foreign Policy and the Ideology of Post-Ideology: The Case of Matteo Renzi's Partito Democratico'. *The International Spectator* 51, no. 1 (2016): 13–27.

Brooke, Steven and Amr Darrag. *Politics or Piety? Why the Muslim Brotherhood Engages in Social Service Provision: A Conversation*. Washington: Brookings Institute, 2016.

Browers, Michaelle L. 'Islamic Political Ideologies'. In *The Oxford Handbook of Political Ideologies*, edited by Michael Freeden, Lyman Tower Sargent and Marc Stears, 627–43. Oxford: Oxford University Press, 2015.

Browers, Michaelle L. 'The Secular Bias in Ideology Studies and the Case of Islamism'. *Journal of Political Ideologies* 10, no. 1 (2005): 75–93.

Brown, Nathan J. *When Victory Becomes an Option: Egypt's Muslim Brotherhood Confronts Success*. Washington, DC: Carnegie Endowment for International Peace, 2012.

Brown, Wendy. *In the Ruins of Neoliberalism: The Rise of Antidemocratic Politics in the West*. The Wellek Library Lectures. New York: Columbia University Press, 2019.

Brumberg, Daniel. 'Authoritarian Legacies and Reform Strategies in the Arab World'. In *Political Liberalization & Democratization in the Arab World*, edited by Rex Brynen, Bahgat Korany and Paul Noble, 229–60. Boulder and London: Lynne Rienner, 1995.

Bugari, Bojan. 'Neoliberalism, Post-Communism, and the Law'. *Annual Review of Law and Social Science* 12, no. 1 (2016): 313–29.

Bulaç, Ali. *Din ve Siyaset*. İstanbul: İnkilap Yayınevi, 2014.

Bulaç, Ali. *Medine Sözleşmesi*. İstanbul: Çıra Yayınları, 2020.

Burgat, François. *Face to Face with Political Islam*. London: I.B. Tauris, 2003.

Burgat, François. 'Islam and Islamist Politics in the Arab World: Old Theories, New Facts?'. In *Islamist Politics in the Middle East: Movements and Change*, edited by Samer S. Shehata, 23–8. Abingdon, Oxon and New York: Routledge, 2011.

Burgat, François and Thomas Hill. *Understanding Political Islam*. Manchester: Manchester University Press, 2019.

Burhani, Ahmad Najib. 'Muslim Televangelists in the Making: Conversion Narratives and the Construction of Religious Authority'. *The Muslim World: A Quarterly Review Of History, Culture, Religions & The Christian Mission In Islamdom* 110, no. 2 (2020): 154–75.

Burke III, Edmund, 'Islam and Social Movements: Methodological Reflections'. In *Islam, Politics, and Social Movements*, edited by Edmund Burke III and Ira M. Lapidus, 17–35. London: University of California Press, 1988.

Buzogany, Aron. 'Illiberal Democracy in Hungary: Authoritarian Diffusion or Domestic Causation?'. *Democratization: Clusters of Authoritarian Diffusion and Cooperation: The Role of Interests vs. Ideology?* 24, no. 7 (2017): 1307–25.

Cammett, Melani and Ishac Diwan. *The Political Economy of the Arab Uprisings*. Boulder: Westview Press, 2014.

Cammett, Melani and Pauline Jones Luong. 'Is There an Islamist Political Advantage?'. *Annual Review of Political Science (Palo Alto, Calif.)* 17 (2014): 187.

Campagna, Joel. 'From Accommodation to Confrontation: The Muslim Brotherhood in the Mubarak Years'. *Journal of International Affairs* 50, no. 1 (1996): 278–304.

Campana, Aurélie and Cédric Jourde. *Islamism and Social Movements in North Africa, the Sahel and Beyond: Transregional and Local Perspectives*. Routledge Studies in Mediterranean Politics; 7. London and New York: Routledge, 2018.

Carothers, Thomas. 'The End of the Transition Paradigm'. *Journal of Democracy* 13, no. 1 (2002): 5–21.

Cavatorta, Francesco. 'Neither Participation nor Revolution: The Strategy of the Moroccan Jamiat Al-Adl Wal-Ihsan'. *Mediterranean Politics* 12, no. 3 (2007): 381–97.

Cavatorta, Francesco. 'The Convergence of Governance: Upgrading Authoritarianism in the Arab World and Downgrading Democracy Elsewhere?'. *Middle East Critique: The Future of Middle Eastern Political Rule through Lenses of the Past: Revisiting the (First) Era of Post-Democratization* 19, no. 3 (2010): 217–32.

Cavatorta, Francesco and Samir Amghar. 'Symposium – Islamism, Islamist Parties, and Economic Policy-Making in the Neo-Liberal Age'. *Politics & Religion* 13, no. 4 (2020): 685–94.

Cavatorta, Francesco and Fabio Merone. 'Moderation through Exclusion? The Journey of the Tunisian Ennahda from Fundamentalist to Conservative Party'. *Democratization* 20, no. 5 (2013): 857–75.

Cavatorta, Francesco and Lise Storm. *Political Parties in the Arab World: Continuity and Change*. Edinburgh: Edinburgh University Press, 2018.

Çavdar, Gamze. 'Islamist New Thinking in Turkey: A Model for Political Learning?'. *Political Science Quarterly* 121, no. 3 (2006): 477–97.

Çavdar, Gamze. 'Islamist Rationality: An Assessment of the Rational Choice Approach'. *Politics & Religion* 5, no. 3 (2012): 584–608.

Cesari, Jocelyne. 'Political Islam: More than Islamism'. *Religions* 12, no. 5 (2021): 299.

Chabot, Sean. 'Dialogue Matters: Beyond the Transmission Model of Transnational Diffusion between Social Movements'. In *The Diffusion of Social Movements: Actors, Mechanisms, and Political Effects*, edited by Rebecca Kolins Givan, Kenneth M. Roberts and Sarah Anne Soule, 99–124. Cambridge: Cambridge University Press, 2010.

Chakravartty, Paula and Sreela Sarkar. 'Entrepreneurial Justice: The New Spirit of Capitalism in Emergent India'. *Popular Communication* 11, no. 1 (2013): 58–75.

Chamkhi, Tarek. 'Neo-Islamism in the Post-Arab Spring'. *Contemporary Politics* 20, no. 4 (2014): 453–68.

Cherribi, Sam and S. Cherribi. *Fridays of Rage: Al Jazeera, the Arab Spring, and Political Islam*. Oxford University Press, 2017.

Christofis, Nikos. 'The Akp's "Yeni Turkiye": Challenging the Kemalist Narrative?' *Mediterranean Quarterly: A Journal of Global Issues* 29, no. 3 (2018): 11.

Çınar, Menderes. 'From Moderation to De-Moderation: Democratic Backsliding of the Akp in Turkye'. In *The Politics of Islamism: Diverging Visions and Trajectories*, edited by J. L. Esposito, Lily Zubaidah Rahim and Naser Ghobazadeh, 127–57. Basingstoke, Hampshire: Palgrave Macmillan, 2017.

Çınar, Menderes. *Siyasal Bir Sorun Olarak Islamcılık: Akp'nin 20 Yılı*. Ankara: Nika Yayınevi, 2021.

Claret-Campana, Maria and Athina Lampridi-Kemou. 'Islamist Forces in Contemporary Egypt: The End of Conventional Dualities'. In *Political Islam in a Time of Revolt*, edited by Ferran Izquierdo, John Etherington and Laura Feliu, 127–52. Basingstoke: Palgrave Macmillan, 2017.

Clark, Janine. 'Social Movement Theory and Patron-Clientelism: Islamic Social Institutions and the Middle Class in Egypt, Jordan, and Yemen'. *Comparative Political Studies* 37, no. 8 (2004): 941–68.

Collier, David. 'Understanding Process Tracing'. *PS, Political Science & Politics* 44, no. 4 (2011): 823–30.

Comaroff, John. 'The End of Neoliberalism?: What Is Left of the Left'. *The Annals of the American Academy of Political and Social Science* 637, no. 1 (2011): 141–7.

Comaroff, Jean and John L. Comaroff. *Millennial Capitalism and the Culture of Neoliberalism*. Durham: Duke University Press, 2001.

Cook, Steven. *Ruling but not Governing: The Military and Political Development in Egypt, Algeria, and Turkey*, Baltimore: Johns Hopkins University Press, 2007.

Crouch, Colin. *Post-Democracy*. Themes for the 21st Century. Cambridge: Polity, 2004.

Crouch, Colin. 'Post-Democracy and Populism'. *The Political Quarterly (London. 1930)* 90 (2019): 124–37.

Dabashi, Hamid. *Being a Muslim in the World: Rethinking Islam for a Post-Western History*. Palgrave Pivot. Basingstoke: Palgrave Macmillan, 2013.

Dabashi, Hamid. *The Arab Spring: The End of Postcolonialism*. London: Zed Books, 2012.

Dağı, İhsan. 'Post-Islamism a la Turca'. In *Post-Islamism: The Changing Faces of Political Islam*, edited by Asef Bayat, New York: Oxford University Press, 2013.

Darwich, May. 'Creating the Enemy, Constructing the Threat: The Diffusion of Repression against the Muslim Brotherhood in the Middle East'. *Democratization: Clusters of Authoritarian Diffusion and Cooperation: The Role of Interests vs. Ideology?* 24, no. 7 (2017): 1289–306.

Das, S. K. *Making the Poor Free?*. Oxford: Oxford University Press, 2015.

De Leon, Cedric, Desai Manali and Tuğal Cihan. *Building Blocs: How Parties Organize Society*. Palo Alto: Stanford University Press, 2015.

Deeb, Lara and Jessica Winegar. *Anthropology's Politics: Disciplining the Middle East*. Ebook Central. Stanford: Stanford University Press, 2016.

Denoeux, Guilain. 'The Forgotten Swamp: Navigating Political Islam'. *Middle East Policy* IX, no. 2 (2002): 56–81.

Devji, Faisal and Zaheer Kazmi. *Islam after Liberalism*. London: Hurst & Company, 2017.

Diwan, Ishac, Philip Keefer and Marc Schiffbauer. 'Crony Capitalism in Egypt'. In *Crony Capitalism in the Middle East: Business and Politics from Liberalization to the Arab Spring*, edited by Ishac Diwan, Adeel Malik and Izak Atiyas, 67–89. Oxford: Oxford University Press, 2019.

Doğan, A. Ekber and Yasin Durak. 'Islami Burjuvazinin Yükselişi Ve Neoliberalizmin Toplumsallaştırılması: Iki Dindar Şehrin Başarı Hikayesinin Perde Arkası'. In *'Yeni Türkiye'ye Varan Yol*, edited by İsmet Akça, Bekmen Ahmet and Özden Barış Alp, 301–18. İstanbul: İletişim Yayınları, 2018.

Drevon, Jerome. 'The Constrained Institutionalization of Diverging Islamist Strategies: The Jihadis, the Muslim Brotherhood, and the Salafis between Two Aborted Egyptian Revolutions'. *Mediterranean Politics: Islamism and Social Movements in North Africa, the Sahel and Beyond: Transregional and Local Perspectives* 22, no. 1 (2017): 16–34.

Ehteshami, Anoushiravan. 'Islam as a Political Force in International Politics'. In *Islam in World Politics*, edited by Nelly Lahoud and Anthony H. Johns, 29–53. London: Routledge, 2005.

Eickelman, Dale F. 'Trans-State Islam and Security'. In *Transnational Religion and Fading States*, edited by Susanne Hoeber and James Piscatori, 27–46. Boulder: Westview Press, 1997.

Eickelman, Dale F. and James Piscatori. *Muslim Politics*. Princeton Studies in Muslim Politics. First edn. Princeton and Oxford: Princeton University Press, 1996.

El Fadl, Khaled Abou. 'Egypt's Secularized Intelligentsia and the Guardians of Truth'. In *Egypt and the Contradictions of Liberalism: Illiberal Intelligentsia and the Future of Egyptian Democracy*, edited by Dalia Faruqi Fahmy and Daanish Faruqi. OneWorld, 2017.

El Fadl, Khaled Abou. 'Failure of a Revolution: The Military, Secular Intelligentsia and Religion in Egypt's Pseudo-Secular State'. In *Routledge Handbook of the Arab Spring: Rethinking Democratization*, edited by Larbi Sadiki, 253–70. London: Routledge, 2016.

El Gannuşi, Raşid. *İslam Devletinde Kamusal Özgürlükler*. İstanbul: Mana Yayınları, 2012.

El Gannuşi, Raşid. *İslam Devletinde Kamusal Vatandaşlık Hakları*. İstanbul: Birleşik Yayıncılık, 1996.

El Gannuşi, Raşid. *Kur'an ve Yaşam Arasında Kadın*. İstanbul: Mana Yayınları, 2011.

El Gannuşi, Raşid. *Laiklik ve Sivil Toplum*. İstanbul: Mana Yayınları, 2010.

El-Ghobashy, Mona. 'The Metamorphosis of the Egyptian Muslim Brothers'. *International Journal of Middle East Studies* 37, no. 3 (2005): 373–95.

El Naggar, Shaimaa. 'The Discursive Construction of Muslim Identities by Contemporary Muslim Televangelists in the West'. ProQuest Dissertations Publishing, 2016.

Elshobaki, Amr. 'The Muslim Brotherhood — Between Evangelizing and Politics'. In *Islamist Politics in the Middle East: Movements and Change*, edited by Samer S. Shehata, 107–19. Abingdon, Oxon and New York: Routledge, 2011.

Eralp, Doga Ulas, *Turkey as a Mediator: Stories of Failure and Success*. Pennsylvania: Lexington Book, 2016.

Erdem, Burcu Kaya. 'Adjustment of the Secular Islamist Role Model (Turkey) to the "Arab Spring": The Relationship between the Arab Uprisings and Turkey in the Turkish and World Press'. *Islam and Christian-Muslim Relations* 23, no. 4 (2012): 435–52.

Esposito, John L. 'Moderate Muslims'. In *Debating Moderate Islam: The Geopolitics of Islam and the West*, edited by M. A. Muqtedar Khan, 25–33. Salt Lake: University of Utah Press, 2010.

Esposito, John L., Lily Zubaidah Rahim and Naser Ghobazadeh. 'Introduction: Theological Contestations and Political Coalition-Building'. In *The Politics of Islamism: Diverging Visions and Trajectories*, edited by J. L. Esposito, Lily Zubaidah Rahim and Naser Ghobazadeh, 1–22. Basingstoke, Hampshire: Palgrave Macmillan, 2017.

Esposito, John L., Lily Zubaidah Rahim and Naser Ghobazadeh. *The Politics of Islamism: Diverging Visions and Trajectories*. Middle East Today. Cham, Switzerland: Palgrave Macmillan, 2018.

Esposito, John L., Lily Zubaidah Rahim and Naser Ghobazadeh. 'Transformations'. In *The Politics of Islamism: Diverging Visions and Trajectories*, edited by J. L. Esposito, Lily Zubaidah Rahim and Naser Ghobazadeh, 267–73. Basingstoke, Hampshire: Palgrave Macmillan, 2017.

Esposito, John L., Sonn Tamara and John O. Voll. *Islam and Democracy after the Arab Spring*. New York: Oxford University Press, 2016.

Euben, Roxanne Leslie and Muhammad Qasim Zaman. *Princeton Readings in Islamist Thought: Texts and Contexts from Al-Banna to Bin Laden*. Princeton Studies in Muslim Politics. Princeton and Oxford: Princeton University Press, 2009.

Eyal, G., I. Szelényi and E. Townsley. 'The Theory of Post-Communist Managerialism'. *New Left Review*, no. 222 (1997): 60–88. https://newleftreview.org/issues/i222/articles/ivan-szelenyi-gil-eyal-eleanor-townsley-the-theory-of-post-communist-managerialism.

Fawaz, Leila T. *An Occasion for War – Civil Conflict in Lebanon and Damascus in 1860*. University of California Press, 1994.

Ferge, Zsuzsa, 'European Integration and the Reform of Social Security in the Accession Countries'. *European Journal of Social Quality* 3, no. 1/2 (2001): 9–25.

Ferhavi, Fuad. 'Abdullah Gül'ün Tunus Ziyareti: Ekonomik Öncelik Ve Bölgesel Eksen Ihtiyacı'. *USAK Analiz* 19 (2012): 1–12.

Foucault, Michel, Michel Senellart and Graham Burchell. *The Birth of Biopolitics: Lectures at the Collège de France, 1978–79*. Houndmills, Basingstoke, Hampshire and New York: Palgrave Macmillan, 2008.

Freeden, Michael. 'Confronting the Chimera of a "Post-Ideological" Age'. *Critical Review of International Social and Political Philosophy* 8, no. 2 (2005): 247–62.

Freeden, Michael. 'Editorial: Fundaments and Foundations in Ideologies'. *Journal of Political Ideologies* 10, no. 1 (2005): 1–9.

Freeden, Michael. *Ideology: A Very Short Introduction*. Oxford: Oxford University Press, 2003.

Freeden, Michael. *Ideologies and Political Theory: A Conceptual Approach*. Oxford and New York: Clarendon Press and Oxford University Press, 1996.

Freeden, Michael. 'The Morphological Analysis of Ideology'. In *The Oxford Handbook of Political Ideologies*, edited by Michael Freeden, Lyman Tower Sargent and Marc Stears, 115–37. Oxford: Oxford University Press, 2015.

Fukuyama, Francis. 'The End of History?'. *The National Interest* 16 (1989): 3–18.

Gamal, Wael. *Lost Capital: The Egyptian Muslim Brotherhood's Neoliberal Transformation*. Carnegie Endowment Middle East Center, 2019.

Gana, Nouri. *The Making of the Tunisian Revolution: Contexts, Architects, Prospects*. Edinburgh: Edinburgh University Press, 2013.

Gardner, Lloyd C. *The Road to Tahrir Square: Egypt and the United States from the Rise of Nasser to the Fall of Mubarak*. London: Saqi, 2011.

Gause, F. Gregory. 'The Price of Order: Settling for Less in the Middle East'. *Foreign Affairs* 101, no. 2 (March/April 2022): 10–21.

George, Alexander L. and Andrew Bennett. *Case Studies and Theory Development in the Social Sciences*. Bcsia Studies in International Security. Cambridge, MA and London: MIT Press, 2005.

Gerges, Fawaz A. *Contentious Politics in the Middle East: Popular Resistance and Marginalised Activism beyond the Arab Uprisings*. Basingstoke: Palgrave Macmillan, 2015.

Ghafar, Adel Abdel and Bill Hess. *Islamist Parties in North Africa: A Comparative Analysis of Morocco, Tunisia and Egypt*. Doha: Brookings Institution, June 2018.

Gidengil, Elisabeth and Ekrem Karakoç. 'Which Matters More in the Electoral Success of Islamist (Successor) Parties – Religion or Performance? The Turkish Case'. *Party Politics* 22, no. 3 (2016): 325–38.

Gill, Stephen. 'The Constitution of Global Capitalism'. The Capitalist World, Past and Present at the International Studies Association Annual Convention, Los Angeles, 2000.

Gillan, Kevin. 'Understanding Meaning in Movements: A Hermeneutic Approach to Frames and Ideologies'. *Social Movement Studies* 7, no. 3 (2008): 247–63.

Gilovich, Thomas and Dale W. Griffin. *Heuristics and Biases: The Psychology of Intuitive Judgment*. Cambridge: Cambridge University Press, 2002.

Givan, Rebecca Kolins, Kenneth M. Roberts and Sarah Anne Soule. *The Diffusion of Social Movements: Actors, Mechanisms, and Political Effects*. Cambridge: Cambridge University Press, 2010.

Göçer, Derya and Marc Herzog, 'Turkey and the Arab Uprisings'. In *Routledge handbook of the Arab Spring: Rethinking Democratization*, edited by Larbi Sadiki, 509. London: Routledge, 2016.

Göle, Nilüfer. 'Snapshots of Islamic Modernities'. *Daedalus* 129, no. 1 (2000): 91.
Gramsci, Antonio, Quintin Hoare and Geoffrey Nowell-Smith. *Selections from the Prison Notebooks of Antonio Gramsci*. Selections from Prison Notebooks. London: Lawrence & Wishart, 1971.
Gümüşçü, Sebnem. 'Class, Status, and Party: The Changing Face of Political Islam in Turkey and Egypt'. *Comparative Political Studies* 43, no. 7 (2010): 835–61.
Habibi, Nader. 'The Economic Agendas and Expected Economic Policies of Islamists in Egypt and Tunisia'. Crown Center for Middle East Studies, 2012.
Hackworth, Jason. 'Religious Neoliberalism(S)'. In *Faith Based. Religious Neoliberalism and the Politics of Welfare in the United States*, 30–47. University of Georgia Press, 2012.
Haenni, Patrick. 'The Reasons for the Muslim Brotherhood's Failure in Power'. In *Egypt's Revolutions*, edited by Bernard Rougier and Stéphane Lacroix, 19–39. New York: Palgrave Macmillan, 2016.
Haenni, Patrick and Tammam Husam. 'Penser Dans L'au-Delà De L'islamisme'. *Revue des mondes musulmans et de la Méditerranée* 123, no. 123 (2008): 179–201.
Hale, William M. *Turkish Foreign Policy, 1774–2000*. London: Frank Cass, 2000.
Hamid, Shadi. 'Political Party Development before and after the Arab Spring'. In *Beyond the Arab Spring: The Evolving Ruling Bargain in the Middle East*, edited by Mehran Kamrava, 131–50. Oxford University Press, 2014.
Hamid, Shadi. *Temptations of Power: Islamists and Illiberal Democracy in a New Middle East*. Ebook Central. Oxford and New York: Oxford University Press, 2014.
Hanafi, Hassan. 'Islamism: Whose Debate Is It?'. In *Islamism: Contested Perspectives on Political Islam*, edited by Richard C. Martin and Abbas Barzegar, 63–6. Stanford: Stanford University Press, 2010.
Hanieh, Adam 'Egypt's "Orderly Economic Transition": Accelerated Structural Adjustment under a Democratic Veneer?' Centre for Development Policy and Research SOAS, University of London, July 2011.
Harnisch, Chris and Quinn Mecham. 'Democratic Ideology in Islamist Opposition? The Muslim Brotherhood's "Civil State"'. *Middle Eastern Studies* 45, no. 2 (2009): 189–205.
Harvey, David. *A Brief History of Neoliberalism*. Oxford: Oxford University Press, 2005.
Hecker, Pierre. 'The "Arab Spring" and the End of Turkish Democracy'. In *Arab Spring: Modernity, Identity and Change*, edited by Eid Mohamed and Dalia Fahmy, 55–78. Basingstoke: Palgrave Macmillan, 2019.
Helbawy, Kamal 'The Muslim Brotherhood in Egypt: Historical Evolution and Future Prospects'. In *Political Islam: Context versus Ideology*, edited by Khālid Ḥarūb, 61–86. Soas Middle East Issues. London: Saqi, 2010.
Hellwig, Martin. '"Capitalism: What Has Gone Wrong?": Who Went Wrong? Capitalism? The Market Economy? Governments? "Neoliberal" Economics?' *Oxford Review of Economic Policy* 37, no. 4 (2021): 664–77.

Hendricks, Joshua D. 'Globalization, Islamic Activism, and Passive Revolution in Turkey: The Case of Fethullah Gülen'. In *The Neoliberal Landscape and the Rise of Islamist Capital in Turkey*, edited by Neşecan Balkan, Erol Balkan and Ahmet Öncü, 235–71. New York and Oxford: Berghahn Books, 2015.

Herrera, Linda. 'Young Egyptians' Quest for Jobs and Justice'. In *Being Young and Muslim: New Cultural Politics in the Global South and North*, edited by Asef Bayat and Linda Herrera, 127–44. New York and Oxford: Oxford University Press, 2010.

Heywood, Andrew. *Political Ideologies: An Introduction*. London: Palgrave, 2017.

Hinnebusch, Raymond. 'Introduction: Understanding the Consequences of the Arab Uprisings - Starting Points and Divergent Trajectories'. *Democratization: From Arab Spring to Arab Winter: Explaining the Limits of Post-uprising Democratisation – Guest Editor: Raymond Hinnebusch* 22, no. 2 (2015): 205–17.

Hinnebusch, Raymond A. 'Political Parties in MENA: Their Functions and Development'. *British Journal of Middle Eastern Studies: Political Parties in the Middle East: Historical Trajectories and Future Prospects* 44, no. 2 (2017): 172.

Hoesterey, James Bourk. *Rebranding Islam: Piety, Prosperity, and a Self-Help Guru*. Studies of the Walter H. Shorenstein Asia-Pacific Research Center. Stanford: Stanford University Press, 2016.

Hoyle, Justin A. 'A Matter of Framing: Explaining the Failure of Post-Islamist Social Movements in the Arab Spring'. *Digest of Middle East Studies* 25, no. 2 (2016): 186–209.

Huffschmid, Jörg. *Economic Policy for a Social Europe: A Critique of Neo-liberalism and Proposals for Alternatives*. Basingstoke: Palgrave Macmillan, 2005.

Huntington, Samuel P. 'Will More Countries Become Democratic?'. *Political Science Quarterly* 131, no. 2 (2016): 237–66.

Ibrahim, Saad Eddin. 'Toward Muslim Democracies'. *Journal of Democracy* 18, no. 2 (2007): 5–13.

İnsel, Ahmet. 'The Akp and Normalizing Democracy in Turkey'. *The South Atlantic Quarterly* 102, no. 2–3 (2003): 293–308.

Iqtidar, Humeira. 'Theorizing Popular Sovereignty in the Colony: Abul A'la Maududi's "Theodemocracy"'. *The Review of Politics* 82, no. 4 (2020): 595–617.

Islam, Maidul. *Limits of Islamism: Jamaat-E-Islami in Contemporary India and Bangladesh*. Cambridge Core. Cambridge: Cambridge University Press, 2015.

Ismail, Salwa. *Rethinking Islamist Politics: Culture, the State and Islamism*. London and New York: I.B. Tauris, 2006.

Izquierdo, Ferran and John Etherington. 'From Revolution to Moderation: The Long Road of Political Islam'. In *Political Islam in a Time of Revolt (Islam and Nationalism)*, edited by Ferran zquierdo, John Etherington and Laura Feliu, 1–34. Basingstoke: Palgrave Macmillan, 2017.

Izquierdo, Ferran, John Etherington and Laura Feliu. *Political Islam in a Time of Revolt*. Islam and Nationalism. Basingstoke: Palgrave Macmillan, 2017.

Jawad, Nazek. 'Democracy in Modern Islamic Thought'. *British Journal of Middle Eastern Studies* 40, no. 3 (2013): 324–39.

Joseph, Jonathan. *The Social in the Global: Social Theory, Governmentality and Global Politics*. Cambridge Studies in International Relations; 122. Cambridge: Cambridge University Press, 2012.

Joya, Angela. 'Neoliberalism, the State and Economic Policy Outcomes in the Post-Arab Uprisings: The Case of Egypt'. *Mediterranean Politics (Frank Cass & Co.)* 22, no. 3 (2017): 339–61.

Kalın, İbrahim. 'The AK Party in Turkey'. In *The Oxford Handbook of Islam and Politics*, edited by John L. Esposito and Emad Eldin Shahin, 423–39. Oxford: Oxford University Press, 2013.

Kandil, Hazem. *Inside the Brotherhood*. Cambridge: Polity Press, 2015.

Kandil, Hazem. *The Power Triangle: Military, Security, and Politics in Regime Change*. New York: Oxford University Press, 2016.

Kamrava, Mehran. 'The Rise and Fall of Ruling Bargains in the Middle East'. In *Beyond the Arab Spring: The Evolving Ruling Bargain in the Middle East*, edited by Mehran Kamrava, 17–46. Oxford University Press, 2014.

Kandiyoti, Deniz. 'The Travails of the Secular: Puzzle and Paradox in Turkey'. *Economy and Society* 41, no. 4 (2012): 513–31.

Kara, İsmail. *Cumhuriyet Türkiye'sinde Bir Mesele Olarak İslam 1*. İstanbul: Dergah Yayınları, 2019.

Kara, İsmail. *Cumhuriyet Türkiye'sinde Bir Mesele Olarak İslam 2*. İstanbul: Dergah Yayınları, 2019.

Karaatlı, Bülent. *Arap Baharı'nda Farklı Bir Ülke: Tunus*. Ankara: Nobel Yayınları, 2018.

Karagiannis, Emmanuel. *The New Political Islam: Human Rights, Democracy, and Justice*. Philadelphia: University of Pennsylvania Press, 2018.

Kenney, Jeffrey T. 'Selling Success, Nurturing the Self: Self-Help Literature, Capitalist Values, and the Sacralization of Subjective Life in Egypt'. *International Journal of Middle East Studies* 47, no. 4 (2015): 663–80.

Kepel, Gilles. *Away from Chaos: The Middle East and the Challenge to the West*. New York: Columbia University Press, 2020.

Ketchley, Neil. *Egypt in Time of Revolution: Contentious Politics and the Arab Spring*. Cambridge: Cambridge University Press, 2017.

Khan, M. A. Muqtedar. 'Islamic Democracy and Moderate Muslims'. In *Debating Moderate Islam: The Geopolitics of Islam and the West*, edited by M. A. Muqtedar Khan, 51–61. University of Utah Press, 2010.

Khatib, Lina and Ellen Lust. *Taking to the Streets: The Transformation of Arab Activism*. Baltimore: Johns Hopkins University Press, 2014.

King, Gary, Robert O. Keohane and Sidney Verba. *Designing Social Inquiry: Scientific Inference in Qualitative Research*. Scientific Inference in Qualitative Research. Princeton: Princeton University Press, 1994.

Kirişci, Kemal. 'The Transformation of Turkish Foreign Policy: The Rise of the Trading State'. *New Perspectives on Turkey* 40 (2009): 29–56.

Kırkıncı, Mehmed. *Hayatım-Hatıralarım*. İstanbul: Zafer Yayınları.

Kirkpatrick, David D. *Into the Hands of the Soldiers: Freedom and Chaos in Egypt and the Middle East*. London: Bloomsbury Circus, 2018.

Kısakürek, Necip Fazıl. *Türkiye'nin Manzarası*. İstanbul: Büyük Doğu Yayınları, 1985.

Kister, M. J. 'Peygamberi'in Pazarı'. *Cumhuriyet Üniversitesi İlahiyat Fakültesi dergisi* 6, no. 2 (2002): 25–30.

Koca, Bayram. 'M. Hayri Kırbaşoğlu Ile Söyleşi: Islam, Sol Ve Akp'. *Birikim Dergisi* July–August, no. 303–304 (2014): 181–91.

Koselleck, Reinhart. *The Practice of Conceptual History: Timing History, Spacing Concepts*. Stanford: Stanford University Press, 2002.

Köseoğlu, Talha. 'Islamists and the State: Changing Discourses on the State, Civil Society and Democracy in Turkey'. *Turkish Studies* 20, no. 3 (2019): 323–50.

Kramer, Gudrun. *Visions of an Islamic Republic: Good Governance According to the Islamists*, edited by Frederic Volpi, 85–95. Political Islam: A Critical Reader. London: Routledge, 2011.

Krastev, Ivan. *Democracy Disrupted: The Politics of Global Protest*. Philadelphia: University of Pennsylvania Press, 2014.

Kuppinger, Petra, Najib B. Hourani and Ahmed Kanna. 'Crushed? Cario's Garbage Collectors and Neoliberal Urban Politics'. *Journal of Urban Affairs* 36, no. 2 (2014): 621–33.

Kurzman, Charles and Ijlal Naqvi. 'Do Muslims Vote Islamic?'. *Journal of Democracy* 21, no. 2 (2010): 50–63.

Laremont, Ricardo René. 'Moving Past Revolution and Revolt: Transitions to Democracy in North Africa'. In *Revolution, Revolt and Reform in North Africa: The Arab Spring and Beyond*, edited by Ricardo René Laremont, 1–14. Abingdon, Oxon and New York: Routledge Studies in Middle Eastern Democratization and Government, 2014.

Lenz, T. M. J. 'EU Normative Power and Regionalism: Ideational Diffusion and Its Limits'. *Cooperation and Conflict* 48, no. 2 (2013): 211–38.

Lenz, T. M. J. and Kalypso Nicolaidis. 'EU-Topia? A Critique of the European Union as a Model'. *Culture, Practice & Europeanization* 4, no. 2 (2019): 92–5.

Lockman, Zachary. *Contending Visions of the Middle East: The History and Politics of Orientalism*. Contemporary Middle East; 3. 2nd edn. Cambridge: Cambridge University Press, 2010.

Lord, Ceren. *Religious Politics in Turkey: From the Birth of the Republic to the Akp*. Cambridge: Cambridge University Press, 2018.

Madi, Ozlem. 'From Islamic Radicalism to Islamic Capitalism: The Promises and Predicaments of Turkish-Islamic Entrepreneurship in a Capitalist System'. *Middle Eastern Studies* 50, no. 1 (2014): 144.

Mahdavi, Mojtaba. 'Wither Post-Islamism: Revisiting the Discourse/Movement after the Arab Spring'. In *Arab Spring: Modernity, Identity and Change*, edited by Eid Mohamed and Dalia Fahmy, 15–38. Basingstoke: Palgrave Macmillan, 2019.

Mahmood, Saba. *Politics of Piety: The Islamic Revival and the Feminist Subject*. Princeton: Princeton University Press, 2011.

Makdisi, Ussama *The Culture of Sectarianism – Community, History, and Violence in Nineteenth-Century Ottoman Lebanon*. University of California Press, 2000.

Mandaville, Peter. *Islam and Politics*. Third edn. London: Routledge, 2020.

Mandaville, Peter. 'Post-Islamism as Neoliberalisation: New Social Movements in the Muslim World'. In *Islam after Liberalism*, edited by Faisal Devji and Zaheer Kazmi, 281–98. London: Hurst & Company, 2017.

March, Andrew F. 'Political Islam: Theory'. *Annual Review of Political Science* 18, no. 1 (2015): 103–23.

Marks, Monica. 'Convince, Coerce, or Compromise? Ennahda's Approach to Tunisia's Constitution'. Brookings Doha Center Analysis Paper, February 2014.

Marks, Monica. 'Tunisia's Islamists and the "Turkish Model"'. *Journal of Democracy* 28, no. 1 (2017): 2.

Marschall, Melissa, Marwa Shalaby and Saadet Konak Unal. 'Municipal Service Delivery, Identity Politics and Islamist Parties in Turkey'. POMEP Studies, September 2017. https://pomeps.org/municipal-service-delivery-identity-politics-and-islamist-parties-in-turkey.

Martin, Richard C. and Abbas Barzegar. 'Introduction: The Debate about Islamism in the Public Sphere'. In *Islamism: Contested Perspectives on Political Islam*, edited by Richard C. Martin and Abbas Barzegar, 1–13. Stanford: Stanford University Press, 2010.

Martin, Richard C. and Abbas Barzegar. *Islamism: Contested Perspectives on Political Islam*. Stanford: Stanford University Press, 2010.

Marzo, Pietro. 'Critical Junctures, Path Dependence and Al-Nahda's Contribution to the Tunisian Transition to Democracy'. *The Journal of North African Studies* 24, no. 6 (2019): 914–34.

Masoud, Tarek E. *Counting Islam: Religion, Class, and Elections in Egypt*. Problems of International Politics. New York: Cambridge University Press, 2014.

Maududi, Abul A'la. *Al Jihad Fil Islam*. Lahore: Idāra Tarjumān-ul-Qur'ān, 2007.

Maynard, Jonathan Leader. 'A Map of the Field of Ideological Analysis'. *Journal of Political Ideologies* 18, no. 3 (2013): 299–327.

McAdam, Douglas, John McCarthy and Mayer Zald. 'Introduction: Opportunities, Mobilizing Structures, and Framing Processes – Toward a Synthetic, Comparative Perspective on Social Movements'. In *Comparative Perspectives on Social Movements: Political Opportunities, Mobilizing Structures, and Cultural Framing*, edited by D. McAdam, J. McCarthy and M. Zald, 1–20. Cambridge: Cambridge University Press, 1996.

McCarthy, Rory. 'Al-Nahda: From Preaching Circles to Politics'. *The Middle East in London* 14, no. 1 (2018): 14–15.

McCarthy, Rory. *Inside Tunisia's Al-Nahda: Between Politics and Preaching*. Cambridge: Cambridge University Press, 2018.

McCarthy, Rory. 'Re-Thinking Secularism in Post-Independence Tunisia'. *The Journal of North African Studies* 19, no. 5 (2014): 733–50.

McCarthy, Rory. 'The Tunisian Uprising, Ennahdha and the Revival of an Arab-Islamic Identity'. In *Political Identities and Popular Uprisings in the Middle East*, edited by S. Holliday and P. Leech, 157–76. London: Rowman & Littlefield International, 2016.

McCarthy, Rory. 'When Islamists Lose: The Politicization of Tunisia's Al-Nahda Movement'. *Middle East Journal* 72 (2018): 365–84.

McKenna, Christopher D. *The World's Newest Profession: Management Consulting in the Twentieth Century*. Cambridge Studies in the Emergence of Global Enterprise. Cambridge: Cambridge University Press, 2006.

Mecham, Quinn. 'Islamist Parties and Foreign Policy in North Africa: Bridging Ideology and Pragmatism'. *The Journal of North African Studies* 24, no. 4 (2019): 640–60.

Mecham, Quinn and Julie Chernow Hwag. 'The New Dynamism of Islamist Parties'. In *Islamist Parties and Political Normalization in the Muslim World*, edited by Quinn Mecham and Julie Chernov Hwang, 175–92. Philadelphia: University of Pennsylvania Press, 2014.

Mellor, Noha. *Voice of the Muslim Brotherhood: Da'wa, Discourse, and Political Communication*. Routledge, 2017.

Metiner, Mehmet. *Yemyeşil Şeriat Bembeyaz Demokrasi*. Doğan Kitap, 2004.

Mohamed, Eid and Dalia Fahmy. *Arab Spring: Modernity, Identity and Change*. Critical Political Theory and Radical Practice. Basingstoke: Palgrave Macmillan, 2019.

Moore, Barrington. *Social Origins of Dictatorship and Democracy [Electronic Resource]: Lord and Peasant in the Making of the Modern World*. Lord and Peasant in the Making of the Modern World. Boston: Beacon Press, 1993.

Morlino, Leonardo. *Democracy between Consolidation and Crisis: Parties, Groups, and Citizens in Southern Europe*. Oxford: Oxford University Press, 1998.

Moussalli, Ahmad S. 'Sayyid Qutb: Founder of Radical Islamic Political Ideology'. In *Routledge Handbook of Political Islam*, edited by Shahram Akbarzadeh, 9–27. London: Routledge, 2012.

Mudge, Stephanie Lee. 'What Is Neoliberalism?' *Socio-economic Review* 6, no. 4 (2008): 703–31.

Müller, Jan-Werner. *What Is Populism?* Philadelphia: University of Pennsylvania Press, 2016.

Mura, Andrea. 'A Genealogical Inquiry into Early Islamism: The Discourse of Hasan Al-Banna'. *Journal of Political Ideologies* 17, no. 1 (2012): 61–85.

Murphy, Emma C. 'The Tunisian Elections of October 2011: A Democratic Consensus'. *The Journal of North African Studies* 18, no. 2 (2013): 231–47.

Nasr, Vali. *The Rise of Islamic Capitalism (Previously Published as Forces of Fortune)*. New York: Free Press, 2009.

Navaro-Yashin, Yael. *Faces of the State: Secularism and Public Life in Turkey*, 223–4. Princeton and Oxford: Princeton University Press, 2002.

Navaro-Yashin, Yael. 'The Market for Identities: Secularism, Islamism, Commodities'. In *Fragments of Culture: The Everyday of Modern Turkey*, edited by Deniz Kandiyoti and Ayşe Saktanber, 221–53. London: I.B. Tauris, 2002.

Netterstrom, Kasper Ly. 'The Islamists' Compromise in Tunisia'. *Journal of Democracy* 26, no. 4 (2015): 110–24.

O'Donnell, Christopher J. *Productivity and Efficiency Analysis: An Economic Approach to Measuring and Explaining Managerial Performance*. Singapore: Springer, 2018.

Ong, Aihwa. *Neoliberalism as Exception [Electronic Resource]: Mutations in Citizenship and Sovereignty*. Durham: Duke University Press, 2006.

Öniş, Ziya. 'The Political Economy of Turkey's Justice and Development Party'. In *The Emergence of a New Turkey: Islam, Democracy, and the Emergence of the AK Parti*, edited by Hakan Yavuz, 207–34. University of Utah Press, 2006.

Osman, Tarek. *Egypt on the Brink: From Nasser to the Muslim Brotherhood*. Updated edn. New Haven: Yale University Press, 2013.

Ounissi, Sayida and Monica Marks. 'Ennahda from Within: Islamists or "Muslim Democrats"?'. In *Rethinking Political Islam*, edited by Shadi Hamid and William F. McCants. New York: Oxford University Press, 2017: 230–43.

Owen, John M. *Confronting Political Islam: Six Lessons from the West's Past*. Princeton: Princeton University Press, 2015.

Özbudun, Ergun. 'From Political Islam to Conservative Democracy: The Case of the JDP in Turkey'. *South European Society and Politics* 11, no. 3/4 (2006): 543–57.

Özkan, Behlül. '"Turkey, DavutoğLu and the Idea of Pan-Islamism"'. *Survival: Global Politics and Strategy* 56, no. 4 (2014): 119–40.

Pargeter, Alison. 'Localism and Radicalization in North Africa: Local Factors and the Development of Political Islam in Morocco, Tunisia and Libya'. *International Affairs* 85, no. 5 (2009): 1031–44.

Pargeter, Alison. *Return to the Shadows: The Muslim Brotherhood and an-Nahda since the Arab Spring*. London: Saqi, 2016.

Pargeter, Alison. *The Muslim Brotherhood: From Opposition to Power*. New edn, Paperback edn. London: Saqi, 2013.

Perekli, Feriha. 'The Applicability of the "Turkish Model" to Morocco: T (Pjd)'. *Insight Turkey* 14, no. 3 (2012): 85–108.

Perkins, Kenneth. 'Playing the Islamic Card: The Use and Abuse of Religion in Tunisian Politics'. In *The Making of the Tunisian Revolution*, edited by Nouri Gana, 58–80. Edinburgh University Press, 2013.

Picchi, Margherita. 'Islam as the Third Way: Sayyid Quṭb's Socio-Economic Thought and Nasserism'. *Oriente Moderno* 97, no. 1 (2017): 177–200.

Piscatori, James P. *Islam, Islamists, and the Electoral Principle in the Middle East*. Leiden: ISIM, 2000.

Piscatori, James P. *Islam in a World of Nation-States*. Cambridge: Cambridge University Press, 1986.

Piscatori, James P. and Amin Saikal. *Islam beyond Borders: The Umma in World Politics*. Cambridge: Cambridge University Press, 2019.

Powers, Colin. 'Run the Country Like a Business? The Economics of Jordan's Islamic Action Front'. *Critical Research on Religion* 7, no. 1 (2019): 38–57.

Pras, Bernard. 'Management Et Islam: Vers Une Convergence De Valeurs'. [In fre]. *Revue Française de Gestion* 33, no. 171 (2007): 91–5.

Qutb, S. *Al-Mustaqbal Li Hadha Al-Din*. Cairo: Maktabat Wahda, 1965.

Rahman, Fazlur. 'Islam and Social Justice'. *Pakistani Forum 1* 1, no. 4–5 (1970).

Ranko, Annette and Justyna Nedza. 'Crossing the Ideological Divide? Egypt's Salafists and the Muslim Brotherhood after the Arab Spring'. *Studies in Conflict and Terrorism* 39, no. 6 (2016): 519–41.

Rethel, Lena. 'Corporate Islam, Global Capitalism and the Performance of Economic Moralities'. *New Political Economy* 24, no. 3 (2019): 350–64.

Roberts, Clayton. *The Logic of Historical Explanation*. University Park: Pennsylvania State University Press, 1996.

Roberts, Adam, Michael J. Willis, Rory McCarthy and Timothy Garton Ash. *Civil Resistance in the Arab Spring: Triumphs and Disasters*. Oxford: Oxford University Press, 2016.

Rodgers, Daniel. 'Bearing Tales: Networks and Narratives in Social Policy Transfer'. *Journal of Global History* 9, no. 2 (2014): 301–13.

Rodinson, Maxime. *Islam and Capitalism*. London: Allen Lane, 1974.

Rogan, Eugene L. 'Sectarianism and Social Conflict in Damascus: The 1860 Events Reconsidered'. *Arabica*, T.51, no. Fasc. 4 (2004): 493–511.

Rogers, Everett M. *Diffusion of Innovations*. 5th edn. New York and London: Free Press, 2003.

Rougier, Bernard and Stephane Lacroix. *Egypt's Revolutions: Politics, Religion, and Social Movements*. Basingstoke: Palgrave Macmillan, 2016.

Rousselin, Mathieu. 'In the Name of Allah and of the Market: The Capitalist Leanings of Tunisian Islamists'. *Science & Society* 80, no. 2 (2016): 196–220.

Roy, Olivier. *Globalized Islam: The Search for a New Ummah*. Ceri Series in Comparative Politics and International Studies. New York: Columbia University Press, 2004.

Roy, Olivier. *The Failure of Political Islam*. London: I.B. Tauris, 1994.

Roy, Olivier. 'The Myth of the Islamist Winter'. *New Statesman* 141, no. 5136 (2012): 23–5.

Rudolph, Susanne Hoeber. 'Introduction: Religion, States, and Transnational Civil Society'. In *Transnational Religion and Fading States*, edited by Susanne Hoeber Rudolph and James P. Piscatori, 1–24. Boulder: Westview Press, 1997.

Sadiki, Larbi. *Routledge Handbook of the Arab Spring: Rethinking Democratization*. London: Routledge, 2016.

Sadiki, Larbi. 'Tunisia's Ennahda: Islamists Turning the Learning Curve of Democracy and Civic Habituation'. In *The Politics of Islamism: Diverging Visions and Trajectories*, edited by J. L. Esposito, Lily Zubaidah Rahim and Naser Ghobazadeh, 87–125. Basingstoke, Hampshire: Palgrave Macmillan, 2017.

Said, Edward W. *Orientalism*. London: Routledge & Kegan Paul, 1978.

Said, Edward W. *Orientalism*. Penguin Classics. London: Penguin Books, 2003.

Saif, Ibrahim and Mohammed Abu Rumman. 'The Economic Agenda of the Islamist Parties'. Carnegie Endowment Middle East Center, 2012.

Sajjad, Fatima and Umbreen Javaid. 'The Civilizational Rift and the Idea of the Turkish Model: A Case Study (2002–2014)'. *Journal of Political Studies* 23, no. 1 (2016): 133–56.

Sargent, Lyman Tower. 'Ideology and Utopia: Karl Mannheim and Paul Ricoeur'. *Journal of Political Ideologies* 13, no. 3 (2008): 263–73.

Sayyid, S. *A Fundamental Fear: Eurocentrism and the Emergence of Islamism*. London: Zed Books, 2015.

Schmidt, Vivien A. 'Taking Ideas and Discourse Seriously: Explaining Change through Discursive Institutionalism as the Fourth "New Institutionalism"'. *European Political Science Review* 2, no. 1 (2010): 1–25.

Schumacher, Tobias. 'The European Union and Democracy Promotion'. In *Routledge Handbook of the Arab Spring: Rethinking Democratization*, edited by Larbi Sadiki, 559–73. London: Routledge, 2016.

Schwedler, Jillian. 'Islamists in Power? Inclusion, Moderation, and the Arab Uprisings'. *Middle East Development Journal* 5, no. 1 (2013): 347–76.

Şengül, Serdar. 'Kategorik Ret ile Kategorik Kabul Arasında Türkiye'de İslam'a ve İslamcılığa Yaklaşımlar'. *Birikim Dergisi* July–August, no. 303–4 (2014): 27–36.

Shehata, Samer S. 'Introduction'. In *Islamist Politics in the Middle East: Movements and Change*, edited by Samer S. Shehata. Abingdon, Oxon and New York: Routledge, 2011.

Shehata, Samer S. 'Political Da'wa: Understanding the Muslim Brotherhood's Participation in Semi-Authoritarian Elections'. In *Islamist Politics in the Middle East: Movements and Change*, edited by Samer S. Shehata, 120–45. Abingdon, Oxon and New York: Routledge, 2011.

Sidahmed, Abdel Salam and Anoushiravan Ehteshami. *Islamic Fundamentalism*. Twentieth Century Religious Thought. Boulder: Westview Press, 1996.

Simon, Herbert A. 'Bounded Rationality'. In *Utility and Probability*, edited by M. Milgate, J. Eatwell and P. Newma, 15–18. Palgrave Macmillan, 1990.

Skinner, Quentin. 'Some Problems in the Analysis of Political Thought and Action'. *Political Theory* 2, no. 3 (1974): 277–303.

Smith, Jackie. 'Transnational Processes and Movements'. In *The Blackwell Companion to Social Movements*, edited by David A. Snow, Sarah Anne Soule and Hanspeter Kriesi. Malden: Blackwell, 2004.

Smith, Zadie. 'Introduction'. In *Recitatif*, edited by Toni Morrison. London: Vintage, 2022.

Snow, David A. 'Framing Processes, Ideology, and Discursive Fields'. In *Blackwell Companion to Social Movements*, edited by David A. Snow, Sarah Anne Soule and Hanspeter Kriesi, 380–412. Malden: Blackwell, 2004.

Snow, David A. and Scott C. Byrd, 'Ideology, Framing Processes, and Islamic Terrorist Movements'. *Mobilization (San Diego, Calif.)* 12, no. 2 (2007): 119–36.

Snyder, Timothy. *The Road to Unfreedom: Russia, Europe, America*. London: The Bodley Head, 2018.

Solingen, Etel. 'Of Dominoes and Firewalls: The Domestic, Regional, and Global Politics of International Diffusion1'. *International Studies Quarterly* 56, no. 4 (2012): 631–44.

Somer, Murat. 'Conquering Versus Democratizing the State: Political Islamists and Fourth Wave Democratization in Turkey and Tunisia'. *Democratization* 24, no. 6 (2017): 1025–43.

Somer, Murat. 'When Is Normalization Also Democratization? Islamist Political Parties, the Turkish Case and the Future of Muslim Polities'. In *Islamist Parties and Political Normalization in the Muslim World*, edited by Quinn Mecham and Julie Chernov Hwang, 40–57. Philadelphia: University of Pennsylvania Press, 2014.

Spiegel, Avi. *Young Islam: The New Politics of Religion in Morocco and the Arab World*. Princeton Studies in Muslim Politics. Princeton: Princeton University Press, 2015.

Springborg, Robert. *Egypt*. Cambridge: Polity, 2018.

Stampnitzky, Lisa. *Disciplining Terror: How Experts Invented 'Terrorism'*. Cambridge Core. Cambridge: Cambridge University Press, 2013.

Stephenson, Niamh and Dimitris Papadopoulos. 'Exit from the Regime of Life Control: Biopolitics, Anticipatory Risk and the Excess of Experience'. *Somatechnics* 1, no. 2 (2011): 412–33.

Svasand, Lars. 'International Party Assistance – What Do We Know About the Effects?' Expertgruppen för bistandsanalys (EBA), 2014.

Tagma, Halit Mustafa, Elif Kalaycioglu and Emel Akcali. '"Taming" Arab Social Movements: Exporting Neoliberal Governmentality'. *Security Dialogue* 44, no. 5–6 (2013): 375–92.

Tamimi, Azzam. *Rachid Ghannouchi: A Democrat within Islamism*. Oxford and New York: Oxford University Press, 2001.

Tammam, Husam and Patrick Haenni. 'Au Diable Les Loosers! Le Succès Et L'achievement, Nouvelles Valeurs Islamiques En Égypte'. *Mouvements (Paris, France: 1998)* 36, no. 6 (2004): 42–53.

Tarrow, Sidney G. *The New Transnational Activism*. Cambridge Studies in Contentious Politics. New York and Cambridge: Cambridge University Press, 2005.

Taşkın, Yücel. 'Arap Baharı ve Türkiye'deki İslamcı çevrelere etkileri: Baharımızı kışa çevirtmeyeceğiz'. *Birikim Dergisi* July–August, no. 303–4 (2014): 105–17.

Taşkın, Yüksel. 'Hegemonizing Conservative Democracy and the Problems of Democratization in Turkey: Conservatism Without Democrats?'. *Turkish Studies* 14, no. 2 (2013): 292–310.

Tezcür, Güneş Murat. *Muslim Reformers in Iran and Turkey: The Paradox of Moderation*. 1st edn. Austin: University of Texas Press, 2010.

Thompson, Helen. *Disorder: Hard Times in the 21st Century*. Oxford: Oxford University Press, 2022.

Tibi, Bassam. *Islamism and Islam*. New Haven and London: Yale University Press, 2012.

Tickell, A. and J. Peck. 'Making Global Rules: Globalization or Neoliberalisation'. In *Remaking the Global Economy: Economic-Geographical Perspectives*, edited by Jamie Peck and Henry Yeung, 163–82. SAGE, 2003.

Trager, Eric. *The Arab Fall: How the Muslim Brotherhood Won and Lost Egypt in 891 Days*. Washington, DC: Georgetown University Press, 2016.

Tripp, Charles. *Islam and the Moral Economy: The Challenge of Capitalism*. Cambridge: Cambridge University Press, 2006.

Tuğal, Cihan. 'Contesting Benevolence: Market Orientations among Muslim Aid Providers in Egypt'. *Qualitative Sociology* 36, no. 2 (2013): 141–59.

Tuğal, Cihan. 'Religious Politics, Hegemony, and the Market Economy: Parties in the Making of Turkey's Liberal-Conservative Bloc and Egypt's Diffuse Islamization'. In *Building Blocs: How Parties Organize Society*, edited by De Leon Cedric, Cihan Tuğal and Desai Manali, 87–122. Palo Alto: Stanford University Press, 2015.

Tuğal, Cihan. *The Fall of the Turkish Model: How the Arab Uprisings Brought Down Islamic liberalism*. Brooklyn: Verso, 2016.

Turner, Bryan S. 'Islam, Capitalism and the Weber Theses'. *British Journal of Sociology* 61, no. Supp. 1 (2010): 147–60.

Türkmen, Hamza. *İslami Mücadelenin Yeni Dili*. İstanbul: Ekin Yayınları, 2013.

Türköne, Mümtazer. *Doğum ile Ölüm arasında İslamcılık*. İstanbul: Kapı Yayınları, 2012.

Turner, Rachel S. 'Neoliberal Constitutionalism: Ideology, Government and the Rule of Law'. *Journal of Politics and Law (Toronto)* 1, no. 2 (2008): 47–55.

Vannetzel, Marie. 'Confronting the Transition to Legality'. In *Egypt's Revolutions: Politics, Religion, and Social Movements*, edited by Bernard Rougier and Stephane Lacroix, 41–60. Basingstoke: Palgrave Macmillan, 2016.

Vannetzel, Marie and Dilek Yankaya. 'Crafting a Business Umma? Transnational Networks of "Islamic Businessmen" after the Arab Spring'. *Mediterranean Politics* 24, no. 3 (2019): 290–310.

Varisco, Daniel M. 'Inventing Islamism: The Violence of Rhetoric'. In *Islamism: Contested Perspectives on Political Islam*, edited by Richard C. Martin and Abbas Barzegar. Stanford: Stanford University Press, 2010: 33–47.

Ventura, Lorella. 'The "Arab Spring" And Orientalist Stereotypes: The Role of Orientalism in the Narration of the Revolts in the Arab World'. *Interventions* 19, no. 2 (2017): 282–97.

Vicini, Fabio. 'Post-Islamism or Veering toward Political Modernity?'. *Sociology of Islam* 4, no. 3 (2016): 261–79.

Volpi, Frédéric. *Political Islam: A Critical Reader*. London: Routledge, 2011.

Volpi, Frederic. *Revolution and Authoritarianism in North Africa*. Oxford University Press, 2017.

Webb, Edward. 'Changing the Player, Not the Game. Ennahda's Homo Islamicus'. *ASPJ Africa & Francophonie* 5, no. 1 (2014): 4–18.
Weber, Max. *Political Writings*. Cambridge Texts in the History of Political Thought. Edited by Peter Lassman and Ronald Speirs. New York: Cambridge University Press, 1994.
Wickham, Carrie Rosefsky. *Mobilizing Islam: Religion, Activism, and Political Change in Egypt*. New York and Chichester: Columbia University Press, 2003.
Wickham, Carrie Rosefsky. *The Muslim Brotherhood: Evolution of an Islamist Movement*. Princeton: Princeton University, 2013.
Wickham, Carrie Rosefsky. 'The Path to Moderation: Strategy and Learning in the Formation of Egypt's Wasat Party'. *Comparative Politics* 36, no. 2 (2004): 205–28.
Wiktorowicz, Quintan. *Islamic Activism: A Social Movement Theory Approach*. Indiana Series in Middle East Studies. Bloomington: Indiana University Press, 2004.
White, Jenny B. 'Islamist Social Networks and Social Welfare Services in Turkey'. In *Islamist Politics in the Middle East: Movements and Change*, edited by Samer S. Shehata, 59–67. Abingdon, Oxon and New York: Routledge, 2011.
White, Jenny B. *Muslim Nationalism and the New Turks*. Princeton Studies in Muslim Politics. Princeton: Princeton University Press, 2013.
Willi, Victor J. *The Fourth Ordeal: A History of the Muslim Brotherhood in Egypt, 1968–2018*. Cambridge: Cambridge University Press, 2021.
Willis, Michael J. 'Evolution Not Revolution? Morocco and the Arab Spring'. In *Routledge Handbook of the Arab Spring: Rethinking Democratization*, edited by Larbi Sadiki, 435–50. London: Routledge, 2016.
Willis, Michael J. 'Morocco's Islamists and the Legislative Elections of 2002: The Strange Case of the Party That Did Not Want to Win'. *Mediterranean Politics* 9, no. 1 (2004): 53–81.
Willis, Michael J. *Politics and Power in the Maghreb: Algeria, Tunisia and Morocco from Independence to the Arab Spring*. London: Hurst, 2012.
Wolf, Anne. 'An Islamist "Renaissance"? Religion and Politics in Post-Revolutionary Tunisia'. *The Journal of North African Studies* 18, no. 4 (2013): 560–73.
Wolf, Anne. *Political Islam in Tunisia: The History of Ennahda*. London: Hurst & Company, 2017.
Woltering, Robbert A. F. L. 'Post-Islamism in Distress? A Critical Evaluation of the Theory in Islamist-Dominated Egypt (11 February 2011–3 July 2013)'. *Die Welt des Islams* 54, no. 1 (2014): 107–18.
Wright, Robin B. *The Islamists Are Coming: Who They Really Are*. Washington, DC: Woodrow Wilson Center Press; United States Institute of Peace Press, 2012.
Yankaya, Dilek. 'Du Cadre D'action Collective Au Programme Partisan: Ancrages Patronaux Des Islamismes En Turquie Et En Tunisie'. *L'année du Maghreb* 22 (2020): 203–22.
Yenigün, Halil Ibrahim. 'The Political and Theological Boundaries of Islamist Moderation after the Arab Spring'. *Third World Quarterly* 37, no. 12 (2016): 2304–21.

Yohanan, Benhaim and Öktem Kerem. 'The Rise and Fall of Turkey's Soft Power Discourse'. *European Journal of Turkish Studies* 21 (2016). https://doi.org/10.4000/ejts.5275.

Zaied, Al-Sayed. 'Da'wa for Dollars: A New Way of Muslim Televangelist'. *Arab Insight* 1, no. 3 (2008): 21–7.

Zubaida, Sami. *Beyond Islam: A New Understanding of the Middle East*. Library of Modern Middle East Studies; 84. London: I.B. Tauris, 2011.

Index

Page numbers followed with "n" refer to endnotes.

Aa Gym. *See* Gymnastair, Abdullah
Abdelkafi, Bedreddine   143
Abdessalem, Rafik   39, 59, 62, 145
Aboul Foutuh, Abdul Moneim   63, 80, 109, 110
Ajami, Fouad   112
Akdogan, Yalçın   36
Akef, Mahdi   31, 52
AKP (*Adalet ve Kalkınma Partisi*)   1–6, 11, 24–6, 32, 36, 42, 43, 47–9, 56, 71, 88–92, 107, 108, 111–13, 115, 117–18, 139, 142, 144, 146, 150, 154, 158–9, 163, 166
   alliance-building   87, 92, 94, 96
   al-Qaradawi as mediator for   68–9
   anti-Morsi coalition   95
   assistance to Ennahda and the Muslim Brotherhood   8
   authoritarianism   134, 137, 153, 157, 158
   ban of   91
   in Cairo   51, 55, 64
   capitalist system   158
   cheap Islamization   133–5
   consolidation of power   92
   corruption investigations against   144
   crises when forming the   75
   cultivating Islamic bourgeoisie   114
   Davutoğlu's policies   48
   democracy   40–1
   democratic reforms   41
   dialogue between the Muslim Brotherhood and   108
   diffused tactics   72, 74
   diffusion process   40, 135
   economic policy   41, 46
   economic strategy   106
   economic vision   107
   effective service delivery techniques   85
   electoral campaigns   78–82
   EU
      accession process   74
      role in Turkish model   43–6
   fourth General Assembly in Ankara   55
   garbage recycling facility   85
   geopolitics   12
   good governance   108
   as good Islamists   40, 42
   governance   37, 45
   Gül's nomination   91
   interaction between Ennahda and   64
   interactions between Muslim Brotherhood and   51–2, 55
   internal rifts   156
   Islamic bourgeoisie   113
   Islamism   11, 116
   legitimacy deficit   45
   local governance   85
   mission to protect Muslim   49
   municipal services   84–6
   Muslim/Conservative democracy   36–40
   Muslim democrats   42
   Muslim politics   34
   neoliberalism   49
      conservatism   158
      governance   116
   neoliberal policies   85
   as non-Arab political party   11
   opinion polls   80
   participation in the EU accession   41, 45
   party institutionalization   76
   piecemeal Islamisation   133–4
   policies and initiatives   26
   political Islam   40–1
   post-Islamist model   12
   power in 2002   25–6

privatization 46
pro-market policies 85
Protestant work ethic 106
refuse disposal trucks 85
relationship
   with MÜSİAD 113
   Muslim Brotherhood and
      Ennahda 11
   with North African parties 5, 8
resisting the military and judicial
      intervention 90
role in Islamism 158
sanitation services 86
social mobilization 84–5
socio-political project 84
state capture 134–5
strategies 46
success 122–3
   in elections 71–2
tacit and cross-class coalition 96
tactics 8
three-party coalition government 44
transactional coalition 156
transformation from Islamism to post-
      Islamism 84
Turkey's debts, reduction of 107
Turkish model 9, 40–3
two-tier formulae 98
winning elections and power 156
al-Afghani, Jamal, *mmah/dar al-Islam* 5
al-Banna, Hasan 16, 20, 29, 30, 76, 106,
   122
   Islamic order (*nizam islami*) 17
   writings of 27, 28
al Fadl, Abou 142
al-Gharbi, Jamel Eddin 59, 60
al-Hudaibi, Hasan 17
al-Hudaibi, Ibrahim 42
al-Ikhwan al-muslimin fi Misr. See Muslim
   Brotherhood (MB)
Al-Ittiḥād Al-'Ālamī li-'Ulamā'
   al-Muslimīn. See IUMS
   (International Union of Muslim
   Scholars)
Al Jazeera TV 67–70, 140
al-Labbad, Mustafa 49
Al Nour Party 109
al-Qaeda 4, 38
   attacks of 11 September 125

al-Qaradawi, Sheikh Yusuf 16, 47,
   67–70, 84, 127, 130, 140–1
al-Radaoui, Reda 146
al-Sadr, Baqir 28
al-Sharia wa-l-Ḥayah 140
Al Sharq Forum 70
Al Sharq TV 141, 150
al-Shater, Khairat 10, 52–5, 63, 109–11,
   114, 155
al-Sherif, Abdel Khaleq 109
al-Shobaki, Amr 88
al-Shuaibi, Riad 165
al-Siba'i, Mustafa 102
al-Sisi, Abdel Fatah 69, 95, 139, 141, 144,
   148–51
Al Watan 141
al-Zomor, Tariq 94, 95, 142
Amin, Samir 103
Amor, Adel Ben Amor 84
Anatolian Tigers or Calvinist
   Muslims 24
Ansar al-Shari'a 60, 144
anti-labour legislation 110
anti-Morsi coalition 95
Arab Uprisings 1, 2, 6–9, 13, 19, 26,
   34, 35, 39–41, 43, 44, 46–9, 61,
   68–70, 77, 83, 86, 100–1, 105,
   132, 138, 153, 154, 159, 163
Arbaoui, Noureddine 123
Assad, Talal 2–3
Atalay, Beşir 22, 25, 57–9, 62, 75, 91,
   122, 123
Atatürk, Mustafa Kemal 20, 23, 53, 133
   modernization model 116
authoritarianism, AKP 134, 137, 153,
   157, 158
authoritarian nationalism 102
Azaiez, Nahdawi Mohammed Ali 76

Babacan, Ali 63, 156
Badie, Mohammad 51, 52, 108–9
banality of governance 13
Bayat, Asef 6, 83, 89, 114, 126, 131–3,
   157, 169
   post-Islamism 37
Beinin, Joel 104
Belaid, Chokri 144, 146
Ben Ali 2, 21–2, 34, 38, 44, 59, 101, 107,
   112, 115, 118, 143

Ben Youssef, Salah 20
Bhiri, Noureddine 143
bilateral relations, Turkey and
    Egypt 150–1
bin Laden, Osama 38
bin Sultan, Bandar 142
Boltanski, Luc 129
bounded rationality 27
bourgeois revolution 113
Bourguiba, Habib 20, 21, 23, 116, 143
Brahmi, Mohamed 144, 146
Brahmi, Zeinab 96
brokers 67–70
a Brotherhood empire 4, 5
Bulaç, Ali 26, 37, 122
Bush, George W. 40

capitalism 101–3, 107, 113, 118, 126,
    129–32, 163, 165–7
CAPMAS (the Central Agency for
    Public Mobilization and
    Statistics) 79–80
cheap Islamization 133–5
Chennoufi, Malek 132
CHP 86, 91
coalition government, of *Doğru Yol Partisi*
    (DYP) 25
Cold War politics 126
communism 102, 125
Congress for the Republic (CPR) 96
conservative bourgeoisie 112
Copenhagen Criteria 44, 74, 157
corruption 100, 105, 108, 110, 114, 123, 134
    investigations 144–7, 164
CPR. *See* Congress for the Republic (CPR)
crisis 74–5, 99, 152, 153
    Islamism 161
    management 46, 74
cronyism 100, 101, 105
Cumhuriyet Mitingleri (Republican
    Rallies) 91

Darrag, Amr 42, 63, 65, 76, 108
Davutoğlu, Ahmet 4, 48–51, 54, 59,
    62–4, 70, 78, 86, 92–5, 156
    total performance 63, 65
da'wa 79, 82, 83, 93, 97–8, 166
democracy 43, 44, 56, 59, 61, 69, 100,
    113, 164, 166

AKP 40–1
    Islam and 22, 61
    and Islamism 152–9
    Muslim/conservative (*see* Muslim/
        conservative democracy)
Democratic Constitutional Rally. *See* RCD
    (*Rassemblement Constitutionnel
    Démocratique*)
democratic governance 38–9, 100
democratic political Islam 69
Destour Party 19
Diab, Amr 131
diffused tactics
    AKP 72, 74
    Ennahda 72
    Tunisian and Egyptian contexts 73
diffusion 2, 6, 8, 11, 27, 34, 35, 39, 71–2,
    123, 142, 163
    actors in 68
    AKP 135
    Arab Uprisings in 70
    brokers in 67–70
    of electoral tactics 77–82
    elite actors in 62–3
    Ennahda 11, 13
    of EU policies 73
    interlocutors in 64–5
    mediated 62, 69
    of MÜSİAD's model 117
    Muslim Brotherhood (MB) 11, 13
    NGOs as interlocutors in 62–3
    non-relational 62
    relational 62
    role of the broker in 67
    transnational 3, 72
Diyanet İşleri Başkanlığı (Presidency of
    Religious Affairs) 133
Driss, Ridha 97, 108, 117

EBDA. *See* Egyptian Business
    Development Association
    (EBDA)
economic liberalism 132
economic system 102
Egyptian Business Development
    Association (EBDA) 111–12,
    114, 116–18
Egyptian coup 138, 139
Egyptian economy 112

Egyptian revolution   6, 10, 32, 36, 40, 43, 44, 51, 55, 74, 95, 110, 154
Egyptian Supreme Court   31, 88, 91, 94
Eickelman, Dale F.   125, 162
election polls   80
electoral politics   166
   Muslim Brotherhood (MB)   17–18
electoral tactics, diffusion of   77–82
elite actors   62–3
end of ideology argument   126, 207 n.25
Ennahda   1–6, 32–3, 35, 36, 45–9, 53, 56, 71, 73, 75, 77, 85, 132, 141, 156, 162, 163, 165, 166
   alliance with Nidaa Tounes   23
   ban of   21, 34
   challenges   34
   as charity organization   77
   coalition   96
      government   58
   dialogue between the AKP and   108
   diffusion process   11, 13, 34, 40, 72
   diversity management task   96
   economic and governance challenges   156
   economic vision of   105–11
   electoral success   58
   establishing the theocratic state   58
   first free elections   97, 98
   ideological revision   22, 169
   imprisonment and exile   22
   interaction between AKP and   64
   internal crisis   145
   internal divisions   22
   Islam and democracy   22, 61
   legalized as political party   57
   legitimacy   34
   money-laundering scheme   146
   Muslim/conservative democracy   39, 97
   Muslim politics   34
   non-violence   38
   normalization for   75
   participation in elections   21, 22, 78, 81, 82
   pluralism   57
   political victory of   7
   post-2013 period   143–7
   rise and decline   11
   rise to power of   74
   and *sharia* law   22
   shura concept   42
   social welfare services   83
   threats and alliances   96–8
   Turkish model   9
   2011 elections   22
   2014 elections   23
   uprising against Saied, Kais   146
   withdrawal from power   144
   for women's rights and economic stability   22
entrepreneurialism   131
Erbakan, Necmettin   23–6, 29–32, 45, 47–9, 112, 145, 164, 183 n.50
   formation of coalition government in 1995   31
   Islamization of success   122
   relationship with Muslim Brotherhood (MB)   31
Erdoğan, Recep Tayyip   1, 4, 26, 29–32, 36, 38–9, 43, 46, 47–51, 55, 58–9, 63–5, 68–70, 76, 80, 84, 86, 91, 104–5, 117, 123, 137, 139–41, 143, 152, 157, 158, 162, 164
   authoritarian and economic policies   156
   concept of legitimacy   164
   corruption investigations against   144
   criticism on   156
   four-fingered symbol   138, 147–8
   Islam and democracy   56
   Islamism   53
   morality politics   133, 134
   pragmatism and the utilitarian value   151
   Rabaa massacre and   148
   relations with Saudi Arabia and the UAE   151
   secularism   52–3, 56, 57
   and Sisi of Egypt   150–1
   support to Morsi government   141
   U-turns vis-a-vis the Muslim Brotherhood (MB)   147–51
   visit
      to Cairo   51–3, 57
      to Tunis   55–6
      to the Zaytouna Mosque   57, 60
Essebsi, Beji Caid   56, 145

Ettakatol Party   96
European Court of Human Rights
    (ECHR) provisions   44
European integration   45
European Union (EU)
  democracy   43
  influence over Turkey   44
  reforms   44
  and Turkish model   43–6

Felhi, Nejmeddin   132
Fidan, Hakan   95–6
financial corruption investigations   146
financialization   46, 103
FJP (Freedom and Justice Party)   2, 7, 19, 43, 74–5, 77, 78, 81, 90, 91, 93, 109, 110, 155, 166
  election campaign   79
  rise and decline   11
  Turkish model   19
foreign policy   7, 42, 45, 48, 63, 65, 162
Foutuh, Abdul Moneim   148
frames/framing   35
  Muslim democracy   36
Freeden, Michael   167–8
Freedom and Justice (al-hurriya wal 'adala)   43

Gaaloul, Ahmed   63, 123, 143
geopolitics   4, 12, 13, 125, 152, 162
Gezi protests   135, 137–9, 164
Ghaffar, Ashraf Abdul   50
Ghannouchi, Rachid   11, 20–4, 30–2, 46, 56, 58, 60, 62, 68, 80, 107, 115, 127, 140, 143, 145, 164–5
  declaration   38
  democratic governance   38–9
  Facebook speech   98
  Islam and modernity   39
  Islamic/Muslim democracy   38–9
  money laundering and inciting violence   145–6
  Public Liberties in the Islamic State   38
  published works   30
  relations with Erdoğan   145
globalization   103, 113, 127, 157
global neoliberal convergence   103
God's sovereignty (*hakimiyya Allah*)   38, 165–6

governance   13, 117, 158, 167
  AKP   37, 45
  banality of   13
  democratic   38
  in Tunisia   11
governmentality   73, 113
grounded theory approach   7
Gül, Abdullah   26, 32, 55, 59, 60, 62–3, 91, 156
  official visit to Cairo   51
Gülen movement   29, 42, 66, 92, 139
Gymnastair, Abdullah   128, 131

Hagia Sophia   133, 134
Hamed, Yehia   155
Harouni, Abdelkarem   42, 87
Haşimi, Cemallettin   65–6
Helsinki declaration   44
hizb al-hurriya wa'l adala. See FJP (Freedom and Justice Party)
homo economicus   104
homo Islamicus   104, 106

ideational diffusion   34
ijtihad   20, 22, 168, 183 n.40
Ikhwan   1, 2, 4, 28, 29, 90, 92–3, 114
Ikhwani   56
Ikhwanweb   140
illiberalism   158
IMF   108, 109
imperialism   103
income inequalities   45
Infitah (Open Door) policies   105
inflation   107, 108, 124, 151
Instalingo case   146
interlocutors and structure   63–7
Iranian revolution of 1979   17, 25, 28, 169
ISIS   60–1
Islam/Islamic   6, 13, 37, 56, 59, 61, 101, 102, 107, 113, 118, 122–3, 169
  activism   142
  bourgeoisie   111–19
  and democracy   22, 61
  economy   102, 107
  and modernity   39
  Muslim and   127
  neoliberalism   104
  political   40, 70

Sufi 29, 131
values 130
Islamic Tendency Group. *See* MTI
  (*Mouvement de tendance
  islamique*)
Islamism 2, 3, 5, 11, 13, 28, 37, 48, 103,
  126, 163, 166, 169, 170
  in aftermath of the Cold War 126
  AKP 11
  as barrier against communism 125
  core objective of 168
  crisis 161
  democracy and 152-9
  Erdoğan 53
  failure 121
  malleability of 170, 170 n.40, 183 n.40
  Muslim Brotherhood (MB) 42
  Orientalist or culturalist approach
    to 15
  popular support 124
  portrayal of 122
  postmodernism 15
  and the Quran 168
  Qutb, Sayyid 165
  revolts on 6
  totalitarian 153
  transnational 5, 7
  Tunisian 20
Islamist political movements
  failures 123
  success 121-4
Islamists
  politics 3, 5-7, 126, 163
  power through elections 124
  principles 103
Islamization 168-9
  AKP 133-5
  cheap 133-5
  piecemeal 133-4
Islamo-nationalism 6
Istanbul 139-41
IUMS (International Union of Muslim
  Scholars) 67-9

Jamaa Islamiyya 20
Jamali, Naofel 42
Jebali, Hamadi 57, 58, 70, 75, 146
Justice and Development Party. *See* AKP
  (*Adalet ve Kalkınma Partisi*)

Kalın, İbrahim 26
KDK (*Kamu Diplomasisi
  Koordinatörlüğü*) 65-6
Kepel, Gilles 4, 5
Keynesian model 107
Khaled, Amr 128-9, 131
Khanfar, Wadah 54, 69, 70, 85
Khashoggi, Jamal 148, 149
Kifaya (Enough) movement 18-19
Kırbaşoğlu, M. Hayri 158
Kırkıncı, Mehmet 29
Kısakürek, Necip Fazıl 29

Labidi, Meherzia 42, 60
Larayedh, Ali 38, 39, 47, 57, 60, 62
legitimacy 33-5, 121, 163-6
  deficit/crisis 37-8
liberalism 169
  economic 132
  Islamic 41, 127, 129
  secular 163
Lourimi, Ajmi 47, 59, 62, 81, 97, 123

majoritarianism 44
Malek, Hassan 110, 111, 114
malleability of Islamism 170, 183 n.40
Management of the Heart (*Manajemen
  Qolbu* - MQ) 131
managerial awakening (*sahwa
  idâriyya*) 129-32
managerialism 73-4, 129-31, 163
  post-Islamism and 124-6
Maqsoud, Salah Abdel 94, 155
Market of Madinah 115
Marx, Karl 168
Marzouki, Moncef 58, 118
Mashhur, Mustafa 29
materialism 102
  Western 102, 167
Maududi, Sayyed Abul A'la 30, 102, 104, 165
mediated diffusion 62, 69
Mekameleen 141, 150
MHP (*Milliyetçi Hareket Partisi*) 91, 92
military threats 89-90
Mill, John Stuart 168
Milli Görüş 23, 26
'*Milli Görüş*' shirt 26
MIT (Milli İstihbarat Teşkilatı) 27-8,
  66, 95

mmah or *dar al-Islam* 5
Mohammad bin Zayed (MBZ) 149
Mohammed VI 12
Moneim, Abdel 110
morality politics 133
Moroccan Justice and Development Party.
 See PJD (*Parti de la Justice et du Développement*)
Morsi, Mohammed 4, 7, 42, 43, 49–50, 52, 53, 55, 63, 66, 68, 76, 81, 85, 89, 90, 92, 94–5, 109, 111, 114, 117, 122, 137–8, 140–2, 150, 151, 155, 164
 death sentence 138–9
 neoliberal economic model 110
 rule 153
 support of Erdoğan to 141
Moussa, Amr 48, 51
MTI (*Mouvement de tendance islamique*) 20–1
Mubarak, Hosni 2, 17, 18, 29, 31, 34, 38, 49, 50, 54, 63, 66, 76, 79, 88–9, 94, 96, 101, 107, 112, 118
 authoritarian regime 79
 corruption and political monopolization 110
 fall of the regime 54, 88, 110
 neoliberal reforms/policies 105, 106, 118
 resignation 51
 visit to Ankara 31
Muhammad Bin Salman (MBS) 148–9
municipalities 84
MÜSİAD (Müslüman İşadamları Derneği) 111–18, 146, 147
Muslim
 democrats 23, 40, 42
 politics 34
 transnationalism 162
 youth 126–9, 131
Muslim Brotherhood (MB) 1–3, 5, 6, 28, 32–3, 35, 36, 45–9, 56, 71, 73, 76–7, 85, 139, 162, 163, 166
 AKP's influence on 54, 55
 Al Wafd Party coalition 29–30
 challenges 34, 87
 charity structure 99
 contact with *Milli Görüş* and *Nurcu*s 29

diffusion process 11, 13, 34, 40, 72
economic vision of 105–11
election campaign/politics 17–18, 78–9, 81
Erbakan's affinity with 31
Erdoğan's meeting with 51
establishing an Islamic state 17–19
full implementation 18
generational divide 54
governance challenges 154
idea of a civil state 18
implementation of AKP's suggestions 93
interactions between AKP and 51–2, 54
internal (generational) divide 18, 19
Islamic finance 105
Islamism 42
large-scale demonstrations 137
learning from AKP's model 42–3
legitimacy 34
Mubarak regime's escalation to 34
Muslim politics 34
Nasser's repression o 17
normalization for 75
participation in election 34, 53, 54
persecution and execution of leaders 17
political Islam 11
political victory of 7
post-2013 period 139–43
protests in Tahrir Square 50
refining the political beliefs 19
rise to power of 74
sharia law 18
social welfare services 83
theoretical principles 18
threats and alliances 87–96
transnational movement 4
Turkish model 9, 12
2005 parliamentary elections 42
Muslim/Conservative democracy 35–6, 70, 97, 166
 origins of 36–40

Nahda Project 110–11
Namaa in Tunisia 111–12, 114–18, 146–7
Nasser, Gamal Abdel 16, 17, 116
nationalism 6, 168

authoritarian 102
   re-emergence 126
   Tunisian 19
   Turkish 29, 134
Nationalist Movement Party. *See* MHP
   (*Milliyetçi Hareket Partisi*)
nation-building 154
Neo-Destour party 19–20
neo-Islamic bourgeoisie 112–14
neoliberal/neoliberalism 44–6, 100–5,
   110, 113, 128, 163, 165–7
   AKP 49
   conservatism 158
   convergence of Islamism and 104
   economic reforms 104, 130
   globalization and financialization 103
   governance 116, 157
   rationality 13
neo-Ottoman 5, 48, 49
new Islamists 12
'new Turkey' 86–7
NGOs. *See* non-governmental
   organizations (NGOs)
Nidaa Tounes party 23
9/11 attacks 18, 125
'nisf-nisf' (half-half) policy 118
non-governmental organizations
   (NGOs) 62–3
non-relational diffusion 62
normalization 74–5
Nour, Ayman 52, 141, 150
Nurcular 29
*Nurcu*s 29

Office of Public Diplomacy. *See*
   KDK (*Kmu Diplomasisi
   Koordinatörlügü*)
Olçok, Erol 81
'one minute' incident 47, 48, 70
opinion polls 79–80
orientational frames 35, 36
Ounnissi, Sayyida 56, 64, 71
Özal, Turgut 24
   liberalization policies 113
   reforms 25

pan-Islamism 3, 5, 6, 48, 49
parliamentary elections in Egypt 78, 81
parliamentary shutdown 88, 91

party institutionalization 74, 76
Pentecostalism 104
piecemeal Islamization 133–4
Piscatori, James P. 125, 162
PJD (*Parti de la Justice et du
   Développement*) 8, 11–12
pluralism 37, 38, 44, 57, 94, 116, 144,
   153
   Ennahda 57
political
   assassinations 144
   confluence 2, 3
   economy 24, 41
   Islam 11, 15, 69, 70
      AKP 40–1
      democratic 69
   polling 79–80
politics, Islamist 3, 5–7
post-Islamism 12, 37, 124–6, 128, 157,
   169
post-Islamist Islamisation 123
postmodern coup 25, 32, 112, 183 n.50
postmodernism 15
poverty 100, 105
presidential election in Egypt 78
private property 103
privatization 46, 100, 104, 106
   of pensions and healthcare 45
prognostic frames 35, 36
Protestantism 129
Protestant work ethic 104–6
Public Liberties in the Islamic State
   (Ghannouchi) 38
pure pragmatism 117

Quran 168
Qutb, Sayyid 17, 20, 29, 38, 102, 104,
   110, 165
   Islamism 165
   writings of 27–8

Rabaa massacre 140, 147, 148, 150
Rabaa Square 137–8
Rady, Bassam Essam 150
Rafah Border 50
rational choice theory 143
RCD (*Rassemblement Constitutionnel
   Démocratique*) 21
relational diffusion 62

reputation, of Islamist parties 83
resurgence of Muslims 138
right to private property 106
Rodinson, Maxime 101
Roy, Olivier 6, 12, 37, 87, 100, 110, 122, 123, 127, 128, 134, 157, 169
RP (*Refah Partisi*) 24–5, 30, 31, 36, 45, 84, 89, 90, 112

Saadet Partisi (Felicity Party) 112, 116
Sadat, Anwar 17, 94, 102
  Infitah (Open Door) policies 105
Sadat, Jehan 43
Sagheir, Oussama 40, 64
Saied, Kais 145–7, 164–5
Salafi-jihadism 61
Sallam, Hesham 43
Saudi Arabia 141–2, 148–51
Sayyid, S. 6, 13
SCAF 122
  anti-labour legislation 110
secular constitution 52
secularism 24, 52–3, 169
  Erdoğan 52–3, 56, 57
secularized intelligentsia, Egypt 94
secular liberalism 163
Selahaddin, Abdurrahman 51, 70
SETA 65, 66, 81
Sezer, Ahmet Necdet 90–1
sharia law 17, 18, 22, 23, 38, 39, 155, 165, 169
sharia state 26
Shariati, Ali 28, 102
shariyya (legitimacy) 163–4
Shehata, Samer S. 79
Shenouda III, Coptic Pope 53
shura 19, 42, 47, 53–4, 62, 63, 84, 87, 93, 109, 123
Sırma, İhsan Süreyya 29
social Islam 83
socialism 102, 103, 107
social justice 102, 105, 108, 165
social protection 45
social welfare services 82–6
Somrani, Maha 39
sovereignty 38
  God 165–6
Strategic Depth (Davutoğlu) 48
Straw, Jack 40

Sufi ethics 131
Sufi Islam 29, 131
Suleimani, Abdel Karim 146
Supreme Council of Armed Forces (SCAF) 88

Tamimi, Abdel Jalil 61
Tantawi, Hussein 51, 89
tawheed (unity of God) 17–18
terrorist attacks, in Tunisia 60–1
TICA (Union Tunisienne de l'Industrie, du Commerce et de l'Artisanat) 115
TIKA (Turkish Cooperation and Coordination Agency) 65, 66
TOBB (*Türkiye Odalar ve Borsacılar Derneği*) 115–16
trade, of Egypt and Turkey 49–50
traditional Islamism 163
translations, of Qutb's writings 27–8
transnational
  activism 142
  diffusion 3, 72
  Islamism 5, 7
  Muslim politics 5
transnationalism 162
Troika (coalition government) 58
Tuğal, Cihan 41, 49, 58, 118, 134
Tunisian Renaissance Party. *See* Ennahda
Tunisia/Tunisian
  constituent assembly elections 78
  cooperation between Turkey and 58–60
  Islamism 20, 28
  model 59
  nationalism 19
  resurgence of terrorist attacks 60–1
  revolution 6
  Salafi-jihadism 61
Turkey/Turkish
  business 50
  cooperation between Tunisia and 58–60
  democratization 26
  EU accession process 93
  financial aid to Tunisia 61
  foreign policy 63, 65
  Islam 28, 29
  Islamism 32–3, 89, 112
  laws 44

municipalities in 84
nationalism 29, 134
neo-Islamic bourgeoisie 112–14
neoliberalization 118
soft power apparatus 65–6
trade with Egypt 49–50
Turkish Intelligence Agency. *See* MIT
  (Milli İstihbarat Teşkilatı)
Turkish model 6, 8–9, 12, 25, 35, 58, 59,
  61, 62, 65, 70, 92, 111, 114, 123,
  157, 166
  AKP 40–3
  democracy 44
  EU and 43–6
  neoliberalism 44–6
  origins of 40–3
  political economy 41
  reform process 44
  reforms in 1982 constitution 44
Türköne, Mümtazer 23, 134, 158
Turks, Devout 29
TÜSİAD (*Türkiye Sanayicileri ve İş*
  İnsanları Derneği) 111, 113

ulama 20, 128, 132, 168
umma 3–6, 69, 116–17, 162

unemployment 107
UTICA 115–17

value cleavages 7
voting behaviour 83

wassatiyya 67
Weber, Max 76, 129
Welfare Party. *See* RP (*Refah Partisi*)
Western
  capitalist system 102
  materialism 102, 167
Westernization 127
World Bank 108

Yaghlane, Boutheina Ben 84
Yarar, Erol 112, 115
Yasser Ali 92
Yavuzer, Necip 29
Yılmaz, Cevdet 59, 60
Yousifi, Bechir 82
Yunus Emre Foundation 66

Zaytouna University 20
Zemni, Sami 118
Ziotun, Lotfi 98

www.ingramcontent.com/pod-product-compliance
Lightning Source LLC
Chambersburg PA
CBHW051635230426
43669CB00013B/2309